ISBN 978-0-331-68634-0
PIBN 11065461

1 MONTH OF
FREE
READING

at

www.ForgottenBooks.com

By purchasing this book you are eligible for one month membership to ForgottenBooks.com, giving you unlimited access to our entire collection of over 1,000,000 titles via our web site and mobile apps.

To claim your free month visit:

www.forgottenbooks.com/free1065461

English
Français
Deutsche
Italiano
Español
Português

www.forgottenbooks.com

Mythology Photography **Fiction**
Fishing Christianity **Art** Cooking
Essays Buddhism Freemasonry
Medicine **Biology** Music **Ancient
Egypt** Evolution Carpentry Physics
Dance Geology **Mathematics** Fitness
Shakespeare **Folklore** Yoga Marketing
Confidence Immortality Biographies
Poetry **Psychology** Witchcraft
Electronics Chemistry History **Law**
Accounting **Philosophy** Anthropology
Alchemy Drama Quantum Mechanics
Atheism Sexual Health **Ancient History**
Entrepreneurship Languages Sport
Paleontology Needlework Islam
Metaphysics Investment Archaeology
Parenting Statistics Criminology
Motivational

QUEEN'S COLLEGE, GALWAY.

FOUNDED A.D. MDCCCXLV.

CALENDAR

FOR

1902–1903.

PUBLISHED BY AUTHORITY OF THE COUNCIL.

DUBLIN:

PRINTED AT THE UNIVERSITY PRESS,

BY PONSONBY AND GIBBS.

1903.

TABLE OF CONTENTS.

Calendar.

1	Wednesday	
2	Thursday	
3	Friday	
4	Saturday	
5	Sunday	
6	Monday	
7	Tuesday	
8	Wednesday	
9	Thursday	
10	Friday	
11	Saturday	
12	Sunday	New Charter, 1863.
13	Monday	
14	Tuesday	
15	Wednesday	
16	Thursday	
17	Friday	
18	Saturday	
19	Sunday	
20	Monday	
21	Tuesday	College Session and First Term begin. Supplementary Examinations begin.
22	Wednesday	
23	Thursday	Examinations for Senior Scholarships, and Junior Scholarships of the Second and Third Years begin.
24	Friday	Matriculation Examination begins.
25	Saturday	
26	Sunday	
27	Monday	Examinations for Junior Scholarships of the First Year begin.
28	Tuesday	
29	Wednesday	
30	Thursday	COLLEGE OPENED, 1849.
31	Friday	

11TH MONTH.]	NOVEMBER, 1902.	[XXX DAYS.

1	Saturday	ALL SAINTS. College Holiday.
2 3 4 5 6 7 8	Sunday Monday Tuesday Wednesday Thursday Friday Saturday	Lectures in Arts, Medicine, and Engineering begin. Examination for the "Dr. and Mrs. W. A. Browne" Scholarship begins.
9 10 11 12 13 14 15	Sunday Monday Tuesday Wednesday Thursday Friday Saturday	King Edward VII born, 1841. Practical Chemistry Classes begin. Supplemental Matriculation Examination begins.
16 17 18 19 20 21 22	Sunday Monday Tuesday Wednesday Thursday Friday Saturday	
23 24 25 26 27 28 29	Sunday Monday Tuesday Wednesday Thursday Friday Saturday	Law Lectures begin.
30	Sunday	

12TH MONTH.]	DECEMBER, 1902.	[XXXI DAYS.
1	Monday	Examination for Blayney Exhibition begins.
2	Tuesday	
3	Wednesday	
4	Thursday	
5	Friday	
6	Saturday	
7	Sunday	
8	Monday	
9	Tuesday	
10	Wednesday	
11	Thursday	Letters Patent appointing Professors and constituting Statutes issued, 1849.
12	Friday	
13	Saturday	
14	Sunday	
15	Monday	
16	Tuesday	
17	Wednesday	
18	Thursday	Lectures end. Examinations for Junior Law Scholarships begin.
19	Friday	
20	Saturday	First Term ends.
21	Sunday	
22	Monday	
23	Tuesday	
24	Wednesday	
25	Thursday	CHRISTMAS DAY.
26	Friday	
27	Saturday	
28	Sunday	
29	Monday	
30	Tuesday	Letters Patent incorporating the College issued, 1845.
31	Wednesday	

1st MONTH.]	JANUARY, 1903.	[XXXI DAYS.
1	Thursday	
2	Friday	
3	Saturday	
4	**Sunday**	
5	Monday	Second Term begins.
6	Tuesday	EPIPHANY. College Holiday.
7	Wednesday	Lectures in Arts, Medicine, Engineering, and Demonstrations in Practical Physics, begin.
8	Thursday	
9	Friday	
10	Saturday	
11	**Sunday**	
12	Monday	
13	Tuesday	
14	Wednesday	
15	Thursday	
16	Friday	
17	Saturday	
18	**Sunday**	
19	Monday	
20	Tuesday	
21	Wednesday	
22	Thursday	
23	Friday	
24	Saturday	
25	**Sunday**	
26	Monday	
27	Tuesday	
28	Wednesday	
29	Thursday	
30	Friday	
31	Saturday	

| 2ND MONTH.] | FEBRUARY, 1903. | [XXVIII DAYS. |

1	Sunday	
2	Monday	
3	Tuesday	Queen's University of Ireland dissolved, 1882.
4	Wednesday	
5	Thursday	
6	Friday	
7	Saturday	
8	Sunday	
9	Monday	
10	Tuesday	
11	Wednesday	
12	Thursday	
13	Friday	
14	Saturday	
15	Sunday	
16	Monday	
17	Tuesday	
18	Wednesday	
19	Thursday	
20	Friday	
21	Saturday	
22	Sunday	
23	Monday	
24	Tuesday	SHROVE TUESDAY. College Holiday.
25	Wednesday	ASH WEDNESDAY. College Holiday.
26	Thursday	Law Lectures begin.
27	Friday	
28	Saturday	

3RD MONTH.]	MARCH, 1903.	[XXXI DAYS.

1	Sunday	
2	Monday	
3	Tuesday	
4	Wednesday	
5	Thursday	
6	Friday	
7	Saturday	
8	Sunday	
9	Monday	
10	Tuesday	
11	Wednesday	
12	Thursday	
13	Friday	
14	Saturday	
15	Sunday	
16	Monday	
17	Tuesday	ST. PATRICK'S DAY. College Holiday.
18	Wednesday	
19	Thursday	
20	Friday	
21	Saturday	
22	Sunday	
23	Monday	
24	Tuesday	
25	Wednesday	LADY DAY. College Holiday.
26	Thursday	
27	Friday	
28	Saturday	
29	Sunday	
30	Monday	
31	Tuesday	

4TH MONTH.]	APRIL, 1903.	[XXX DAYS.
1	Wednesday	
2	Thursday	
3	Friday	Lectures end.
4	Saturday	Second Term ends.
5	Sunday	
6	Monday	
7	Tuesday	
8	Wednesday	
9	Thursday	
10	Friday	GOOD FRIDAY.
11	Saturday	
12	Sunday	EASTER SUNDAY.
13	Monday	
14	Tuesday	
15	Wednesday	
16	Thursday	
17	Friday	
18	Saturday	
19	Sunday	
20	Monday	Third Term begins.
21	Tuesday	Lectures begin.
22	Wednesday	
23	Thursday	
24	Friday	
25	Saturday	Medical Session ends.
26	Sunday	
27	Monday	
28	Tuesday	Charter of Royal University of Ireland granted, 1880.
29	Wednesday	
30	Thursday	

5TH MONTH.]		MAY, 1903.	[XXXI DAYS.
1	Friday		
2	Saturday		
3	Sunday		
4	Monday		
5	Tuesday		
6	Wednesday		
7	Thursday		
8	Friday		
9	Saturday		
10	Sunday		
11	Monday		
12	Tuesday		
13	Wednesday		
14	Thursday		
15	Friday		
16	Saturday		
17	Sunday		
18	Monday		
19	Tuesday		
20	Wednesday		
21	Thursday	Ascension Day. College Holiday.	
22	Friday		
23	Saturday	Lectures end.	
24	Sunday	Queen Victoria *b.* 1819.	
25	Monday		
26	Tuesday		
27	Wednesday		
28	Thursday		
29	Friday		
30	Saturday		
31	Sunday		

6TH MONTH.]	JUNE, 1903.	[XXX DAYS.

1	Monday	Sessional Examinations begin.
2	Tuesday	
3	Wednesday	
4	Thursday	
5	Friday	
6	Saturday	
7	Sunday	
8	Monday	
9	Tuesday	
10	Wednesday	
11	Thursday	CORPUS CHRISTI. College Holiday.
12	Friday	
13	Saturday	Third Term ends. End of Session.
14	Sunday	
15	Monday	
16	Tuesday	
17	Wednesday	
18	Thursday	
19	Friday	
20	Saturday	
21	Sunday	
22	Monday	
23	Tuesday	
24	Wednesday	
25	Thursday	
26	Friday	
27	Saturday	
28	Sunday	
29	Monday	
30	Tuesday	

7TH MONTH.]	JULY, 1908.	[XXXI DAYS.

1	Wednesday	
2	Thursday	
3	Friday	
4	Saturday	
5	Sunday	
6	Monday	
7	Tuesday	
8	Wednesday	
9	Thursday	
10	Friday	
11	Saturday	
12	Sunday	
13	Monday	
14	Tuesday	
15	Wednesday	
16	Thursday	
17	Friday	
18	Saturday	
19	Sunday	
20	Monday	
21	Tuesday	
22	Wednesday	
23	Thursday	
24	Friday	
25	Saturday	
26	Sunday	
27	Monday	
28	Tuesday	
29	Wednesday	
30	Thursday	
31	Friday	Colleges Act, 1845.

8TH MONTH.]	AUGUST, 1903.	[XXXI DAYS.
1	Saturday	
2	Sunday	
3	Monday	
4	Tuesday	
5	Wednesday	
6	Thursday	
7	Friday	
8	Saturday	
9	Sunday	
10	Monday	
11	Tuesday	
12	Wednesday	
13	Thursday	
14	Friday	
15	Saturday	
16	Sunday	
17	Monday	
18	Tuesday	
19	Wednesday	
20	Thursday	
21	Friday	
22	Saturday	
23	Sunday	
24	Monday	
25	Tuesday	
26	Wednesday	
27	Thursday	
28	Friday	
29	Saturday	
30	Sunday	
31	Monday	

9TH MONTH.]	SEPTEMBER, 1903.	[XXX DAYS.
1 Tuesday 2 Wednesday 3 Thursday 4 Friday 5 Saturday		
6 Sunday 7 Monday 8 Tuesday 9 Wednesday 10 Thursday 11 Friday 12 Saturday		
13 Sunday 14 Monday 15 Tuesday 16 Wednesday 17 Thursday 18 Friday 19 Saturday		
20 Sunday 21 Monday 22 Tuesday 23 Wednesday 24 Thursday 25 Friday 26 Saturday		
27 Sunday 28 Monday 29 Tuesday 30 Wednesday		

10TH MONTH.]	OCTOBER, 1903.	[XXXI DAYS.

1	Thursday	
2	Friday	
3	Saturday	

4	Sunday	
5	Monday	
6	Tuesday	
7	Wednesday	
8	Thursday	
9	Friday	
10	Saturday	

11	Sunday	
12	Monday	New Charter, 1863.
13	Tuesday	
14	Wednesday	
15	Thursday	
16	Friday	
17	Saturday	

18	Sunday	
19	Monday	
20	Tuesday	College Session and First Term begin. Supplementary Examinations begin.
21	Wednesday	
22	Thursday	Examinations for Senior Scholarships, and Junior Scholarships of the Second and Third Years, begin.
23	Friday	Matriculation Examination begins.
24	Saturday	

25	Sunday	
26	Monday	Examinations for Junior Scholarships of the First Year begin.
27	Tuesday	
28	Wednesday	
29	Thursday	
30	Friday	COLLEGE OPENED, 1849.
31	Saturday	

11TH MONTH.]	NOVEMBER, 1903.	[XXX DAYS.

1	Sunday	ALL SAINTS.
2	Monday	
3	Tuesday	Lectures in Arts, Medicine, and Engineering begin.
4	Wednesday	Examination for the "Dr. and Mrs. W. A. Browne" Scholarship begins.
5	Thursday	
6	Friday	
7	Saturday	
8	Sunday	
9	Monday	Practical Chemistry Classes begin.
10	Tuesday	
11	Wednesday	Supplemental Matriculation Examination begins.
12	Thursday	
13	Friday	
14	Saturday	
15	Sunday	
16	Monday	
17	Tuesday	
18	Wednesday	
19	Thursday	
20	Friday	
21	Saturday	
22	Sunday	
23	Monday	
24	Tuesday	
25	Wednesday	
26	Thursday	Law Lectures begin.
27	Friday	
28	Saturday	
29	Sunday	
30	Monday	

12TH MONTH.]	DECEMBER, 1903.	[XXXI DAYS.

1	Tuesday	Examination for Blayney Exhibition begins.
2	Wednesday	
3	Thursday	
4	Friday	
5	Saturday	

6	Sunday	
7	Monday	
8	Tuesday	
9	Wednesday	
10	Thursday	
11	Friday	Letters Patent appointing Professors and constituting Statutes issued, 1849.
12	Saturday	

13	Sunday	
14	Monday	
15	Tuesday	
16	Wednesday	
17	Thursday	Lectures end. Examinations for Junior Law Scholarships begin.
18	Friday	
19	Saturday	First Term ends.

20	Sunday	
21	Monday	
22	Tuesday	
23	Wednesday	
24	Thursday	
25	Friday	CHRISTMAS DAY.
26	Saturday	

27	Sunday	
28	Monday	
29	Tuesday	
30	Wednesday	Letters Patent Incorporating the College issued, 1845.
31	Thursday	

NOTE.—Lectures of the Second Term begin on the 7th January, 1904.

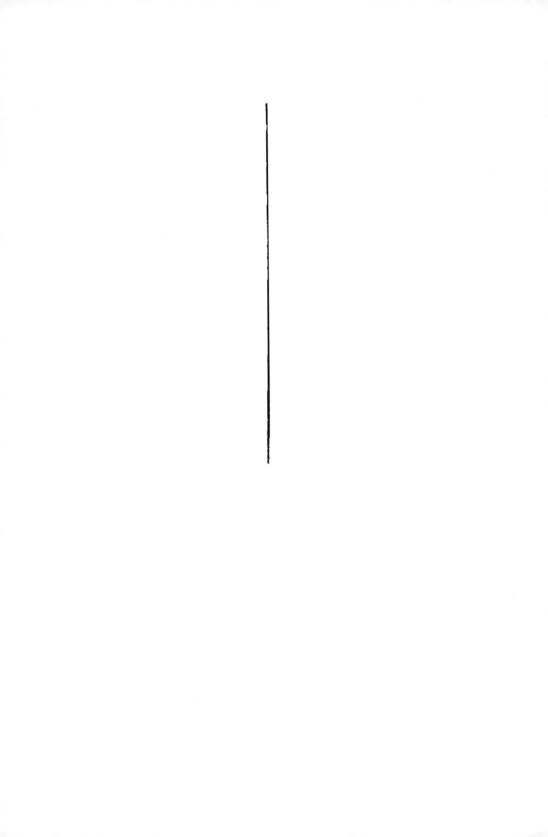

QUEEN'S COLLEGE, GALWAY.

FOUNDED A.D. MDCCCXLV.

—◦◦◦—

FOUNDATION AND CONSTITUTION.

THE Colleges of the Queen's University were founded under the provisions of the Act 8 and 9 Victoria, cap. 66, intituled "An Act to enable Her Majesty to endow new Colleges for the Advancement of Learning in Ireland." Under the powers given by this Act, it was determined to found three Colleges. Belfast, Cork, and Galway were selected as their sites; and on the 30th of December, 1845, Letters Patent were issued incorporating them under the name and style of "THE PRESIDENT, VICE-PRESIDENT, AND PROFESSORS OF QUEEN'S COLLEGE, [BELFAST, CORK,] GALWAY.

The Colleges were opened for Students on the 30th October, 1849. The Presidents and Vice-Presidents of the Three Colleges constituted a Board of Government till the foundation of the Queen's University in 1850. By the University Education (Ireland) Act of 1879 provision was made for the foundation of the Royal University and the dissolution of the Queen's University, within two years from the date of the Charter of the Royal University. All Graduates and Matriculated Students of the Queen's University at the time of dissolution became Graduates and Students of the Royal University, and all existing Professors of the Queen's Colleges continued to be University Professors. The Charter of the Royal University was granted on the 27th of April, 1880, and the Queen's University was dissolved on the 3rd of February, 1882.

B

COLLEGE BUILDINGS.

THE College, erected in 1848, is situated on the west side of the River Corrib, which divides its grounds from the town of Galway. It is built of cut limestone from the neighbourhood, in the form of a quadrangle. The style is Gothic of the 14th century. Over the principal entrance facing the town is a clock tower, 108 feet high. The private residences of the President and Registrar with the Examination Hall occupy the west side. The Library, over 130 feet in length, extends along the first floor of the north side. It contains upwards of 35,000 volumes in the various departments, to which constant additions are made of the most recent standard works. Beneath it are the Drawing school and Lecture rooms of the Engineering department, the Pharmacy Laboratory, the Mathematics and Modern Languages Lecture rooms. Corresponding to it on the south side is the Museum of Natural History, under which are the Laboratory, Museum, and Lecture rooms of Natural Philosophy. The Laboratories of Chemistry and of Practical Physiology with the Museums of Geology and Mineralogy and of Gynæcology, which are described under the departments to which they belong, and various Lecture rooms occupy the rest of the main buildings. The Anatomical School is situated in the north-west corner of the grounds. The Botanical Gardens, the cricket and football fields, the tennis and racquet courts are in the grounds surrounding the principal Building, as are also the Meteorological instruments, which are in charge of one of the College officers. The majority of the students reside during term in Salthill, which lies on Galway Bay, about a mile distant from the College.

SESSION 1902–1903.

THIS College is a Corporation, founded by Letters Patent under the Great Seal of Ireland, under the name and style of the "President and Professors of Queen's College, Galway."

The general government and administration of the College is vested in a Council consisting of the President and six Professors elected by the Corporate Body.

Visitors:

THE RIGHT HONOURABLE THE CHIEF SECRETARY FOR IRELAND.
THE RIGHT REVEREND THE LORD BISHOP OF TUAM.
THE RIGHT HONOURABLE THE LORD CHIEF JUSTICE OF IRELAND.
THE REVEREND THE MODERATOR OF THE GENERAL ASSEMBLY.
THE PRESIDENT OF THE ROYAL COLLEGE OF PHYSICIANS.
THE PRESIDENT OF THE ROYAL COLLEGE OF SURGEONS.

President:

ALEXANDER ANDERSON, M.A., CAMB., Hon. LL.D. Glasgow, late Fellow of Sidney Sussex College, Cambridge; Member of the Senate of the Royal University of Ireland.

Professors:

Greek, ...	R. KNOX MCELDERRY, M.A., Fellow of St. John's College, Cambridge; late J.F.R.U.I.
Latin, ...	PHILIP SANDFORD, M.A. DUB., F.R.U.I.
Mathematics, . . .	THOMAS JOHN I'ANSON BROMWICH, M.A., Fellow of St. John's College, Cambridge; Examiner, R.U.I.
Natural Philosophy, . .	THE PRESIDENT.
History, English Literature, and Mental Science, }	WILBRAHAM FITZJOHN TRENCH, M.A., M.R.I.A.; Examiner R.U.I.
Chemistry, . . .	ALFRED SENIER, PH.D. BERLIN.
Natural History, . . } *Mineralogy and Geology,* . }	RICHARD J. ANDERSON, M.A., M.D. R.U.I., M.R.C.S. ENG.; Examiner, R.U.I.
Modern Languages, . .	VALENTINE STEINBERGER, M.A., F.R.U.I.
Jurisprudence and Political Economy, . . }	CHARLES FRANCIS BASTABLE, LL.D. DUB., B.L.
English Law, . . .	WILLIAM B. CAMPION, B.A. DUB., Serjeant-at-Law.
Anatomy and Physiology, .	JOSEPH P. PYE, M.D., M.CH., D.SC., F.R.U.I.
Practice of Medicine, . .	JOHN ISAAC LYNHAM, M.D., M.CH., M.A.O., F.R.U.I.

Professors—*continued:*

Practice of Surgery,	. .	WILLIAM W. BRERETON, L.R.C.S.I., M.R.C.P.I.
Materia Medica,	. .	NICHOLAS W. COLAHAN, M.D., M.CH., R.U.I.
Midwifery,	. . .	RICHARD JOHN KINKEAD, B.A., M.D. DUB., L.R.C.S.I.
Civil Engineering,	. .	EDWARD TOWNSEND, M.A. DUB., D.SC., Examiner, R.U.I.

(*The above compose the Corporate Body.*)

Council, 1902–1903:

THE PRESIDENT.

PROFESSOR LYNHAM.	PROFESSOR SENIER.
,, STEINBERGER.	,, TOWNSEND.
,, SANDFORD.	,, KINKEAD.

Office-Bearers:

Registrar,	. . . .	PROFESSOR TOWNSEND.
Bursar,	. . . .	,, LYNHAM.
Acting Librarian,	. .	,, STEINBERGER.

Deans of Residences:

Church of Ireland,	. . .	REV. JAMES F. BERRY, B.D.
General Assembly of the Presbyterian Church in Ireland,	. . . .	REV. J. COURTENAY CLARKE, D.D.
Methodist Church,	. . .	REV. HUGH M'GAHIE.

———

1902–1903.

Lecturers:

Medical Jurisprudence,	.	{ PROFESSOR KINKEAD.
		,, SENIER.
Clinical Fever,	. .	,, COLAHAN.
Pathology,	. .	WILLIAM A. SANDYS, M.B., B.CH., B.A.O.
Theory of Music,	. .	WALTER WILLIAMS, A.R.C.M., F.R.C.O.

Demonstrators and Assistants:

Natural Philosophy,	.	JAMES WARNOCK, B.A.
Chemistry,	. .	THOMAS WALSH, B.A.
Demonstrator of Anatomy,		SAMUEL PORTERFIELD, B.A.
Assistant in English,	.	JOHN J. O'NEILL, M.A.
Assistant in Biology,	.	JOHN BYRNE.
Assistant in Electrical Engineering,	. . .	F. ALWYN HAIGH, B.SC. Vict., A.I.E.E.

Senior and other *Scholars* also act as Assistants and Demonstrators to the Professors in the various departments, as required by the Council.

REGISTRAR'S AND BURSAR'S OFFICES.

The Offices of the Registrar and of the Bursar are open on week days during Session from 10 A.M. to 4 P.M., for the receipt of Fees, and transaction of other business. During recess, *letters* addressed to the Registrar will receive attention.

College Clerk,   .   .   .   JAMES M'CLELLAND.

THE COLLEGE SESSION.

The College Session commences on the third Tuesday in October, and, in the Faculty of Arts and the School of Engineering, continues until the second Satrrday in June; it is divided into three Terms.

The First Term of the Session 1902–1903 commences on October 21, and ends on December 20, 1902.

The Second Term commences on January 5, and ends on April 4, 1903.

The Third Term commences on April 20, and ends on June 13, 1903.

In the Faculties of Law and Medicine the Sessions terminate in April, 1903.

LECTURES.

Lectures in Arts, Medicine, and Engineering begin :—

In the First Term on November 4, 1902.
In the Second Term on January 7, 1903.
In the Third Term on April 21, 1903.

Lectures in Law begin :—

In the First Term on November 27, 1902.
In the Second Term on February 26, 1903.

DUTIES OF MATRICULATED STUDENTS.

" Every Matriculated Student shall obey the Statutes of the College, conform to all Decrees and other Regulations made by the authorities of the College for the maintenance of discipline and good conduct, and assist the College authorities in enforcing the same."—*Statutes.*

Every Matriculated Student is required to wear a cap and gown.

GENERAL REGULATIONS.

I.—MATRICULATION.

THE Matriculation Examination is held at the commencement of the first Term of each Session. In the Session 1902–1903, it will commence on Friday, 24th October, at 10 o'clock, A.M.

An additional Matriculation Examination will be held on 7th November.

Each Candidate, before being admitted to the Matriculation Examination, is required to pay to the Bursar the *Matriculation fee* of ten shillings. This fee will not be returned to Students who may fail to pass the Examination; but such Students may present themselves at any subsequent Matriculation Examination in the same year without additional payment.

All Students are required to appear in the Registrar's office for the purpose of having their names entered on the College books.

The Council will admit any Student to Matriculation, without examination, who has passed the Entrance Examination of either of the Queen's Colleges, Belfast or Cork, or of the Royal or any other University within the United Kingdom empowered to grant Degrees in the several Faculties of Arts, Law, Medicine, and School of Engineering. Provided that—

(*a*) His certificate of Matriculation be lodged with the Registrar:

(*b*) He pass any portion of the Matriculation Examination of the College that is not included in the Entrance Examination of such other College or University:

(*c*) His College Fees have been paid:

(*d*) His standing be counted from the date of his having passed the Entrance Examination of such College or University.

A certificate of Matriculation will not be granted to any Student until he has paid the whole of the *Class Fees* for the Session, and commenced attendance on Lectures.

———

II.—AD-EUNDEM STUDENTS.

Any Student who has pursued part of his Collegiate Studies in any one of the Queen's Colleges, or in any University empowered to grant Degrees in Arts, Law, Medicine, and Engineering, or a Student of any School of Law, Medicine, or Engineering, recognized by the Council, may, on passing such Examinations, and fulfilling such other conditions as the Council shall prescribe, take corresponding rank in this College ; and may also compete for Junior Scholarships or other Prizes of the corresponding year : provided he shall not hold at the same time a Scholarship or other office of emolument in any other University, College, or Medical School.

———

III.—NON-MATRICULATED STUDENTS.

Non-Matriculated Students may attend the Lectures of any Professor. They are required to pay to the Bursar the Fees for the Classes they propose to attend, and a College Fee of ten shillings, and to sign an engagement to observe order and discipline in the College. They are not entitled to compete for Scholarships or other Collegiate distinctions.

During the term of their attendance on College Lectures they are admitted to read in the Library, and are permitted to take out books on loan under the same regulations as Matriculated Students.

———

IV.—ADMISSION OF WOMEN.

Women may attend the Lectures of the Professors, and present themselves at the College Examinations. By a recent alteration in the statutes all Scholarships and Prizes are open to Students of either sex.

V.—FEES PAYABLE BY STUDENTS.

To be paid to Bursar at commencement of First Term.

College Fee—

	£	s.	d.
For each and every year, including Matriculation,	0	10	0

CLASS FEES.

Pass Courses—

	£	s.	d.
For each Course,	2	0	0
Re-attendance on same,	1	0	0

Except for the following :—

	£	s.	d.
Anatomy and Physiology (First Course),	3	0	0
First Re-attendance on Physiology (by Junior Students),	2	0	0
Practical Anatomy,	3	0	0
*Practical Physiology,	2	0	0
Practical Anatomy (Post-Graduate and Six Months Honour Courses),	5	0	0
Practical Physiology (Post-Graduate and Six Months Honour Courses),	5	0	0
*Practical Histology,	2	0	0
Practical Chemistry,	3	0	0
Practical Chemistry (Post-Graduate and Six Months Honour Courses),	5	0	0
Hebrew or Sanskrit,	3	0	0
†Practical Biology (3 months),	2	0	0
Practical Biology (3rd Year),	2	0	0
Practical Physics (Second and Third Terms),	2	0	0
Medical Jurisprudence,	2	0	0
Pathology,	2	0	0

Honour Courses—

	£	s.	d.
In all subjects of the 1st and 2nd Years,	2	0	0
‡In all subjects of the 3rd Year,	3	0	0

SCHOLARS.

Junior Scholars are exempted from the payment of one-half of the Class Fees for *Pass Courses*, prescribed to Students of their Faculty and standing, when attended for first time.

VI.—RULES RELATING TO ATTENDANCE ON LECTURES.

All Matriculated Students are required to attend Lectures in Academical Costume.

No Student shall be admitted to Lectures until he has paid his College and Class Fees to the Bursar, and entered his name with the Registrar.

---

* Conjoint Fee, £3.

† Students of Natural History are admitted to the Practical Biology Class on payment of £1. Additional Attendances £1 per month.

‡ Except in Jurisprudence and Political Economy, in which the fees are £2 each.

Attendance on Lectures includes preparation for Lectures; and a Professor, who on any occasion is not satisfied with the preparation of a Student, may refuse him credit for attendance.

In cases where Students pass from the Faculty of Arts to a different Faculty or School, they are exempted from re-attendance upon such Courses in Arts as they have already attended, which would otherwise be necessary for keeping the Academic year.

In cases of absence arising from illness, or other unavoidable cause, the Student is required, on resuming attendance, to lodge with the Registrar a letter or certificate explaining his absence, to be laid before the Council.

VII.—LIBRARY REGULATIONS.
ORDERS OF COUNCIL.
(I.) General.

The Library shall be opened and closed as follows:—

OPEN.

March 1 to June 30, from 10 a.m. to 5 p.m.
August 1 to September 30, from 11 a.m. to 3 p.m.
October 1 to February 28, from 10 a.m. to 4 p.m.

CLOSED.

During July, a week at Christmas and at Easter, and on College holidays.

The Librarian shall attend in the Library each day from 11 a.m., to 3 p.m.

The Librarian shall enter the name of every new book in the Departmental Catalogue.

No book shall be issued, placed in the Professors' Room, or taken away by a Professor or Officer, until the invoice of the parcel which contained it shall have been examined by at least one Member of the Library Committee, the name of the book shall have been entered in the Catalogue, the book itself shall have been stamped, and its place in the Library shall have been marked on it.

Dictionaries, Grammars, Cyclopædias arranged in alphabetical order, works the chief value of which consists in plates and embellishments, and such books as the Library Committee shall enumerate, shall be issued only by special permission of the Library Committee.

The Librarian shall each day examine the recall book, and call in all books therein required.

If a book be not brought back when due or when required, the Librarian shall write to demand its immediate return, and if the demand be not complied with, he shall report the same to the Council.

The Librarian shall call in all books towards the close of the Second Term ; and shall report to the Council the names of all persons in default.

Every book brought back to the Library shall be set aside by the Librarian's Assistant, until it shall have been inspected by the Librarian, and the said book shall not be re-issued (unless to the same borrower) until it shall have been so inspected.

The Librarian shall inspect each book returned, if not re-issued to the same borrower.

In case of a book or books being lost or injured, the Library Committee shall estimate the cost of such loss or injury, and the borrower shall pay same : or the amount may be deducted from the deposit lodged with the Bursar. The privilege of borrowing shall cease until the loss has been made good, or the deposit made up to the full amount.

No books shall be ordered except through the Librarian.

The Professors' room shall be kept strictly private.

(II.) Issuing of Books.

No one shall borrow any book from the Library without first delivering a note for it to the Librarian or Assistant, signed by the borrower, and specifying, in the borrower's handwriting, the title of the book and the date on which it is borrowed.

The Librarian or Assistant shall compare the notes delivered for books borrowed with the books themselves, before they are taken away, and shall keep all such notes until the books to which they refer are brought back to the Library. When all the books specified in any note are brought back, the note shall be delivered up to the person by whom they are brought ; when only some of the books specified are returned, their titles shall be crossed out on the note at the time, the borrower being responsible for each book until its title is so crossed out.

To Professors and Office-Bearers.

A Professor may borrow whatever books from his own department he may require for the working of the same.

A Professor or Officer of the College may borrow books from any department other than his own, provided that the number of such volumes in his possession at any one time do not exceed twenty ; each volume to be returned within one month.

A Professor or Officer of the College requiring a larger number of books for any special purpose, shall make application on each occasion for the same to the Library Committee, stating fully the grounds on which he requires them.

A Professor or Officer requiring a book which is out may enter its name in a recall book to be kept for that purpose in the Professors' Room, and on its return shall have priority.

A Professor may, through the Librarian, call in any book lent from his department : and such book shall immediately be returned to the Library by the borrower.

The last number of any periodical shall not be removed from the Professors' Room until after the time limited by the posted notice, and the Librarian shall report to the Library Committee every infringement of this rule.

To Students.

No Student shall be admitted to the Library, except in full academical costume.

No Student shall be allowed to read in, or borrow books from, the Library until he shall have subscribed the following declaration :—

"I, the undersigned, do hereby promise to the President and Council of Queen's College, Galway, that I will not mark, turn down the leaves of, or write on paper placed upon, or in any way whatsoever soil, deface, injure or remove without permission, any book or document in the Library of said College. I also promise that I will not injure the Library furniture : that I will faithfully observe all the rules made for the regulation of the Library ; and that I will acquaint the College Authorities with any serious instance of violation of the said rules which may come under my notice."

A Student, after depositing with the Bursar £1, may borrow three volumes, or on depositing £2, six volumes, at a time.

A Scholar can comply with this rule by giving the Bursar an order on his Scholarship for the amount of the deposit.

On the production, by a Student, of a certificate from the Librarian that all books borrowed by him from the Library

have been returned uninjured, the Bursar shall, at the end
of the term, repay the deposit.

The Library Committee may grant special permission to a
Senior Scholar to borrow more books than the number of
volumes specified in these rules, application for this privilege
to contain the names of the books required, and to be counter-
signed by the Professor of the Department.

A Student shall not retain a book borrowed from the Library
longer than one fortnight; but on returning it, may renew
the loan, if it has not been in the meantime applied for.

On receiving at any time notice from the Librarian, a
Student shall return within 48 hours any books borrowed
from the Library. On failure to comply with this rule he
incurs a penalty of sixpence per volume for each day the
book or books are retained, until the amount of fine equals
the deposit.

To others than Professors or Students.

Any person resident in Galway may, by permission of the
Council or of the Library Committee, obtain the privilege of
borrowing books from the Library.

Each person on obtaining such permission, shall deposit
the sum of £1 with the Bursar, which shall be refunded
when he ceases to avail himself of the privilege, on presenting
a certificate from the Librarian that all books borrowed by
him have been returned uninjured.

No person may have more than two volumes on loan from
the Library at the same time.

The borrower may not retain a book for longer than a
fortnight, but may, on returning it, renew the loan if the
book has not in the meantime been applied for.

Books shall not be issued to persons other than Professors,
Office-Bearers, or Students, except between 12 and 3 p.m. on
Wednesdays and Saturdays.

VIII.—SESSIONAL EXAMINATIONS.

An Examination is held at the close of the Session in the
subjects upon which Lectures have been delivered. Any Professor may, with the sanction of the Council, conduct the
Sessional Examinations in any of his Classes by means of Term
Examinations. Notice of this method shall be given to the
Class at the beginning of the Session. Prizes may be awarded
for distinguished answering in these Examinations; but no
prize can be obtained by a student who fails in any of the
subjects prescribed. Students to whom prizes are awarded

must order their books from the College booksellers before the 1st of the following December, otherwise their prizes will be forfeited.

A Supplementary Examination in the same subjects is held at the commencement of the following Session. Candidates intending to present themselves at the Supplementary Examination must give a fortnight's notice to the Registrar.

No Student is admitted to the Sessional or Supplementary Examination who has not attended at least three-fourths of the Lectures delivered in the prescribed Courses.

Every Matriculated Student in Arts, Law, and Engineering, must attend the Courses of Lectures prescribed to Students of his class and standing, and must pass either the Sessional or the Supplementary Examination, before his name can be entered on the College Register as having completed the Session.

The Sessional Examination, completing a course of lectures, may be passed (except for the retention of Scholarships or Exhibitions) by passing the corresponding Examination of the Royal University in the same year, in so far as this Examination includes the subjects of the lectures.

IX.—SCHOLARSHIPS.

No Student can compete for a Scholarship in any Course substantially the same as, or included in, one in which he has already held a Scholarship or Exhibition in this, or in either of the other Queen's Colleges.

No Scholarship will be awarded to a Candidate who is not, in the opinion of the Examiners, sufficiently qualified in the prescribed Course.

A.—Senior Scholarships.

The Council is empowered to award by Examination Eight Senior Scholarships of the value of £40 each to Matriculated Students, whose answering is reported as meritorious, and who shall have, during *three College Sessions* (of which *two at least* shall have been attended in Queen's College, Galway*), attended such Courses of Lectures, and passed such Examinations as shall be prescribed in that behalf by the Council,

---

* The *third* Session above referred to, as in the Statute relating to Senior Scholarships, may have been attended by Candidates in any one of the Queen's Colleges in Ireland, or in a College of any University in the United Kingdom.

and who shall have passed the necessary Examinations within five years from the date of Matriculation, and who shall have complied with such further conditions as the Council shall impose, provided he shall not have previously obtained a Senior Scholarship in the same department in this or in either of the other Queen's Colleges.

Of these Scholarships one is awarded for proficiency in each of the following departments :—

1. Ancient Classics.
2. English and Modern Languages.
3. Mathematics.
4. Natural Philosophy.
5. Metaphysics, Political Science, and History.
6. Chemistry.
7. Natural History.
8. Engineering.
9. See note *.

All Senior Scholars are required to be in attendance in the College during their period of office, and to assist the Professors in such ways and under such regulations as the Council shall prescribe.

Senior Scholars, except in Engineering and Medicine, who have not taken the Degree of B.A., shall attend the Courses prescribed for the third year in Arts.

Senior Scholars in Engineering, who have not taken the Degree of B.E., shall attend the Courses prescribed for the Students in Engineering of the Third Year.

Senior Scholars not assisting the Professor must attend at least one Honour Course of three Terms.

For the date of these Examinations, see page 20. For the Courses in the various branches, see pages 57, *sqq.*

B.—Junior Scholarships.

The Council is empowered to award Forty-five Junior Scholarships, tenable for one year, which are allocated as follows :—

(*a*) In the Faculty of Arts, thirty (value £24 each).
(*b*) In the Faculty of Law, two (value £25 each).
(*c*) In the Faculty of Medicine, eight (value £25 each).
(*d*) In the School of Engineering, five (value £20 each).

---

* One Senior Scholarship in *Anatomy and physiology*, value £40, will also be open for competition at commencement of Session 1902–1903, tenable for one year, by a Student who shall have attended the Medical School of this College for at least Two Sessions, and shall have obtained a Degree in Arts or Medicine, or a Diploma in Medicine from a Licensing Body. The Senior Scholar shall act as Demonstrator, if appointed, and shall assist the Professor in such way as the Council shall prescribe.

(*a*) Of the thirty Junior Scholarships assigned to the FACULTY OF ARTS, ten—five Literary and five Science*†—are awarded to Students of the *First Year ;* ten others—five Literary and five Science*—to Students of the *Second Year ;* ten—five Literary and five Science—*to Students of the *Third Year.*

For Courses, see pages 48, *sqq.*

(*b*) Of the two Junior Scholarships appropriated to the FACULTY OF LAW, *one* is tenable by a Student of the *First* Year, *one* by a Student of the *Second* Year.

For Courses, &c., see pages 63, *sq.*

(*c*) Of the eight Junior Scholarships appropriated to the FACULTY OF MEDICINE, *two* are tenable by Students of the *First* Year, *two* by Students of the *Second* Year, *two* by Students of the *Third* Year, and *two* by Students of the *Fourth* Year.

For Courses, &c., see pages 78, *sqq.*

(*d*) Of the five Junior Scholarships appropriated to the SCHOOL OF ENGINEERING,† *two* are tenable by Students of the *First* Year, *two* by Students of the *Second* Year, and *one* by a Student of the *Third* Year.

For Courses, see page 87.

Junior Scholars in any Faculty are exempted from the payment of one half of the Class Fees for the *Pass Courses prescribed to Students of their faculty and standing.* (See pages 27, 62, 65, and 82).

The Examinations for Junior Scholarships are held at the beginning of the first term of the Session.

No Student can compete for any Scholarship until—

(*a*) He has Matriculated.‡

(*b*) He has paid the College and Class Fees.

---

* The Council may withhold Scholarships in either department on the ground of insufficient answering, and may assign Scholarships so withheld to the other department.
If a Candidate be placed *first* in the order of merit in *both* departments, he is entitled to two Junior Scholarships, but in no other case can the same person hold two Scholarships simultaneously.
† Candidates for Junior Scholarships of the First Year in Arts or Engineering must declare which they intend to compete for, as competition for both is inadmissible.
‡ Non-Matriculated Students, who satisfy the Registrar that they have been *bonâ fide* Candidates at the Current Matriculation Examina-

(*c*) He has entered his name with the Registrar.

(*d*) He has (except when a candidate for a Junior Scholarship of the First Year) completed the course of the previous year in any one of the Queen's Colleges, or in any University empowered to grant Degrees.

Scholars failing to attend the prescribed Courses of Lectures, and to pass the Sessional Examinations, vacate their Scholarships. Students attending Honour Lectures must pass the Sessional Examinations in the subjects of such Lectures.

For the days and hours of examination for these Scholarships see pages 20, 21, 22.

C.—The "Dr. and Mrs. W. A. Browne" Scholarship.

An Examination for a Scholarship of the yearly value of about £37, founded and endowed by Dr. W. A. Browne, on behalf of and in memory of his wife Caroline Charlotte Browne, F.Z.S., is held early in the First Term of each year.

The Scholarship is awarded for proficiency in the French and German languages, a competent colloquial knowledge of both languages being required.

It is open to any Matriculated Student of Queen's College, Galway, of either sex, who is a natural born subject of His Majesty, if not more than two years have elapsed from the 1st of January following his, or her, Matriculation.

The Scholarship shall be held for one year only; but the successful candidate, if otherwise qualified, may compete in succeeding years, provided that no Student shall hold the Scholarship more than three times.

The Scholar, during the year of tenure of the Scholarship, shall attend the lectures prescribed to Students of his, or her, faculty and standing, and shall pursue Honour Courses in French and German Literature in the College, and shall qualify for a Sessional Prize in these subjects.

The Scholarship may be held along with any other Scholarship.

---

tion of the Royal University, may be admitted to the Scholarship Examinations on payment of the stated Fees, but cannot be elected to Scholarships unless they produce to the Registrar Certificates of having passed that Matriculation Examination, on or before the day on which the Scholarships are awarded.

One-half of the Scholarship will be paid in January, and one-half in the following July, provided the holder shall have satisfied the conditions stated above.

The Council retains the power of withholding the whole or of awarding only a portion of the Scholarship, if sufficient merit be not shown. In case the whole or part of the Scholarship be not expended in any year, the Council shall apply the money so accruing to the purpose of giving an additional Scholarship in the next or following years, in the same subjects and under the same regulations.

Scholars.

1899–1900,*	.	.	.	Steinberger, Cecil Lucy Marian.
1900–1901,	.	.	.	Steinberger, Cecil Lucy Marian.
1901–1902,	.	.	.	Steinberger, Cecil Lucy Marian.
1902–1903,	.	.	.	Minnis, Samuel.

D.—RESEARCH SCHOLARSHIP.

A Research Scholarship in Science (value £150 per annum, tenable for two years, subject to a satisfactory report at the end of the first year) has been offered by the Royal Commission for the " 1851 Exhibition," to students of science of at least three years' standing who have been recommended by the authorities of this College. For information respecting the nomination for 1903–1904 given to this College by the Royal Commission, application may be made to the Registrar.

1892–93,	.	.	.	. Gannon, William, M.A.
[1893–94,	.	.	.	. Gannon, William, M.A.†]
1894–95,	.	.	.	. M'Clelland, John A., M.A.
1895–96,	.	.	.	. M'Clelland, John A., M.A.
1896–97,	.	.	.	. Henry, John, M.A., B.E.
1897–98,	.	.	.	. Henry, John, M.A., B.E.
1898–99,	.	.	.	. Ryan, Hugh, M.A.
[1899–1900,	.	.	.	. Ryan, Hugh, M.A., D.SC.‡]
1900–1901,	.	.	.	. Mills, William S., M.A.
1901–1902,	.	.	.	. Mills, William S., M.A.
1902–1903,	.	.	.	. Mills, William S., M.A.
1902–1903,	.	.	.	. Goodwin, William.

---

* The answering of Mr. Edward H. M'Grath was very favourably reported on by the Examiner.

† Resigned Scholarship on being appointed to Lectureship in the Owens College, Manchester.

‡ Resigned on being appointed Professor of Chemistry in the Catholic University School of Medicine, Dublin.

X.—EXHIBITIONS.

The Council may award Exhibitions, tenable for one year, to Matriculated Students at the Examinations for Junior Scholarships.

No Student is allowed to compete for an Exhibition in any Course substantially the same as that in which he has already held a Scholarship or Exhibition.

Exhibitioners failing to attend the prescribed Courses of Lectures, and to pass the Sessional Examinations, forfeit their Exhibitions.

THE "BLAYNEY" EXHIBITION.

An Examination for one Exhibition, value about £30, in connection with the "Blayney" Bequest, is held in the month of December of each year, on the following conditions :—

1. No Candidate is eligible if more than two and a-half years have elapsed from the date of his Matriculation in this College to the time of the Examination.

2. The Holder of the Exhibition must attend Honour Classes, as required by the Council in this College, during the Session in which he shall have obtained the Exhibition ; he must pass the College Sessional Examinations at the close of the same Session, and he must qualify for First Class Prizes at these Examinations in the subjects in which he shall have obtained the Exhibition.

3. The Council retain the power of withholding, or of awarding only a portion of the Exhibition.

4. The "Blayney" Exhibition may be held along with any Scholarship.

5. One-half of the Exhibition will be paid in January, and one-half in the following month of July, provided the Holder shall have satisfied the conditions stated above.

The Exhibition is awarded in alternate years for Classical and Scientific merit, respectively.　In 1902 the Course is in Classics.

The following is the Course :—

1. Composition in Greek and Latin Prose.
2. Higher Grammar and Philology (Giles' *Manual of Comparative Philology*, and Lindsay's *Short Historical Latin Grammar*).
3. Translation of unprescribed passages.
4. The following authors :—

> *Greek*—Aristophanes, *Acharnians* and *Wasps*; Aristotle, *Poetics*.
> *Latin*—Lucretius, book i. Cicero, *Ad Atticum*, viii. Plautus, *Aulularia*.

The Examinations begin on Monday, 1st December, 1902. Intending Candidates must give in their names to the Registrar a fortnight before this date.

" BLAYNEY " EXHIBITIONERS.

1890 (*Classics*),	. . .	Mahon, John S. (Sch.)
1891 (*Science*),	. . .	M'Clelland, John A. (Sch.)
1892 (*Classics*),	. . .	M'Gregor, William (Sch.)
1893 (*Science*),	. . .	None awarded.
1894 (*Classics*),	. . .	Johnston, James (Sch.)
		(Mills, John (Sch.), *proxime accessit.*)
1895 { (*Science*), } { (*Classics*), }	. . .	{ Carmichael, John S. (Sch.) { Reid, John (Sch.)
1896 (*Classics*),	. . .	Hezlett, James (Sch.)
1897 (*Science*),	. . .	McLean, Andrew H. (Sch.)
1898 (*Classics*),	. . .	Williams, William J. (Sch.), in part.
1899 (*Science*),	. . .	Strain, Thomas G. (Sch.)
1900 (*Classics*),	. . .	O'Neill, Joseph J. (Sch.)
1901 (*Science*),	. . .	Perry, Agnes M. (Sch.)
1902 (*Classics*),	. . .	Thompson, Frances L. (Sch.)

XI.—THE PRESIDENT'S MEDAL.

This Medal for excellence in Oratory and English Composition, founded by the late President, Sir Thomas Moffett, will be awarded annually in connection with the Literary and Debating Society, by the President.

Medalists.

1895–96,	. . .	Farley, William J., B.A.
1896–97,	. . .	Curry, David S., B.A.
1897–98,	. . .	O'Grady, Henry G.
1898–99,	. . .	Moore, William Irwin.
1901–1902,	. . .	Minnis, Samuel.

I.—Supplementary Examinations for First, Second, and Third Year Students will be held on Tuesday, the 21st October and Wednesday, the 22nd October, 1902, from 10 a.m. to 1 p.m., and 2 p.m. to 5 p.m.

II.—Days and Hours of Matriculation and Scholarship Examinations, October, 1902.

DAYS.	HOURS.	FIRST YEAR.	SECOND YEAR. JUNIOR SCHOLARSHIPS.	THIRD YEAR. JUNIOR SCHOLARSHIPS.	SENIOR SCHOLARSHIPS.
Thursday, 23rd Oct.	10—1		Arts.—Latin.	Arts.—Latin.	Latin.
	2—5		Arts.—Greek.	Arts.—Greek.	Greek.
Friday, 24th Oct.	10—11¾ 11¾—1 11¾—1	MATRICULATION. English. Latin. Greek.	{ Arts.—English. Engin.—Geometrical Drawing, &c. } 10—1	{ Arts.—English. } 10—1	French.
	2—3½ 3½—5	French or German or Italian. Mathematics.	{ Arts.—English. Engin.—Geometrical Drawing, &c. } 2—5	{ Arts.—English. } 2—5	German. Italian.
Saturday, 25th Oct.	10—1	Experimental Physics.	Arts.—Latin.	Arts.—Latin.	Latin.
	2—5		Arts.—Greek.	Arts.—Greek.	reek.

Day	Time	Jun. SCHOLARSHIPS			
Monday, 27th Oct.	10—1	Arts.} Med.} English.	Arts. Med. Engin.} Modern Languages.	Arts.—Modern Lang. / Engin.—Engineering.	Engineering. Political Science.
	2—5	Arts.} Med.} Greek.	Arts.—Modern Languages.	Engin.—Engineering. / Arts.—Modern Lang.	Engineering. Modern History.
Tuesday, 28th Oct.	10—1	Arts.} Med.} Latin.	Med.} Engin.} Theoretical Chemistry.	Arts.—Chemistry.	Theoretical Chemistry.
	2—5	Arts.} Med.} Greek.		Arts,} Engin.} Math. Physics.	Mathematical Physics.
Wednesday, 29th Oct.	10—1	Arts.} Med.} Latin.	Arts. †Med. †Engin.} Experimental Physics.	Arts.—Experimental Physics.	Exper. Physics.†
	2—5	Arts.} Med.} Engin.} Arithm. Algebra.	Arts. Engin.} Mathematics.	Arts.—Mathematics.	Metaphysics.
Thursday, 30th Oct.	10—1	Arts.} Med.} Engin.} Geom. Trig.	Arts. Engin.} Med.—Anatomy. } Mathematics.	Arts.—Mathematics. / Engin.—Mathematics.	Mathematics.
	2—5	Arts.} Med.} Celtic.	Med.—Anatomy.	Arts.—Logic.	English.
Friday, 31st Oct.	10—1	Arts.} Med.} German.		Arts.—Geology.	English. Nat. History.
	2—5	Arts.} Med.} French.	Med.—Natural History.	Arts.—Nat. History.	Practical Chemistry.*
Monday,	10—1	Italian.			Engin.—Practical

III.—DAYS AND HOURS OF THE EXAMINATIONS FOR MEDICAL SCHOLARSHIPS OF THE THIRD AND FOURTH YEARS, 1902.

DAYS.	MONTHS.	HOURS.	SUBJECTS.
THURSDAY,	30th October,	{ 10—1, 2—5,	Anatomy. Physiology.
FRIDAY,	31st October,	{ 10—1, 2—5,	Materia Medica. Surgery.
MONDAY,	3rd November,	{ 10—1, 2—5, 10—1,	Midwifery. Medicine. Practical Chemistry.
TUESDAY,	4th November,	{ 10—11½, 11½—1, }	Medical Jurisprudence.

Examinations for JUNIOR LAW SCHOLARSHIPS will be held on the 18th and 19th December, 1902.

MATRICULATION EXAMINATION,*

SESSION 1902-1903.

[For **Regulations and date see pages 6 and 20.**]

A.—*In the Faculties of Arts, Law, and Medicine.*

Subjects :

i. *Latin.*
ii. Any one of the following languages :—*Greek, French, German, Italian.*
iii. *English.*
iv. *Mathematics.*
v. *Experimental Physics.*

The following are the particulars of the foregoing subjects of Examination :—

i. *Latin,* . . Virgil—*Georgics,* i.
Cicero—*Pro Archia* ; *Divinatio in Q. Caecilium.*
Outlines of Roman History, from 390 B.C. to 27 B.C. (Smith's smaller *History of Rome.*)
[NOTE.—A paper will be set in Latin Grammar, and easy sentences will be set for translation into Latin.]

ii. {

Greek, . . Plato—*Euthyphro, Crito.*
Euripides—Scenes from *Bacchae.* (Longmans.)
Outlines of Grecian History, from 560 B.C. to 322 B.C. (Smith's smaller *History of Greece.*)
[NOTE.—A paper will be set in Greek Grammar touching on Declensions, Conjugations, and Rules of Syntax.]

French, . . About—*Le Roi des Montagnes.*
Coppée—*Le Trésor.*
Elements of French Grammar.
Easy sentences for translation into French.
Oral Examination.

German, . . Kohlrausch—*Das Jahr 1813.*
Elements of German Grammar.
Easy sentences for translation into German.
Oral Examination.

Italian, . . Goldoni—*Il Burbero benefico.*
Tasso—*Gerusalemme Liberata,* Cantos i., ii., iii.
Elements of Italian Grammar.
Easy sentences for translation into Italian.
Oral Examination.

* Matriculation Certificates of the Queen's Colleges, Belfast and Cork, and of the Royal University of Ireland, and of other Universities, are accepted by this College.

iii. *English,* . . English Grammar and Composition.
Scott—*Waverley.*
Milton—*Paradise Lost,* Book vi.

iv. *Mathematics,* . Arithmetic, including Principles of Notation and the four rules, Vulgar and Decimal Fractions, Proportion and its applications, and the Extraction of the Square Root.
Algebra, including Fractions, and the solution of Simple Equations.
Geometry—Euclid, Books i., ii., iii.

v. *Experimental Physics :* The Elementary Principles of Dynamics and Hydrostatics, as treated in Everett's Elementary Text-book of Physics.

B.—*In the School of Engineering.**

Subjects :

i. *Mathematics.*—Same as Course in Faculty of Arts.

ii. *History, Geography, and the English Language.* History—Outlines of History of Great Britain and Ireland. Geography—Outlines of Geography. English Language — English Grammar and Composition.

iii. *Experimental Physics :* Same as Course in Faculty of Arts.

---

*See footnote, p. 23.

LECTURES.

DAYS AND HOURS OF LECTURES.

Subjects.	Terms.	Mon.	Tues.	Wed.	Thrs.	Fri.	Sat.
1st YEAR.							
French (Honour),	1, 2, 3,	10	—	—	10	—	—
French (Pass),	1, 2, 3,	—	10	—	—	10	—
German,	1, 2, 3,	—	1	—	—	—	10
*Italian,	1, 2, 3,	—	—	—	—	—	—
Latin (Honour),	1, 2, 3,	12	—	12	—	12	—
Latin (Pass),	1, 2, 3,	—	11	—	11	—	*
Greek (Honour),	1, 2, 3,	—	2	—	2	—	2
Greek (Pass),	1, 2, 3,	12	—	12	—	12	—
Mathematics,	1, 2, 3,	1	—	1	—	1	—
Mathematics (Honour),	1, 2, 3,	—	1	—	1	—	1
†English,	1, 2, 3,	11	—	—	—	11	—
Experimental Physics,	1, 2, 3,	—	12	—	12	—	12
2nd YEAR.							
French (Pass),	1, 2, 3,	—	12	—	12	—	—
,, (Honours,)		—	—	2	—	—	12
†German,	1, 2, 3,	9	—	—	9	—	—
*Italian,		—	—	—	—	—	—
†Greek,	1, 2, 3,	—	11	—	11	—	11
Latin,	1, 2, 3,	11	—	11	—	—	—
,, (additional for Honours),	1, 2, 3,	—	10	—	—	11	—
Mathematics (Pass),	1, 2, 3,	—	1	—	1	—	1
Mathematics (Honour),	1, 2, 3,	—	11	—	11	—	11
Logic,	1, 2,	1	—	1	—	—	—
† English,	1, 2, 3,	—	—	10	—	10	—
*History,	1, 2,	—	—	—	—	—	—
Mathematical Physics (Honour),	1, 2, 3,	—	—	9	—	—	9
Mathematical Physics (Pass),	1, 2, 3,	10	—	—	—	10	—
Experimental Physics,	1, 2, 3,	—	9	—	9	—	—
Chemistry (Pass and Honour),	1, 2, 3,	12	—	12	—	12	—
Chemistry, Laboratory (Pass),	3 Mths.	3	—	3	—	3	—
*Chemistry, Laboratory (Honour),							
Biology,	1, 2, 3,	—	3	—	3	—	3
Practical Biology (Honour),	3 Mths.	—	—	—	—	—	—
Mineralogy and Geology,	1, 2,	10	—	10	—	10	—
*Practical Physics,	2, 3,	—	—	—	—	—	—

* At hours and on days to be arranged.
† Honour Students receive special instruction.

DAYS AND HOURS OF LECTURES—*continued.*

Subjects.	Terms.	Mon.	Tues.	Wed.	Thrs.	Fri	Sat.
3rd YEAR.							
Zoology or Botany,	1, 2, 3,	—	3	—	3	—	3
*Practical Biology (3 Months) Honour,	—	—	—	—	—	—	—
Physiology,	1, 2,	9	—	9	—	9	—
*Chemistry (Honour),	1, 2, 3,	—	—	—	—	—	—
*Chemistry, Laboratory (Honour)	1, 2, 3,	—	—	—	—	—	—
English Literature (Honour),	1, 2, 3,	—	10	—	10	—	—
*Metaphysics,	1, 2,	—	—	—	—	—	—
*History,	—	—	—	—	—	—	—
*Logic,	—	—	—	—	—	—	—
French,	1, 2, ,	11	—	—	11	—	—
German,	1, 2, ,	—	11	—	—	11	—
*Italian,	1, 2,	—	—	—	—	—	—
Latin,	1, 2,	10	—	10	—	10	—
„ (additional for Honours)*	1, 2 ,	—	—	—	—	—	—
Greek,	1, 2; 3,	11	—	11	—	11	—
Ethics,	—	—	—	—	—	—	—
*Political Economy,	1, 2,	—	—	—	—	—	—
Mathematics (Pass),	1, 2, 3,	—	11	—	11	—	11
Mathematics (Honour),	1, 2, 3,	—	12	—	12	—	12
Mathematical Physics,	1, 2, 3,	—	10	—	10	—	10
Experimental Physics (Honour),	1, 2, 3,	11	—	11	—	—	—
*Practical Physics,	2, 3,	—	—	—	—	—	—
†Mineralogy and Geology,	1, 2,	10	—	10	—	10	—
*Jurisprudence,	—	—	—	—	—	—	—
4th YEAR.							
For Post-Graduate Classes see various Departments.							

* At hours and on days to be arranged.

† Honour Students receive special instruction.

COURSES OF LECTURES.

—

Faculty of Arts.

[The Course of Study extends over three Sessions.]

PRESCRIBED PASS COURSES.

For Students of the First Year.

- I. Latin.
- II. Any one of the following:—Greek, French, German, Italian.
- III. English Language and Literature.
- IV. Mathematics.
- V. Experimental Physics.

Students may substitute Honour Courses in Latin, Greek, Mathematics, and Modern Languages for the Pass Courses in these subjects.

For Students of the Second Year.

- I. Latin.
- II. Greek.
- III. English Language and Literature.
- IV. Any one of the following languages:—French, German, Italian.
- V. Logic (Two Terms).
- VI. Mathematics.
- VII. Mathematical Physics.
- VIII. Experimental Physics.
- IX. Chemistry.
- X. Natural History.
- XI. Geology (including Mineralogy and Physical Geography).

Students must attend in four of the foregoing subjects, one of which must be Latin or Mathematics.

Honour Students may take Honour for Pass Courses in any of the subjects, and a Fifth (optional) Honour Course.

For Students of the Third Year.

    I. Latin.
    II. Greek.
  III. English, and any one of the following languages:—French, German, Italian.
   IV. Logic, and any one of the following:—Metaphysics, Ethics, History of Philosophy, Political Economy.
    V. Mathematics.
   VI. Mathematical Physics.
 VII. Experimental Physics.
VIII. Chemistry.
   IX. Physiology.
    X. Botany and Zoology.
   XI. Geology (including Mineralogy and Physical Geography).

Students may attend, at their option, in any one of the following groups of subjects:—

  A. (1) Latin; (2) Greek; and (3) any one other of the above subjects.

  B. (1) Latin; (2) Logic, Metaphysics, with History of Philosophy; and (3) either Ethics or Political Economy.

  C. (1) Mathematics; and (2) (3) two others of the above subjects, one of which must be one of those enumerated under heads VI. to XI.

Or Honour Lectures in any one of the following Groups:—

    I. Latin and Greek Languages and Literatures.
   II. English, and any two of the following languages:—French, German, Italian.
*III. Logic, Metaphysics, Ethics, and History of Philosophy.
   IV. Civil and Constitutional History, Political Economy, and General Jurisprudence.
    V. Mathematics and Mathematical Physics.
   VI. Mathematical and Experimental Physics.
  VII. Any two of the following subjects:—

       i. Experimental Physics.
      ii. Chemistry.
     iii. Botany and Zoology.
     iv. Physiology *or* Geology.

[For the regulations as to University Examinations in Arts, see Appendix.]

---

* Any Candidate selecting Group No. III. will be at liberty to substitute for Ethics any one of the three subjects included in Group No. IV.

I.—GREEK.

The books to be read in the Greek class-room for Session 1902–1903 will be selected so as to prepare students for the several Examinations in the Royal University and corresponding Examinations.

Students of the *First Year* will read—

> In *Pass* Class—Homer, *Od.*, ix., x.; Demosthenes—*Leptines*. Greek *History* from B.C. 560 to B.C. 429; Greek *Literature*—Lyric Poets—Life in the Homeric Age, and Outlines of the Homeric Controversy; *Antiquities* (Gow., chaps. x., xi., xix.).
>
> In *Honour* Class, in addition to the above, Euripides, *Hercules Furens*; Herodotus, Book viii.; Plato—*Menon*.
>
> The *Pass* Class meets at 2 P.M. on Tuesdays, Thursdays, and Saturdays; the *Honour* Class at 12 noon on Mondays, Wednesdays, and Fridays during three terms.

Students of the *Second Year* will read—

> In *Pass* Class—Sophocles, *Antigone;* Thucydides, Book 6, *History*, from 431 to 387 B.C.; *Literature*, History of the Drama, The Historians; *Antiquities* (Gow, chaps. xii.–xv., xviii., xx., xxi.):
>
> In *Honour* Class, in addition to the above—Homer, *Iliad*, 16, 21, 22; Plato, *Phaedo*. *Literature*—(*Grote*, chaps. 58–62, Abbott's *Pericles*, Jebb's *Homer*, Jevons' *Hist. of Greek Literature*, Part 1, Book 3).
>
> The Class meets at 11 A.M. on Tuesdays, Thursdays, and Saturdays.

Students of the *Third Year* will read—

> In *Pass* Class—Jebb's Selections from the Attic Orators—*Antiphon, Andocides, Lysias*; Demosthenes, *De Falsa Legatione;* Aeschylus, *Prom. Vinct.* Special Portions of History, Literature, and Antiquities.
>
> In *Honour* Class, in addition to the above, Aristotle, *Poetics;* Aesch., *Ag.* and *Eum.*; Aristoph., *Acharnians* and *Frogs*; Theocr., 1, 2, 3, 6, 7, 9, 10,; Pindar, *Nemeans*, i.–vi.
>
> The Class meets at 11 A.M. on Mondays, Wednesdays, and Fridays.

Obs.—The hours of attendance may possibly require readjustment; as, for instance, if Pass Students in the Second or Third Year should present themselves.

In all the years Students are exercised in Prose Composition. The required portions of Greek History and Antiquities are also studied.

All Students must provide themselves with annotated text-books such as are published by the leading booksellers for use in schools and colleges; with a Greek Grammar and a copy of the smaller edition of King and Cookson's "Introduction to the Comparative Grammar of Greek and Latin."

Students will have at their disposal in the Library the larger and more expensive editions of the works that are studied in class-room. They will also there find Dictionaries, Lexicons, Dictionaries of History, Geography, Antiquities; in fact, all the requisite works for general reference. Books of general reference can only be consulted in the Library. Books not of general reference may be borrowed for home-study.

II.—LATIN.

Lectures are delivered during three terms on the *Language* and *Literature* of Ancient Rome. Special portions of the *History* and *Antiquities* are studied in connection with the authors read. *Latin Prose Composition*, taught orally as well as by written exercises, forms an important part of each Course. Arrangements are made for the instruction in writing *Latin Verse* of such Students as are anxious to cultivate the art. The elements of *Classical Philology* and *Textual Criticism* are part of the work of the senior classes.

The Books read in class are chosen with a view to the requirements of Students who are preparing for Examinations in the Royal University of Ireland.

Lectures for Students of the First Year:—

(*a*) The *Pass* Class meets on Tuesdays and Thursdays, at 11 A.M., during three terms.
Books appointed for Session 1902–1903:—Livy, Book xxxv. Virgil, *Aeneid* Book vi. Roman History, A.U.C. to 133 B.C. (Pelham, Rivington's.) Literature (Wilkins' Primer).

(*b*) Additional Lectures for *Honour* Students are delivered on Mondays, Wednesdays, and Fridays, at 12 noon.

Books appointed for Session 1902-1903:—Virgil—*Æneid*, ii., and *Georgics*, iv. Horace, *Odes*, ii. Cicero—*Philippic*, ii. History—From 216 to 167 B.C. (*Mommsen*, vol. II., bk. iii., 6–10). Antiquities (Ramsay, chaps. ii.–vi.). Literature (Student's Companion to Latin Authors, ch. iii. ; Mackail, ch. ii.).

[These Lectures include the Courses prescribed for the First Year's Examination in the Royal University, for the Sessional Examination in Q. C. G., and for the Latin portion of the Second Year's Literary Scholarship in Q. C. G.]

Lectures for Students of the Second Year :—

(*a*) The class meets on Mondays and Wednesdays at 11 a.m. The special books appointed for the Session 1902-1903 are :— Cicero—*Tusc. Disp.* ii. and iii. ; Tacitus—*Agricola* ; Juvenal— *Satires*, 4, 5, 7, 8, 10 ; History of the period from B.C. 31 to A.D. 68 (Student's Roman Empire, chaps. 1–18 (omitting 4, 6, 7, 8). Antiquities—The Public Lands, Financial Administration of the Republic ; Law and Justice ; Roman Money ; Roman Measures (Ramsay, chaps. 7, 8, 9, 13, and Roby L. G. i., App. D). Literature—Student's Companion to Latin Authors, chap. ii. Mackail, chap. i.

(*b*) Additional Lectures for *Honour* Students are delivered on Tuesdays at 10 a.m., and Fridays at 11 a.m., when the following will be studied :—*Lucretius*, i. ; Martial—*Liber Spec.* and Books i.–iv. (Stephenson's edition); Cicero—*In his Letters*, xli. to lxxx. (Tyrrell's edition); Tacitus—*Hist.* iii., iv., v. The special Honour course in History is Mommsen, *Provinces of the Roman Empire*, vol. i., pp. 1–194 (Eng. Trans.) Literature and Antiquities.

[These Lectures include the Courses prescribed for the Second Year's Examination in the Royal University, for the Sessional in Q. C. G., and for the Latin portion of the Third Year's Literary Scholarship Q. C. G.]

Lectures for Students of the Third Year :—

The class meets at 10 a.m. on Mondays, Wednesdays, and Fridays, and arrangements are made for additional Lectures for *Honour* Students. The subjects of Lecture during the Session 1902-1903, will be:—Virgil—*Æneid*, ii., iv., vi. ; Horace—*Odes*, ii. and iii. ; Tacitus—*Annals*, xiii.–xvi. ; Lucretius, Book i. ; Plautus— *Asinaria* and *Captivi* ; Cicero—*Ad Atticum*, iv., v., vi. ; Persius (omitting *Sat.* iv.); History, A.D. 68 to A.D. 138 (Student's Roman Empire) ; Mommsen—*History of Rome*, vol. v., bk. v., chaps. 8–11) ; Literature—Student's Companion to Latin Authors ; Sellar—*Poets of the Republic*, chaps. i.–vii. ; Antiquities—Law and Justice ; Religion, The Calendar ; the Military and Naval Organisation of the Republic (Ramsay, chaps. 9 to 12.)

[These Lectures embrace the Courses prescribed for the Royal University B.A. Examination, for the Sessional of the Third Year in Q. C. G., and for the Senior Scholarship in Q. C. G.]

[Arrangements may be made with the Professor for additional Lectures if necessary.]

Students are expected to provide themselves with texts and the ordinary editions for College use in class. The larger modern editions and Books of Reference may be consulted in the Library. For *Pass* Students of the *First* Year, Bradley's edition of Arnold's *Latin Prose Composition* is used as a basis of instruction in Prose Composition; for all the other classes Bradley's *Aids to Latin Prose Composition.*

III.—MATHEMATICS.

Instruction is given in this department by means of Lectures. Students are expected to prepare for the Lectures by reading, and also to work out the examples set in the classes to the best of their ability. The Lectures are adapted for those preparing for the Examinations of the Royal University in their respective years.

The Courses in the Faculty of Arts are as follows :—

I. For all Students of the First Year—

Elements of Plane Geometry, Algebra and Plane Trigonometry.

II. For Honour Students of the First Year, and Pass Students of the Second Year—

Elements of Solid Geometry; Plane Trigonometry; Elements of the Theory of Equations, of Analytical Geometry and of Conic Sections. First principles of the Differential Calculus, *or* (for Second Year Pass Students) Spherical Trigonometry.

III. For Honour Students of the Second Year, and Pass Students of the Third Year—

Algebra and Trigonometry; Analytical Geometry; Differential and Integral Calculus; Theory of Equations.

IV. For Honour Students of the Third Year—

Analytical Geometry of Two and of Three Dimensions, including Higher Plane Curves; Differential and Integral Calculus; Differential Equations.

A Class may be arranged with the Professor for Students reading the Course in Mathematics for the M.A. Degree in the Royal University.

An additional Course of Lectures is given by the Senior Scholar to Pass Students of the First Year.

The College Library contains a large collection of standard mathematical works and Journals, to which regular additions are made. The following may be mentioned, in addition to the usual text-books :—

> Works of *Lagrange, Jacobi, Gauss, Cayley, Weierstrass, &c., Journals of Crelle* and *Liouville, Acta Mathematica, Quarterly Journal of Mathematics, Proceedings of the London Mathematical Society, Jahrbuch der Fortschritte der Mathematik, Annali di Matematica, American Journal of Mathematics.*

IV.—NATURAL PHILOSOPHY.

[In this Department Courses of Study are pursued in both Experimental Physics and Mathematical Physics.]

A.—Experimental Physics.

Instruction in this subject is imparted by means of Lectures illustrated by experiments, by the use of suitable text-books, and by Courses of practical work in the Laboratory.

Lecture Courses.—Separate Courses of Lectures are given to Students of the First, Second, and Third Years.

The Class for Students of the *First Year* meets on three days of the week during the whole Session. The Lectures are designed to give Students in Arts, Medicine, and Engineering a thorough grounding in the general principles of *Mechanics, Hydrostatics, Heat, Sound, Light, Magnetism*, and *Electricity*, and are adapted for those preparing for the First University Examinations of the Royal University of Ireland, and similar Examinations. Special attention is given to the subjects of *Heat, Light*, and *Sound*, to meet the requirements of those intending to compete for Honours at the First University Examination in Arts.

The Class for Students of the *Second Year* meets on two days of the week during the whole Session. The subjects chosen are those prescribed for the Second University Examination in Arts of the Royal University. These subjects are dealt with as completely as the Mathematical attainments of the Class will permit.

The Class for Students of the *Third Year* meets on two days of the week during the whole Session for Pass Students, and an additional Lecture every week is delivered to those who intend to compete for Honours at the B.A. Examination of the Royal University. The subjects chosen are those prescribed for this Examination, and the Lectures aim at making Students familiar with the present state of physical science, and with the results and methods of modern physical research. A Class may also be arranged with the Professor for Students reading the M.A. Honour Course of the Royal University.

Text-Books.

The Text-books recommended for the First Year Course are h Cambridge Natural Science Manuals, by R. T. Glazebrook.

For the Second Year Course the Text-books recommended are Deschanel's Natural Philosophy, edited by Professor Everett, Joubert's Electricity and Magnetism, and Balfour Stewart's Heat.

For the Third Year Course the Text-books recommended are Deschanel's Natural Philosophy, edited by Professor Everett; Preston's Theory of Light; Preston's Theory of Heat; Fleming's Alternate Current Transformer, vol. i.; Maxwell's Heat; Cours de Physique, by J. Violle; Ewing's Magnetic Induction.

Laboratory Courses.—Separate Courses of practical instruction in the Laboratories, at which the Demonstrator assists, are given to Students in the Faculties of Arts, Medicine, and Engineering. These Courses, which are continued for three months of the Session, are designed to prepare Students for the Examinations in Practical Physics of the Royal University, and similar Examinations; but facilities are afforded to Students desirous of pursuing a more extended course of practical work. The Physical Laboratories are supplied with electrical power from the Galway Electric Light Company's Station, and provided with storage batteries, continuous current dynamo, alternator, and transformer. The Museum of Natural Philosophy, in connection with the Laboratories, contains a very complete collection of physical apparatus suitable for lecture illustration and research work.

B.—MATHEMATICAL PHYSICS.

Instruction in this subject is imparted by means of Lectures and by the use of text-books.

Lecture Courses.—Three Courses of Lectures are delivered extending over the whole Session—one to Pass Students of the Second Year, one to Honour Students of the Second Year, and one to Honour Students of the Third Year. Pass Students of the Third Year attend the Honour Course of the Second Year. A Class for Students reading the M.A. Honour Course of the Royal University in Mathematical Physics may be arranged with the Professor. An additional Course of Lectures is given by the Senior Scholar to Pass Students of the Second Year.

The subjects treated in the Courses of the Second Year are those branches of Mathematical Physics prescribed for the Second University Examinations of the Royal University in Arts and Engineering. The Third Year Course includes those branches of Mathematical Physics prescribed by the Royal University for the Degrees of B.A. and B.E. with Honours.

Text-Books.

The Text-books recommended for the Second Year Courses are, Loney's Mechanics and Hydrostatics for Beginners, Loney's Treatise on Elementary Dynamics, Greaves' Statics, Heath's Elementary Optics, Greaves' Hydrostatics, Parker's Astronomy.

For the Third Year Course, the following Text-books are recommended :—Routh's Statics, vols. i. and ii. ; Williamson and Tarleton's Dynamics, Routh's Elementary Rigid Dynamics, Heath's Geometrical Optics, Besant's Hydromechanics, Part I.; Godfray's Astronomy, Frost's Newton.

LIBRARY :—The College Library contains a large collection of standard works on the various branches of Mathematical and Experimental Physics, and their allied subjects, and receives many British and foreign scientific periodicals and journals.

V.—ENGLISH LANGUAGE AND LITERATURE.

Lectures to *First Year* Students are delivered during the whole Session on Mondays and Fridays, at 11 a. m. The Course prescribed in the First University Examination in the R.U.I. supplies the subjects specially dealt with in these Lectures.

The Lectures for Students of the *Second Year* are given during the three terms. Additional Lectures are given to Students reading for Honours.

In the *Third Year*, Honour Lectures are given throughout the Session.

In each year the Books prescribed for the Examinations of the Royal University form the subjects of special study.

Courses of Honour Lectures deal with the history of English Literature during the periods prescribed for the several years: these Lectures aim especially at imparting an intelligent apprehension of the origin, development, and characteristics, of successive literary movements; rather than a knowledge of the names of individual writers and their works.

The Students are also instructed and exercised in the writing of essays.

Students are expected to provide themselves with the text-books in the study of which the classes are respectively engaged. They will find the College Library, especially as their studies become more advanced, a great assistance, for it contains a large collection of standard editions of English poets and prose writers, as well as the principal works in literary criticism and on the history of literature, and also works that will aid in the linguistic study of English.

Arrangements may be made with the Professor for a post-graduate class, with a view to the examination for M.A. Degree in the R.U.I.

VI.—MODERN HISTORY.

Lectures will be given to *Second Year* Students during two terms.

Lectures are also given to *Third Year* Students, the Course including the History of Great Britain and Ireland, and of France, from 1589 to 1815.

VII.—MENTAL SCIENCE.

Logic.—The Courses of Lectures for *Second Year* Students are delivered during two terms, at 1 p.m., on Mondays and Wednesdays.

The Lectures for *Third Year* Students extend over two terms.

Metaphysics.—Lectures are delivered during two terms. The Lectures deal with the principles of Psychology and Ontology.

In the various Courses of Lectures, the portions of the subjects for each class are chosen to meet the requirements of Students who are preparing for Examination in the Royal University, and special arrangements may be made for Students who are studying for other public Examinations.

VIII.—CHEMISTRY.

Chemistry is studied throughout the Session: (1), by means of Lectures in which an acquaintance is made with the chief facts upon which the science is based, by experiments conducted on the Lecture-table These are carefully observed and their scientific bearing considered; (2), by experiments conducted by the Students themselves, each working independently in the laboratory, under the supervision of the Professor or Demonstrator; (3), by the use of text-books; by reference to the Dictionaries of Chemistry, and to the Chemical Journals which are available in the Library.

(1) LECTURE COURSES.

(*a*) *Second Year Course for Pass and Honours. Inorganic Chemistry.*—The class meets at 12 o'clock on Mondays, Wednesdays, and Fridays throughout the Session, but attendance is not required on Mondays, between the Christmas recess and the close of Medical Lectures. The Lectures embrace a consideration of the leading facts of Inorganic Chemistry, and include both the Pass and Honour subjects required for the Second University Examination in Arts of the Royal University, or for other corresponding Examinations.

About forty Lectures are devoted to a detailed study of the non-metallic elements, their reactions, and the constitution of the compounds they form. The remaining Lectures embrace a review of the general facts established, including the weight and volume relation in chemical reactions, the molecular hypothesis, the atomic hypothesis, and the relative weight of molecules and atoms. The leading metals and their more important compounds are also briefly considered.

(*b*) *Third Year Course for Honours.*— *Organic Chemistry.*— A class in Advanced Organic Chemistry, adapted to the requirements of the B.A. *Honour* Examination of the Royal University, will, if required, be formed to meet throughout the Session at hours to be arranged ; also a *Fourth Year* (*Post-Graduate*) *Course for Honours*, to meet the requirements of Students preparing for the M.A. *Honour* Examination of the Royal University. Students wishing to avail themselves of these classes must arrange with the Professor at the beginning of the First Term.

(2) LABORATORY COURSES, PRACTICAL CHEMISTRY.

Students are admitted to the Laboratory at the hours given in the time-table, and at other times by arrangement with the Professor. A separate bench is allotted to each Student. These courses of experiment afford a means of acquiring manipulative skill, and of attaining a more intimate knowledge of the science of chemistry.

(*a*) *Second Year Course for Pass.*—This course consists of about forty Lectures of two hours each, commencing in the first term, and ending at the close of the second term. The work done is adapted to the requirements in Practical Chemistry of the Pass Second Examination in Arts. A *Second Year Six Months' Course for Honours*, adapted to the Honour Second Examination in Arts of the Royal University, will be arranged for Students who desire it.

(*b*) *Third Year Course for Honours.*—This Course is arranged to meet the requirements of the B.A. *Honour* Examination of the Royal University and of other corresponding Examinations. The Class works throughout the Session at hours to be arranged. Fee, five pounds. *Fourth Year (Post-Graduate) Courses for Honours* will be organized, if desired, to meet the requirements of Students preparing for the M.A. *Honour* Examination of the Royal University, or for other Examinations. These Classes will commence work at the beginning of the Session. Post-Graduate Courses may also be arranged in other departments of Pure or Applied Chemistry, including Agriculture, Brewing, Food Analysis, etc., to meet individual requirements. Fee, five pounds.

(3) TEXT-BOOKS, CHEMISTRY DEPARTMENT OF LIBRARY, CHEMISTRY MUSEUM.

(*a*) *Text-Books recommended.*—For Second Year Lecture Course :—

Thorpe, Inorganic Chemistry, 2 vols.; Newth, Inorganic Chemistry; Remsen, College Chemistry; or Richter, Inorganic Chemistry (trans. Smith).

For Third Year Honour and Post-Graduate Lecture Courses :—

Roscoe and Schorlemmer, Treatise on Chemistry, vols. i. and ii.; Richter, Organic Chemistry (trans. Smith); Nernst, Theoretical Chemistry (trans. Palmer); Hjelt, Principles of General Organic Chemistry (trans. Tingle); L. Meyer, Outlines of Theoretical Chemistry (trans. Bedson and Williams); Van't Hoff, The Arrangements of Atoms in Space (trans. Eiloart); Walker, Introduction to Physical Chemistry; Van't Hoff, Lectures on Theoretical and Physical Chemistry (trans. Lehfeldt); Lehfeldt, Physical Chemistry.

For Laboratory Courses :—

Qualitative Analysis—Clowes, Practical Chemistry. For Quantitative Analysis—Fresenius. Quantitative Analysis, (trans. Vacher and Groves), or Clowes and Coleman, Quantitative Analysis; Hempel, Gas Analysis (trans. Dennis). For Preparations—Fischer, Organic Compounds (trans. Kling); Gattermann, Practical Methods of Organic Chemistry (trans. Shober); Lassar-Cohn, Manual of Organic Chemistry (trans. Smith). Erdmann, Chemical Preparations (trans. Dunlap). H. Meyer, Determination of Radicals in Carbon Compounds (trans. Tingle). Cohen, Practical Organic Chemistry.

(b) *Chemistry Department of Library.*—Chief works of reference :—

Morley and Muir, Watt's Dictionary of Chemistry; Thorpe, Dictionary of Applied Chemistry; Beilstein, Organische Chemie; Richter, Lexicon der Kohlenstoffverbindungen; Roscoe and Schorlemmer, Treatise on Chemistry; L. Meyer, Modern Theories of Chemistry (trans. Bedson); Ostwald, Lehrbuch der Allgemeinen Chemie; Kopp, Geschichte der Chemie; E. Meyer, History of Chemistry (trans. M'Gowan); Comey, Dictionary of Solubilities; Allen, Commercial Organic Analysis; Green, Fermentation; Menschutkin, Analytical Chemistry (trans. Locke).

Principal Journals containing original Memoirs :—

Journal of the Chemical Society; Liebig's Annalen der Chemie; Berichte der Deutschen Chemischen Gesellschaft; Chemisches Central-Blatt; Zeitschrift für Physikalische Chemie; Annales de Chemie et de Physique; Journal of the Society of Chemical Industry; Chemical News.

IX.—NATURAL HISTORY.

The Department of Natural History comprehends the Sections of Zoology, Botany, Practical Biology, Geology, Mineralogy, and Physical Geography.

1. ZOOLOGY.

The Class in Zoology meets at 3, on Tuesdays, Thursdays, and Saturdays, during the months of November, December, January, and February. The Course consists of at least forty Lectures.

Introduction—The Kingdoms of Nature. The Characters of Organized Bodies. Protoplasm. Cells. Tissues. Organs. Development. Classification of Animals. Distribution in Time and Space. Theories of Evolution. The Anatomy, Physiology, and Life-History of selected types. Systematic Zoology.

The Museum.

This Museum contains a series of specimens illustrating the Animal Sub-Kingdoms. The specimens are arranged in a series, commencing with the simpler and proceeding to the higher Forms. Disarticulated Skulls, Glass and Papier-Maché Models may be used by the Students. A revolving Microscope, Panoramic Diagrams, and Dissected Specimens of Animals are included in the Collection.

Text-Books.

Thomson's Zoology, Huxley's Vertebrata.

Books recommended to Senior and Honour Classes:—Wiedersheim, Lang, Sedgwick, Parker and Haswell.

Works of Reference

The works of Ray Lankester (Oxford Zoology); The Cambridge Zoology; Bronn's Tier-Reich; Brehm, Tier-Leben; Cuvier, Règne Animal; Marey, D'Arsonval and others, Physique Biologique; Owen, Odontography; Owen, Comparative Anatomy; Ludwig's Leunis; Fuerbringer, Birds; Bateson, Materials for Variation; Ellenberger, Anatomy of the Dog; Hertwig, Embryology; Krause, Anatomy of the Rabbit; A. Russel Wallace, Distribution of Animals; C. Darwin, Animals and Plants under Domestication; Tarrell, British Birds and British Fishes; Fürbringer, Untersuchungen zur Morphologie und Systematik der Vögel; British Museum Zoological Catalogues; Macalister, Animal Morphology and Comparative Anatomy of Vertebrates Topinard, Anthropology.

Journals.

Journ. Zoological Society, Journ. Linnean Society, Challenger Reports, The American Naturalist, Annales des Sciences Naturelles. Kölliker's Zeitschrift für Wissenschaftliche Zoologie, Gegenbaur's Morphologisches Jahrbuch, Journ. of Marine Biological Association, Zoologischer Jahresbericht, Naples; Zoologische Jahrbücher, Spengel.

Several small Aquaria in the Museum and passages contain living specimens.

2. BOTANY.

The Course in Botany extends over three months. The Class meets on at least three days in the week at 3 o'clock. The Lectures will embrace :—

Definitions. Plant Life; Histology and Physiology. Morphology. Systematic Botany, Cryptogams and Phanerogams. The course is fully illustrated with Microscopic specimens.

The Morphology and minute Anatomy of Plants, Plant Physiology. Systematic Botany. The Characters of the Chief Natural Orders. The Life History of selected types—Phanerogams and Cryptogams; General conditions of Plant Life.

Text-Books.

Strasburger's Botany, Vines' Botany, Hooker's British Flora.

Senior Classes.—Le Maout and Decaisne, Sachs, Geobel, Pfeffer; and the Practical manuals of Bower, Vines, Detmer, and Darwin.

Works of Reference.

Leunis' Synopsis; Kerner and Oliver, Natural History of Plants; Sowerby, English Botany; J. Lubbock, Seedlings; Vines, Physiology of Plants; Massee, Plant Diseases; Scott, Structural Botany; De Candolle, Monographae Phanerogamarum C. Darwin, Insectivorous Plants.

Journals.

Just's Botanischer Jahresbericht, Annales des Sciences Naturelles, Linnean Society's Journal and Transactions.

A centrifugal machine to show Knight's experiment, a Growth lever Registering Drum, and other apparatus are included in the Museum of this department.

3. BIOLOGY.

This Class meets on two or three days each week during the first three months of the Session.

During this Course the following Animals are dissected by the Students:—the Rabbit, Pigeon, Frog, Codfish or Dogfish, Sepia, Snail, Mussel, Blatta, Crayfish or Lobster, Cockroach, Earthworm, Leech, Hydra ; Microscopic preparations of the organs are examined, fresh or preserved. The Plants studied are (*a*) Flowering Plant, Arabis or Wallflower, Tulip; (*b*) The Fern ; (*c*) Chara, Penicillium, Mucor, Yeast. Sections of stems, leaves, roots, and flowers are made by the Students, who are expected to make drawings. Paramaecium, Vorticella, Acineta, Amoeba, Noctiluca, Spongilla, and Rotifers may be studied.

Third Year.—*Honour Students* meet on an extra day in the week, and are supplied with other specimens in addition to the above. All animals are supplied to the Students free of cost. Dissections take place under the superintendence of the Professor of Natural History and the Assistant in Biology.

Senior Zoological Classes have opportunities afforded them of dissecting, amongst other types, Helix, Blatta, Oniscus, Actinia, Taenia, and cartilaginous fishes.

Senior Botanical Classes are provided with chemicals, microscopes, and other apparatus for the study of the minute structure of composite types, and the conditions under which elementary organisms live. All animals are supplied to Students free of charge, and dissections are superintended by the Professor and his assistants.

Text-Books.

The Biological Works of Marshall and Hurst, and of Parker are recommended. Marshall's Frog. The Practical Botanical Works of Bower, Vines, and Francis Darwin.

4. MINERALOGY, GEOLOGY, AND PHYSICAL GEOGRAPHY.

Lectures on Mineralogy, Geology, and Physical Geography are delivered during the First and Second Terms. The Class meets on Mondays, Wednesdays, and Fridays at 10 A.M.

The Lectures will embrace :—

(A.) MINERALOGY.—Crystallography. Physical Characters and Chemical Constitution of Minerals. Classification.

Text-Books.

Rutley or Dana's Class Book, Mineralogy, Gurney's Crystallography, Rutley's Rocks.

Books recommended to Senior Students:—Dana's Text-book and System of Mineralogy, Bauermann's Mineralogy, Maskelyne's Crystallography, Lewis' Crystallography.

Works of Reference.

Die Mikroskopische Beschaffenheit der Mineralien und Gasteine. Dana's System of Mineralogy. Miller's Mineralogy. Bonney Volcanoes.

Journals.

The Mineralogical Magazine. Bulletin de la Société française de Mineralogie. Neues Jahrbuch f. Mineralogie u. Geologie.

(B.) GEOLOGY.—Definitions—The Materials of the Earth's Crust. The General Structure and the Size of the Earth. The Density of the Earth. Comparison with other Heavenly Bodies. The Nebular Hypothesis. The Rotation of the Earth. The Effects of the Sun and Moon on the Earth. Underground Temperature. Temperature of the outer Crust. Temperature in the Past. Climate. Limitation of Geographical Regions. Process of Denudation. Air. Water. Ice. Process of Depositing. Stratification, Jointing, Dip, Strike, Contortion, Faults, Synclinal and Anticlinal Folds. The Clinometer. Volcanic Agencies.—Active Volcanoes, and Earthquakes. Igneous Rocks, Granites, Porphyries and Volcanic Rocks, Lavas, Tuffs, and Ashbeds. Configuration and Structure. Classification of Animals and Plants. General Distribution. Biological Theories. Systematic Stratigraphical Geology.

Text-Books.

Watt's Geology (Students are recommended to read Harrison's Elementary Geology early in the Session), *or* Geikie's Class-book, Lyell's Student's Elements, Wood's Palæontology.

Senior Students are advised to read:—Lapworth's Geology, Geikie's Class-book, and Woodward's Palæontology.

Works of Reference.

Etheridge and Seely—Geology. Prestwich—Geology. Kinahan—Geology of Ireland. Hull—Coalfields. Woodward—Palæontology of Vertebrates. Schimper—Traité de Palæcntologie Végétale. Greene's Geology. Jukes Browne—Geology. Zittel—Palæontology. Lapparent's Geology. Bonney—Story of our Planet. Scott—Studies in Fossil Botany. Jukes Browne—Stratigraphical Geology.

Journals.

The Geological Magazine. Palæontologie française. Quarterly Journal of the Geological Society. The Transactions of the Palæontological Society.

(C.) PHYSICAL GEOGRAPHY.—The Earth. General Geographical Considerations, Continents, Islands, Varieties of Land Surfaces, Proportion of Land to Water, Rivers, Lakes, Water in Interior of Earth, Snow, Ice, The Atmosphere, Winds, Climate, Weather, Volcanoes, Earthquakes.

Text-Books.

Geikie (to be read early), Mill's Realm of Nature, Gregory's Physical Geography.

Books recommended to Honour and Senior Students :—The advanced Text-books of Thornton and Simmon.

Works of Reference.

Sir Wyville Thompson's Voyage of the Challenger, Wallace's Australasia, Wallace's Island Life, Darwin's Beagle, Stansford's Compendium, Réclu's Universal Geography ; also the works of Baker, Burton, Cameron, Cook, Kane, Livingstone, M'Clintock, and M'Clure. Prevalsky—Mongolia.

Journals.

The Geographical Journal, Geographical Magazine, Journal of the Geographical Society of London.

THE MUSEUM OF MINERALOGY AND GEOLOGY.

The Museum, founded by the late Professor King, contains a series of Fossils illustrating the Geological Formations. The Museum contains also a large collection of Minerals and Ores, and a small Chemical Cabinet.

Instruments have been provided for the use of Senior Students and for Class Purposes, including a Goniometer, a Clinometer, a Spectroscope, and an apparatus to illustrate Crystalline forms. A large Globe and several Maps, with the Land Surfaces in relief, are at the disposal of Students.

Newton's large Revolving Lantern, with Microscopic, Vertical, and other attachments has been placed in this Museum. A second Lantern, which is supplied with numerous slides, is placed in the larger room.

Senior Students are permitted to work in the Museum on one or two days in each week.

X.—MODERN LANGUAGES.

Subjects : French, German, Italian.

There are three Classes, for Students of the First, Second, and Third Year of their Academical Course. In each of these Classes separate Lectures for Pass and Honour Candidates will be given. The different Classes meet at the hours set down in the Time Table of the College Calendar. The Lectures are arranged to suit the requirements of Students preparing for the several Examinations in the Royal University and for similar Examinations.

Pass Classes.

The business of these Classes is conducted by Lectures on Grammar and (in the Second and Third Year) on the Elementary History and some particular period of Literature of the language, by translations from and into English, by written exercises and examinations.

Honour Classes.

The Course of Instruction comprises advanced Composition, Translation, Critical Readings, and (in the Second and Third Year) Lectures on the History and Literature of the Romance and Teutonic languages.

The Third Year Honour Class is conducted in the vernacular of the language which is being studied.

M.A. Class.

A Class may be arranged with the Professor for Students reading the Course in Modern Languages for the M.A. Degree in the Royal University.

XI.—JURISPRUDENCE AND POLITICAL ECONOMY.

See pp. 62, 63.

XII.—PHYSIOLOGY.

For Course see Faculty of Medicine, page 71.

XIII.—THEORY OF MUSIC.

Arrangements were made for a Course of Lectures in the above subject during the Second and Third Terms of the Session 1901–1902.

The Course embraced that prescribed for the First Year in Music at the Royal University, and included Harmony, Counterpoint, and Elementary Composition.

These Lectures will, if possible, be continued during the ensuing Session. Intending Students should communicate with the Registrar before the end of the First Term.

COURSES FOR SCHOLARSHIP EXAMINATIONS,

SESSION 1902–1903.

———

[No Candidate can take Celtic as a subject at any of the Scholarship Examinations unless he has given the Registrar notice of his intention at least six weeks before the date of Examination.]

I.—JUNIOR SCHOLARSHIPS OF THE FIRST YEAR.

[For Regulations see pp. 14 sqq.　For dates of Examinations see pp. 20 and 21.]

1. Faculty of Arts.

A.—*Literary Scholarships of the First Year.*

Subjects:

i. *Latin.*

ii. Any one of the following languages :—*Greek, French, German, Italian, Celtic.*

iii. *English.*

Note.—In Group ii., embracing Greek, French, German, Italian, Celtic, the candidates must answer in one subject, may answer in two, but not in more.

Detailed Courses:

[The maximum mark is attached to each subject, and no mark under one-fifth of this is taken into account.]

i. *Latin* (150), . Livy—*Book* xxii.
　　　　　　　　Sallust—*Catilina.*
　　　　　　　　Horace—*Odes,* Book iii. (omitting 6, 15, 22), and Book iv; *Epistles,* Books i. and ii., i. and ii.
　　　　　　　　A piece of unprescribed Latin.
　　　　　　　　A paper on Latin Grammar.
　　　　　　　　Roman History—133–65 b.c. (Student's Rome).
　　　　　　　　Composition in Latin Prose.

Greek (150), . Homer—*Iliad*, Book vi., and *Odyssey* Book i.
Demosthenes—*De Corona.*
Isocrates—*Panegyricus.*
A piece of unprepared Greek.
A paper in Greek Grammar (Accidence, ordinary Rules of Syntax, and idiomatic Constructions).
Grecian History—560 to 322 B.C. (The Students' Greece, or Oman's History of Greece), and outlines of Greek Literature (Jebb's Primer).
Composition in Greek Prose.

French (100), . Erckmann-Chatrian—*L'Invasion.*
Sandeau—*Mademoiselle de la Seiglière.*
About—*Le Roi des Montagnes.*
French Grammar. Translation from English into French.

ii. Oral Examination.

German (100), . Wachenhusen—*Vom ersten bis zum letzten Schuss.*
Schiller—*Der dreissigjährige Krieg*, Book iv.
German Grammar. Translation from English into German.
Oral Examination.

Italian (100), . Machiavelli—*Istorie Fiorentine*, Books i. and ii.
Alfieri—*Saul.*
Monti—*Caio Gracco.*
Italian Grammar. Translation from English into Italian. Oral Examination.

Celtic (100), . *Eachtra Lomnochtdin an t-Sléibhe-Riffe* (Mac Neil).
Irish Phrase-Book (Hogan).
Handbook of Irish Idioms (Hogan), p. 64 to end.
Grammar and Composition.
Keating's *History of Ireland*, Bk. i., Pt. i. (Joyce).

iii. English (100), . Shakspere—*Julius Cæsar, Coriolanus.*
Bacon—Essays: *of Truth; of Revenge; of Adversity; of Goodness and Goodness of Nature; of Nobility; of Atheism; of Travel; of Wisdom for a Man's Self; of Innovations; of Friendship; of Discourse; of Riches; of Ambition; of Nature in Men; of Custom and Education; of Youth and Age; of Studies; of Praise; of Anger; of Vicissitudes of Things.*
English Grammar and Composition.

B.—*Science Scholarships of the First Year.*

Subjects:

i. *Arithmetic—*
Including Vulgar and Decimal Fractions, Proportion and its applications, and the extraction of the Square Root.

ii. *Algebra—*
Including the Solution of Simple and Quadratic Equations, Progressions, Permutations and Combinations, the Binomial Theorem for a positive Integral exponent, the nature and use of Logarithms, Graphical methods, Representation of Functions by Curves, Problems.

iii. *Geometry*—
   Euclid, Books i.–vi., or the subjects thereof.   Deductions.
iv. *Plane Trigonometry*—
   So far as to include the Solution of Triangles.   Problems.
   v. The use of Logarithmic and Trigonometrical Tables.

2. Faculty of Law.

One Junior Scholarship is awarded in the First Year.
Examination to be held in December (see page 22).
For the Course (see pages 62, *sqq.*).

3. Faculty of Medicine.

Two Junior Scholarships are awarded in the First Year.
(See page 14).

The Course for one is the same as that prescribed for *Literary* Scholarships of the First Year in the Faculty of Arts (pages 48, *sqq.*), and the Course for the other is the same as that prescribed for *Science* Scholarships of the First Year in the Faculty of Arts (page 49, *sq.*). But the Council may withhold either Scholarship if sufficient merit be not shown, and may assign the Scholarship so withheld to the other department.   Exhibitions may also be awarded.

4. School of Engineering.

Two Junior Scholarships are awarded in the First Year.

The Course for these Scholarships is the same as that prescribed for the *Science* Scholarships of the First Year in the Faculty of Arts (page 49, *sq.*). The Council may withhold the Scholarships, or award Exhibitions as in the Faculty of Arts.

II.—JUNIOR SCHOLARSHIPS OF THE SECOND YEAR.

1. Faculty of Arts.

A.—*Literary Scholarships of the Second Year.*

Subjects:

i. *Latin.*
ii. Any one of the following languages :—
   Greek, French, German, Italian.
   [Candidates may select two, but not more, of these four languages.]
iii. *English.*

Detailed Courses:

[The maximum mark is attached to each subject, and no mark under one-fifth of this is taken into account.]

i. *Latin* (200), . Horace—*Odes*, Bk. iii.
Virgil—*Georgics*, ii., and *Aeneid*, ii. and vi.
Livy—*Book* xxxiv.
Cicero—*Philippics*, ii.
Translation at sight.
Latin Prose Composition, and Questions on Grammar and Philology.
Roman History—from B.C. 241 to B.C. 196. (*Mommsen*, vol. ii., Book iii., chaps. 3–8).
Literature—The Augustan Age (Student's Companion to Latin Authors, chap. iii.). Mackail's Latin Literature, chap. ii.

ii.

Greek (200), . Euripides—*Hercules Furens*.
Homer—*Odyssey*, v., vi., and vii.
Herodotus—*Book* viii.
Plato—*Meno*.
Demosthenes—*Leptines*.
Translation at sight.
Greek History—from B.C. 560 to 429 B.C..
Greek Prose Composition, and Questions on Greek Grammar and Philology.

French (150), . Guizot—*Guillaume le Conquérant*.
Maineau—*Les deux Sourds*.
Corneille—*Polyeucte*.
Questions on the Works and Lives of the Authors prescribed.
French Grammar.
Translation from English into French.

German (150), . Uhland—*Ausgewählte Gedichte* (Macmillan).
Benedix—*Die Hochzeitsreise*.
Fontane—*Vor dem Sturm*.
German Grammar.
Translation from English into German.
Questions on the Works and Lives of the Authors prescribed.

Italian (150), . Manzoni—*I Promessi Sposi*.
De Amicis—*Gli Amici di Collegio*.
Tasso—*Gerusalemme Liberata*, Cantos v. to viii., inclusive.
Italian Grammar.
Translation from English into Italian.
Questions on the Works and Lives of the Authors prescribed.

Celtic, . . The Love Songs of Connacht.
The Fate of the Children of Lir.
Translation into Irish Prose.
Irish Grammar and Idioms.
History of Ireland from the commencement of Danish incursions to the reign of Henry II. (inclusive).

iii. *English* (150),   .   Shakspere—*Macbeth*.
Pope—*Essay on Man*.
Johnson—*Life of Pope. Rasselas.*
Gray—*Elegy;* Odes on *Spring, Eton, Adversity,
the Progress of Poesy;* the Bard.
Addison—*Critical Papers* (Arnold's edition).
History of English Literature from 1688 to 1790.
English Composition.

B.—*Science Scholarships of the Second Year.*

Subjects :

(1.) MATHEMATICS.

The Course appointed for Science Scholarships of the First Year, and in addition the following :—

Algebra—

Nature and Simpler Transformations of Equations. Determinants of the Third Order.

Geometry—

Elements of Solid Geometry—Euclid, Book xi., Propositions 1 to 21, inclusive, with easy deductions from them ; Elementary Properties and Mensuration of the Prism, Pyramid, Cone of Revolution and Sphere.

Trigonometry—

Plane Trigonometry (including Mensuration of Plane Figures, Determination of Heights and Distances, Properties of the Circumscribed, Inscribed, and Escribed Circles, and the Use of Tables).

Analytical Geometry—

Discussion of the Equations of the Right Line and Circle in Cartesian and Polar Co-ordinates ; Equations of the Conic Sections, deduced from their Geometrical Definitions, with their Elementary Properties. Easy Problems.

Differential Calculus—

Differentiation of Algebraic and Trigonometrical Functions of a single variable ; *Easy* applications to tangents and normals of plane curves ; Maxima and Minima of Functions of a single variable,

(2). EXPERIMENTAL PHYSICS.

The Elementary Principles of Mechanics, Hydrostatics, Pneumatics, Sound, Heat, Light, Electricity and Magnetism.

2. Faculty of Law.

One Junior Scholarship (value £25) is awarded in the Second Year.
For the date of Examination see page 22.
For the Course see pages 62, *sqq.*

3. Faculty of Medicine.

Two Junior Scholarships (value £25 each) are awarded in the Second Year.
For days and hours of Examination see page 21.
For the Course see page 79.

4. School of Engineering.

Two Junior Scholarships (value £20 each) are awarded in the Second Year.
For days and hours of Examination see pages 20, 21.
For the Course see page 87.

III.—JUNIOR SCHOLARSHIPS OF THE THIRD YEAR.

1. Faculty of Arts.

A.—*Literary Scholarships of the Third Year.*

Subjects:

i. *Latin.*

ii. Any one of the following languages :—

Greek, French, German, Italian, Celtic.

[Candidates may select two, but not more than two of these five languages.]

iii. *English.*

iv. *Logic* (Optional).

v. *History* (Optional).

Detailed Courses:

[The maximum mark is attached to each subject, and no mark under one-fifth of this is taken into account.]

i. *Latin* (200), . Tacitus—*Agricola*; Juvenal—*Satires*, 4, 5, 7, 8, 10 ; Cicero—*In his Letters*, xli. to lxxx. (Tyrrell's edition); *Tusc. Disp.* ii. and iii. ; Lucretius—*Book* i. ; Martial (Macmillan), *Lib. Spec.* and *Epig.* i.–iv.

Translation at Sight.

Latin Prose Composition, and questions on Grammar and Philology.

Roman History—*Mommsen's Provinces of the Roman Empire*, vol. pp. 1–194 (Eng. Trans.); and history of the period from 31 B.C. to 68 A.D. Bury—*Student's Roman Empire*, chaps. i.–xviii. (omitting chaps. 4, 6, 7, 8).

Literature—*Student's Companion to Latin Authors*, chaps. ii. and iii.; Mackail, chap. i.; Sellar—*Roman Poets of the Republic*, chaps. 1, 2, 10, 11, 14.

Greek (200), . Homer—*Iliad*, xvi., xxi., xxii.; Sophocles—*Philoctetes*; Plato—*Phaedo* ; Thucydides, Book vi.

Translation at Sight.

Greek Prose Composition, and questions on Grammar and Philology.

French (150), . Boileau—*L'Art Poétique.*

Molière—*Le Misanthrope.*

Corneille—*Polyeucte* and *Le Cid.*

Merlet—*Etudes littéraires*—Corneille, Racine, Molière, Boileau.

Translation from English into French.

Darmesteter—*Histoire de la langue française, première partie (phonétique).*

German (150) . Schiller—*Die Piccolomini*; *Wallensteins Lager.*

Goethe—*Wahrheit und Dichtung*, i. ii. iii.

Raumer—*Der erste Kreuzzug.*

ii. Behaghel—*Historical Grammar of the German Language*, up to page 87.

Translation from English into German.

German Literature—Kluge, sections 41–57.

Italian (150), . Goldoni—*Un Curioso Accidente.*

Alfieri—*Oreste.*

Machiavelli—*Istorie Fiorentine*, Bks. i.–iv. incl.

Dante—*Inferno.*

Demattio — *Grammatica Storica della lingua Italiana-parte prima.*

Translation from English into Italian.

Fornaciari—*Litteratura Italiana*, chapters 1–9.

Celtic, . . . Diarmid and Grainne.

Cath Rois na Riogh (*later version*).

Translation into Irish Prose.

Irish Grammar and Idioms.

History of Ireland from Richard I. to Henry VIII. (inclusive.)

Detailed Courses (*continued*) :

iii. *English* (150), . Shakspere—*Hamlet* and *Merchant of Venice.*
Spenser—*Faëry Queene,* Book i.
Milton—*Paradise Lost,* i. and ii.
Bacon—*Essays,* i. to xxv. (omitting iii. viii., x.,
xvi., xvii.).
Sidney—*Defence of Poesie.*
History of English Literature, 1579–1616.
English Composition.
iv. *Logic* (50), . . Deductive Logic.
v. *History* (50), . History of England, Ireland, and France, from
1558 to 1689.
History of the Thirty Years' War.

B.—*Science Scholarships of the Third Year.*

Subjects :

i. *Mathematics.*
ii. *Mathematical Physics.*
iii. *Experimental Physics.*
iv. *Chemistry.*
v. *Natural History.*
vi. *Geology, Mineralogy, and Physical Geography.*

Detailed Courses :

[The maximum mark is attached to each subject.]

i. *Mathematics* (140), Algebra and Theory of Equations, including
Infinite Series, Determinants, Probability, and
the solution of Cubic and Biquadratic Equations.
Plane Geometry and Elementary Solid Geometry.
Plane and Spherical Trigonometry.
Analytical Geometry, including Trilinear Co-
ordinates, and the discussion of the General
Equation of the Second Degree.
Differential and Integral Calculus.

ii. *Mathematical
Physics* (100), Mechanics, Hydrostatics, Geometrical Optics, and
Astronomy, as treated by the simpler mathe-
matical methods.

iii. *Experimental
Physics* (100), The Course for this Examination includes that
for the Science Scholarship of the Second
Year ; but a more extensive knowledge of the
subject is required. In addition Candidates
are required to show proficiency in Physica
Manipulation and Measurements.
Schuster and Lee's Practical Physics is recommended.

E

iv. *Chemistry* (100); Lecture Course prescribed for Arts Students of the Second Year. (See page 37.)

v. *Natural History* (100), . Subject of Natural History Lectures and Practical Biology Demonstrations of Second Year Arts.
Students are recommended to read A. Thomson's Zoology, Marshall and Hurst's Practical Biology, Vines' Botany.

vi. *Geology, Mineralogy, and Physical Geography* (100), . . Subjects of Geological Lectures delivered to Second Year Arts Students.
Geikie's Class Book. Dana's Class Book of Mineralogy. Gregory's Physical Geography.

Candidates must answer in two, may answer in three, but not more of the foregoing subjects.

2. Faculty of Medicine.

Two Junior Scholarships (value £25 each) are awarded in the Third Year.
For days and hours of Examination see page 22.
For the Courses see page 80.

3. School of Engineering.

One Junior Scholarship (value £20) is awarded in the Third Year.
For days and hours of Examination see page 21.
For the Course see page 87.

IV.—JUNIOR SCHOLARSHIPS OF THE FOURTH YEAR.

Faculty of Medicine.

Two Junior Scholarships (value £25 each) are awarded in the Fourth Year.
For days and hours of Examination see page 22.
For the Courses see page 81.

V.—SENIOR SCHOLARSHIPS.

[For Regulations see pp. 13, 14.]

1.—ANCIENT CLASSICS.

Greek, . . Pindar—*Nemeans*, i–vi.
Aristotle—*Poetics.*
Æschylus—*Agamemnon*, and *Choephoræ.*
Aristophanes—*Acharnians*, and *Wasps.*
Andocides and Lysias (Jebb's Selections).
Translation from an unprescribed author.
Grecian History.
Composition in Greek Prose.
Higher Greek Grammar and Philology.

Latin, . . Tacitus—*Annals*, xv., xvi.
Lucretius—*Book* i.
Plautus—*Asinaria, Rudens.*
Cicero—*Ad Atticum*, v., vi., vii.
Virgil—*Aeneid*, v., vi., vii.
Horace—*Odes*, ii. and iii.
Persius—*Sat.* 1, 2, 3, 5, 6. .
Roman History. Mommsen's *Provinces of the Roman Empire*, vol. i.
Giles—*Manual of Comparative Philology* (Parts i. and ii.)
Student's Companion to Latin Authors, chaps. 2, 3, 4.
Latin Prose Composition.
Sellar—*Poets of the Republic*, chaps. 1–7.

2.—ENGLISH AND MODERN LANGUAGES.

(i.) *English*, 100, . Chaucer—*The Prologue.*
Shakspere—*Lear* and *Richard III.*
Wordsworth—*Excursion*, i., ii.
Byron—M. Arnold's *Selections* (including Preface).
Coleridge—*Lectures and Notes on Shakspere* (Bohn's Series, pp. 183–394).
Coleridge—*Biographia Literaria*, ch. xiv. to ch. xxii.
Cowper—*Task.*
History of English Literature, 1800–1850.
English Essay.

E 2

(ii.) Any two of the following : —*French, German Italian, Celtic.*

French, 100, . Taine—*L'Ancien Régime*, ii., iii., iv.
Sanson—*Littérature française—Le XVII. Siècle.*
Corneille—*Le Cid.*
Voltaire—*Mérope.*
Molière—*Les Précieuses Ridicules.*
Buffon—*Discours sur le style.*
Darmesteter et Hatzfeld—*Tableau de la Littéra-
ture au seizième Siècle.*
Darmesteter—*Histoire de la langue française,
deuxième partie (Morphologie).*
Translation from English into French.
Essay in French.

German, 100, . Schiller—*Die Braut von Messina.*
Goethe—*First Part of Faust.*
Freytag—*Die Verlorene Handschrift*, Buch I.
Schiller—*Wilhelm Tell.*
Kluge—History of German Literature, sections
41–64.
Behaghel—History of the German Language, to
page 87.
Translation from English into German.
Essay in German.

Italian, 50, . Dante—*Il Purgatorio.*
Monti—*In Morte di Ugo Basseville, In Morte di
Lorenzo Mascheroni.*
Fogazzaro—*Piccolo Mondo Antico.*
Tasso—*La Gerusalemme Liberata.*
Manzoni—*Il Conte di Carmagnola.*
Gino Capponi—*Storia della Republica di Firenze,*
books 1, 2.
Translation from English into Italian.
Elements of the History of the Italian Language.
History of Italian Literature from the death of
Boccaccio to Tasso.
Essay in Italian.

Celtic, 50, . The Life of Alexander the Great.
Cath Rois na Riogh (older version).
Prose Composition in Irish.
Windisch's Irish Grammar, with Lessons at the
end.
The Prosody of the Irish Language.
History of Ireland from the reign of Edward VI.
to the reign of Elizabeth (inclusive).

3.—MATHEMATICS.

In addition to the Mathematical Course appointed for Science Scholarships of the third year:—

Analytical Geometry of two and of three dimensions, including Higher Plane Curves.

Differential and Integral Calculus, including applications to Geometry.

Differential Equations.

4.—NATURAL PHILOSOPHY.

Mathematical Physics—

Statics, with the Elementary Theory of Attractions.
Dynamics of a Particle.
The Elementary Principles of the Dynamics of Rigid Systems.
Hydrostatics.
Geometrical and Physical Optics.
Spherical Astronomy.

Experimental Physics—

The subjects treated in Everett's Translation of Deschanel's Natural Philosophy, Preston's Theory of Light, Preston's Theory of Heat, Fleming's Alternate Current Transformer, Part I., and Ewing's Magnetic Induction.

Candidates will be required to show a practical knowledge of the use of Physical apparatus.

5.—METAPHYSICS, POLITICAL SCIENCE, AND HISTORY.

I. (A) *General Metaphysics—*

(i.) Object, methods, and chief divisions of Metaphysics.

(ii.) Notion of Being. Conceptions of Existence, Essence, Substance. Quality, Accident, Nature, Subsistence, Personality, Unity, Number, Identity, Diversity, Simplicity, Extension, Quantity, Space, Duration, Finite, Infinite; Relation; Possibility; Cause and Effect.

(B) *Psychology—*

(i.) Analysis of Psychological Phenomena, as Consciousness, Sensation, Imagination, Remembrance, Judgment, Reasoning, Appetite, Emotion, Volition, Freedom of Will.

(ii.) Subject, Object, and their relation in cognition. Perception, Conception. Laws of mental development, and Association of mental phenomena. The Nature and Properties of the Human Mind; mutual relations of the Mind and Body. Immortality.

(C) *Outlines of the History of Philosophy*, from Descartes to Kant (inclusive).

Candidates will be required to answer on the foregoing Course—

Either according to the principles of the philosophy of Aquinas, as expounded by Maher, Rickaby, &c.

Or according to the principles of Sir W. Hamilton's Psychological and Metaphysical system ; with special reference to Hamilton's Lectures on Metaphysics, Lectures XVI. to XL., and Notes A, B, C, in his edition of Reid, excluding the merely historical matter contained in those notes.

II. (A) *Political Science* (100).

(B) *Jurisprudence—*

> Austin—*Jurisprudence* (Student's Ed.).
> Holland—*Jurisprudence.*
> Maine—*Ancient Law.*
> > *Early History of Institutions.*
> > *Early Law and Custom.*

(C) *Economics—*

> Marshall—*Elements of Economics,* vol. i. (Third Edition).
> J. S. Mill—*Political Economy* (Books iii. and v.).
> C. S. Devas—*Political Economy* (Second Edition).
> Gibbins—*Industry in England* (Second Edition).
> J. S. Nicholson—*Money* (Fifth Edition).
> G. Clare—*Money-market Primer* (Second Edition).

III. *Modern History—*

> The History of Great Britain and Ireland, France and Germany, from 1688 to 1815.

6.—CHEMISTRY.

(i.) *Theory of Chemistry*—inorganic and organic—

Books recommended :

Roscoe and Schorlemmer's *Treatise on Chemistry,* non-metals and metals.
Perkin and Kipping—*Organic Chemistry, or*
Richter—*Organic Chemistry* (translated by Smith).
L. Meyer—*Outlines of Theoretical Chemistry* (translated by Bedson and Williams).
Hjelt—*General Organic Chemistry* (translated by Tingle).

(ii.) *Laboratory Experiments*—Qualitative and simple quantitative (volumetric and gravimetric) analysis—

Books recommended :

Clowes—*Practical Chemistry.*
Clowes and Coleman—*Quantitative Analysis.*

7.—NATURAL HISTORY.

The Examination for the Senior Scholarship in Natural History will include the subjects of the Third Year Honour Course in Arts.

Candidates are advised to pay attention to the practical work.

8.—ENGINEERING.

For the necessary qualification of Candidates and the Course prescribed for Examination see pp. 13, 87.

9.—ANATOMY AND PHYSIOLOGY.

For the conditions of Candidature see pp. 13, 82.

Faculty of Law.

COURSE OF STUDY.

Courses of Twenty-four Lectures are delivered to each Class, commencing in the First Term, on days and hours that are arranged with the Professors.

The following Course of Study is prescribed :—

FIRST YEAR.—The Law of Real Property and the Principles of Conveyancing; Jurisprudence.

SECOND YEAR.—Equity, Personal Property, Contracts, and Bankruptcy; Civil Law.

LAW CLASSES.

FIRST YEAR. — *Jurisprudence.* — Course of Twenty-four Lectures in the First and Second Terms.

Books Recommended.

Holland—Jurisprudence.
Austin—Jurisprudence (Student's edition).
Maine—Ancient Law.
Maine—Early History of Institutions.
Maine—Early Law and Custom.

SECOND YEAR. — *Roman Law.* — Course of Twenty-four Lectures in the First and Second Terms.

Justinian—Institutes (Sanders).
Mackenzie—Studies in Roman Law.

ARTS CLASSES.

Pass.—Courses of Twenty-four Lectures during the First and Second Terms are delivered on :—

(*a*) POLITICAL ECONOMY.

Books Recommended.

Marshall—Elements, vol. i.
Devas—Political Economy.
Nicholson—Money.

Honours.—Additional Lectures supplementing the Pass Course.

Books Recommended.

J. S. Mill—Political Economy.
Ingram—History of Political Economy.
Gibbins—Industry in England.

(*b*) JURISPRUDENCE.—(Honour Course).

Books Recommended.

Holland—Jurisprudence.
Austin—Jurisprudence (Student's edition).
Maine—Ancient Law.
Maine—Early History of Institutions.
Maine—Early Law and Custom.

EXAMINATIONS.

MATRICULATION.

The same Course as for Arts, page 23.

JUNIOR SCHOLARSHIPS.

One (value £25) tenable by a Student of the FIRST YEAR.

Subjects :

Law of Property, &c.—

Williams—Real Property.
Goodeve—Modern Law of Real Property.

Jurisprudence—

Holland—Jurisprudence.
Austin—Jurisprudence (Student's edition).
Maine—Ancient Law.
Maine—Early History of Instituuons.
Maine—Early Law and Custom.

One (value £25) tenable by a Student of the SECOND YEAR.

Equity—

Snell—Principles of Equity.
White and Tudor—Leading Cases in Equity, vol. i.

Law of Property, &c.—

Williams—Personal Property.
Smith—Lectures on the Law of Contract.

E 8

Jurisprudence and Roman Law—

Jurisprudence as for First Year's Scholarship.
The Elements of Roman Law.
Mackenzie—Studies in Roman Law.

Students intending to proceed for the Certificate of the Law Professors, so as to entitle them to serve an apprenticeship of *four* years instead of *five*, under the provisions of the Attorneys and Solicitors (Ireland) Act, 1886*, are required to enter their names with the Registrar, *either as Matriculated or Non-Matriculated* Students, and pay the necessary College and Class Fees to the Bursar before the commencement of the Law Lectures in each Session.

Such Students are required to attend all the Lectures and pass all the Examinations prescribed for the first and second years of the Course of Study for Candidates for the Diploma of Elementary Law.

For the Degrees of LL.B. and LL.D., see Regulations of Royal University (Appendix).

---

* Every person who, as a Matriculated or as a Non-Matriculated Student of the University of Dublin or of any of the Queen's Colleges in Ireland, shall have attended or shall attend any prescribed Lectures, and shall have passed or shall pass any prescribed Examinations of the Professors of the Faculty of Law in the said University of Dublin or in any of the said Queen's Colleges, for a period of Two Collegiate Years, and who shall have duly served as an Apprentice under Indentures for the term of four years, in like manner as by this Act provided respecting the service for the term of five years, shall at any time after the expiration of five years from the commencement of such attendance on Lectures, or of such period of service, which shall first happen, be qualified to be sworn and to be admitted as an Attorney or Solicitor respectively, according to the nature of his service, of the several and respective superior Courts of Law or Equity in Ireland, as fully and effectually to all intents and purposes as any person having been bound and having served five years is qualified to be sworn, and to be admitted or enrolled and registered an Attorney or Solicitor under or by virtue of this Act.—EXTRACT.—29 & 30 Victoria, cap. 84.

Faculty of Medicine.

COURSE OF STUDY AND EXAMINATION.

The attention of Students is specially directed to the absolute necessity for their being registered with the Branch Medical Council not later than fifteen days after the commencement of those Courses of Lectures, certificates of attendance on which they have to produce.

No student can be registered until he has passed the *Preliminary Examination in General Education* required by the General Medical Council, or one of the other examinations recognised as qualifying for registration, among which are included :—

The Matriculation Examination of the Royal University. (Certificate to include the required subjects.)

The Preliminary Examination of the Royal College of Surgeons of Ireland. (The required subjects to be passed at one time.)

Intermediate Education of Ireland :—

Middle Grade Examination. (The required subjects to be passed at one time.)

Senior Grade Examination. (Certificates to include the required subjects.)

The Preliminary Examination in General Education, required to be passed previous to Registration as a Medical Student, shall be as follows :—

(*a*) ENGLISH; (Paraphrasing; Grammar; Composition; questions on English History and Geography).

(*b*) LATIN; (Grammar; Translation into English from unprescribed Latin books; Translation into Latin of a continuous English passage and of short idiomatic English sentences).

(*c*) MATHEMATICS; (Arithmetic; Algebra including easy quadratic equations; Geometry including the subject-matter of Euclid, Books I., II., and III., and simple deductions).

(*d*) One of the following subjects :—

    (*a*) GREEK (Grammar; Translation into English from unprescribed Greek books; Translation into Greek of short idiomatic English sentences) ; or

    (*β*) A MODERN LANGUAGE (Grammar; Translation into English from unprescribed books; Translation of a continuous English passage, and of short idiomatic sentences).

Course of Study.

The Curriculum extends over at least five years, and comprises the following* :—

COURSE OF STUDY.

Natural Philosophy.
Practical Physics.
Chemistry.
Practical Chemistry.
Botany with Herborizations for practical study, and Zoology.
Anatomy and Physiology.
Practical Anatomy.

Practical Physiology.
Materia Medica and Pharmacy.
Theory and Practice of Surgery.
Obstetrics and Gynæcology.
Theory and Practice of Medicine
Medical Jurisprudence.
Pathology.

The Courses prescribed to Scholars of the several years are given on pp. 78–82.

DAYS AND HOURS OF LECTURES.

Subjects.	Months.	Mon.	Tues.	Wed.	Thrs.	Fri.	Sat.
French, ...	VI.	—	10	—	10	—	10
German, ...	VI.	—	—	9	—	—	9
Botany and Zoology,† .	VI.	2‡	3	2‡	3	2‡	3
Natural Philosophy, . .	VI.	—	12	—	12	—	12
Practical Physics,§ .	—	9	—	—	—	9	—
Chemistry (Pass and Honour),	VI.	12	—	12	—	12	—
Chemistry, Laboratory (Pass or Honour),	III.	3	—	3	—	3	—
Physiology, . . .	VI.	9	9	9	9	9	—
Anatomy, ...	VI.	1	1	1	1	1	—
Practical Pharmacy, .	III.	—	3	—	—	—	3
Materia Medica, . .	III.	—	2	—	2	—	2
Anatomy, ...	VI.	1	1	1	1	1	—
Practical Physiology, and Practical Histology, }	III.	2	—	2	—	2	—
Surgery, . . .	VI.	—	12	—	12	12	—
Midwifery, . . .	VI.	2	—	2	—	2	—
Medicine, ...	VI.	—	2	—	2	—	2
Pathology,‖ . . .	III.	—	—	—	—	—	—
Medical Jurisprudence, } Toxicology,‖ . . }	IV. {	12	—	12	—	—	—

* The Regulations of Licensing Bodies whose requirements differ from the above Curriculum may be learned on application to the Professors of the Faculty of Medicine.

† Students taking Practical Biology and Natural History are admitted to both Classes on payment of a fee of £3.

‡ These Lectures are delivered in the last week of November, and in December, January, and February. Students may attend these lectures alone, and obtain a certificate.

§ The Class in Practical Physics begins at the beginning of the Second Term, and lasts till the end of the Session.

‖ At hours to be arranged.

Attendance on Lectures is strictly obligatory.

The Lectures of the Professors in the Medical School of Queen's College, Galway, and the Clinical Instruction in the Galway Hospitals, are recognised as qualifying for the Diplomas of the Royal College of Physicians and Surgeons of Ireland, England, and Scotland, and for the Medical Degrees of the University of London, and the Royal University of Ireland.

CLINICAL TEACHING.

Clinical Teaching is carried on in THE GALWAY HOSPITAL, established as a Public General Hospital (in the place of the County Galway Infirmary) by Act of Parliament (1892).

The appointment of the Medical Staff being vested, by the Act, in the Local Government Board, that Board has made the following appointments :—

Physicians—
PROFESSOR KINKEAD.
PROFESSOR LYNHAM.

Surgeons—
PROFESSOR PYE.
PROFESSOR COLAHAN.
PROFESSOR BRERETON.

Gynæcologist—
PROFESSOR KINKEAD.

The interests of Students are expressly recognised and secured by section 2 of the Act, which provides that—

"The Hospital shall be available as a Clinical School for Medical Students attending the Queen's College, and such Students may attend the Hospital at such times, and subject to such regulations, as may be prescribed."

For further information application may be made to—

PROFESSOR PYE,

*Hon. Secretary of the Medical
Staff of Galway Hospital.*

In addition to this, the GALWAY FEVER HOSPITAL* is open to Students of the Clinical Class.

---

* The Royal University and other Licensing Bodies require a certifi-cate of attendance for three months at an hospital devoted to the treatment of fever.

Medical Officers—

PROFESSOR COLAHAN.

M. A. LYDON, L.R.C.S., L.R.C.P. EDIN.

Apothecary—

N. GREALY, L.R.C.S., L.R.C.P. EDIN.

Here opportunities are afforded for studying the various forms of Fever and Zymotic disease admitted during the College Session.

The Medical Faculty has also made arrangements with the Medical Officers for the admission of Students to the GALWAY UNION HOSPITAL.

Medical Officers—

PROFESSOR COLAHAN, M.D., M.CH.

M. A. LYDON, L.R.C.S., L.R.C.P.

*Apothecary—*N. GREALY, L.R.C.S., L.R.C.P. EDIN.

This Hospital affords an extensive field for the study of all classes of disease, acute and chronic. A special ward is set apart for the diseases of children, in which Students will have an opportunity of studying this important class of cases.

Opportunities for Extern Practice and Vaccination are afforded at GALWAY DISPENSARY, No. 1.

Medical Officer—

MARTIN F. LYDEN, L.R.C.S., L.R.C.P., EDIN.

Students whose names are on the Clinical Roll of THE GALWAY HOSPITAL may attend any of the above-named Institutions without further charge.*

I.—NATURAL PHILOSOPHY.

(For Courses see Faculty of Arts, p. 33.)

II.—CHEMISTRY.

(1) LECTURE COURSE.

First Year Course for Pass and Honours. Inorganic and Organic Chemistry.—The class meets at 12 o'clock on Mondays, Wednesdays, and Fridays throughout the Medical Session.

* For further information as to the arrangements for clinical teaching (which are liable to alteration) application should be made to Professor Pye, Hon. Sec. of Medical Staff of Galway Hospital.

The Lectures embrace a consideration of the leading facts of Inorganic and Organic Chemistry, and include both the Pass and Honour subjects required for the First Examination in Medicine of the Royal University, or for other corresponding Examinations.

About forty Lectures are devoted to a detailed study of the non-metallic elements, their reactions, and the constitution of the compounds they form. The general facts established are then reviewed, including the weight and volume relation in chemical reactions, the molecular hypothesis, the atomic hypothesis, and the relative weight of molecules and atoms. The leading metals and their more important compounds are briefly considered, and the remaining Lectures are devoted to Elementary Organic Chemistry, embracing the general methods of study of organic compounds, their identification, qualitative and quantitative composition, the constitution of molecules, isomerism, and including the reactions of the chief members of the fatty and aromatic groups.

(2) LABORATORY COURSES, PRACTICAL CHEMISTRY.

Second Year Course for Pass.—This course consists of about forty Lectures of two hours each, commencing early in the first term, and ending at the close of the second term. The class works from 3 to 5 o'clock on Mondays, Wednesdays, and Fridays. The experiments are adapted to the requirements of the Pass Second Examination in Medicine of the Royal University, and of other corresponding Examinations. A *Second Year Six Months' Course for Honours*, adapted to the Honour Second Examination in Medicine of the Royal University, will be arranged for Students who desire it.

(3) TEXT-BOOKS.

For Lecture Course.—Newth, Inorganic Chemistry; or Richter, Inorganic Chemistry (trans. Smith); Turpin, Organic Chemistry, and Perkin and Kipping, Organic Chemistry (vol. ii.), or for Elementary Examinations, Luff and Page, Manual of Chemistry.

For Laboratory Courses.—Clowes and Coleman, Elementary Qualitative Analysis, or Clowes, Practical Chemistry; also Rideal, Practical Organic Chemistry.

III.—NATURAL HISTORY.

(For Courses see Faculty of Arts, p. 40.)

IV.—MODERN LANGUAGES.

(For Courses see Faculty of Arts, p. 46.)

V.—ANATOMY AND PHYSIOLOGY.

A. The Course laid down for Students in ANATOMY comprises :—

(*a*) *Descriptive Anatomy.*—A Course of Systematic Lectures on the Human Body. In the First Term, Osteology and Arthrology are taken up, and special attention is paid to the cultivation of a power of accurate observation and precise description.

Later on, more attention is gradually directed to the Topographic Anatomy of regions that are of medical or surgical importance.

The dissections for these Lectures are made by Prosectors appointed from amongst the best Students.

Casts, plates, and permanent dissections are used, sparingly at first, to a larger extent towards the end of the Course.

(*b*) *Dissections*, made by each Student independently, under the supervision of the Professor and Demonstrator. The Students are advised to learn Topographic Anatomy by means of a series of mental pictures; and, in order to secure vivid pictures, it is pointed out that careful and methodical dissections must be made.

The results of dissections are compared with the special information obtained by frozen sections, as well as with surface Anatomy of the living body, and the knowledge of its deeper organs obtained by auscultation and percussion.

B. In PHYSIOLOGY three Classes are formed:—Junior, Senior, and Practical.

To the *Junior Class* Lectures are delivered on the Histology and functions of the tissues, and of the organs of vegetable life, to which is added a special account of the structure and functions of muscle and nerve.

In the *Senior Class* the highest animal functions are taken first, beginning with a study of the nervous system and organs of sense.

The great facts of Physiology are studied by an examination of the original evidence, and, when practicable, by a repetition of the experiments that establish them.

For this purpose special portions of Physiology are taken each year.

The *Practical Class* meets in the second and third terms, on three days weekly. Each meeting occupies two hours. A separate table in the Laboratory is provided for each Student. In succession the Students undertake:—

I. PRACTICAL HISTOLOGY.—A Microscope and accessories are at the disposal of each Student.
About 60 preparations of the tissues and organs are made, which become the property of the preparer.

II. PRACTICAL EXPERIMENTAL PHYSIOLOGY.—The phenomena of muscle and nerve, of circulation and respiration, and of the sense organs, are studied experimentally.

III. PRACTICAL CHEMICAL PHYSIOLOGY.—Analysis of the various animal substances and fluids referred to in the General Course of Lectures are made by each Student, special attention being paid to work that is important from a clinical point of view.
A dark room for photographic work and for the use of the Laryngoscope and Ophthalmoscope is in readiness.
The *Laboratory* contains an excellent collection of instruments used in physiological work.

MUSEUM.

To the Physiological Department is attached the Museum of Human and Comparative Anatomy. The preparations in this Museum are arranged in physiological series according to functions of organs.

They form a valuable addition to the teaching facilities in Physiology; enabling the Professor to illustrate his Lecture by extended references to Comparative Physiology.

This Museum was founded by the late Dr. CROKER KING, some time Professor of Anatomy and Physiology in this College, afterwards Medical Commissioner of the Local Government Board. It was remodelled and enlarged by his successor in the Chair, PROFESSOR CLELAND, F.R.S., now Professor of Anatomy in the University of Glasgow. To Professor Cleland the College is indebted for many valuable specimens which form a permanent record of his work here.

VI.—PRACTICE OF MEDICINE.

Six Months' Course.

On Tuesdays, Thursdays, and Saturdays, at 2 o'clock. The Course is divided into two parts. The first comprises a general introduction to the study of Medicine, and a series of Lectures on the classification of diseases; the general principles of ætiology, semeiology, diagnosis, and therapeusis; the method of clinical examinations; body temperature, and pulse in disease, and kindred subjects.

In the second and longer portion, the specific infections and constitutional diseases, and the diseases of the various systems and organs of the body, are taken up in regular order. The morbid anatomy and pathology, the symptoms, course, duration, and treatment are reviewed; and in addition, the causation, complications, and sequelæ, prognosis, vital statistics, differential diagnosis, prophylaxis, &c., receive attention.

The Lectures are illustrated by pathological preparations—both macroscopic and microscopic—apparatus, instruments, drawings, &c.; and the Professor, being one of the Physicians to the Galway Hospital, has an excellent opportunity of demonstrating to the Class the facts and methods treated of in the Lectures.

Examinations are frequently held during the Session, and by this means attention is paid to the progress of each member of the Class.

VII.—SURGERY.

The Surgical Lectures are delivered by the Professor of Surgery, at the College, on three days each week during the Session.

During the *First Term*, inflammation, general Surgical diseases, theory of treatment of wounds, &c., furnish the subjects of the Lectures. The class-books recommended are "Walsham's Surgery," "Erichsen's Surgery," and "Green's Pathology."

Early in the *Second Term*, fractures and dislocations form the subject of the Lectures, where much assistance is given by dry specimens of bones, both normal and abnormal.

Special injuries and surgical diseases form the subjects of Lecture during the remainder of the Session.

Treves' System of Surgery and Cassell's Clinical Manuals in connection with the subjects of the Lectures are recommended.

Surgical instruments are shown in connection with the Lectures, so as to give the Students the opportunity of learning the special use of each instrument.

At the termination of the Session an Examination is held, the questions being taken from different portions of the Course, and prizes given for high answering.

VIII.—MATERIA MEDICA.

Lectures are delivered at 2 P.M. on Tuesdays, Thursdays, and Saturdays. The Course comprises a study of the Drugs, organic and inorganic, of the British Pharmacopœia, and a review of the more important Drugs that are not officinal.

The earlier Lectures include a study of :—

1. The general method of classifying drugs.
2. The sources and natural conditions of medicines.
3. The selection and collection of medicines.
4. The active principles of medicines derived from the vegetable kingdom.
5. The modes of administration of drugs.
6. The several circumstances that influence the action of drugs in the system.
7. Prescription-reading and prescription-writing.

Several Lectures are next devoted to a critical study of the Official Pharmacopœia.

The succeeding Lectures include the study of individual drugs, organic and inorganic, according to a pre-arranged therapeutical grouping, and after the following method:— Source (geographical, botanical); characters and tests; impurities and incompatibilities; preparations and doses; therapeutic value.

At the commencement of each Lecture the Class are examined on the previous day's work.

THE MUSEUM is enlarged and replenished from year to year, so that the drugs exhibited may be as fresh and characteristic as possible, and contains a complete set of the official drugs, and an extensive collection of drugs not official. These are exhibited to Students during Lecture, and ample opportunity is given them to investigate the physical properties and characteristic appearance of each specimen.

Text-Books.

Whitla—*Pharmacy, Materia Medica and Therapeutics* (6th edition): White—*Materia Medica,* &c.; Mitchell Bruce—*Materia Medica,* &c.: F. T. Roberts—*The Officinal Materia Medica;* C. L. Semple—*Elements of Materia Medica.*

Works of Reference.

Ringer—*Therapeutics;* Farquharson—*Guide to Therapeutics;* Binz—*Elements of Therapeutics;* Lauder Brunton—*Pharmacology, Therapeutics, and Materia Medica, Tables of Materia Medica.*

PRACTICAL PHARMACY.

1. Is taught in the new Laboratory, which is fitted up with all the appliances, and supplied with all the drugs necessary for a comprehensive study of the subject.

2. Lectures commence early in the first Term, and continue for three months. Not less than two Lectures are delivered in each week. Tuesdays and Saturdays at 3 o'clock.

3. Each Student is obliged to carry out personally the different manipulations and experiments suggested by the Professor in the course of study followed.

4. The earlier Lectures are devoted to a study of the more important pharmaceutical processes—

> Sub-division of Drugs.
> Weighing.
> Measuring.
> Sifting.
> Elutriation, Suspension, Emulsions.
> Solution (Pharmacopœial Solvents).
> Crystallization, Evaporation, Precipitation, and Sublimation.

During the study of the above the Students are obliged to prepare some of the more important pharmaceutical preparations involving the processes enumerated.

5. Attention is next directed to the study of incompatibility, after which several Lectures are devoted to the preparation of plants for pharmaceutical purposes, separation of active principles, &c.

6. The concluding Lectures are devoted to the practical study of prescribing, compounding, and dispensing.

The Professor, at the commencement of each Lecture, supplies the notes necessary for the day's work.

IX.—MIDWIFERY.

1. *Obstetrics.*

The Course occupies six months, and covers :—Anatomy of pelvic organs, mechanism of delivery, conception, pregnancy (including diseases of pregnancy), abortion, normal and abnormal labour, obstetric operations, puerperal diseases.

Gynæcology.

Instruments; methods of examination; operations; and diseases peculiar to women.

Lectures are delivered on Mondays, Wednesdays, and Fridays, from 2 to 3 P.M., during the Session.

THE MUSEUM.

The important Museum, collected by the late Dr. MONTGOMERY, and purchased for this Department, contains many very valuable Physiological and Pathological specimens, models, and diagrams. A large collection of Obstetric and Gynæcological instruments has been added.

The Library of the Department is very complete, and to it are added each year, as they are published, the best books and journals on Obstetrics, Gynæcology, and Pædiatrics.

Text-Books.

Playfair's or Leishman's Midwifery.
Barnes—Obstetric Operations.
MacNaughton Jones—Diseases of Women.
Hart and Barbour—Diseases of Women.
Goodall—Lessons on Gynæcology.
Lawson Tait—Diseases of Women and Abdominal Surgery.
Kelly—Operative Gynæcology.

X.—MEDICAL JURISPRUDENCE.

A. *Forensic Medicine.*—From 12 to 1 on Mondays and Wednesdays.

> Poisoning, Suspicion and Symptoms of ; Process of Law ; Evidence ; Signs of Death ; Post-mortem Examinations ; Crimes against the Person ; Starvation ; Suicide ; Heat and Cold ; Insanity, &c.

B. *Toxicology.*—At hours to be arranged with the Professor of Chemistry at the commencement of the Session. The Lectures are based on experiments made partly by the Lecturer and partly by the Students, and embrace the methods of detecting the leading poisons.

The *Library* in this department includes not only the standard works on Forensic Medicine, but those on Criminal Anthropology, on Public Health, Inebriety and Insanity. The *Law* Library is also available for reference.

Text-Books.

> Luff's Text-Book of Forensic Medicine and Toxicology ; Taylor's Medical Jurisprudence (Stevenson) ; Tidy's Legal Medicine ; Guy and Ferrier's Medical Jurisprudence ; Kinkead's Medical Practitioner's Guide.

XI.—FEVER.

This Course of Lectures, including Clinical Instruction, will be delivered at days and hours to be arranged.

XII.—PATHOLOGY.

The Course for 1901-1902 was for three months—two Lectures a week in Theoretical Pathology, and three meetings of the Class weekly in Practical Pathology.

The Laboratory is supplied with Microscopes, Apparatus, and Re-agents.

There is an extensive and valuable collection of Pathological preparations and specimens at the disposal of the Lecturer for use in the Class.

EXAMINATIONS.

MATRICULATION.

See the Regulations, pages 6 and 23.

SCHOLARSHIPS.*

A. FIRST YEAR.—For one Scholarship the Course is the same as that prescribed for the Literary Scholarships of the First Year; for the other Scholarship the Course is the same as that prescribed for Science Scholarships of the First Year, in the Faculty of Arts.†

A Scholar or Exhibitioner of the First Year shall attend the following Courses‡ :—

Anatomy,	French or German.
Chemistry,	Natural Philosophy, treated
Natural History.	Experimentally.

---

* For Conditions of Tenure and for Exhibitions, see pages 13, 14, By a recent regulation of the Council, all Scholarships and Exhibitions of the Second, Third, and Fourth Years may now be competed for by Students who have attained the requisite standing in any Medical School recognised by the College Council, and have passed the Matriculation Examination in the College.

† See pages 46, 47, and 48.

‡ Scholars of the First Year shall be exempt from attendance on Lectures in French (or German), and Physics, who shall produce Certificates of (a) having passed a University Examination, which includes these two subjects, or (b) of having attended a Course of Lectures in these two subjects in any Institution recognised by the Council of this College. In place of French (or German), the Council may accept another language as an alternative.

B. Second Year.—A Student, in order to compete for a Scholarship of the Second Year, must have Matriculated, and must be of one year's standing, and not more.

Subjects of Examination.

1. *Anatomy* (100).—Osteology and Arthrology; also the Myology of the Limbs.

Candidates may be examined on specimens placed before them.

2. *Chemistry* (100).—The First Year Lecture Course in Chemistry, for which see page 68.

3. *Natural History* (100).—Vertebrata and Invertebrata.

Structural and Physiological Botany; Principles of Classification; Characters of the more common Natural Orders.

4. *Natural Philosophy* (50). — Elements of Mechanics, Hydrostatics, Pneumatics, Acoustics, Optics, Heat, Electricity, and Magnetism, treated principally from an Experimental point of view.

5. *Practical Physics* (50).—The First Year Practical Course, see page 33.

And either of the following—

6. *French* (50).* *German* (50).*

For the Courses, see the Second Year Scholarship in Arts, page 51.

No mark under one-fifth of the maximum shall be taken into account in any subject.

Scholars or Exhibitioners of the Second Year shall attend the following Courses :—

Physiology.	Practical Anatomy.
Practical Chemistry (if not taken in the First Year).	Materia Medica.

* The Candidates may select either French or German. When entering his name with the Bursar, the Candidate shall declare the subjects which he selects for Examination.

C. THIRD YEAR.—In order to compete for a Scholarship of the Third Year, a Student must—

(*a*) Have Matriculated.

(*b*) Be of two years' standing and not more.

(*c*) Have attended in this, or some Medical School recognised by the College Council, Courses of Lectures in at least four of the following subjects :—

Anatomy and Physiology.   Practical Chemistry.
Chemistry.   Practical Anatomy.
Botany.   Materia Medica.
Zoology.

Subjects of Examination.

1. *Physiology* (100).—Physiology of Muscle and Nerve, Organs and Functions of Digestion, Absorption, Circulation, Respiration, and Urination, together with the Blood and its Elaboration.   The Examination will include practical work.

2. *Practical Anatomy* (100).—Joints, Muscles, Vessels, Viscera, and Brain.
During the Examination, Candidates may be called on to make dissections, or to describe structures placed before them.

3. *Materia Medica and Therapeutics* (100).—The Medicines and Compounds in the British Pharmacopœia.   Candidates will be required to identify specimens and write prescriptions.

4. *Laboratory Experiments (Practical Chemistry)* (100).— The Second Year Laboratory Course for Pass described, page 69.
No mark under 30 shall be taken into account in any subject.
A Student to whom a Third Year Scholarship has been awarded shall attend, during the year of his election, four at least of the following Courses :—

Anatomy and Physiology.   Midwifery and Diseases of Women.
Practical Anatomy.   Theory and Practice of Medicine.
Theory and Practice of Surgery.   Medical Jurisprudence.

D. FOURTH YEAR.—In order to compete for a Scholarship of the Fourth Year, a Student must—

(*a*) Have Matriculated.

(*b*) Be of three years' standing and not more.

(*c*) Have attended in this or some School recognised by the College Council, Lectures in Anatomy and Physiology, and three at least of the following Courses:—

Materia Medica and Therapeutics.	Theory and Practice of Surgery.
Medical Jurisprudence.	Obstetrics and Gynæcology.
Theory and Practice of Medicine.	

Subjects of Examination.

1. *Anatomy and Physiology* (100).—Functions of Cerebro-spinal Axis, Cranial Nerves, Sense Organs and Larynx. Analysis of Bile, Urine, Blood (including quantitative determination of Grape-sugar and Urea, and the use of the Spectroscope).

And *any three* of the following in which he has attended Lectures :—

2. *Materia Medica and Therapeutics* (100).—The Medicines and Compounds of the British Pharmacopœia, together with the Physiological action and Therapeutical effects of the following substances:—Iron, Mercury, Iodine, Arsenic, Aconite, Opium, Digitalis, Alcohol, Nux Vomica, Cinchona. [Candidates will be required to write prescriptions, and identify specimens.]

3. *Medical Jurisprudence* (100).—Abortion ; Wounds ; Insanity ; the Principal Poisons.

4. *Theory and Practice of Medicine* (100).—Diseases of the Digestive, Urinary, and Nervous Systems.

5. *Theory and Practice of Surgery* (100).—Wounds and their treatment ; Fractures and Dislocations ; Surgery of the Abdomen.

6. *Obstetrics and Gynæcology* (100).—Normal and Abnormal Labour ; Obstetric operations ; Menstruation.

No mark under 30 shall be taken into account in any subject. When entering his name with the Bursar, the Candidate shall declare the subjects which he selects for Examination.

F 2

Scholars of the Fourth Year shall attend during the year of their election two at least of the following Courses, viz. Medicine, Surgery, Obstetrics, Medical Jurisprudence.

E. SENIOR SCHOLARSHIP IN ANATOMY AND PHYSIOLOGY.— The Scholar will be required to act as Demonstrator in these subjects, and the Examination will be directed to ascertaining his fitness for that position. The Examination will be on the structure and functions of the Human Body, and will include the preparation and recognition of specimens and the description of Museum preparations. Candidates are recommended to practise diagram work. An Examination will be held in the Physiological Laboratory at which Candidates will be required to show a practical acquaintance with the working of Physiological apparatus.

School of Civil Engineering.

Students in the School of Engineering can obtain in the Royal University of Ireland, the Degree of Bachelor of Engineering, Master in Engineering, or a Diploma in Engineering; for the regulations regarding these, see Appendix.

PRESCRIBED COURSE OF STUDY.

First Session.

Mathematics (First Course); Chemistry; *Experimental Physics; Practical Physics; Geometrical Drawing and Descriptive Architecture; Office Work.

Second Session.

Mathematics (Second Course); Mathematical Physics; Practical Chemistry; Civil Engineering and Constructive Architecture; Office Work and Field Work.

---

* Students shall be exempt from attendance on Lectures in Experimental Physics, who shall produce a Certificate of having passed a University Examination, or of having attended a Course of Lectures in any Institution recognised by the College Council, in this subject.

Third Session.

Mathematical Physics ; Civil and Mechanical Engineering ; Office Work and Field Work ; Geology and Physical Geography.

Attendance on these Courses in all cases includes passing such Examinations as may be appointed by the College Council, as well as the Catechetical parts of the Courses of Lectures.

Some modification of the order in which the subjects shall be studied will be admitted on the recommendation of the Council.

DAYS AND HOURS OF LECTURES.

Subjects	Terms.	Mon.	Tues.	Wed.	Thrs.	Fri.	Sat.
1st YEAR.							
Experimental Physics, . .	1, 2, 3,	—	12	—	12	—	12
Practical Physics, . .	2, 3	—	3	—	3	—	—
Chemistry (Pass and Honour),	1, 2, 3,	12	—	12	—	12	—
Mathematics, . . .	1, 2, 3,	1	—	1	—	1	—
Mathematics (Honour), .	1, 2, 3,	—	1	—	1	—	1
Geometrical Drawing and Descriptive Architecture, .	1, 2, 3,	11	—	11	—	11	—
Office Work, . . .	1, 2, 3,	2	—	2	—	2	—
2nd YEAR.							
Civil Engineering, . .	1, 2, 3,	1	—	1	—	1	—
Office Work and Field Work,	1, 2, 3,	2	—	2	—	2	—
Chemistry, Laboratory (Pass or Honour),	3 Mths.	3	—	3	—	3	—
Mathematical Physics (Pass),	1, 2, 3,	10	—	—	—	10	—
Mathematical ,, (Honour),	—	—	9	—	—	—	9
Mathematics (Honour), .	1, 2, 3,	11	—	11	—	11	—
Mathematics (Pass), . .	1, 2, 3,	—	1	—	1	—	1
3rd YEAR.							
Civil and Mechanical Engineering, . . .	1, 2, 3,	12	—	12	—	12	—
Office Work and Field Work,	1, 2, 3,	2	—	2	—	2	—
Mathematical Physics, .	1, 2, 3,	—	—	9	---	—	9
Geology and Physical Geography, ...	1, 2,	10	—	10	—	10	—

I.—MATHEMATICS.

The Courses in Mathematics in the School of Civil Engineering coincide in a great measure with those in the Faculty of Arts (see p. 30), but are slightly more extensive.

In particular, the Pass Course for the First Year includes the elements of Solid Geometry and the use of Logarithmic and Trigonometrical Tables.

The Pass Course for the Second Year includes the elements of the Differential and Integral Calculus, as well as of Spherical Trigonometry.

On the other hand, the Theory of Equations, and the methods of Polar and Trilinear Co-ordinates, do not form part of the Course in this School.

When no other arrangements are made, the Lectures on the above additional subjects to Honour Students in the Faculty of Arts are open to Pass Engineering Students.

The Library contains books of Mathematical Tables which will be useful to those who wish for practice in computation.

II.—NATURAL PHILOSOPHY.

(For Courses see Faculty of Arts, p. 33.)

III.—CHEMISTRY.

(1) LECTURE COURSE.

First Year Course for Pass and Honours. Inorganic Chemistry.—The class attends the Lectures given to Students of the Faculty of Arts at 12 o'clock on Mondays, Wednesdays, and Fridays throughout the Session. Attendance will, however, not be required on Mondays between the Christmas recess and the close of the Medical Lectures. The Lectures embrace a consideration of the leading facts of Inorganic Chemistry, and include both the Pass and Honour subjects required for the Second Professional Examination in Engineering of the Royal University, or for other corresponding Examinations. For syllabus see Faculty of Arts.

(2) Laboratory Courses, Practical Chemistry.

Second Year Pass Course.—This course consists of about forty Lectures of two hours each, commencing in the first term, and ending at the close of the second term. The work done is adapted to the requirements in Practical Chemistry of the Pass Second Professional Examination in Engineering of the Royal University. A *Second Year six months' Course for Honours*, adapted to the Honour Second Professional Examination of the Royal University, will be organized for Students who desire it.

(3) Text-Books.

For Lecture Course.—Thorpe, Inorganic Chemistry; Newth, Inorganic Chemistry ; Remsen, College Chemistry : or Richter, Inorganic Chemistry (trans. Smith).

For Laboratory Courses.—Clowes and Coleman, Elementary Qualitative Analysis, or Clowes, Practical Chemistry.

For Reference.—Blount and Bloxam, Chemistry for Engineers; Butterfield, Gas Manufacture; Thorpe, Dictionary of Applied Chemistry.

IV.—MINERALOGY AND GEOLOGY.

(For Courses see Faculty of Arts, p. 43.)

V.—CIVIL ENGINEERING.

First Year—Subjects of Lectures.

Scales, Curves, Descriptive Geometry, Orthographic and Isometric Projections, Shadows, Perspective and Descriptive Architecture.

Text-Books and Works of Reference.

Miller's Descriptive Geometry. Winter's Geometrical Drawing. Buck on Oblique Bridges. Clarke on Perspective. Carpenter's and Joiner's Assistant. Engineer and Machinists' Drawing Book. Rickman's Gothic Architecture. Ferguson's History of Architecture—(chapters on Greece, Rome, and England). Stuart and Revett's Antiquities of Athens. Oxford Glossary. Classic and Early Christian Architecture—Smith and Slater. Gothic and Renaissance Architecture—Smith. An Introduction to the Study of Gothic Architecture by Parker.

Second Year—Subjects of Lectures.

Instruments, Surveying, Levelling, Railway Curves, Measurement of Earthwork, Constructive Architecture, Measurement of the Flow of Water, Roads, Tramways, and Streets (excluding electrical theory of Electric Tramways). Materials—including, stone, brick, concrete, timber, and iron (their composition, production, and uses).

Text-Books and Works of Reference.

Rankine's Civil Engineering. Gillespie's Surveying. Rivington's Building Construction, Parts I., II., III. Bidder's Tables. Sir John M'Neill's Tables. Turner and Brightmore—Principles of Water Supply Engineering. (Chapter on Hydraulics.) Carpenter's and Joiner's Assistant. Clarke on Tramways. Clarke on Roads. Carriage-ways and Footways by Boulnois. Moore's Sanitary Engineering.

Third Year—Subjects of Lectures.

Materials used in Construction, Stresses in Structures, Principles of Construction of Bridges, Roofs, Canals, Sewerage Works, Harbours, Arterial and Thorough Drainage, Water-works, Locomotive Engine, Pumping Engines and Pumps, Railways, County and Municipal Work.

Text-Books and Works of Reference.

Fairbairn's History of the Manufacture of Iron. Rankine's Civil Engineering. Rankine on the Steam Engine. Rivington's Building Construction, Parts III. and IV. Redgrave's Calcareous Cements. Stoney on Stresses. Cotteril's Applied Mechanics, chaps. xii., xiii., xiv., xv., xx. Humber on Bridges. Strength of Materials by Ewing. Buck on the Oblique Arch. Simms on Tunnelling. Latham on Sanitary Engineering. Moore's Sanitary Engineering. Hill on Thirlmere Works. Deacon on Vyrnwy Works, Proc. I. C. E., vol. cxxvi. Drainage of Lands, Towns, and Buildings, by Dempsey, with recent Practice by D. R. Clarke. Sewage Disposal Works by Santo Crimp. Purification of Sewage and Water, by W. J. Dibdin. Turner and Brightmore—Principles of Water Supply Engineering. Pumps and Pump Motors by Philip R. Björling. Vernon Harcourt on Harbours. Vernon Harcourt on Canals and Rivers. Steam Engine by Holmes omitting Thermodynamical Theory). Bowen Cook, British Locomotives. Mills' Railway Construction. Barry's Railway Appliances. Fairbairn on Mills and Millwork. Bodner's Hydraulic Motors. Tredgold on Carpentry. Carpenter's and Joiner's Assistant. Timber and Timber Trees by Ward. Shelly's Workshop Appliances. Records of Modern Engineering.

The Students of each year are engaged during each term in preparing working drawings of Structures in Architecture and Engineering.

Students of the Second and Third Years make Surveys and Sections in the field.

EXAMINATIONS.

MATRICULATION.
(See page 24.)

*SENIOR SCHOLARSHIP.

The Course for the Examination consists of the Civil and Mechanical Engineering, Office Work and Field Work, prescribed for Engineering Students of the Third Year (see p. 83).

JUNIOR SCHOLARSHIPS.

Two are tenable by Students of the First Year.
Two   ,,   ,,   Second Year.
One is   ,,   a Student ,,   Third Year.

First Year Scholarships.

To compete for a Scholarship of the First Year a Student must have Matriculated.

The Course is that prescribed for Science Scholarship of the First Year in the Faculty of Arts (see pp. 49, 50).

Second Year Scholarships.

To compete for a Scholarship of the Second Year a Student must have Matriculated, and be of one year's standing, and not more.

The Course consists of the subjects of study prescribed for Students of the First Year (see p. 82). French or German may be taken as a voluntary subject.

The subjects of Examination in French or German, and Experimental Physics, are the same as those prescribed for Medical Scholarships of the Second Year (see p. 79). Candidates are also required to show efficiency in Physical Manipulation and Measurements.

Third Year Scholarships.

To compete for a Scholarship of the Third Year a Student must have Matriculated, and be of two years' standing, and not more.

The Course consists of the subjects of study prescribed for Students of the Second Year (see p. 82).

---

* For Regulations *see* pp. 13, 14.

CHANGES IN THE MATRICULATION AND SCHOLAR-SHIP COURSES FOR THE SESSION 1903–1904.

The Courses for 1903–1904 will be the same as those prescribed for 1902–1903, with the following alterations :—

Faculty of Arts.

I. *Matriculation.*

Latin, . . Cicero—*The Fourth Verrine* (for Cicero as at page 21).
Virgil—*Aeneid*, i. (for *Georgics*, i.).

Greek, . . Xenophon—*Hellenica*, i. (for Plato, as at page 21).
Euripides—*Medea* (omitting choral odes) (for *Bacchæ*).

French, . . Souvestre—*Un philosophe sous les toits* (for About—*Le Roi des Montagnes*).

German, . Schiller—*Der dreissigjährige Krieg, Buch* iv. (for *Das Jahr 1813*).

English, . Thackeray—*Addison, Steele, Goldsmith*, from *English Humorists* (for Milton as at page 22).
Macaulay—*Life of Johnson* (for Scott as at page 22.)

II. *Junior Scholarships of the First Year.*

Latin, . . Livy—Bk. xxiii (for Bk. xxii).
Horace—*Odes*, i. (omitting 13, 19, 23, 25, 33) ; *Satires*, Bk. i., 1, 5, 6, 9 (for Horace as at page 44).

Greek, . . Homer—*Iliad*, Book vi.
Euripides—*Heraclidæ*.
Thucydides—Bk. vii.

(For Homer, Demosthenes, and Isocrates as at page 45.)

French, . . Erckmann-Chatrian—*Le Conscrit* (for *L'Invasion*).
Coppée—*Le Trésor* (for *Le Roi des Montagnes*).

| German, . | . Goethe — *Poems* :—*Mignon, Der Sänger, Der Erlkönig, Der König von Thule, Der Schatzgräber, Der Zauberlehrling* (for *Vom ersten bis zum letzten Schuss*). |

Italian, . . Tasso—*La Gerusalemme Liberata*, Cantos i., ii., iii. (for Monti—*Caio Gracco*).

English, . . Shakespeare—*Henry IV.*, i. and ii. (for *Julius Cæsar* and *Coriolanus*).
Pope—*Iliad*, 18 to 24 inclusive (for Bacon's Essays).

The rest as at page 45.

III. *Junior Scholarships of the Second Year.*

Latin, . . Horace—*Odes*, Bk. ii. (for iii.).
Virgil—*Georgics*, Bk. iv. (for ii.).
Livy—Bk. xxxv. (for xxxiv.).
Roman History—216-167 B.C. [Mommsen, vol. II., Bk. iii., chaps. 6-10 (for 3–8)].

Greek, . . Homer—*Odyssey*, ix., x. (for v., vi., vii.).

English, . . Gray—Omit *Odes* on *Spring* and *Adversity*.
The rest as at page 48.

IV. *Junior Scholarships of the Third Year.*

[No Change.]

V. *Senior Scholarships.*

1. ANCIENT CLASSICS.

Greek, . . Æschylus—*Eumenides* (for *Choephori*).
Aristophanes—*Frogs* (for *Wasps*).

Latin, . . Virgil—*Æneid*, ii., iv., vi. (for v., vi., vii.).
Plautus—*Captivi* (for *Rudens*).
Cicero—*Ad Atticum*, iv., v., vi. (for v., vi., vii.).
Roman History—*Mommsen*, vol. v., Bk. v., chaps. 8–11 (for *Provinces of the Roman Empire*, vol. i.).
Students' Companion to Latin Authors.—The whole (for chaps. ii., iii., iv.).

2. English and Modern Languages.

English, . . Wordsworth—M. Arnold's Selections, from p. 115 to end, and Preface (for *Excursion*).
Cowper—*Task*, Books i., iv., v.
Coleridge—*Lectures and Notes on Shakspere*, pp. 183–242 (for pp. 183–394).

3. Mathematics.

Two papers will be set instead of one ; the first paper on Wednesday, October 28.

Course for the Blayney Exhibition, 1903.

The Mathematical Course appointed for the Junior Science Scholarship of the Second Year, and in addition :—

General Theory of Infinite Series.

The *Binomial, Exponential,* and *Logarithmic Series.*

Analytical Geometry of Two Dimensions, including the discussion of the *General Equation of the Second Degree.*

Differential and *Integral Calculus,* excluding *Differential Equations.*

Newton's *Principia*, Book i., Sections 1, 2, 3.

Elementary *Statics.*

Elementary *Dynamics,* including easy applications to the plane motion of rigid bodies.

Elementary *Hydrostatics.*

Elementary *Optics.*

Elementary *Astronomy.*

FORMER PROFESSORS AND OFFICERS.

Appointed.		Vacated.
1845.	Very Rev. J. W. Kirwan, President, . . Died,	1849
1845.	Edward Berwick, Vice-President, appointed President, ... Resigned,	1849
1849.	Thomas Drane, M.A., Professor of Civil Engineering, ... Resigned,	1849
1850.	Very Rev. J. P. O'Toole, Vice-President, Resigned,	1852
1849.	Morgan W. Crofton, M.A., Professor of Natural Philosophy, ... Resigned,	1852

[Fellow of the Royal Society, 1868 ; late Professor of Mathematics, R.M. Academy, Woolwich ; late Fellow of the Royal University of Ireland ; Author of Papers in *Philosophical Transactions*, 1868–69.]

1849.	Patrick G. Fitzgerald, Bursar, . . . Died,	1853
1849.	John Mulcahy, LL.D., Professor of Mathematics, ... Died,	1853

[Author of " Principles of Modern Geometry," 1852.]

1849.	W. E. Hearn, M.A., LL.D., Professor of the Greek Language, ... Resigned,	1854

[Late Dean of the Faculty of Law in the University of Melbourne. Author of " Plutology," 1864 ; " The Government of England " ; and " The Aryan Family."

1849.	William Nesbitt, M.A., Professor of the Latin Language, appointed to the Greek Professorship, ... Resigned,	1854
1849.	Cornelius Mahony, Professor of the Celtic Languages, ... Resigned,	1854

1849.   Bernard O'Flaherty, Registrar,   . . Resigned, 1855

1849.   James Hardiman, Librarian,   . . . Died, 1855

[Author of "History of Galway," 1820; and of "Irish Minstrelsy or Bardic Remains of Ireland," 1831.]

1849.   Edmond Ronalds, PH.D., Professor of Chemistry, ... Resigned, 1856

[Editor of the Journal of the Chemical Society, joint Editor with Dr. T. Richardson of Knapp's "Chemistry in its applications to the Arts and Manufactures," 1848–1851. Author of papers:—"Ueber die Oxydation des Wachses durch Salpetersäure," *Liebig Ann.* 1842, and "Excretion of Phosphorus," 1853, *Phil. Trans.*]

1853.   G. Johnstone Stoney, M.A., Professor of Natural Philosophy, appointed Secretary of the Queen's University, . . . Resigned, 1857

[Fellow of the Royal Society, 1861; late Secretary to the Queen's University in Ireland. Author of numerous Scientific and Philosophical Papers in *Phil. Trans.*, *Trans. of Royal Dublin Society*, and *Philosophical Magazine.*]

1849.   H. Law, B.A., Professor of English Law,   Resigned, 1858

[Solicitor-General, 1873; M.P. for Londonderry, 1874; Attorney-General, 1880; Lord Chancellor of Ireland, 1881.]

1849.   Denis C. Heron, LL.D., Professor of Jurisprudence and Political Economy, . . Resigned, 1859

[Serjeant-at-Law; M.P. for county of Tipperary, 1870. Author of "An Introduction to the History of Jurisprudence," 1860, and "History of the University of Dublin."]

1849.   Wm. B. Blood, B.A., Professor of Civil Engineering, ... Resigned, 1860

[Author of Paper on "Stresses in Girders," *Min. Proc., I.C.E.*]

1849.   Charles Croker King, M.D., Professor of Anatomy and Physiology, . . . Resigned, 1863

[M.R.I.A.; late Medical Commissioner, Local Government Board for Ireland. Author of numerous Papers on Anatomy and Physiology.]

1852. Joseph O'Leary, B.A., Vice-President, Professor of History and English Literature, . Died, 1864
[Author of various Legal works.]

1853. Arthur Ireland, Bursar, ... Died, 1864

1852. William Nesbitt, M.A., Professor of the Greek Language, ... Resigned, 1864

[Late Professor of Latin, Queen's College, Belfast. Author of the Article, "Horae Taciteae" in *Hermathena*, Vol. III.]

1849. Thos. Skilling, Professor of Agriculture, . Died, 1865

1849. Augustus Bensbach, M.D., Professor of Modern Languages, ... Died, 1868
[Author of "Sketch of German Literature."]

1854. Richard Blair Bagley, M.A., Professor of Latin, Died, 1869

1859. John E. Cairnes, M.A., Professor of Jurisprudence and Political Economy, . . Resigned, 1870

[Sometime Whately Professor of Political Economy in the University of Dublin ; late Professor of Political Economy in the University College, London. Author of "The Definition and Logical Method of Political Economy," 1875, 2nd Edition ; "The Slave Power," 1862 ; Essays on Political Economy ; Political Essays ; Some Leading Principles of Political Economy ; and of other works.]

1853. William Lupton, M.A., Registrar, appointed Professor of Jurisprudence and Political Economy, ... Resigned, 1870

1849. Simon M'Coy, Professor of Materia Medica, Resigned, 1873
[Author of numerous papers on Medical and Surgical Science.]

1849. Richard Doherty, M.D., Professor of Midwifery, Died, 1876
[Author of papers on Obstetric Science.]

1870. William Lupton, M.A., Professor of Jurisprudence and Political Economy, . . . Died, 1876

1856. John H. Richardson, B.A., Librarian, . Resigned, 1876

1849. Edward Berwick, B.A., President, . . . Died, 1877

1863.   John Cleland, M.D., D.SC., LL.D., Professor of
        Anatomy and Physiology.   .   .   Resigned,   1877

        [Fellow of the Royal Society, 1872. Professor
        of Anatomy in the University of Glasgow.
        One of the Editors of the 7th Edition of
        Quain's "Elements of Anatomy;" Author
        of "Scala Naturae and other Poems," 1887;
        and of "Animal Physiology," "Variations
        of the Skull," and other important papers
        in the *Philosophical Transactions.*]

1870.   Thomas W. Moffett, LL.D., Registrar, ap-
        pointed President, ...   Resigned,   1877

1873.   Joseph P. Pye, M.D., M.CH., Professor of
        Materia Medica, ...   Resigned,   1877

1849.   Nicholas Colahan, M.D., Professor of Practice
        of Medicine, ...   Resigned,   1879

1857.   Arthur Hill Curtis, M.A., LL.D., Professor of
        Natural Philosophy, .   .   .   Resigned,   1879

        [Late Assistant Commissioner of Intermediate
        Education ; late Senator of the Royal Uni-
        versity of Ireland.   Author of Papers :—
        " On the Integration of Linear and Partial
        Differential Equations," in the *Cambridge
        and Dublin Mathematical Journal*, 1854 ;
        " Sur la Surface Lieu des Centres de Cour-
        bure Principaux d'une Surface Courbe," in
        Liouville's *Journal de Mathématiques pures et
        appliquées*, 1858 ; A Mathematical Deduction
        of the principal properties of the Gyroscope,
        Dublin, 1862 ; and of numerous Papers in
        *The Oxford, Cambridge, and Dublin Messenger
        of Mathematics, The Messenger of Mathe-
        matics*, New Series; *The Quarterly Journal
        of Pure and Applied Mathematics ;* and *The
        Philosophical Magazine.*]

1877.   Arthur Hill Curtis, M.A., LL.D., Registrar, Resigned,   1879

1869.   Thomas Maguire, LL.D., Professor of Latin, Resigned,   1880
        [Late Fellow of Trinity College, Dublin, and
        Professor of Moral Philosophy in the Uni-
        versity of Dublin. Author of "An Essay on
        the Platonic Idea," 1866 ; of "Essays on
        the Platonic Ethics"; of "Lectures on
        Philosophy"; and of numerous Articles in
        Hermathena, Vols. I.–VI. Editor of "The
        Parmenides of Plato," 1882.]

Appointed.   Vacated.

1849. Alexander G. Melville, M.D., D.SC., Professor
       of Natural History, ... Resigned, 1882

       [Joint Author of " The Dodo and its kindred,"
       and of papers on Anatomy and kindred
       subjects.]

1876. Robert Cather Donnell, M.A., LL.D., Professor
       of Jurisprudence and Political Economy,   . Died, 1883

       [Sometime Professor of Political Economy in
       the University of Dublin.]

1849. William King, D.SC., Professor of Mineralogy
       and Geology and Natural History,   . Resigned, 1883

       [Author of " Monograph of Permian Fossils of
       England, " published by the Palæonto-
       graphical Society, 1850 ; and of " Report on
       the Superinduced Divisional Structure of
       Rocks, called Jointing, and its Relation to
       Slaty Cleavage," *Transactions of the Royal
       Irish Academy*, Vol. XXV., 1875, and of
       numerous Papers in the *Annals of Natural
       History*, and in other Scientific Journals.
       Also Author in conjunction with Dr. T. H.
       Rowney of a Paper on " Eozoon Canadense "
       in the *Quarterly Journal of the Geological
       Society*, and of other Papers on the same
       subject in various Scientific Journals.]

1880. Joseph Larmor, M.A., D.SC., Professor of
       Natural Philosophy, ... Resigned, 1885

       [Secretary of the Royal Society, 1901 ; late
       Fellow of the Royal University of Ireland ;
       Fellow of St. John's College, Cambridge.
       Author of various Papers in the *Proceedings
       of the Cambridge Philosophical Society ;
       Philosophical Transactions of the Royal
       Society ; Proceedings of the London Mathe-
       matical Society ; The Quarterly Journal of
       Pure and Applied Mathematics ; The Mes-
       senger of Mathematics*, New Series; *The
       Philosophical Magazine*.]

1868. Charles Giesler, PH.D., D.LIT., Professor of
       Modern Languages, ... Died, 1886

       [Late Fellow of the Royal University of Ire-
       land.]

1849. James V. Browne, M.D., Professor of Surgery, Died, 1887

1880. John Fletcher Davies, M.A., D.LIT., Professor
         of Latin, ... Died,   1889

> [Late Fellow of the Royal University of Ire-
> land. Editor of "The Agamemnon, The
> Choephoroe, and The Eumenides of Æschy-
> lus." Author of several Articles in *Herma-
> thena*, contributed largely to *Kottabos* and
> *Dublin Translations*.]

1856. Thomas H. Rowney, PH.D., D.SC., Professor
         of Chemistry, ... Resigned, 1889

> [Author of numerous memoirs in Organic Che-
> mistry, especially on the Fatty Acids and
> their Amides, *Journal of the Chemical
> Society*; and in conjunction with Dr. Wm.
> King of a Paper on "Eozoon Canadense"
> in the *Quarterly Journal of the Geological
> Society*, and of other Papers in various
> Scientific Journals.]

1889. Augustus E. Dixon, M.D., Professor of Che-
         mistry, ... Resigned, 1891

> [Professor of Chemistry, Queen's College, Cork.
> Author of Papers on Organic Chemistry in
> the *Journal of the Chemical Society*.]

1853. George Johnston Allman, LL.D., D.SC., Pro-
         fessor of Mathematics, Senator of the Royal
         University of Ireland, Fellow of the Royal
         Society, 1884, ... Resigned, 1893

> [Member of the Senate of the Queen's Uni-
> versity in Ireland, 1877. Editor of the
> Lectures of Professor MacCullagh on "The
> Attraction of Ellipsoids," *Transactions of the
> Royal Irish Academy*, Vol. XXII., 1853.
> Author of a Paper, "On Some properties of
> the Paraboloids," *The Quarterly Journal of
> Pure and Applied Mathematics*, 1874; of
> Articles on "Greek Geometry from Thales
> to Euclid " in *Hermathena*, Vols. III.-VI.,
> 1878-1887, subsequently published as a
> Volume of the Dublin University Press
> Series, 1889; also of "Ptolemy (Claudius
> Ptolemaeus) " and other Articles in the 9th
> edition of the *Encyclopædia Britannica*.]

1864. George Johnston Allman, LL.D., D.SC.,
         Bursar, ... Resigned, 1893

1849. Sir Thomas Moffett, LL.D., D.LITT., Professor
of Logic and Metaphysics ; Professor of
History, English Literature, and Mental
Science, 1863; Registrar, 1870 ; President,
1877 ; Senator of the Royal University of
Ireland.   Author of "Selections from
Bacon's Works," translated with commentary, and numerous Literary and Philosophical Papers, ...   Resigned, 1897

1897. William Joseph Myles Starkie, M.A., D.LITT. ;
late Scholar of Trinity College, Cambridge ;
ex-Fellow of Trinity College, Dublin ;
President, and Professor of History, English
Literature, and Mental Science, 1897 ;
Senator of the Royal University of Ireland ;
Resident Commissioner of National Educa-
tion (Ireland); Editor of "Aristophanes'
Vespae," and Author of many Papers on
Classical Subjects, ...   Resigned, 1899

1893. Alfred Cardew Dixon, SC.D., M.A., Professor of
Mathematics; late Fellow of Trinity College,
Cambridge ; Fellow of the Royal University
of Ireland.   Author of the "Elementary
Properties of Elliptic Functions," 1894 : and
of numerous papers in *Philosophical Transactions, Quarterly Journal of Mathematics,
Proceedings of London Mathematical Society,*
and *Messenger of Mathematics,* .   .   Resigned, 1901

1864. D'Arcy W. Thompson, M.A., D.LITT., Professor of Greek, and Librarian,   .   .   .   Died, 1902

[Late Fellow of the Royal University of Ireland.   Author of "Daydreams of a
Schoolmaster," "Sales Attici, the wit and
wisdom of the Athenian Drama," "Way-
side Thoughts," being lectures delivered in
the Lowell Institute in Boston, and
numerous literary papers.]

FORMER DEANS OF RESIDENCES.

Appointed.		Vacated.
1857.	Rev. Wm. Lough, ...	Resigned, 1860
1860.	Rev. Robert Huston, ...	Resigned, 1863
1863.	Rev. John Duncan, ...	Resigned, 1866
1866.	Rev. Hugh Moore, ...	Resigned, 1867
1858.	Rev. John Lewis, ...	Resigned, 1867
1867.	Rev. James Murdock, ...	Resigned, 1868
1849.	Rev. John Treanor, ...	Resigned, 1868
1868.	Rev. Wm. Jarrett, ...	Resigned, 1868
1868.	Rev. Mortlock Long, ...	Resigned, 1871
1871.	Rev. Oliver M'Cutcheon, . . .	Resigned, 1874
1874.	Rev. J. C. Moore, B.A., . . .	Resigned, 1878
1874	Rev. Colin M'Cay, ...	Resigned, 1876
1876.	Rev. F. Elliot, ...	Resigned, 1879
1879.	Rev. T. W. Baker, ...	Resigned, 1882
1880.	Rev. J. G. Robb, LL.B., D.D., . .	Died, 1881
1880.	Rev. John Kydd, ...	Resigned, 1881
1882.	Rev. Thomas C. Maguire, . . .	Resigned, 1885
1885.	Rev. John Carson, ...	Resigned, 1887
1868.	Venerable Archdeacon O'Sullivan, . [Bishop of Tuam, 1890.]	Resigned, 1890
1887.	Rev. Henry Shire, ...	Resigned, 1890
1890.	Rev. Richard Little, ...	Resigned, 1893
1893.	Rev. Robert Boyd, M.A., . . .	Resigned, 1896
1896.	Rev. Wm. Crook, D.D., . . .	Died, 1879
1897.	Rev. Henry J. F. Ranson, . . .	Resigned, 1901

GRADUATES.

Adair, James J., ..	.. ..	B.A. 1858; M.D. 1861.
Adams, Archibald,	.. ..	M.D., M.CH. 1872.
Adams, David O.,	.. ..	B.A. 1873; M.A. 1882.
e Adams, John A., ..	.. ..	B.A. 1888; M.B., R.CH., B.A.O. 1890.
c Agnew, Samuel, ..	.. ..	B.A. 1868; M.D. 1871; M.CH., Dip. Obs. 1872; M.A. 1882.
e Aimers, Margaret M.,	.. ..	B.A. 1900.
Allen, Alfred, ..	.. ..	M.D., M.CH., Dip. Obs. 1876.
Allen, Robert, ..	.. ..	M.B., B.CH., B.A.O. 1893.—Demonstrator of Anatomy, Queen's College, Galway; Travelling Medical Scholar, Royal Univ. of Ireland, 1894; Studentship in Pathology R.U.I. 1900.
a Allen, William, ..	.. ..	M.D., M.CH., Dip. Obs. 1877.—Demonstrator of Anatomy, Univ., Glasgow.
Ambrose, Daniel,	.. ..	M.D. 1865.
Ambrose, Robert,	.. ..	B.A. 1876.
a Anderson, Alexander,	.. ..	B.A. 1880; M.A. 1881; Hon. LL.D., Glasgow. — Late F. R. U. I., late Fellow S.S. Coll. Camb., Professor of Natural Philosophy, Queen's College, Galway; President of Queen's College, Galway, 1899; Memb. of Senate, R.U.I.
Anderson, Edward,	.. ..	M.D. 1867.
Anderson, Joseph J.,	.. ..	M.B., B.CH., B.A.O. 1901.
Anderson, Joseph R.,	.. ..	B.A. 1878; M.A. 1882.
c Andrews, John, ..	.. ..	M.D., M.CH. 1883.
a Angus, Samuel, ..	.. ..	B.A. 1902.
Armstrong, Thomas M.,	.. ..	M.D. 1869.
e Arnold, Pierce, ..	.. ..	B.A. 1856; M.A. 1882.
a Atkinson, Rt. Hon., John,	..	B.A. 1861; LL.B. 1865; M.A., LL.D. 1882; K.C.; Bencher of the Honourable Society of King's-Inns, Dublin; Attorney-General for Ireland; P.C.
Atkinson, Miles H. C.,	.. ..	M.D. 1879; M.CH. 1880.
Atkinson, William,	.. ..	M.D. 1879.
Atock, Arthur, ..	.. ..	M.D. 1885; M.CH. 1886; B.A.O. 1888.
Atock, Martin H.,	.. ..	M.D., M.CH. 1882; B.A.O. 1889.
Bacon, Theophilus,	.. ..	M.D., M.CH. 1878.
e Bain, John A., ..	.. ..	B.A. 1880; M.A. 1882.
a Barker, Alexander A.,	.. ..	B.E. 1877; M.E. 1882.
Barnes, Leopold J. J.,	.. ..	M.D. 1869.
Barr, Andrew, ..	.. ..	B.A. 1899.

---

a With First Honours. *c* Naval Medical Service. *e* With Second Honours.

Bartley, William., ...	M.D., M.CH. 1884 ; B.A.O. 1890.
a Bateman, Richard C., ...	B.A. 1857 ; M.A. 1882.
Beattie, Charles J., ...	M.B., B.CH., B.A.O. 1889.
Beattie, Robert, ...	M.D., M.CH. 1876; Dip. Obs. 1879.
Beattie, Robert A., ...	B.A. 1891.
Beatty, John, ...	B.A. 1893.
Beatty, John W., ...	M.D. 1879.
Bell, James, ...	B.A. 1888.
Bell, Robert, ...	M.D., M.CH. 1884.
Best, Robert, ...	M.B., B.CH., B.A.O. 1902.
Binns, Edmund T., ...	B.A. 1892 ; B.E. 1893.
a Binns, Henry A., ...	B.E. 1883.
d Binns, William N., ...	B.E. 1888.
b Black, John G., ...	M.D., Dip. Obs. 1881; M.CH. 1882.
Bligh, John, ...	M.D., M.CH. 1865.
b Blood, Robert, ...	M.D., M.CH. 1871.
Booth, Samuel, ...	B.A. 1899.
Bournes, William H., ...	M.D. 1859.
Boycott, W. Douglass, ...	B.A. 1883.
Boyd, Robert J., ...	M.D., M.CH. 1886 ; B.A.O. 1890.
Bradshaw, George B., ...	Dip. Agric. 1857.
Breen, John, ...	B.A. 1857.
Breen, Michael, ...	B.A. 1857 ; M.D. 1861.
Bright, John S., ...	B.A. 1895.
b Brodie, James F., ...	M.D., M.CH., Dip. Obs. 1876.
e Brooke, John, ...	B.A. 1867 ; M.A. 1870.
a Brooke, William, ...	B.A. 1867 ; M.D. 1874 ; M.A. 1882.
e Browmlow, Thomas D., ...	M.D. 1863.
Brown, Henry, ...	B.A. 1897.
e Brown, John I., ...	B.A. 1879 ; M.A. 1882.
a Brown, William, ...	B.A. 1879 ; M.A. 1882 ; LL.B. 1887.
Browne, Andrew, ...	M.D. 1864.
Browne, David, ...	B.A. 1891 ; M.A. 1893.
e Browne, William A., ...	B.A. 1853 ; M.A. 1882.
Bryant, William V., ...	B.A. 1900.
Buchanan, L. Dobbin, ...	M.D. 1861.
Buckley, Thomas, ...	B.A. 1882 ; LL.B. 1889.
e Bunton, Christopher L. W., ..	M.B., B.CH., B.A.O. 1891.—Demonstrator, Queen's Coll., Galway.
Burke, Edward, ...	B.E. 1870.
Burke, John, ...	B.A. 1865 ; M.D. 1872.
Burke, John P., ...	M.D. 1861.
b Burke, John R., ...	M.D. 1861.
Burke, Martin J., ...	B.A. 1858 ; M.D. 1859.
a Burke, Michael J., ...	B.A. 1863 ; M.D. 1867.
b Burkitt, James P., ...	B.A. 1891 ; B.E. 1892 ; County Surveyor of Fermanagh.

---

a With First Honours.   *b* Army Medical Service.
c Naval Medical Service.
d Harbour Engineer and Borough Surveyor of Galway.
e With Second Honours.

Cairnes, John E., ..	.. ..	B.A. 1887 ; M.A. 1889.
Caldwell, William H.,	.. ..	M.D., M.CH., Dip. Obs. 1880.
a Campbell, James A.,	..	B.A. 1879 ; M.A. 1882.
e Carbery, Edward O. B.,	..	M.B., B.CH., B.A.O. 1897.
Card, David,	.. ..	B.A. 1887.
Card, William,	.. ..	B.A. 1886.
Carey, Patrick,	.. ..	B.A. 1868.
a Carmichael, John S.,	..	B.A., B.E. 1897.
ab Carpenter, William,	..	M.D. 1862.
Carroll, Henry,	.. ..	B.A. 1884.
Carroll, James,	..	M.D., M.CH. 1883 ; B.A.O. 1889.
Carroll, Richard,	..	M.D. 1862.
Carroll, William S.,	..	M.B., B.CH., B.A.O. 1895.
Charlton, Robert J.,	..	B.A. 1887.
a Chestnutt, Joseph W.,	..	B.A. 1860; M.D. 1865 ; M.A. 1882.
e Clancy, John J.,	..	B.A. 1866 ; M.A. 1868; B.L. (Ir.) ; M.P.
Clarke, John A.,	..	B.A. 1898.
a Clarke, Margaret,	..	B.A. 1900.
e Clarke, Samuel B.,	..	B.A. 1880 ; M.A. 1882.
Clarke, Thompson R.,	..	M.D., M.CH. 1866.
Clarke, William,	..	B.A. 1859.
Clarke, William A.,	..	B.A. 1886 ; LL.B. 1890.
Clements, Francis H.,	..	M.B., B.CH., B.A.O. 1892.
Clements, John,	..	M.B., B.CH., R.A.O. 1902.
Clements, Joseph A.,	..	M.B., B.CH.. B.A.O. 1895.
Clements, Robert W.,	..	B.A. 1894 ; M.B., B.CH., B.A.O. 1895.
Clements, Robert,	..	M.D. 1873 ; Medical Inspector Local Government Board (Ireland).
b Climo, William H.,	..	M.D. 1860.
Clinch, Patrick J.,	..	B.E. 1882.
Coates, George J.,	..	M.D., M.CH., Dip. Obs. 1880.
Coates, William,	..	M.D., M.CH., Dip. Obs. 1876 ; M.A.O. 1887.
be Colahan, John,	..	M.D. 1857.
Colahan, Nicholas W.,	..	M.D., M.CH. 1872.—Professor of Materia Medica, Queen's College, Galway.
c Colahan, William H. W.,	..	M.D., M.CH. 1870.
e Cole, James A.,	..	B.A. 1901.
b Comerford, Henry,	..	M.D., M.CH. 1865.
a Concannon, Patrick,	..	B.A. 1871 ; M.A. 1874.
e Condon, Daniel E.,	..	B.E. 1879 ; M.B. 1882.
e Connolly, Thomas J.,	..	B.A. 1891; M.B., B.CH., B.A.O. 1893.
Conolly, James,	..	B.A. 1858 ; M.D. 1866.
e Conolly, Patrick W.,	..	B.A. 1861 ; M.A. 1865.—Civil Service of Ceylon, Second place.
Considine, P. Oswald,	..	M.D. 1878.
e Conway, John K.,	..	M.D. 1866.
a Copithorne, James G.,	..	B.A. 1879 ; M.A. 1882.

---

a With First Honours.	*c* Naval Medical Service.
b Army Medical Service.	*e* With Second Honours.

a Corley, Anthony H.,	M.D. 1863 ; D.SC. *Honoris Causa*, 1882.
Corry, John G.,	M.B., B.CH., B.A.O. 1897.
Costello, Michael J. B.,	M.B., B.CH., B.A.O. 1891.
Costello, Thomas B.,	M.D., B.CH., B.A.O. 1888.
Craig, Samuel R.,	B.A. 1869.
Crean, Martin J.,	M.D. 1857.
Creighton, Robert W.,	B.E. 1883.
e Croke, J. O'Byrne,	B.A. 1871 ; M.A. 1874.
Crone, Alexander,	B.A. 1877.
Crooks, William,	B.A. 1865.
Crotty, Richard D.,	B.A. 1861 ; Resident Magistrate.
Crowley, Patrick,	M.B., B.CH., B.A.O. 1890.
Cullin, Henry C.,	B.A. 1871.
ee Cummins, Robert J.,	B.E. 1900 ; B.A. 1901.
Cuningham, John S. A.,	M.D. 1866.
e Cunningham, William,	B.A. 1861 ; M.A. 1882.
Cuppage, William B.,	M.D., M.CH. 1871 ; Dip. Obs. 1877.
Curran, Anthony,	B.A. 1902.
Curry, David S.,	B.A. 1898.
a Curry, Samuel,	B.A. 1893.
Daly, John H. C.,	M.B., B.CH., B.A.O. 1897.
e Davidson, Andrew G.,	B.A. 1887.
Davies, W. Naunton,	M.D. 1880 ; M.CH., Dip. Obs. 1881.
b Davis, John N.,	M.D. 1862.
Davis, John W.,	M.D. 1869.
Davis, William,	M.D. 1874 ; M.CH. 1875.
Davy, Alfred,	Dip. Eng. 1867 ; M.D. 1870 ; B.E. 1882.
b Davy, Francis A.,	M.D. 1867.
Davys, Frank,	B.A. 1858.
e Daxon, William,	M.D. 1862.—Resident Physician, District Asylum, Ennis.
e Deane, Henry,	B.A. 1865 ; M.A. 1882 ; Engineer-in-Chief of Railways under the Government, Victoria (Australia).
Deans, John,	B.A. 1890.
Deans, William,	B.A. 1891.
e Delmege, Alfred G.,	M.D. 1868.
b Delmege, J. P. De G.,	M.D. 1862.
Dempsey, Alexander,	M.D. 1874.
e Dick, James,	B.A. 1864 ; M.A. 1866.
Dick, John,	M.D. 1869.—Surgeon, Mount Ida District Hospital, Otago, New Zealand.
b Dickenson, Frederick F.,	M.D. 1863.
Dickey, Samuel,	M.D., M.CH., Dip. Obs. 1879.
Dickson, John D.,	M.D., M.CH., Dip. Obs. 1876.

a With First Honours.　　*c* Naval Medical Service.
b Army Medical Service.　　*e* With Second Honours.

Divers, Edward, ... M.D. 1860; D.SC. *Honoris Causa*, 1897; F.R.S.—Emeritus Professor of Chemistry in the Imperial University, Tokyo, Japan.

a Dobbyn, John S., ... M.D. 1875.

a Dodds, Robert, ... B.A. 1878; M.A. 1879.

Dooley, John L., ... B.A. 1873.

Dooley, Michael S., ... B.A. 1865; Dip. Eng. 1865; M.B. 1882.—Telegraph Department, India.

Dougan, George, ... M.D., M.CH., Dip. Obs. 1875.

Dowling, Jeremiah J., ... B.A. 1853; M.D. 1858.

Dowling, Patrick A. S., ... B.A. 1895; B.E. 1898.

e Downard, Thomas, ... B.A. 1890; M.B., B.CH., B.A.O., 1898.

Doyle, Peter John, ... M.D. 1883.

e Drummond, Michael, ... B.A. 1869; M.A. 1870.—Q.C. (Ir.)

Drury, Richard J., ... B.A. 1869; M.D. 1873; Dip. Obs. 1874.

b Drury, Robert, ... M.D. 1870.

e Duffy, Francis, ... M.D. 1864; M.CH. 1865.

a Duggan, Charles W., ... B.A. 1852; M.A. 1853.—Inspector National Schools.

Duke, Alexander W., ... M.D. 1867.

Dundee, Isaac C., ... B.A. 1874; M.D. 1877; M.CH. 1878.

Dwyer, Peter J., ... M.D. 1869.

a Eagleton, John F., ... M.B., 1885; M.CH. 1886.

Eaton, Richard, ... M.D. 1855.—Resident Physician, Asylum, Ballinasloe.

e Eaton, Thomas, ... B.A. 1868; M.A. 1871.

Edge, John D., ... M.D. 1870.

e Ekin, Edward, ... B.A. 1880; M.A. 1881.

Eldon, Joseph, ... M.B., B.CH., B.A.O. 1889; M.D., M.CH. 1895.

Emerson, T. Gilbert, ... M.D., M.CH. 1875.

Emerson, Thomas, ... B.A. 1891.—Civil Service of India,

England, William G., ... B.A. 1880; B.L. (Ir.)

e Entrican, Samuel W., ... B.A. 1894; M.A. 1896.

Evans, Isaac Rennison, B.A. 1885.

Evans, John, ... B.A. 1852.

b Evatt, George G. J. H., .. M.D. 1863.

Evatt, Humphrey, ... B.A. 1859. — Surveyor-General, Sierra Leone.

Fairbrother, Jacob, ... M.D., M.CH. 1884.

a Falkiner, George A., ... B.E. 1871; M.E. 1882.

e Falkiner, Richard D., ... Dip. Eng. 1861; M.E. 1882.—Engineer, Public Works of India.

Farley, William J., ... B.A. 1896.

---

a With First Honours.   *b* Army Med. Service.   *e* With Second Honours.

e Farrelly, Michael J., ... B.A. 1876; M.A. 1882; LL.B. 1890; LL.D. 1892; B.L. (Ir.)—Formerly Member of Senate of the Royal University.

Farrelly, Thomas, ... M.D, M.CH. 1883.
Feeny, Dominick, ... B.A. 1863.
b Ferguson, Frederick, ... M.D. 1862.
Finnucane, Thomas E., ... B.B. 1889.
e Fisher, John M., ... B.E. 1875; M.E. 1882.
Fisher, Joseph R., ... B.A. 1876; B.L. (Eng.)
Fitzgerald, Gerald H., ... M.D. 1874; M.CH. 1875.
e Fitzpatrick, John, ... B.A. 1868; M.A. 1869.
c Fitzpatrick, Joseph A., ... M.D., M.CH. 1865.
Fitzsimon, C. Collingwood, .. M.D., Dip. Obs. 1875.
e Flack, William T., ... B.A. 1894; M.A. 1900.
a Flatley, William P., ... B.E. 1880; M.E. 1882.
Fleming, George H., ... B.E. 1899.
Fleming, Samuel H., ... B.A. 1894; *e* B.E. 1902.
Fleming, William, ... M.D. 1871; M.CH. 1872.
Flood, John C., ... M.D., M.CH., Dip. Obs. 1875.
Foley, Charles H., ... M.B., B.CH., B.A.O. 1893.
Foley, Thomas H., ... M.B., B.CH., B.A.O. 1890.
a Forde, Patrick F., ... B.A. 1854; M.A. 1856.
Forde, Michael J., ... M.B., B.CH., B.A.O. 1900.
Foreman, Robert L., ... B.A. 1864.—Civil Service of India.
Forman, William J., ... B.A. 1876.
a Forsyth, Samuel M'C., ... B.A. 1865; M.A. 1882.
Forsythe, Anderson, ... B.A. 1869; M.D. 1871.
e Foy, Alexander R., ... B.A. 1881; M.A. 1882.
d French, John G., ... M.D., M.CH. 1870.—First Place, Indian Medical Service.
a Freyer, John, ... B.A. 1882.
ad Freyer, P. Johnson, ... B.A. 1872; M.D., M.CH., Dip. Obs. 1874; M.A. 1882.—First Place, Indian Medical Service.
Freyer, Samuel, ... B.A. 1884.

e Gahan, Charles J., ... B.A. 1881; M.A. 1882.
Gahan, Garner, ... B.A. 1878.
Gailey, Andrew, ... B.A. 1889.
Gailey, John, ... B.A. 1882.
Gallagher, Stephen G., ... B.E. 1896.
e Gannon, William J., ... B.A. 1889; M.A. 1892.—Elected to Science Research Scholarship by H.M. Exhibition (1851) Commissioners; Lecturer, the Owens College, Manchester; Head Master of the Municipal School of Science, Stafford; Science Master and Inspector to the Staffordshire County Council.

---

a With First Honours.　　*c* Naval Medical Service.
b Army Medical Service.　　*d* Indian Medical Service.
e With Second Honours.

Garry, Thomas G.,	.. ..	M.D., M.CH., Dip. Obs. 1883; M.A.O. 1886.
e Gaston, James, ..	• ..	B.A., B.E. 1897.
Geoghegan, A. Osmond,	..	M.D. 1878; M.CH. 1879.
Geoghegan, F. Meagher,	..	M.D. 1876.
Gibson, William W.,	.. ..	M.D. 1881; M.CH. 1882.
Gilchrist, Andrew,	.. ..	B.A. 1891.
Gill, Peter T., ..	.. ..	B.A., B.E. 1897.
e Gillespie, George,	.. ..	B.A. 1884; M.A. 1885.
Gillespie, James J.,	.. ..	B.A. 1880.
Gillespie, Michael,	..	B.A. 1867; M.D. 1872, M.CH., Dip. Obs. 1873.
Gillespie, William H.,	..	B.A. 1889; M.A. 1890.
e Glover, R. Francis,	..	B.A. 1869; M.A. 1882.
a Glover, R. Stephen,	..	B.E. 1869; M.E. 1882.
Glynn, John,	.. ..	M.D. 1883.
Gordon, John,	.. ..	B.A. 1873; LL.B. 1876; LL.D. 1882.—K.C. (Ir.)
b Gore, Albert A., ..	.. ..	M.D. 1860.
c Gorham, Anthony,	..	M.D. 1866.—Fleet-Surg. R.N.
e Gorham, James J.,	..	B.A. 1872; M.D., M.CH., Dip. Obs. 1875; M.A. 1882.
Gorham, John,	.. ..	B.A. 1877.
Gormley, John,	.. ..	B.A. 1861.
b Gormley, Joseph A.,	..	M.D., M.CH. 1873.
b Gouldsberry, V. Skipton,	..	M.D. 1862.
Graham, George,	..	M.B., B.CH., B.A.O. 1900.
Grealy, John,	.. ..	B.A. 1861.
Green, Joseph J.,	.. ..	B.A. 1862.
Greenfield, John K.,	..	B.A. 1875.
Greenway, Alfred G.,	..	M.D. 1870; M.CH. 1895.—House Physician, General Hospital, Birmingham.
Gregg, Andrew C.,	.. ..	B.A. 1886.
Gregory, William J.,	.. ..	M.B., B.CH., B.A.O. 1889.
Griffin, John,	.. ..	B.A. 1863.
e Griffin, Thomas, ..	.. ..	B.A. 1867; M.A. 1882.
Griffith, William,	.. ..	B.A. 1860.
a Hackett, Edward A.,	..	B.E. 1880; M.E. 1882.—County Surveyor of Tipperary.
ab Hackett, Robert I. Dalbey,	..	B.A. 1877; M.D., M.CH. 1880; M.A. 1882.
c Hall, Arthur A., ..	.. ..	B.A. 1898; B.E. 1899.
Hall, Charles B.,	.. ..	M.D. 1878; M.CH. 1880.
Hall, John,	.. ..	B.A. 1902.
e Hall, Thomas Andrew, ..	..	B.E. 1888; B.A. 1889.
e Hallidy, Robert J.,	.. ..	B.E., B.A. 1898.

---

a With First Honours.	*e* Naval Medical Service.
b Army Medical Service.	*e* With Second Honours.

Hamilton, James,	.. ..	M.B., B.CH., B.A.O. 1889.
Hamilton, James,	.. ..	M.D., M.CH., Dip. Obs. 1875.
Hamilton, Samuel,	.. ..	B.A. 1889 ; M.B., B.CH., B.A.O. 1891.
Hanly, Edward, ..	.. ..	M.D., M.CH. 1879.
e Hanly, John J., ..	.. ..	B.A. 1880 ; M.A. 1881.
Hanly, Joseph F.,	.. ..	B.E. 1897.
e Hanna, James, ..	.. ..	B.A. 1874 ; M.A. 1876.
e Hanna, Robert K.,	.. ..	B.A. 1894.
b Hanrahan, James J.,	.. ..	M.D. 1864.
Hardiman, James,	.. ..	Dip. Agric. 1853.
Hardiman, James J.,	.. ..	B.A., B.E. 1900.
Hare, Gustavus J. C.,	.. ..	B.A. 1863 ; M.A. 1865.
Harkin, James C.,	.. ..	M.B., B.CH., B.A.O. 1889.
Harper, Henry, ..	.. ..	M.D. 1881.
Harrington, Denis,	.. ..	M.D., M.CH., Dip. Obs. 1877.
a Harrison, John H.,	.. ..	B.A. 1870 ; M.A. 1872.—Civil Service of India.
Harrison, Thomas,	.. ..	B.A. 1892.
Hart, James C., ..	.. ..	B.A. 1858.
e Haslam, George J.,	.. ..	M.D. 1880.
e Hayes, John C., ..	.. ..	B.A 1892.
Hayes, John S., ..	.. ..	M.D. 1875.
Hayes, Patrick, ..	.. ..	B.A., B.E. 1890.
Heany, James H.,	.. ..	M.B., B.CH., B.A.O. 1890.
Hegan, Edwin, ..	.. ..	M.B., B.CH., B.A.O. 1891.
Hegarty, John, ..	.. ..	M.D., M.CH. 1872.
a Henderson, John,	.. ..	B.A. 1878 ; M.A. 1882.
Henderson, Robert W., ..	.. ..	M.D., M.CH. 1883.
Henderson, S. Dunlop, ..	.. ..	M.D., M.CH. 1882.
e Henderson, Thomas,	.. ..	B.A. 1877 ; M.A. 1882.
a Henry, Augustine,	.. ..	B.A. 1877 ; M.A. 1878.—Consular Med. Service, China.
e Henry, Joseph, ..	.. ..	M.D. 1874.
Henry, John W. R.,	.. ..	B.A. 1857.
e Henry, Moses, ..	.. ..	B.A. 1886 ; M.A. 1888.
Henry, Moses, ..	.. ..	M.B., B.CH., B.A.O. 1897.
a Henry, William E.,	.. ..	B.A. 1869 ; M.A. 1870.—President, Wesleyan Coll., St. John's, N.B.
a Henry, John,	.. ..	B.A. 1893 ; M.A. (with Special Prize) 1894 ; B.E. 1895.— Elected to Science Research Scholarship by H. M. Exhibition (1851) Commissioners, 1896 ; Demonstrator of Physics, Queen's College, Galway ; Junior Fellowship in Natural Philsophy, R.U.I., 1899.

a With First Honours.   *e* With Second Honours.
b Army Medical Service.

Heuston, Francis T.,	.. ..	M.CH., M.D. 1878.—Professor of Anatomy, Royal College of Surgeons in Ireland ; Consult-Surgeon to the Coombe Lying-In Hospital, Dublin ; Consulting Surgeon to the Cripples' Home, Bray ; Surgeon to the Adelaide Hospital, Dublin ; Member of the Council, Royal College of Surgeons in Ireland.
Hewitt, David W.,	.. ..	M.B., B.CH., B.A.O. 1895.
e Hezlett, James M.,	.. ..	B.A. 1897 ; Demonstrator of Physics, Queen's College, Galway ; Civil Service of India.
b Hickman, Arthur,	.. ..	M.D. 1880.
a Hickman, James,	.. ..	B.A. 1874 ; M.A. 1877.
Hickman, William,	.. ..	M.D., M.CH. 1872.
e Hilton, Hugh, ..	.. ..	B.A. 1889.
b Hinds, William R. G., ..	.. ..	M.D. 1863.
e Hoctor, William F.,	.. ..	B.A 1866 ; M.A. 1882.
Hogg, T. Simpson,	.. ..	B.A. 1883.
Holland, John J.,	.. ..	M.D., M.CH., Dip. Obs. 1872.
Holmes, Arthur P.,	.. ..	M.D. 1859.
Holmes, Robert A. K., ..	.. ..	B.A. 1866 ; M.D. 1870 ; M.A. 1882.
a Hooper, Charles J.,	.. ..	B.A. 1855; M.A. 1856 ; LL.B. 1858 ; LL.D. 1862.
Hooper, Robert, ..	.. ..	M.D. 1861.
Horkan, Peter Joseph,	.. ..	M.D., M.CH. 1884.
Houston, James D. C., ..	.. ..	B.A. 1872.
a Huey, John, ..	.. ..	B.A. 1868; M.A. 1869.
Huggard, William R., ..	.. ..	M.D., M.CH. 1875 ; B.A. 1876 M.A. 1879.
b Hughes, John H.,	.. ..	M.D. 1863.
e Hughes, Patrick J.,	.. ..	B.A. 1853 ; M.A. 1882.—Consular Service of China.
e Hughes, William,	.. ..	B.A. 1866; Dip. Eng., 1867; M.A., M.E. 1882.—Engineer, Public Works of India.
a Hume, George A.,	.. ..	B.A. 1878; M.A. 1879 ; LL.B. 1880 ; LL.D. 1882 ; B.L. (Ir.)
a Humphreys, John,	.. ..	B.A. 1890.
a Hunter, Charles W.,	.. ..	B.A. 1877 ; M.A. 1879.
Hunter, Charles H.,	.. ..	B.A. 1893.
c Hurley, Francis B.,	.. ..	B.A. 1856 ; M.D. 1860.
e Hurley, Patrick, ..	.. ..	B.A. 1862 ; M.A. 1882.—Civil Service of India.
e Hutchinson, James,	.. ..	M.D. 1861.
Hynes, Michael, ..	.. ..	Dip. Eng. 1859 ; B.E. 1882.
Hynes, Mortimer,	.. ..	M.B., B.CH., B.A.O. 1895.

a With First Honours.	*c* Naval Medical Service.
b Army Medical Service.	*e* With Second Honours.

Ievers, Robert W.,	.. ..	B.A. 1870; M.A. 1882.—Ceylon Civil Service, First Place; Acting Colonial Secretary for Ceylon, 1891.
Ireland, Arthur J.,	.. ..	M.D. 1861.
Irwin, Albert J.,	.. ..	B.A. 1888.
Jackson, Burton, ..	.. ..	B.A. 1858; M.D. 1862.
Jackson, Mark, ..	..	M.D. 1882.
Jackson, Joseph Brown, ..	..	M.D., M.CH., 1883.
a Jackson, William J.,	.. ..	B.A. 1880; M.A. 1882.
James, Arthur, ..	.. ..	B.A. 1879.
Jaquet, J. Lewis,	.. ..	M.D. 1881.
b Jenings, Ulick A.,	.. ..	M.D., M.CH. 1865.
Jennings, Edward C.,	.. ..	B.E. 1899.
Jennings, Michael,	.. ..	M.D., 1881; M.CH. 1885.
Johnson, Alexander M.,	.. ..	M.D., M.CH. 1883.
Johnson, Samuel,	.. ..	M.D., M.CH. 1870.
Johnson, Samuel W.,	.. ..	M.D. 1881.
a Johnston, James,	.. ..	B.A. 1895.—Civil Service of India (Third Place.)
e Johnston, J. Wesley,	.. ..	B.A. 1854; M.A. 1882.
Johnston, William,	.. ..	B.A. 1852; M.A. 1882.
Johnston, William M.,	.. ..	B.A. 1866; M.A. 1868.
e Jones, James, ..	.. ..	B.A. 1894; M.A. 1895.
e Jordan, Michael J.,	.. ..	B.A. 1886.
Jordan, William,	.. ..	B.A. 1881; M.A. 1882.
Joyce, Patrick K.,	.. ..	B.A. 1872; M.B., B.CH., B.A.O. 1893.—Head Master, Royal School, Banagher.
b Joynt, Christopher,	.. ..	M.D. 1855.
b Joynt, E. Hearne,	.. ..	M.D., M.CH. 1870.
Kane, John, ..	.. ..	B.A. 1866.
a Kane, Thomas, ..	.. ..	B.A. 1891.
a Keane, C. Marceet,	.. ..	B.A. 1853; Dip. El. Law, 1865
Kearney, Daniel,	.. ..	B.A. 1854.
e Keating, William H.,	.. ..	B.A. 1882; M.A. 1883.
e Keegan, David M.,	.. ..	B.A. 1894.
c Keegan, James M.,	.. ..	B.A. 1886; M.A. 1887; M.B., B.CH., B.A.O. 1890.
e Keenan, John F.,	.. ..	B.A. 1892; Demonstrator of Chemistry, Queen's College, Galway.
Keers, James, ..	.. ..	B.A. 1886.
a Kelly, Michael, ..	.. ..	B.A. 1874; M.A. 1876; M.D. 1882; M.CH., Dip. Obs. 1883.
Kelly, Patrick J.,	.. ..	M.D. 1857.
Kennedy, John, ..	.. ..	M.D., M.CH., Dip. Obs. 1881.

a With First Honours.   *b* Army Medical Service.   *e* With Second Honours.

a Kennedy, William,	.. ..	B.A. 1888 ; M.A. 1890.—University Student, R.U.I., B.A. (Gold Medalin Classics), T.C.D.1893 ; The Madden Prize at Fellowship Examination, T.C.D., 1899 ; Fellowship T.C.D., 1901.
Kenny, John D.,	.. ..	M.D., M.CH. 1884.
Keogh, Alfred H.,	.. ..	M.D., M.CH., Dip. Obs. 1878 ; M.A.O. 1892.
Kernaghan, Thomas W.,	..	B.A. 1896.
e Kerr, Æneas,	.. ..	B.A. 1876 ; M.A.1882.
Kidd, Charles, ..	.. ..	M.B., B.CH., B.A.O. 1899.
a Killen, James B.,	.. ..	B.A. 1863 ; M.A. 1868 ; LL.B. 1868. —B.L. (Ir.)
a Killen, John M., ..	.. ..	B.A. 1866 ; M.D. 1870.
King, Ælian A., ..	.. ..	B.A. 1862 ; M.A. 1882.—District Judge, Ceylon.
King, William, ..	.. ..	B.A. 1853 ; D.SC. *Honoris causa*, 1882.—Staff of Indian Geological Survey.
Kingston, William Y.,	.. ..	M.D., M.CH., Dip. Obs. 1873.
e Kirker, H. Fitzwalter,	.. ..	B.A. 1881 ; M.A. 1882.
e Kirwan, James St. L.,	.. ..	B.A.1893; M.B., B.CH., B.A.O. 1896.
e Kirwan, Robert J.,	.. ..	B.A. 1892 ; B.E. 1893.
Knight, William J. R., ..	.. ..	M.D. 1881 ; M.CH. 1885
Lalor, James,	.. ..	B.A. 1855.
Lavertine, Charles,	.. ..	B.A. 1875.
Lavertine, Richard A.,	.. ..	B.E. 1876.
Lawlor, J. Stanislaus,	.. ..	M.D., M.CH. 1877.
Lawson, J. Henry,	.. ..	M.D. 1860.—Lecturer and Surgeon, St. Mary's Hospital, London.
Leary, Joseph W.,	.. ..	B.A. 1862.
Legate, George W.,	.. ..	B.A. 1867 ; M.A. 1869.
b Lestrange, Edward,	.. ..	M.D. 1856.
e Lewis, John P., ..	.. ..	B.A. 1876 ; M.A. 1882.—Civil Service of Ceylon.
a Lewis, W. Llewellyn,	.. ..	B.A. 1869 ; M.A. 1871.
Lightbody, Robert,	.. ..	Dip. Eng. 1864 ; B.E. 1882.
e Livingstone, John L.,	.. ..	M.B., M.CH., M.A.O. 1886.
Loane, Thomas, ..	.. ..	M.D., M.CH. 1874.
Loftus, Joseph J.,	.. ..	M.B., B.CH., B.A.O. 1889.
Longworth, Peter,	.. ..	M.D. 1868.
Lough, William J.,	.. ..	B.A. 1867.
Love, George C.,	.. ..	B.A. 1876 ; M.A. 1877.
b Love, Robert L., ..	.. ..	B.A. 1876 ; M.D., M.CH. 1877.
e Lowe, William J.,	.. ..	B.A. 1880 ; M.A. 1881.
Lundy, Joseph, ..	.. ..	B.A. 1892.

---

a With First Honours.   *e* With Second Honours.
b Army Medical Service.

Lupton, Henry, ...	M.D. 1864 ; M.CH. 1866.
Lyden, Michael J., ...	M.D., M.CH. 1877.
Lydon, Patrick J., ...	B.A. 1902.
e Lynam, Edward W., ..	B.E. 1878. ; M.E. 1882 ; Inspector of Board of Works (Ireland).
e Lynam, James, ...	B.A. 1859 ; M.A. 1882.
a Lynam, James, ...	B.A. 1872 ; M.A. 1882.
c Lynam, Joseph D., ...	B.A. 1881; M.A.1882.—F.R.C.PRE. Lond. ; Inspector of National Schools, Ireland, (December, 1893).
a Lynam, Patrick, ...	B.E. 1872 ; M.E. 1882. — First Place Civil Service of Ceylon ; County Surveyor of Louth.
c Lynam, William P., ...	Dip. Eng, 1866; B.E. 1880 ; M.E. 1882.—Engineer, Public Works of India.
a Lynam, Francis J., ...	B.E. 1884.—County Surveyor of North Tyrone, (Nov., 1895).
a Lynham, John I., ...	M.D., M.CH. 1875.—F.R.U.I. ; Professor of Medicine, Queen's College, Galway.
e Lyons, Frederick W., ...	B.A. 1896.—Inspector, Imperial Chinese Customs, Swatow.
Lyons, James A., ...	B.A. 1902.
Lyons, Robert W. S., ...	M.D., M.CH. 1881 ; Dip. Obs., M.A.O. 1888.
Macartney, James, ...	M.D. 1865.
e Macaulay, Colman P., ...	B.A. 1867 ; M.A. 1868. — Civil Service of India; Financial Secretary, Government of Bengal.
c Macauley, Charles A., ...	M.D., M.CH., Dip. Obs. 1872.
e Macauley, Roger, ...	M.D. 1873.
a MacDonnell, Sir Anthony P., ..	B.A. 1864 ; M.A. 1873 ; D. LIT. *Honoris causa.*—Civil Service of India ; K.C.S.I. ; Member of Council of the Viceroy of India ; Lieut.-Governor of the North-West Provinces and Oudh ; Under-Secretary to the Lord-Lieutenant of Ireland.
MacFeeters, William E., ..	M.D., M.CH. 1886.
Macnamara, John Maurice, ..	B.A. 1879 ; M.B., M.CH. 1887
ad Macnamara, Robert J., ...	M.D., M.CH. 1884.
Madden, Henry M., ...	M.D. 1868 ; M.CH. 1870.
Madden, Henry J., ...	M.D. 1865.
Madden, Thomas P., ...	M.D., M.CH. 1879.
Madill, Thomas, ...	B.A.1861 ; LL.B. 1878 ; LL.D. 1879.
Maguire, Connor J. O'L. ..	M.D., M.CH., Dip. Obs. 1882 ; M.A.O. 1892.

e Maguire, Edward,	.. ..	B.A. 1854 ; M.A. 1882.
e Maguire, Thomas M.,	.. ..	B.A. 1867 ; M.A. 1870 ; LL.D. 1874 ; B.L. (Eng.)
Maguire, Joseph P.,	.. ..	M.B., B.CH., B.A.O. 1895.
Maher, Newenham E.,	.. ..	M.D. 1866.
a Mahon, John S.,	.. ..	B.A. 1891 ; M.A. 1892 ; Inspector of Schools, First Place.
Mahon, Ralph B.,	.. ..	M.B., M.CH. 1885.
Mahon, William,	.. ..	B.A. 1883 ; M.A. 1884.
a Mahony, John,	.. ..	B.A. 1854 ; M.A. 1882.
Mairs, William C.,	.. ..	B.A. 1901 ; B.E. 1902.
e Mallagh, Joseph	.. ..	B.A., B.E. 1896.
e Mangan, Denis,	.. ..	B.A. 1890 ; Inspector of National Schools, Ireland.
Mann, Samuel,	.. ..	B.E. 1900.
a Mapother, Edward D.,	.. ..	M.D. 1857.—Late Professor of Anatomy and Physiology, Royal College of Surgeons, Ireland, &c. &c.
Marks, C. Ferdinand,	.. ..	M.D. 1874.
Marks, Edward G. K.,	.. ..	M.D., M.CH. 1876.
e Marshall, John,	.. ..	B A. 1867 ; M.A. 1869 ; M.D., M.CH. 1870.
Martin, James H.,	.. ..	B.E. 1868 ; M.E. 1882.—Surveyor-ship, Demerara.
Martin, John,	.. ..	M.D., Dip. Obs. 1879 ; M.CH. 1880.
Martin, John W.,	.. ..	M.D., M.CH. 1868.
a b Martin, William T.,	.. ..	B.A. 1859 ; M.D. 1862 ; M.A. 1882.
Maunsell, Charles A.,	.. ..	M.D. 1862.
Maxwell, Sydney L.,	.. ..	B.A. 1883.
e Maxwell, William H.,	.. ..	B.A., 1872 ; M.A. 1874.
May, William G.,	.. ..	B.A. 1859.
e Maybin, Hugh,	.. ..	B.A. 1896.
a Maybin, W.,	.. ..	B.A. 1873 ; M.A. 1882.—Principal of Belfast Academy.
a Maybury, Lysander,	.. ..	M.D., M.CH., Dip. Obs. 1878.
Maybury, William A.,	.. ..	M.D., M.CH. 1871 ; Dip. Obs. 1872.
M'Afee, Alexander,	.. ..	B.A 1887.
M'Afee, William,	.. ..	M.D., M.CH., Dip. Obs. 1876.
M'Aleer, John,	.. ..	M.D., M.CH. 1885 ; B.A.O. 1888.
M'Askie, William J.,	.. ..	B.A. 1890.
a M'Auliffe, Michael,	.. ..	B.A. 1860 ; M.A. 1882.
M'Auliffe, Thomas B.,	.. ..	M.D., M.CH. 1868.
M'Bride, John B.,	.. ..	B.A. 1856.
M'Call, Robert A.,	.. ..	B.A. 1867 ; M.A. 1868 ; LL.D. *Honoriscausa*,1882.—K.C.(Eng.); Bencher of the Middle Temple.
b M'Carthy, David J.,	.. ..	M.D. 1862 ; M.CH. 1875.
b M'Carthy, James,	.. ..	M.D., M.CH. 1871.
M'Causland, Joseph,	.. ..	B.A. 1901.

a With First Honours. *b* Army Med. Service. *e* With Second Honours.

M'Cay, Daniel, ...	..	B.E., 1893.
a M'Cay, Francis,	..	B.A. 1889 ; B.E. 1890.
a M'Clelland, John A.,	..	B.A. 1892.—Special Prize at Degree M.A. 1893. Elected to Science Research Scholarship by H. M. Exhibition (1861) Commissioners, 1894 : Junior Fellowship in Natural Philosophy, R.U.I., 1895 ; Research Degree, Cambridge, 1898 ; Professorship of Natural Philosophy in University College, Dublin, 1900 ; Fellowship in Natural Philosophy, R.U.I., 1901.
b M'Conaghey, John, ..	..	M.D., M.CH. 1871.
M'Conaghy, William, ..	..	M.D. 1869.
M'Connell, Edward, ..	..	M.D. 1881 ; M.CH. 1882.
M'Connell, Thomas S., ..	..	M.D. 1881 ; M.CH. 1882.
M'Cormick, John J.,	..	M.D., Dip. Obs. 1879 ; M.CH. 1882.
M'Cormick, Henry,	..	M.D., Dip. Obs. 1879.
M'Corry, Peter, ..	..	M.D. 1861.
e M'Cosh, John, ..	..	B.A. 1876 ; M.A. 1881.
M'Crea, Samuel, ..	..	M.D. 1864.
M'Cully, William J.,	..	B.A. 1866.
a M'Cune, Thomas H.,	..	B.A. 1883 ; M.A. 1884.
c M'Dermott, B. P. Sarsfield,	..	B.A., M.D., M.CH. 1878.
e M'Dermott, Cornelius, ..	..	B.A. 1878 ; M.A., M.D., M.CH. 1882.
e M'Dermott, Dominick L.,	..	B.A. 1853 ; M.A. 1882.—War Office.
e M'Donagh, Redmond, ..	..	B.A. 1882 ; M.A. 1883.
M'Donagh, Thomas J., ..	..	B.A. 1894.
d M'Donnell, James O'M.,	..	M.D., M.CH. 1869.
c M'Donnell, Joseph R., ..	..	M.D. 1881 ; M.CH. 1882.
M'Donnell, Mark A.,	..	M.D., M.CH., Dip. Obs. 1876.—M.P.
M'Dowell, Thomas H., ..	..	B.A. 1879.
M'Elfatrick, Thomas A.,	..	B.A. 1896.
e M'Elney, Robert,	..	B.A. 1884 ; M.A. 1887.
M'Elrea, William,	..	B.E. 1879.
M'Elwaine, Robert,	..	M.D. 1883 ; M.CH. 1884.
ce M'Elwee, John, ..	..	B.A. 1884 ; M.D., M.CH. 1887.
M'Farland, Beattie,	..	M.D. 1881 ; M.CH. 1883.
e M'Farlane, Hugh,	..	B.A. 1878 ; M.A. 1879.
a M'Farlane, Robert A.,	..	B.A. 1867 ; M.A. 1869.
M'Gennis, John, ..	..	M.D., B.CH., B.A.O. 1890.
M'Gloin, Patrick F.,	..	M.D. 1863 ; M.CH. 1865.
M'Granahan, James,	..	B.A. 1882.
M'Granahan, William, ..	..	B.A. 1876.

a With First Honours.   *d* Indian Medical Service.
b Army Medical Service.   *e* With Second Honours.
c Naval Medical Service.

M'Grath, Edward H., ...	B.A. 1901; M.A. 1902.
e MacGregor, William, ...	B.A. 1893 ; M.A. 1894 ; LL.B. 1897.
M'Ilroy, John, ...	M.D., B.A.O. 1883.
M'Ilveen, John, ...	B.A. 1868.
M'Ilwaine, Robert, ...	B.A. 1893; M.A. 1894; LL.B. 1895 ; Assistant Magistrate, Salisbury, British South Africa.
a M'Kane, John, ...	B.A. 1860; M.A. 1862.—Late Barrington Lecturer, Professor of English Law, Queen's College, Belfast ; B.L. (Ir.)
e M'Kee, William J., ...	B.A. 1887.
M'Kelvey, Thomas, ...	M.B., B.CH., B.A.O. 1898.
M'Kenzie, John, ...	B.A. 1865 ; M.A. 1871.
M'Kinlay, John, ...	M.D., Dip. Obs. 1878; M.CH. 1879.
M'Kinley, David, ...	B.A., 1896 ; B.E. 1898.
M'Kinney, Hugh G., ...	Dip. Eng. 1867; M.E. 1882.— Engineer, Public Works of India.
e M'Kinney, Samuel B. G., ..	B.A. 1870 ; M.A. 1882.
M'Lachlan, John S., ..	B.A. 1902.
a M'Laren, James B., ...	B.A. 1881; M.A. 1882.
M'Laughlin, John, ...	M.D. 1880.
M'Lean, Andrew H, ...	B.E. 1899.
M'Lean, Robert J., ...	B.A. 1898.
e M'Loughlin, Francis, ...	M.D. 1881.
e M'Mahon, George Y., ...	B.A., Dip. El. Law, 1852 ; M.A. 1860. — Late Professor of Modern Languages, Royal College, Mauritius.
ce M'Mahon, William, ...	M.D, 1862.
M'Manus, Leonard S., ...	M.D., M.CH. 1882.
M'Millan, Hugh, ...	M.D., M.CH., Dip. Obs. 1873.
M'Millan, John, ...	B.A. 1875.
M'Mordie, Elijah, ...	B.A. 1873 ; M.A. 1874.
M'Mullan, Hugh S., ...	M.A.
b M'Nally, Christopher J., ..	M.D., M.CH. 1871.
e M'Namara, John W., ...	B.A. 1873 ; M.D. 1879.
M'Namara, Joseph C., ...	B.A. 1874.—Inspector of National Schools.
d M'Namara, William J. U., ..	B.A. 1875; M.D., M.CH. 1878; M.A. 1880.—Ind. Med. Serv., First Place; Demonstrator, Queen's College, Galway.
M'Neill, John R., ...	M.D., M.CH. 1881.
M'Quaid, Peter J., ...	M.D., M.CH. 1872.
M'Sherry, Edward H., ...	M.D., M.CH., M.A.O. 1886.

M'Swinney, George H.,	..	M.D., M.CH. 1871.
a M'Swinney, Robert F.,	..	B.A. 1866 ; M.A. 1868 ; LL.B. 1870; LL.D. 1882.—First Law Studentship, Inns of Court, London, 1871 ; B,L. (Eng.)
M'Vittie, R. Blake,	.. ..	M.D. 1876.
Megarry, James,	.. ..	B.A. 1872.
Megaw, Robert T.,	.. ..	B.A. 1877 ; LL.B. 1885 ; LL.D. 1887.
Meharry, John B.,	.. ..	B.A. 1868.
Millea, William C.,	.. ..	B.A. 1891.
Millar, William J.,	.. ..	B.A. 1881; M.A. 1882 ; LL.B. 1887. —District Inspector, R.I.C.
Milligan, William,	.. ..	M.D., M.CH., M.A.O. 1886.
Mills, John A., ..	.. ..	B.A. 1897; M.B., B.CH., B.A.O. 1900.
Mills, Samuel, ..	.. ..	B.A. 1862.
e Mills, William S.,	.. ..	B.A. 1898 ; M.A. 1900 ; Demonstrator of Chemistry, Queen's College, Galway; elected to Science Research Scholarship by H. M. Exhibition (1851) Commissioners, 1900.
e Milward, Edwin O.,	.. ..	B.A. 1873 ; M.A. 1875.
Minniken, John, ..	.. ..	B.A. 1877.
Mitchell, Andrew A.,	.. ..	M.D. 1879 ; M.CH. 1891.
Mitchell, Campbell M., ..		M.D., M.CH. 1883.
Mitchell, Charles A. P.,	..	M.D., M.CH., Dip. Obs. 1879.
e Mitchell, Robert,	.. ..	B.A. 1871 ; M.A. 1882.
Mitchell, Robert,	.. ..	M.D., M.CH. 1879.
a Mitchell, Robert J.,	.. ..	B.A. 1854 ; M.A. 1860 ; D. LIT. *Honoris causa.*—Late Inspector of National Schools ; Inspector, Registrar General's Office, Ireland.
Mitchell, W. J., ..	.. ..	M.D. 1883.
Moffett, Samuel, ..	.. ..	B.A. 1867.
e Molloy, Mark, ..	.. ..	B.A. 1881 ; M.A., LL.B. 1882.; LL.D. 1883.
Molony, Henry G.,	.. ..	B.A. 1873 ; M.D., M.CH. 1876.
Molony, John, ..	.. ..	B.A. 1874.
e Molony, John S.,	.. ..	B.A. 1874 ; B.E. 1877 ; M.E. 1882.
Molony, Timothy,	.. ..	M.D., M.CH. 1872.
a Monroe, John, ..	.. ..	B.A. 1857 ; M.A. 1859 ; LL.B. 1862 ; LL.D. 1882.—Studentship, Inns of Court, London ; Judge of High Court of Ireland.
a Monroe, Samuel H., ..	..	B.A. 1873 ; M.A. 1882.
e Montgomery, Alexander W.,	..	B.A. 1895; M.B., B.CH., B.A.O. 1897.
Moody, John, ...	..	B.A. 1882.

---

a With First Honours.   *e* With Second Class Honours.

Moody, Samuel, ...	B.A. 1863.
Moody, William, ...	B.A. 1887; M.B., B.CH., B.A.O. 1893.
e Moon, Frederick W., ...	B.E. 1897.
Moon, James R., ...	B.E. 1870.
Moon, Robert A., ...	B.E. 1890.
a Moore, John H., ...	B.A. 1858; M.D. 1861; M.A. 1882.
Moore, William D., ...	M.D., M.CH. 1880.
Moore, William Irwin, ...	B.A. 1899.
a Moorhead, William R., ..	B.A. 1865; M.A. 1866; M.D. 1869.
a d Moorhead, James, ..	B.A. 1871; M.A. 1872; M.D. 1875. — First Place Indian Medical Service.
a Moorhead, John, ...	B.A. 1855; M.D. 1856; M.A. 1857.
a Moorhead, John R., ...	B.A. 1881; LL.B. 1886.
a Moran, John, ...	B.A. 1870; M.A. 1872; LL.B. 1878; LL.D. 1879.—Inspector of National Schools.
e Moran, John, ...	B.A. 1891; B.E. 1898.
Moran, Michael, ...	M.B., B.CH., B.A.O. 1897.
Morris, Arthur E., ...	M.D., M.CH 1883.
c Morris, John James, ..	M.D., Dip. Obs. 1873; M.CH. 1874.
Morris, Michael O'K., ...	B.A. 1854; M.D. 1857; M.CH. 1865.
Morrow, Henry W., ...	B.A. 1881; M.A. 1882.
Morton, David, ...	B.A. 1887.
Morton, John H., ...	B.A. 1881.
Moylan, Hannah A., ...	B.SC. 1896.
Moylan, Michael J., ...	B.A. 1873.
Moynan, Joseph, ...	B.E. 1881.
Moynan, Richard M., ...	M.D., M.CH. 1882.
Moynan, William A., ...	M.D., M.CH. 1881.
b Moynan, W. E. Bonsall, ..	M.D., M.CH., Dip. Obs. 1872.
e Mulholland, William, ..	B.A. 1863; M.A. 1882.—Barrington Lecturer; K.C. (Eng.)
a Mullally, Michael, ...	B.A. 1871; M.A. 1873.—Inspector of National Schools.
Mullally, William T., ...	M.D., M.CH. 1880.
c Mullen, Douglas, ...	M.D. 1872; M.CH., Dip.Obs.1873.
b Mullen, Jarlath J., ...	M.D., M.CH., Dip. Obs. 1873.
Mullen, St. Laurence, ...	M.D., M.CH. 1868.
b Mullen, Thomas F., ...	M.D. 1864; M.CH. 1865.
a Mulligan, James, ...	B.A. 1869; M.A. 1871; B.L. (Eng.), Bencher of Gray's Inn.
e Mullin, James, ...	B.A. 1874; M.D., M.CH., Dip. Obs. 1880; M.A 1882.
Mullin, John F. L., ...	M.D. 1880; M.CH. 1881.
e Munro, William H., ...	B.A. 1880; M.A. 1882; M.D., M.CH. 1885.
Murphy, Michael E., ...	M.D. 1868.

a With First Honours.　　*c* Naval Medical Service.
b Army Medical Service.　　*d* Indian Medical Service.
e With Second Class Honours.

Murray, Charles F. K., ...	M.D. 1868; M.CH. 1884.
Murray, G. Stanley, ...	M.D., M.CH. 1875.
Neilson, Robert A., ...	M.B., B.CH., B.A.O. 1898.
a Nelson, Thomas E., ...	B.A. 1880; M.A. 1881; LL.B. 1884; LL.D. 1886.
Newell, Peter, ...	B.A. 1882.—Inspector of National Schools.
Nicholls, John W., ...	M.D., M.CH., Dip. Obs. 1873.
Nicholson, William, ...	M.B., B.CH., B.A.O. 1900.
Nicholson, George F., ...	M.D. 1875.
d Nightingale, Walter H., ..	B.E. 1880; M.E. 1882.
c Nixon, John C., ...	B.A. 1893; M.B., B.CH., B.A.O. 1895.
Norris, Patrick J., ...	M.D. 1869.
Norton, Bernard G., ...	B.A. 1860.—Late Judge of Superior Court, British Guiana.
O'Brien, Daniel, ...	M.D., M.CH. 1869.
O'Brien, Michael, ...	M.D. 1875.
O'Brien, Thomas M., ...	M.D., M.CH., 1877; Dip. Obs. 1879.
b O'Connell, David V., ...	M.D., Dip. Obs. 1881; M.CH. 1882; M.A.O. 1893.
a O'Connor, George, ...	B.A. 1874; M.A. 1875.
O'Connor, Patrick, ...	M.D., M.CH. 1877.
O'Connor, P. Fenelon, ...	B.A. 1871; M.D., M.CH., Dip. Obs. 1874.
e O'Connor, Thomas P., ...	B.A. 1866; M.A. 1873.—M.P.
O'Dea, Martin, ...	M.B., B.CH., B.A.O., 1893.
O'Dea, Simon, ...	B.E. 1899.
d Odling, Charles W., ...	Dip. Eng. 1865; M.E. 1882.—Chief Engineer and Secretary to the Government, North Western Provinces, in the Public Works Department, India.
O'Donel, Claudius, ...	M.D. 1883.
O'Donnell, Charles J., ...	B.A. 1868; M.A. 1870.—Civil Service of India.
a O'Donnell, Francis, ...	B.A. 1865; M.A. 1868.—Late M.P.
be O'Farrell, Thomas, ...	B.A. 1861; M.A. 1863; M.D. 1864.
a O'Feely, Timothy O'B., ...	B.A. 1856; LL.B. 1857; LL.D. 1860.
ac O'Flaherty, Thomas A., ...	M.D. 1859.
O'Gorman, Patrick, ...	M.D. 1882; MC.H. 1883.
a O'Hara, Charles, ...	Dip. Agric. 1855; B.A. 1860; M.D. 1865; M.A. 1882.
O'Hara, Robert F., ...	B.A. 1873; B.L. (Ir.)
e O'Hara, Thomas, ...	Dip. Agric. 1852; B.A. 1860; M.A. 1882.—Inspector of National Schools.
O'Kelly, Thomas, ...	M.D. 1879.

a O'Kinealy, James,	.. ..	B.A. 1858 ; M.A. 1882 ; LL.D. *Honoris Causa.*—Civil Service of India.
a O'Kinealy, Michael,	.. ..	Dip. Eng. 1855 ; M.E. 1882.
a O'Kinealy, Peter,	.. ..	B.A. 1874 ; M.A. 1875 ; LL.B. 1875 ; LL.D. 1882 ; B.L. (Eng.)
O'Malley, David J.,	.. ..	M.D., M.CH. 1881.
a O'Neill, Geroge F.,	.. ..	B.A. 1858 ; M.A. 1862.—Inspector of National Schools.
a O'Neill, Joseph J.,	.. ..	B.A. 1901 ; *e*M.A. 1902.
O'Neill, Peter J.,	.. ..	B.A. 1872 ; B.L. (Ir.)
a Oram, John E., ..	.. ..	B.E. 1868 ; M.E. 1882. — Late Prof. Univer., Windsor, Nova Scotia ; late Librarian and Chief Clerk Royal University of Ireland.
O'Reilly, Myles W.,	.. ..	M.D., Dip. Obs. 1879 ; M.CH. 1880.
O'Reilly, Walter W. J.,	.. ..	M.D. 1870 ; M.CH. 1871.
b O'Reilly, Henry W. H.,	.. ..	M.B., B.CH., B.A.O. 1891.
e O'Shaughnessy, Michael M.,	.. ..	B.E., 1884.
b O'Sullivan, Patrick J., ..	.. ..	M.D., M.CH. 1875.
c O'Sullivan, Thomas,	.. ..	M.D., M.CH. 1869 ; Dip. Obs. 1878.
e Padin, Thomas, ..	.. ..	B.A. 1864 ; M.A. 1882.
Paisley, William,	.. ..	M.B., B.CH., B.A.O. 1899.
b Palmer, Dean P.,	.. ..	M.D. 1864.
Parker, James D.,	.. ..	B.A. 1854 ; Dip. El. Law, 1855 ; LL.B. 1857 ; LL.D. 1864.
d Parker, Joseph, ..	.. ..	M.D., M.CH. 1874.
Parry, Edward J.,	.. ..	M.D. 1881.
Patterson, Samuel,	.. ..	B.A. 1881.
e Paul, John, ..	.. ..	B.A. 1890.
Pearson, James D.,	.. ..	B.A. 1897 ; B.E. 1898.
Peterson, Richard A.,	.. ..	M.D. 1868.
Pierse, Gerard J.,	.. ..	M.D., B.CH., B.A O. 1889.
Pillow, Henry,	.. ..	M.D., M.CH. 1886.
Porterfield, Samuel,	.. ..	B.A. 1902.
Potter, Robert, ..	.. ..	M.D. 1862.
Powell, George H.,	.. ..	M.D., M.CH., Dip. Obs. 1881.
Pritchard, Thomas,	.. ..	M.D. 1880 ; M.CH. 1883.
Purcell, Matthew,	.. ..	M.B., M.CH. 1887.
b Purefoy, John W.,	.. ..	M.D. 1864.
a Pye, Joseph P., ..	.. ..	M.D., M.CH. 1871 ; D.SC. *Honoris Causa* 1882.—F.R.U.I. ; Professor of Anatomy and Physiology, Queen's College, Galway.
Quinn, Martin, ..	.. ..	B.A. 1863.
Quinton, John H.,	.. ..	B.A. 1871 ; B.E. 1872.
Quirk, Martin, ..	.. ..	M.D., M.CH., Dip. Obs. 1875.

---

a With First Honours.   *c* Naval Medical Service.
b Army Medical Service.   *d* Indian Medical Service.
e With Second Class Honours.

Raddin, George H.,	..	..	B.A., B.E. 1892.
Rankin, William J.,	..	..	M.D. 1865.
c Rathborne, Charles A.,	..	..	M.D., M.CH. 1870.
b Raye, Daniel O'C.,	..	..	M.D. 1865.
a Rea, Thomas,	..	..	B.A. 1899 ; M.A. 1900 ; Junior Fellowship in Modern Languages, R.U.I., 1901.
Read, Richard,	..	..	M.D., M.CH. 1872.
Reade, Hector M.,	..	..	B.A. 1877.
a Reed, Sir Andrew,	..	..	B.A. 1859; LL.B. 1877 ; LL.D. 1878; M.A. 1882.—Knt. C.B. ; Inspector-General, R.I.C.
c Reed, Matthew,	..	..	M.D., M.CH. 1870.
b Reid, Robert,	..	..	B.A. 1854.
e Reid, William Joseph,	..	..	B.A. 1861 ; M.A. 1882.
Reidy, Charles,	..	..	B.A. 1880.
Rentoul, Robert R.,	..	..	M.D. 1880 ; Direct Represertative of the Registered Practitioners of England on the General Medical Council.
e Rentoul, James Alex.,	..	..	B.A. 1869 ; LL.B. 1874 ; LL.D. 1875 ; K.C. (Eng.) ; a Judge of the City of London Court, 1901.
Reynolds, T. Taylor.	..	..	M.D., M.CH. 1879.
Richards, Henry E. S.,	..	..	M.B., B.CH., B.A.O. 1901.
Richardson, John H.,	..	..	B.A. 1852.
Riordan, Daniel,	..	..	M.D. 1878 ; Dip. Obs. 1879.
e Rishworth, Frank S.,	..	..	B.E. 1898 ; B.A. 1899 ; Instructor in Engineering under the Egyptian Ministry of Education.
Roe, William,	..	..	M.D. 1868.—Professor of Midwifery, Royal College of Surgeons, Ireland, late Examiner in Q. U. Ireland.
Roseingrave, Thomas W.,	..	..	B.E. 1881.
Ross, David R.,	..	..	M.D., M.CH. 1875.
Ross J., Alexander,	..	..	M.D. 1868 ; M.CH. 1869.
Ross, John R.,	..	..	B.A. 1863 ; M.D. 1866.
Rosten, William M.,	..	..	M.D. 1874.
Roulston, Robert J.,	..	..	M.D., M.CH., Dip. Obs. 1880.
Rowney, George A. H.,	..	..	B.A. 1882 ; B.E. 1883.
Rusk, John,	..	..	B.A. 1886 ; M.B., B.CH., B.A.O. 1894.
Rutherford, Robert L.,	..	..	M.D. 1881 ; M.CH .1882.
Rutherford, William,	..	..	M.D., M.CH. 1871 ; Dip. Obs. 1873 ; M.A.O. 1885.
Rutledge, Andrew,	..	..	B.A. 1892.
Rutledge, John G.,	..	..	B.A. 1893 ; M.A. 1894.
e Ryan, Dominick D.,	..	..	B.A. 1852 ; M.A. 1882.

---

a Ryan, Hugh, ...   B.A. 1895; M.A. 1897; D.Sc. 1899. Awarded a Gold Medal for highly distinguished answering; Demonstrator of Chemistry, Queen's College, Galway; elected to Science Research Scholarship by H. M. Exhibition (1851) Commissioners, 1898; University Student R.U.I., 1898; Professor of Chemistry in the Catholic University School of Medicine (Dublin), 1899; Fellowship in Chemistry, R.U.1., 1900.

Ryan, John, ...   M.D., M.CH., M.A.O. 1885.

Ryan, John, ...   B.A., B.E. 1893.

Sandys, William A., ...   M.B., B.CH., B.A.O. 1901; Demonstrator of Anatomy, Queen's College Galway.

Saunderson, James E., ...   B.A. 1862; M.D., M.CH. 1866.

Saunderson, Robert, ...   M.D. 1870.

b Saunderson, William H.,   ..   B.A. 1863; M.A. 1864.

Scott, Ernest F., ...   M.B, R.CH., B.A.O. 1901.

Scott, Frederick S., ...   M.B., B.CH., B.A.O. 1898.

Semple, Martin, ...   M.B., M.CH. 1888.

a Semple, Robert J., ...   B.A. 1888; M.A. 1889, University Student, R.U.I.

Semple, Samuel, ...   B.A. 1881; M.A. 1882.

Sexton, William, ...   M.D., M.CH., M.A.O. 1885.

Shannon, Owen J., ...   B.A. 1883; M.A. 1889.

Shannon, Patrick J., ...   M.D. 1864; M.CH. 1865.

a Sharkey, Edmund de la Garde, ..   B.A. 1863; M.A. 1866.—Civil Service of India.

b Sharpe, William, ...   M.D. 1866; M.CH. 1868.

b Shaw, John A., ...   M.D. 1863.

a Shiel, Joseph R., ...   B.A. 1871; M.A. 1873; LL.B. 1874; LL.D. 1882.

Shine, Eugene, ...   B.A. 1879.

*ad*Shore, Robert ..   ..   ..   B.A. 1875; M.A. 1877; M.D. 1880.

Sigerson, George   ..   ..   M.D. 1859; M.CH. 1865—F.R.U.I., Professor of Botany and Zoology, Catholic Univ. Medical School.

Simms, John M., ...   B.A. 1879.

Simpson, William, ...   M.D. 1872; M.CH., Dip. Obs. 1873.

Skilling, Thomas, ...   Dip. Agric. 1852 — Director of Model Farm, Royal Park, Melbourne.

---

a With First Honours.   *b* Army Medical Service.
d Indian Medical Service.

Sloan, John, ...	M.B., B.CH., B.A.O. 1898.	
Sloane, George, ..	.. B.A. 1883.	
*d*Smith, Henry, ...	.. B.A. 1883; M.D., M.CH., M.A.O. 1888.	
Smith, Joseph, ...	.. B.A. 1884 ; LL.B. 1887.	
*e*Smith, J. Anderson, ..	.. B.A. 1853 ; M.A. 1882.	
Smith, Robert J., ..	.. B.A. 1861.	
Smithwick, Richard H.,	.. B.E. 1879.	
*e*Smylie, Archibald, ..	.. B.A. 1864 ; M.A. 1874 ; LL.B. 1877 ; LL.D. 1877 ; B.L. (Australia).	
Smyth, John, ...	.. M.D., M.CH. 1879.	
Smyth, Thomas C., ..	.. B.A. 1880 ; M.A. 1882.	
Smith, William J., ..	.. B.A. 1865 ; M.D. 1872 ; M.A. 1882.	
Somerville, Richard N.,	.. B.A. 1871 ; B.E. 1873. — County Surveyor, Cavan.	
Spence, J. Beveridge, ..	.. M.D., M.CH. 1869.	
Spencer, William F., ..	.. M.D., M.CH. 1872.	
Steen, James R., ..	.. M.B., M.CH., B.A.O. 1890.—Travelling Medical Scholar, Royal University of Ireland, 1890.	
a Steinberger, Cecilia L. M., ..	B.A. 1902.	
Stephens, William, ..	.. M.D. 1866.	
Stewart, Joseph, ..	.. M.B., M.CH., M.A.O. 1887.—Travelling Medical Scholar, Royal University of Ireland, 1889 ; Demonstrator of Anatomy, Queen's College, Galway.	
Stewart, Robert F., ..	.. B.A. 1861.	
Stewart, Washington S.,	.. B.A. 1866.	
Stoker, Sir Thornley, ..	.. M.D. 1666 ; M.CH. *Honoris Causa* 1895.—Surgeon, Richmond Hospital ; F.R.U.I. ; late Prof. of Practical Anatomy, R.C.S., Ireland ; President, R.C.S.I.	
Stokes, William, ..	.. M.D. 1878 ; M.CH., Dip. Obs. 1880.	
*a*Stoney, Edward W., ..	.. Dip. Eng. 1863 ; B.E. 1872 ; M.E. 1882.	
Stoney, John H. L., ..	.. M.D. 1861.—Late Surgeon, City of Dublin Hospital ; late Demonstrator, Royal College of Surgeons, Dublin.	
Strain, James K. C., ..	.. B.A. 1896.	
Stratford, John, ...	.. B.E. 1881.	
Stuart, James, ...	.. B.A. 1895.	
Stuart, Simson, ...	.. M.D. 1880 ; M.CH. 1883.	
*a*Stuart, Thomas, ...	.. B.A. 1895 ; M.A. 1896 ; D.SC. 1900 ; Demonstrator of Physics, Queen's College, Galway; Junior Fellowship in Mathematical Science, R.U.I. 1902.	

---

a With First Honours. *d* Indian Medical Service.
e With Second Class Honours.

Sugars, John C., ..	.. ..	M.D., M.CH. 1868.
Sullivan, John, ..	.. ..	B.A. 1878.
Talbot, Bertram H.,	.. ..	B.A. 1869.
Tate, Davis D., ..	.. ..	M.D. 1868.
Tatham, Garnett G.,	.. ..	M.D. 1877.
Taylor, William J.,	.. ..	M.B., B.CH., B.A.O. 1888.
Thomas, William R.,	.. ..	M.D., M.CH. 1875.
*a*Thompson, Atwell,	.. ..	B.E. 1886 ; B.A. 1887.
Thompson, David,	.. ..	B.A. 1871.
Thompson, George,	.. ..	B.A. 1865.—Master, Doveton College, Calcutta.
Thompson, Henry G., ..	.. ..	M.D., M.CH. 1877.
Thompson, James,	.. ..	B.A. 1883.
*a*Thompson, William H.,	..	M.D., M.CH. 1883 ; Dip. for Mental Diseases, 1886.—Professor of Physiology, Queen's College, Belfast.
e Thompson, William J.,	..	B.E. 1882.
Thomson, Sir William,	..	B.A. 1867 ; M.D., M.CH. Dip. Obs. 1872 ; M.A. *Honoris Causa* 1881. —Surgeon, Richmond Hospital, Examiner, R.C.S.; Member of Senate, R.U.I. ; Examiner, late Queen's University, Ireland ; President R.C.S.I. ; Direct Representative for Ireland on the General Medical Council ; Surgeon in Ordinary to his Excellency the Lord Lieutenant.
Thorpe, Joseph C,	.. ..	M.D. 1864.
Threfall, Richard B.,	.. ..	M.B., B.CH., B.A.O. 1898.
*a*Thynne, Henry,	.. ..	B.A. 1859 ; LL.B. 1873 ; M.A. 1882 ; LL.D. 1882. — C.B. ; Deputy Inspector-General, R.I C.
Tierney, Daniel,	..	B.A. 1856 ; Dip. Eng. 1857 ; B.E. 1882.
*a*Todd, Andrew, ..	..	B.A. 1876 ; LL.B. 1879 ; M.A. 1882 ; LL.D. 1882 ; B.L. (Ir.).
*e*Todd, Robert H.,	..	B.A. 1870 ; M.A. 1871 ; LL.B. 1873 ; LL.D. 1875.
*a*Torrens, James,	..	B.A. 1866 ; M.A. 1867 ; M.D. 1883 ; M.CH. 1884.
e Townsend, Thomas A., ..	..	B.E. 1869 ; M.E. 1882.
Twigg, William, ..	..	M.D. 1862.
Vance, George, ..	.. ..	M.D., M.CH. 1886 ; B.A.O. 1888.
a Vance, Robert, ..	.. ..	B.A. 1879 ; M.A. 1880.
Vinrace, Felix C.,	.. ..	M.D. 1881.

---

a With First Honours.   *e* With Second Honours.

Waddell, Sydney,	.. ..	M.B., B.CH., B.A.O., 1900.
Wadsworth, William A.,	.. ..	M.D. 1884; B.CH. 1888.
Walker, Andrew J.,	..	B.A. 1895; Demonstrator of Chemistry, Queen's College, Galway; PH.D., Heidelberg, 1898; Lecturer in Chemistry, Borough Polytechnic Institute, London; Head of Chemistry Department, Municipal Technical College, Derby.
Walker, Cuthbert F.,	.. ..	B.A. 1897.
Walker, William,	.. ..	B.A. 1894; B.E. 1895.
Waller, Edmund W.,	.. ..	Dip. Eng. 1861; B.E. 1882.
e Walsh, Michael, ..	..	B.A. 1867; M.D., M.CH., Dip. Obs. 1873.—Demonstrator of Anatomy, Queen's College, Galway.
Walsh, Thomas, ..	..	B.A. 1899.—Robert Platt Physiological Research Scholar, Owens College, Manchester, 1901.
Ward, Peter,	.. ..	B.A. 1867.
a Warnock, James,	..	B.A. 1901; Demonstrator of Physics, Queen's College, Galway.
Warnock, William,	.. ..	M.B., B.CH., B.A.O. 1902.
Warren, J. Monteith,	.. ..	M.D., M.CH. 1874.
Warren, William E.,	.. ..	B.A. 1871; M.D. 1873.
Warren, William H.,	.. ..	M.D. 1866.
e Waters, Eaton W.,	.. ..	M.B., M.CH. 1886; M.A.O. 1887.
Waters, George A.,	.. ..	M.D., M.CH. 1884.
Waters, Horace R.,	.. ..	B.E. 1885.
Waters, Joseph J.,	.. ..	M.B., B.CH., B.A.O. 1899.
a Waterworth, Hugh,	.. ..	B.A. 1877; M.A. 1879.
Watson, John, ..	.. ..	B.A. 1897.
e Watt, George, ..	.. ..	B.A. 1896.
Watters, Francis O. M.,	...	B.A. 1880; M.A. 1881.
e Watters, William,	.. ..	B.A. 1877; M.A. 1882; M.D., M.CH. 1883.
Watts, Walter A.,	.. ..	B.A. 1856; M.A. 1857.—Late Prof. Training College, Toronto.
Wells, Charles, ..	.. ..	M.D. 1880.
Wenyon, Charles,	.. ..	M.D., M.CH. 1880.
West, John D., ..	.. ..	B.A. 1859.
a West, Sir Raymond,	..	B.A. 1855; M.A. 1869; LL.D. *Honoris causa*, 1882.—Judge of the High Court of Bombay: Vice-Chancellor, University of Bombay; Member of the Council of the Government of Bombay.

---

a With First Honours.   *e* With Second Honours.

White, James F.,	.. ..	M.D. 1880; M.CH., Dip. Obs. 1881.
White, Michael, ..	.. ..	M.D., M.CH. 1878.
White, Patrick B.,	.. ..	M.D., M.CH. 1883 ; Dip. Obs. 1884 ; M.A.O. 1885.
a White, Sinclair, ..	.. ..	M.D., M.CH., Dip. Obs. 1879 ; Lecturer on Physiology and Hygiene, Firth College, Sheffield.
e White, Thomas R.,	.. ..	M.D. 1862.
Whitton, Joseph,	.. ..	B.E. 1899 ; B.A. 1900.
Williams, J. O'Brien,	.. ..	M.D., M.CH. 1877.
Williams, William,	.. ..	M.D., M.CH. 1869.
e Wilson, David, ..	.. ..	B.A. ; B.E. 1895.
Wilson, James, ..	.. ..	M.D. 1879.
Wilson, John, ..	.. ..	B.A. 1865 ; M.A. 1866.
b Wilson, J. Bower,	.. ..	M.D. 1871.
e Wilson, Robertson B. S.,	..	B.A. 1869 ; M.A. 1870.
e Wilson, Samuel L.,	.. ..	B.A. 1875 ; M.A. 1876.
a Wilson, Thomas N.,	.. ..	B.A. 1861 ; M.A. 1882.—Civil Service of India.
e Wilson, William N.,	.. ..	B.A. 1865 ; M.A. 1866.
e Winder, James, ..	.. ..	B.A. 1865 ; M.A. 1882.
Wise, Charles H.,	.. ..	M.D. 1882.
Wood, George V.,	.. ..	M.D., M.CH. 1866.
e Wood, John E., ..	.. ..	B.A. 1864 ; M.A. 1882.—Inspector of National Schools.
e Woods, Richard J.,	.. ..	B.E. 1874 ; M.E. 1882.—Engineer, Public Works of India.
e Zouche, Isaiah de,	.. ..	M.D. 1865.

DIPLOMATES IN ENGINEERING.

Stuart, William, 1893.
Howley, Richard J., 1895.

---

a With First Honours.   *b* Army Medical Service.
e With Second Honours.

SCHOLARS.

SESSION 1849-50.

Faculty of Arts.

JUNIOR SCHOLARSHIPS.

FIRST YEAR.

Literary Division.

Richardson, John H.
Norton, Bernard G.
M'Mahon, George Y.
M'Dermott, Dominick.
Fynn, Peter J.
Murphy, Thadeus.
Power, Richard.
M'Mullen, James A.
Kyle, Christopher.
O'Maher, William.
Fitzgerald, Nicholas.
Johnston, William.
Eaton, Richard.
Hughes, Patrick J.
Kelly, Patrick.
Gibson, John.
O'Kelly, Edmond.
Irwin, George.
Pall, Joshua.
Hearne, John Henry.
Dopping, James H.
Hurly, Joseph.
Scott, William A.

Science Division.

Duggan, Charles W.
Ford, Patrick F.
Ryan, Dominick D.
M'Grath, John.
Powell, John.
Scott, Patrick.
Howze, John.
O'Feely, Timothy O'B.
Eames, Richard F.
Blake, Joseph V.
Evans, John.
Johnston, John.
Ferguson, Robert.
Tully, Joseph.
Skerrett, Peter.
Duggan, Joseph.
Walkinshaw, Robert.
King, William.
St. George, Henry.
M'Mahon, Thomas A.

School of Engineering.

FIRST YEAR.

Drysdale, Charles. | Gardiner, Martin.

School of Agriculture.

FIRST YEAR.

Skilling, Thomas. | O'Hara, Thomas.

SESSION 1850-51.

Faculty of Arts.

SECOND YEAR.

Literary Division.

Richardson, John H.
M'Dermott, Dominick.
Kyle, Christopher.
M'Mahon, George.
Murphy, Thadeus.
Johnston, William.
Irwin, George.
Hughes, Patrick J.

Science Division.

Scott, Patrick.
Powell, John.
Ryan, Dominick D.
Duggan, Charles W.
Howze, John.
Duggan, Joseph.
Johnston, John.
Evans, John.
O'Feely, Timothy O'B.
King, William.
Walkinshaw, Robert.
Fynn, Peter J.

FIRST YEAR.

Literary Division.

M'Gowan, Robert.
Smith, J Anderson.
M'Grath, Thomas.
Montgomery, James. ⎫ *equal.*
Mitchell, Robert J. ⎬
Berwick, John.
Browne, William A.
Kilkelly, Garrett H.
Perrin, Patrick.
Lalor, James.

Science Division.

Warrell, James.
Stephens, Robert.
Moorhead, John.
Jackson, Burton.
Comyns, William.
Hurly, Joseph.
Roach, Edward.
Slater, James.
Gardiner, Martin.
O'Doherty, John.
Gilmore, Charles.

Faculty of Law.

SECOND YEAR.

Ryan, Dominick D.

FIRST YEAR.

Keane, C. Marceet.

Faculty of Medicine.

SECOND YEAR.

Eaton, Richard. | O'Leary, John.

FIRST YEAR.

Skerrett, Peter. | Kelly, Patrick J.

School of Engineering.

SECOND YEAR.

Drysdale, Charles.

FIRST YEAR.

Eames, Richard F.

School of Agriculture.

SECOND YEAR.

Skilling, Thomas. | O'Hara, Thomas.

FIRST YEAR.

O'Hara, Charles. | Comyns, Patrick J.

SESSION 1851–52.

Faculty of Arts.
JUNIOR SCHOLARSHIPS.
THIRD YEAR.

Literary Division.
Richardson, John H.
Johnston, William.
Murphy, Thadeus.

Science Division.
Duggan, Charles.
Scott, Patrick.
Evans, John.
Howze, John.
Walkinshaw, Robert.
King, William.
Duggan, Joseph.

SECOND YEAR.

Literary Division.
Mitchell, Robert J.
Browne, William A.
Berwick, John.
Smith, J. Anderson.
Hughes, Patrick J.
Mahony, John.
Fynn, Peter J.
Kilkelly, Garrett.

Science Division.
Ford, Patrick F.
Breen, Michael.
Maguire, Edward.
Roach, Edward.

FIRST YEAR.

Literary Division.
Moffett, James.
Fleming, William.
Dunlop, Charles.
Hurley, Francis B.
Jackson, Burton. } *equal.*
Hooper, Charles J.
Arthur, John.
Ireland, Arthur J.

Science Division.
M'Shane, John.
Kearney, Daniel. } *equal.*
Johnson, J. Wesley.
Colahan, John. } *equal.*
Atkinson, Samuel.

Faculty of Law.
THIRD YEAR.
Ryan, Dominick D.

SECOND YEAR.
Keane, C. Marceet.

FIRST YEAR.
Stephens, Robert.

H

Faculty of Medicine.

THIRD YEAR.

Eaton, Richard. | O'Leary, John.

SECOND YEAR.

Kelly, Patrick J. | Skerrett, Peter.

FIRST YEAR.

Joynt, Christopher. | Moorhead, John.

School of Engineering.

SECOND YEAR.
Powell, John.

FIRST YEAR.
O'Doherty, John.

School of Agriculture.

SECOND YEAR.
O'Hara, Charles.

FIRST YEAR.

Short, William. | M'Grath, John

SESSION 1852-53.

Faculty of Arts.

SENIOR SCHOLARSHIPS.

Ancient Classics, ...	.. Richardson, John, B.A.
Metaphysical and Economic Science,	.. Johnston, William, B.A.
Natural History, ...	.. Duggan, Charles, B.A.

JUNIOR SCHOLARSHIPS.

THIRD YEAR.

Literary Division.	*Science Division.*
Hughes, Patrick J.	M'Dermott, Dominick.
Mitchell, Robert J.	Smith, John A.
Browne, William A.	Powell, John.
Berwick, John.	Ford, Patrick F.
Mahony, John.	Roach, Edward.

SECOND YEAR.

Literary Division.	*Science Division.*
Jackson, Burton.	Maguire, Edward.
Hooper, Charles J.	Kearney, Daniel.
Hurley, Francis B.	Atkinson, Samuel.
Johnson, John W.	Colahan, John.
Clarke, William.	

FIRST YEAR.

Literary Division.	*Science Division.*
* West, Raymond.	* West, Raymond.
Treanor, W. Stanley.	Breen, Daniel.
Charters, William. } *equal.*	Gilmore, Stewart.
Arnold, Pierce.	Stephens, Samuel.
Davys, Frank.	Dillon, Gerald.

Faculty of Law.

SENIOR SCHOLARSHIPS.

Ryan, Dominick D., B.A.

THIRD YEAR.

Keane, C. Marceet.

SECOND YEAR.

O'Feely, Timothy O'B.

FIRST YEAR.

Walkinshaw, Robert.

---

* Having obtained *First* place in both divisions, retains both Scholarships.

Faculty of Medicine.

SENIOR SCHOLARSHIP.

Therapeutics and Pathology, ...   O'Leary, John.

THIRD YEAR.

Blake, James V. | Kelly, Patrick.

SECOND YEAR.

Moorehead, John. | Joynt, Christopher.

FIRST YEAR.

*West, Raymond. | Ireland, Arthur J.
Crinnian, P.

School of Engineering.

SECOND YEAR.
Breen, John.

FIRST YEAR.
Howze, John.

School of Agriculture.

SECOND YEAR.
M'Grath, John. | Hardiman, James.

FIRST YEAR.
M'Donagh, William. | M'Mahon, Thomas.

---

* Resigned.

SESSION 1853-54.

Faculty of Arts.

SENIOR SCHOLARSHIPS.

Ancient Classics, ...	Dowling, Jeremiah J., B.A.
Modern Languages and Modern History,	Hughes, Patrick J., B.A.
Metaphysical and Economic Science, ..	Browne, William A., B.A.
Natural History, ...	M'Dermott, Dominick, B.A.

JUNIOR SCHOLARSHIPS.

THIRD YEAR.

Literary Division.	*Science Division.*
† Charters, William.	Maguire, Edward.
Clarke, William. } equal.	Hurley, Francis B.
Hooper, Charles J. }	Colahan, John.
Johnston, John W.	Kearney, Daniel.
Jackson, Burton.	Atkinson, Samuel.

SECOND YEAR.

Literary Division.	*Science Division.*
*West, Raymond.	*West, Raymond.
Treanor, W. Stanley.	Tierney, Daniel.
Fleming, William.	Dillon, Gerald.
Arnold, Pierce.	Stephens, Samuel.
Davys, Frank.	Short, William.

FIRST YEAR.

Literary Division.	*Science Division.*
Thomson, Alfred B.	Adair, James J.
Coffie, Edward. } equal.	Dowman, William.
Henry, John W. R. }	Gormley, John.
Stirke, Julius W.	Watts, Walter A.
Conolly, James.	Breen, John.

* Having obtained *First* place in both divisions, retains both Scholarships.
† According to Minute of Council.

Faculty of Law.

SENIOR SCHOLARSHIP.

Keane, C. Marceet, B.A.

THIRD YEAR.

Stephens, Robert.

SECOND YEAR.

Mason, William.

FIRST YEAR.

Perrin, Patrick.

Faculty of Medicine.

SENIOR SCHOLARSHIP.

Anatomy and Physiology, ..	.. ..	Blake, Joseph V.
Therapeutics and Pathology,	.. ..	Kelly, Patrick J.

THIRD YEAR.

Moorhead, John.	Joynt, Christopher.

SECOND YEAR.

Ireland, Arthur J.	Purcell, Patrick J.

FIRST YEAR.

Mahony, John.

School of Engineering.

SECOND YEAR.

M'Donagh, William.

FIRST YEAR.

Meharg, William.

School of Agriculture.

SECOND YEAR.

M'Donagh, William.

FIRST YEAR.

Carrick, Daniel.	O'Leary, Arthur.

SESSION 1854-55.

Faculty of Arts.

SENIOR SCHOLARSHIPS.

Ancient Classics, ...	Mahony, John, B.A.
Mathematics, ...	Ford, Patrick F., B.A.
Natural Philosophy, ...	Maguire, Edward, B.A.
Metaphysical and Economic Science, ..	Kearney, Daniel, B.A.
Chemistry, ...	M'Dermott, Domk., B.A.
Natural History, ...	Parker, James D., B.A.

JUNIOR SCHOLARSHIPS.

THIRD YEAR.

Literary Division.	*Science Division.*
*West, Raymond.	*West, Raymond.
Arnold, Pierce.	Tierney, Daniel.
Treanor, W. Stanley.	
Davys, Frank.	

SECOND YEAR.

Literary Division.	*Science Division.*
Henry, John W. R.	Gormley, John.
Conolly, James.	Watts, Walter A.
	Dowman, William.
	O'Hara, Thomas.

FIRST YEAR.

Literary Division.	*Science Division.*
Lane, George.	Moore, John H.
Hooper, Robert.	Bateman, Richard C.
Monroe, John.	Bruen, Patrick.
Reddan, John.	Ross, Cornelius P.
Stewart, Robert F.	Thane, Charles H.

Faculty of Law.

THIRD YEAR.
Mason, William.

SECOND YEAR.
Perrin, Patrick.

FIRST YEAR.
Hooper, Charles J.

---

* Having obtained *First* place in both divisions, retains both Scholarships.

Faculty of Medicine.

SENIOR SCHOLARSHIP.

Therapeutics and Pathology, ...   Duggan, Joseph.

SECOND YEAR.

Colahan, John.	Crean, Martin J.

FIRST YEAR.

Hurley, Francis B.	O'Brien, James.

School of Engineering.

SECOND YEAR.
O'Kinealy, Michael.

FIRST YEAR.
O'Kinealy, James.

School of Agriculture.

SECOND YEAR.

Carrick, Daniel.	Keane, John E.

FIRST YEAR.

Gouldsberry, V. Skipton.	Wall, Walter S.

SESSION 1855-56.

Faculty of Arts.

SENIOR SCHOLARSHIPS.

Ancient Classics, ...	.. West, Raymond, B.A.
Modern Languages and Modern History, ..	Mahony, John, B.A.
Natural Philosophy, ...	.. Ford, Patrick F., B.A.
Metaphysical and Economic Science,	.. Hooper, Charles J., B.A.
Chemistry, ...	.. Maguire, Edward, B.A.
Natural History, ...	.. Moorhead, John, B.A.

JUNIOR SCHOLARSHIPS.

THIRD YEAR.

Literary Division.
Conolly, James.
Henry, John W. R.

Science Division.
Watts, Walter A.
Gormley, John.
O'Hara, Thomas.
Breen, John.

SECOND YEAR.

Literary Division.
Monroe, John.
Treanor, Arthur.
Bateman, Richard C.
West, John D.
Stewart, Robert F.

Science Division.
Thane, Charles H.
Adair, James J.
Burke, Martin J.
Moore, John H.

FIRST YEAR.

Literary Division.
Hunter, John.
Stewart, Washington S.
Evatt, Humphrey.
Hart, James C.

Science Division.
Thynne, Henry.
O'Kinealy, James.
Quinn, Martin.
O'Neill, George F.
Grealy, John.

Faculty of Law.

THIRD YEAR.
O'Feely, Timothy O'B.

FIRST YEAR.
Arnold, Pierce.

H 3

Faculty of Medicine.

SENIOR SCHOLARSHIP.

Therapeutics and Pathology, ... Morris, Michael O'K., B.A.

THIRD YEAR.

Colahan, John. | Crean, Martin J.

SECOND YEAR.

Hurley, Francis B. | O'Flaherty, Thomas A.

FIRST YEAR.

Sigerson, George. | M'Bride, John B.

School of Engineering.

SECOND YEAR.
Quinn, Michael.

FIRST YEAR.
Weir, John.

School of Agriculture.

SECOND YEAR.

Gouldsberry, V. Skipton. | O'Donohoe, Patrick.

FIRST YEAR.

Bradshaw, George B. | Killery, Henry.

SESSION 1856–57.

Faculty of Arts.

SENIOR SCHOLARSHIPS.

Ancient Classics, &c., ...	Arnold, Pierce, B.A.
Mathematics, ...	Maguire, Edward, B.A.
Metaphysical and Economic Science, ..	O'Feely, Timothy O'B., B.A.
Chemistry, ...	Watts, Walter A., B.A.
Natural History, ...	Mahony, John, B.A.

JUNIOR SCHOLARSHIPS.

THIRD YEAR.

Literary Division.	*Science Division.*
Monroe, John.	Adair, James J.
Bateman, Richard C.	Moore, John H.
Stewart, Robert F.	Greene, Joseph R.
West, John D.	Burke, Martin J.

SECOND YEAR.

Literary Division.	*Science Division.*
O'Neill, George F.	Thynne, Henry. } *equal.*
Hunter, John H.	O'Kinealy, James. } *equal.*
Hart, James C.	Grealy, John.
	Quinn, Martin.

FIRST YEAR.

Literary Division.	*Science Division.*
Lawson, Charles H.	Reed, Andrew A.
(*Also a prize of* £10.)	Weir, John.
M'Mahon, William.	Martin, William T.
*Martin, William T. } *equal.*	May, William G.
Martin, William. } *equal.*	*Lawson, Charles H.
O'Brien, Julius.	O'Hara, Charles.
Lynam, James.	

Faculty of Law.

SENIOR SCHOLARSHIP.

Parker, James D., B.A.

THIRD YEAR.
Perrin, Patrick.

FIRST YEAR.

*Lawson, Charles H.	O'Hara, Thomas.

* Ineligible, having obtained Scholarship in other division.

Faculty of Medicine.

SENIOR SCHOLARSHIPS.

Anatomy and Physiology,	.. ..	Reid, Robert, B.A.
Therapeutics and Pathology,	.. ..	Colahan, John.

THIRD YEAR.

O'Flaherty, Thomas A. | Killery, St. John.

SECOND YEAR.

Burke, John P. | Bournes, William H.

FIRST YEAR.

Literary Division. | *Science Division.*
Lane, George. | Gormley, John.

School of Engineering.

SECOND YEAR.

Blake, Martin P.

FIRST YEAR.

Cullen, Alexander.

School of Agriculture.

SECOND YEAR.

Bradshaw, George B. | King, Nicholson.

FIRST YEAR.

Bligh, John. | Clarke, Denis.

SESSION 1857-58.

Faculty of Arts.

SENIOR SCHOLARSHIPS.

Ancient Classics, &c., ...	Monroe, John, B.A.
Modern Languages and Modern History,	Arnold, Pierce, B.A.
Mathematics, ...	Tierney, Daniel, B.A.
Natural Philosophy, ...	Bateman, Richard C., B.A.
Metaphysical and Economic Science, ..	M'Mahon, George Y., B.A.
Chemistry, ...	Hurley, Francis B., B.A.
Natural History, ...	Maguire, Edward, B.A.

JUNIOR SCHOLARSHIPS.

THIRD YEAR.

Literary Division.	*Science Division.*
O'Neill, George F.	O'Kinealy, James.
Hart, James C.	Thynne, Henry.
	Quinn, Martin.

SECOND YEAR.

Literary Division.	*Science Division.*
Stewart, Washington S.	Reed, Andrew A.
Martin, William T.	May, William G.
Lynch, Martin.	Griffith, William.
Lynam, James.	Weir, John.
Conolly, Patrick W.	

FIRST YEAR.

Literary Division.	*Science Division.*
Nicoll, Robert.	Cunningham, William.
M'Auliffe, Michael.	Murray, John.
Hopkins, Jacob B.	Davison, William.
Potter, Robert.	Burdge, William E.
Smith, Robert J.	O'Farrell, William.

Faculty of Law.

SENIOR SCHOLARSHIP.

O'Feely, Timothy O'B., B.A.

SECOND YEAR.
Madill, Thomas.

FIRST YEAR.
West, John D.

Faculty of Medicine.

SENIOR SCHOLARSHIP.

Therapeutics and Pathology .. .. O'Flaherty, Thomas A

THIRD YEAR.

Burke, John P.	Burke, Martin J.

SECOND YEAR.

Hooper, Robert.	Divers, Edward.

FIRST YEAR.

Literary Division.	*Science Division.*
M'Mahon, William.	Moore, John H.

School of Engineering.

SECOND YEAR.

Connolly, Michael.

FIRST YEAR.

Mac Farlane, Alexander.

School of Agriculture.

SECOND YEAR.

Bligh, John.	Clarke, Denis.

FIRST YEAR.

Rorke, Patrick.	Burke, John R.

SESSION 1858-59.

Faculty of Arts.

SENIOR SCHOLARSHIPS.

Ancient Classics, &c.,	Mitchell, Robert J., B.A.
Modern Languages and Modern History,	O'Neill, George F., B.A.
Mathematics,	O'Kinealy, James, B.A.
Natural Philosophy,	Moore, John H., B.A.
Metaphysical and Economic Science,	Monroe, John, B.A.
Chemistry,	Breen, Michael, B.A.
Natural History,	Bateman, Richard C., B.A.

JUNIOR SCHOLARSHIPS.

THIRD YEAR.

Literary Division.	*Science Division.*
Norton, Bernard G.	Reed, Andrew A.
Conolly, Patrick W.	May, William G.
Martin, William T.	Griffith, William.
	Evatt, Humphrey.
	Grealy, John.

SECOND YEAR.

Literary Division.	*Science Division.*
M'Auliffe, Michael.	Davison, Thomas.
O'Brien, Julius.	Ireland, Edward.
Smith, Robert J.	O'Farrell, William.
	O'Hara, Charles.

FIRST YEAR.

Literary Division.	*Science Division.*
* Wilson, Thomas N.	* Wilson, Thomas N.
Greer, James R.	† Blood, Bindon.
Blood, Bindon.	Dowman, Charles
Greer, John H.	Atkinson, John.
Madill, Thomas.	† Greer, James R.
	M'Dermott, Brian. } equal.
	O'Farrell, Thomas. }

* Having obtained *First* place in both divisions, retains both Scholarships.

† Ineligible, having obtained Scholarship in other division.

Faculty of Law.

SENIOR SCHOLARSHIP.

Hooper, Charles J., B.A.

SECOND YEAR.
West, John D.

FIRST YEAR.

M'Kane, John. | Monroe, John.

Faculty of Medicine.

SENIOR SCHOLARSHIPS.

Anatomy and Physiology, ...   Maguire, Edward, B.A.
Therapeutics and Pathology, ...   Burke, Martin J., B.A.

THIRD YEAR.
Climo, William H. | Hooper, Robert.

SECOND YEAR.
M'Mahon, William. | Davis, John N.

FIRST YEAR.

Literary Division. | *Science Division.*
M'Kane, John. | White, Thomas R.
M'Cracken, Thomas. |

School of Engineering.

SECOND YEAR.
Thynne, Henry.

FIRST YEAR.
Galwey, Charles.

School of Agriculture.

SECOND YEAR.
Bright, William A.

FIRST YEAR.

Mullins, John. | Rentoul, James.

SESSION 1859-60.

Faculty of Arts.

SENIOR SCHOLARSHIPS.

Ancient Classics, &c., ...	M'Mahon, George Y., B.A.
Modern Languages and Modern History,	Mitchell, Robert J., B.A.
Natural Philosophy, .. .: ..	Thynne, Henry, B.A.
Metaphysical and Economic Science,	O'Neill, George F., B.A.
Chemistry, ...	O'Kinealy, James, B.A.

JUNIOR SCHOLARSHIPS.

THIRD YEAR.

Literary Division.
M'Auliffe, Michael.

Science Division.
O'Hara, Charles.
Davison, Thomas.
Ireland, Edward.

SECOND YEAR.

Literary Division.
* Wilson, Thomas N.
Cunningham, William.
Crotty, Richard D.
Madill, Thomas.
Smith, Washington.

Science Division.
* Wilson, Thomas N.
Atkinson, John. ⎫
Dowman, Charles. ⎬ *equal.*
M'Dermott, Brian.
Reid, William J.

FIRST YEAR.

Literary Division.
Hurley, Patrick. ⎫
O'Connor, John. ⎬ *equal.*
Saunderson, James E.
Mills, Samuel.
Madden, Henry M.

Science Division.
Burke, Michael J.
King, Ælian A.
Stokes, George.
Falkiner, Richard D. ⎫
M'Enery, Edward. ⎬ *equal.*

Faculty of Law.

JUNIOR SCHOLARSHIPS.

SECOND YEAR.
Monroe, John, B.A.

FIRST YEAR.
Louden, John J.

---

* Having obtained *First* place in both divisions, retains both Scholarships.

Faculty of Medicine.

SENIOR SCHOLARSHIPS.

Anatomy and Physiology,	..	.. ..	Climo, William H.
Therapeutics and Pathology, ..	..	..	Divers, Edward.

THIRD YEAR.

Davis, John N. | Evans, Charles.

SECOND YEAR.

White, Thomas R. | Potter, Robert.

FIRST YEAR.

Literary Division. | *Science Division.*
Connolly, Patrick. | Howse, John.

School of Engineering.

SECOND YEAR.

Waller, Edmund W.

FIRST YEAR.

Grealy, John.

School of Agriculture.

SECOND YEAR.

Killery, Henry. | Mullins, John.

FIRST YEAR.

Greaven, Dominick. | Burke, Edward.

SESSION 1860–61.

Faculty of Arts.
SENIOR SCHOLARSHIPS.

Ancient Classics, &c., ...	M'Auliffe, Michael, B.A.
Modern Languages and Modern History,	Conolly, James, B.A.
Mathematics, ...	Thynne, Henry, B.A.
Natural Philosophy, ...	O'Kinealy, James, B.A.
Metaphysical and Economic Science, ..	O'Hara, Thomas, B.A.

JUNIOR SCHOLARSHIPS.
THIRD YEAR.

Literary Division.
Cunningham, William.
Wilson, Thomas N.
Crotty, Richard D.
Madill, Thomas.
Smith, Washington.

Science Division.
Atkinson, John.
O'Farrell, Thomas.
Reid, William J.
Johnson, John.

SECOND YEAR.

Literary Division.
Greene, Joseph J.
Leary, Joseph W.
Hurley, Patrick.
Mills, Samuel.
Saunderson, James E.
M'Kenzie, John.

Science Division.
King, Ælian A.
* Leary, Joseph W.
Burke, Michael J.

FIRST YEAR.

Literary Division.
Sharkey, Edmund de la Garde
Feeny, Dominick.
† Mac Donnell, Anthony P.
Crooks, William.
Padin, Thomas.

Science Division.
Saunderson, William H.
Young, Robert.
Griffin, John.
Callaghan, Patrick.
Daly, William.

Faculty of Law.
JUNIOR SCHOLARSHIPS.
THIRD YEAR.
Monroe, John.

SECOND YEAR.
Louden, John J.

FIRST YEAR.
Costigan, Thomas J.

---

* Ineligible, having obtained Scholarship in other division.
+ Mr. Mac Donnell was awarded an Exhibition in the Medical Faculty in lieu of this Scholarship.

Faculty of Medicine.

SENIOR SCHOLARSHIPS.

Anatomy and Physiology, ...	Davis, John N.
Therapeutics and Pathology, ...	Gouldsberry, V. Skipton.

THIRD YEAR.

Comerford, Michael.	Potter, Robert.

SECOND YEAR.

King, Charles E.	Hughes, John H.

FIRST YEAR.

Literary Division.	*Science Division.*
Hanrahan, James J.	Bligh, John.

School of Engineering.

SECOND YEAR.
Falkiner, Richard D.

FIRST YEAR.
Stoney, Edward W.

School of Agriculture.

FIRST YEAR.

O'Flynn, John T.	Kearney, Ambrose.

SESSION 1861-62.

Faculty of Arts.
SENIOR SCHOLARSHIPS.

Ancient Classics, ...	Wilson, Thomas N., B.A.
Modern Languages and Modern History,	Conolly, Patrick. M'Auliffe, Michael. } *equal.*
Mathematics, ...	Atkinson, John, B.A.
Natural Philosophy, ...	O'Hara, Charles, B.A.
Metaphysical and Economic Science,	Cunningham, William, B.A.
Chemistry, ...	Reid, William J., B.A.
Natural History, ...	O'Farrell, Thomas, B.A.

JUNIOR SCHOLARSHIPS.
THIRD YEAR.

Literary Division.	*Science Division.*
Leary, Joseph W.	Leary, Joseph W.
Greene, Joseph J.	King, Ælian A.
Hurley, Patrick.	
Mills, Samuel.	
Saunderson, James.	

SECOND YEAR.

Literary Division.	*Science Division.*
Sharkey, Edmund de la Grade	Griffin, John.
Hare, Gustavus J. C.	Saunderson, William H.
Mulholland, William.	Daly, William.
Feeny, Dominick.	Moody, Samuel.
Padin, Thomas.	M'Enery, Edward.

FIRST YEAR.

Literary Division.	*Science Division.*
Wood, John E.	Foreman, Robert L.
Smylie, Archibald.	Winder, James.
Mac Donnell, Anthony P.	Thompson, George.
Thynne, Andrew.	Burke, John.
Droughton, Edward.	Dooley, Michael S.

Faculty of Law.
SENIOR SCHOLARSHIP.
Monroe, John, M.A.

THIRD YEAR.
Louden, John J.

SECOND YEAR.
Costigan, Thomas J.

FIRST YEAR.
M'Dermott, Brian.

. Faculty of Medicine.

SENIOR SCHOLARSHIPS.

Anatomy and Physiology, ...	White, Thomas R. (£40).
Therapeutics and Pathology, ...	Davis, John N.

THIRD YEAR.

M'Mahon, William. | Dickenson, Frederick F.

SECOND YEAR.

Bligh, John. | Lightbody, William H.

FIRST YEAR.

Literary Division. | *Science Division.*
Lynch, Martin. | Thomson, William.

School of Engineering.

SECOND YEAR. .
Stoney, Edward W.

FIRST YEAR.
Stanley, Alexander.

School of Agriculture.

FIRST YEAR.

Corbett, Thomas. | Nally, William.

SESSION 1862-63.

..Faculty of Arts.

SENIOR SCHOLARSHIPS.

Ancient Classics, ...	Conolly, James, B.A.
Modern Languages and Modern History,	Conolly, Patrick W., B.A.
Mathematics, ...	King, Ælian A., B.A.
Natural Philosophy, ...	Atkinson, John, B.A.
Metaphysical and Economic Science, ..	Wilson, Thomas N., B.A.
Chemistry,..	O'Farrell, Thomas, B.A.

THIRD YEAR.

Literary Division.	*Science Division.*
Hare, Gustavus J. C.	Griffin, John.
Mulholland, William.	Saunderson, William H.
Feeny, Dominick.	Moody, Samuel.
Crooks, William.	
M'Kenzie, John.	

SECOND YEAR.

Literary Division.	*Science Division.*
Wood, John E.	Foreman, Robert L.
Mac Donnell, Anthony P.	*Wallace, John.
Smylie, Archibald.	Burke, John.
Wallace, John.	Winder, James.
Droughton, Edward.	Dooley, Michael S. } *equal.*
	Thompson, George. }

FIRST YEAR.

Literary Division.	*Science Division.*
Wilson, William N.	Deane, Henry.
M'Farlane, Robert A.	Moorhead, William R
Persse, William D.	Gaynor, William. } *equal.*
Killen, John M.	Gibbons, Thomas. }
Torrens, James.	Greaven, Dominick.

Faculty of Law.

THIRD YEAR.
Costigan, Thomas J.

SECOND YEAR.
M'Dermott, Brian.

* Ineligible, having obtained Scholarship in other division.

Faculty of Medicine.

SENIOR SCHOLARSHIPS.

Anatomy and Physiology, ...	Hinds, William R. G.
Therapeutics and Pathology, ...	Dwyer, Peter J.

THIRD YEAR.

Comerford, Henry. | Hanrahan, James J.

SECOND YEAR.

Saunderson, James E. | Thomson, William.

FIRST YEAR.

Literary Division. | *Science Division.*
Baldwin, H. | Smith, William A.

School of Engineering.

SECOND YEAR.

Stanley, Alexander.

FIRST YEAR.

Odling, Charles W.

School of Agriculture.
FIRST YEAR.

Chambers, Thomas. | Boyd, John S.

SESSION 1863-64.

Faculty of Arts.
SENIOR SCHOLARSHIPS.

Ancient Classics, ...	Sharkey, Edmund de la Garde, B.A.
Modern Languages and Modern History,	King, Ælian A., B.A.
Mathematics, ...	Griffin, John, B.A.
Natural Philosophy, ...	Saunderson, William H., B.A.
Metaphysical and Economic Science, ..	Mulholland, William, B.A.
Chemistry, ...	O'Hara, Charles, B.A.
Natural History, ...	Chestnut, Joseph W., B.A.

THIRD YEAR.

Literary Division.	*Science Division.*
Mac Donnell, Anthony P.	Foreman, Robert L.
Wood, John E.	Daly, William.
Maybin, William.	Dooley, James.
Droughton, Edward.	Dooley, Michael S.
Smylie, Archibald.	Thompson, George.

SECOND YEAR.

Literary Division.	*Science Division.*
M'Farlane, Robert A. } equal. Wilson, William N. }	Deane, Henry. } equal. Moorhead, William R. }
Persse, William D.	Forsyth, Samuel M'C.
Mac Donald, Francis.	Greaven, Dominick.
Meharry, John B.	Grealy, Nicholas.

FIRST YEAR.

Literary Division.	*Science Division.*
M'Swinney, Robert F.	Walsh, Thomas.
Legate, George W.	Hughes, William.
Macaulay, Colman P.	Hoctor, William F.
O'Connor, Thomas P.	Griffin, Thomas.
Gillespie, Michael.	Brooke, John.

Faculty of Law.

THIRD YEAR.
Atkinson, John, B.A.

FIRST YEAR.
Atkinson, Nicholas.

I

Faculty of Medicine.

FOURTH YEAR.

Anatomy and Physiology, ...	Comerford, Henry (£25).
Therapeutics and Pathology, ...	Wilson, William J. (£25).
Therapeutics (*Special Exhibition*), ..	Lupton, Henry (£18).

THIRD YEAR.

Bligh, John. | Conway, John K.

SECOND YEAR.

Boyd, John S. | Gorham, Anthony.

FIRST YEAR.

Literary Division.	*Science Division.*
Holmes, Robert A. K.	Walsh, Anthony.

School of Engineering.

THIRD YEAR.

M'Kelvey, Thomas.

SECOND YEAR.

Odling, Charles W. | Potter, Michael.

FIRST YEAR.

Lynam, William P. | Walker, Richard.

SESSION 1864-65.

Faculty of Arts.

SENIOR SCHOLARSHIPS.

Ancient Classics, ...	Dick, James, B.A.
Modern Languages and Modern History, ...	{ MacDonnell, Anthony P., B.A. } *equal* { Sharkey, Edmund de la } { Garde, B.A. }
Natural Philosophy, ...	Griffin, John, B.A.
Metaphysical and Economic Science,	Conolly, Patrick W., B.A.
Chemistry, ...	Conolly, James, B.A.
Natural History, ...	Wood, John E., B.A.

THIRD YEAR.

Literary Division.	*Science Division.*
Wilson, William N.	Winder, James.
M'Donald, Francis.	Burke, John.
Persse, William D.	Deane, Henry.
Meharry, John B.	Forsyth, Samuel M'C.
M'Farlane, Robert A.	Moorhead, William R.

SECOND YEAR.

Literary Division.	*Science Division.*
Moffett, Samuel.	Brooke, John.
M'Swinney, Robert F.	Hughes, William.
Killen, John M.	Griffin, Thomas.
Clancy, John J.	Lough, William J.
Dickey, Conly.	Walsh, Thomas.

FIRST YEAR.

Literary Division.	*Science Division.*
* Ward, Peter.	* Ward, Peter.
Maguire, Thomas M.	Brooke, William.
	Matthews, William.
	Ievers, Henry.
	Walsh, Michael.
	Colahan, William H. W.

Faculty of Law.

SENIOR SCHOLARSHIP.

Atkinson, John, B.A.

THIRD YEAR.
Mulholland, William.

SECOND YEAR.
Atkinson, Nicholas.

FIRST YEAR.
Crooks, William.

---

* Having obtained *First* place in both divisions, retains both Scholarships.

Faculty of Medicine.

FOURTH YEAR.

Bligh, John. | Saunderson, James E.

THIRD YEAR.

Burke, Michael J. | Gorham, Anthony.

SECOND YEAR.

Sharpe, William. | Warde, Michael.

FIRST YEAR.

Literary Division.

Reed, Matthew. | Cleary, Michael J.

School of Engineering.

THIRD YEAR.
Odling, Charles W.

SECOND YEAR.
Lynham, William P.

FIRST YEAR.

Davy, Alfred. | Taaffe, Michael.

SESSION 1865-66.

Faculty of Arts.

SENIOR SCHOLARSHIPS.

Ancient Classics, ...	Wilson, William N., B.A.
Modern Languages and Modern History,	Sharkey, Edmund de la Garde, B.A.
Mathematics, ...	Deane, Henry, B.A.
Natural Philosophy, ...	Foreman, Robert L., B.A.
Metaphysical and Economic Science, ..	Moorhead, William R., B.A.
Chemistry, ...	Forsyth, Samuel M'C., B.A.
Natural History, ...	Wilson, John, B.A.

THIRD YEAR.

Literary Division.	*Science Division.*
Moffett, Samuel.	Brooke, John.
M'Swinney, Robert F.	Hughes, William.
Killen, John M.	Griffin, Thomas.
Clancy, John J.	Lough, William.
Dickey, Conly.	Walsh, Thomas.

SECOND YEAR.

Literary Division.	*Science Division.*
Macaulay, Colman P.	Brooke, William.
Maguire, Thomas M.	Colahan, William H. W.
Gillespie, Michael.	Walsh, Michael.
Marshall, John.	Ward, Peter.
	Gaynor, William.

FIRST YEAR.

Literary Division.	*Science Division.*
M'Donald, Charles.	M'Ilveen, John.
Fitzpatrick, John.	Smith, Oliver.
Dooley, John L.	M'Kenna, Thomas.
Howley, James.	Colahan, Nicholas W.
Talbot, Bertram H.	Lewis, W. Llewellyn.

Faculty of Law.

SENIOR SCHOLARSHIP.

Mulholland, William, B.A.

THIRD YEAR.

Atkinson, Nicholas.

SECOND YEAR.

[None.]

FIRST YEAR.

M'Donald, Francis, B.A.

Faculty of Medicine.

FOURTH YEAR.

Conway, John K. | Conolly, James.

THIRD YEAR.

Davy, Francis A. | Sharpe, William.

SECOND YEAR.

Saunderson, William H. | Sugars, John C.

FIRST YEAR.

Literary Division.	*Science Division.*
Murphy, Michael E.	Hegarty, John.

School of Engineering.

THIRD YEAR.

Lynam, William P.

SECOND YEAR.

Davy, Alfred. | Grealy, Nicholas.

FIRST YEAR.

Nightingale, Walter H. | Chaster, Walter T.

SESSION 1866-67.

Faculty of Arts.

SENIOR SCHOLARSHIPS.

Ancient Classics, ...	M'Swinney, Robert F., B.A.
Modern Languages and Modern History,	O'Connor, Thomas P., B.A.
Mathematics, ...	*Foreman, Robert L., B.A.
Natural Philosophy, ...	Hughes, William, B.A.
Metaphysical and Economic Science,	M'Donald, Francis, B.A.
Chemistry, ...	Hoctor, William F., B.A.

THIRD YEAR.

Literary Division.	*Science Division.*
Macaulay, Colman P.	Brooke, William.
Maguire, Thomas M.	Colahan, William H. W.
Gillespie, Michael.	Walsh, Michael.
Marshall, John.	Ward, Peter.
Agnew, Samuel.	Gaynor, William.

SECOND YEAR.

Literary Division.	*Science Division.*
Fitzpatrick, John. } *equal.*	Smith, Oliver.
M'Donald, Charles.	Colahan, Nicholas W.
Howley, James.	Fahy, Edward.
Craig, Samuel R.	M'Ilveen, John.
Dooley, John L.	Eaton, Thomas.

FIRST YEAR.

Literary Division.	*Science Division.*
Drummond, Michael.	Drury, H. D'Olier.
Henry, William E.	Glover, Ralph F.
Mitchell, Robert.	M'Kinney, Samuel B. G. } *equal*
Ievers, Robert W.	Nealon, William.
Drury, Richard J.	Duncan, James.

Faculty of Law.

FIRST YEAR.

M'Farlane, Robert A.

Faculty of Medicine.

FOURTH YEAR.

Kearney, Ambrose. | Clayton, Nicholas.

THIRD YEAR.

Saunderson, William H. | Sugars, John O.

SECOND YEAR.

M'Donnell, James O'M. | O'Brien, Daniel.

FIRST YEAR.

Literary Division. | *Science Division.*
Pye, Joseph P. | M'Swinney, George H.

School of Engineering.

THIRD YEAR.

M'Kinney, Hugh G.

SECOND YEAR.

Nightingale, Walter H. | Oram, John E.

FIRST YEAR.

Concannon, Patrick. | Glover, R. Stephen.

SESSION 1867–68.

Faculty of Arts.

SENIOR SCHOLARSHIPS.

Ancient Classics, ...	Marshall, John, B.A.
Modern Languages and Modern History,	M'Donald, Francis, B.A.
Natural Philosophy, ...	Brooke, William, B.A.
Metaphysical and Economic Science, ..	M'Farlane, Robert A.
Chemistry, ...	Walsh, Michael, B.A.
Natural History, ...	Gillespie, Michael, B.A.

JUNIOR SCHOLARSHIPS.

THIRD YEAR.

Literary Division.	*Science Division.*
Fitzpatrick, John.	Colahan, Nicholas W.
M'Donald, Charles.	Fahy, Edward.
Howley, James.	M'Ilveen, John.
Craig, Samuel R.	Eaton, Thomas.
Dooley, John L.	Huey, John.

SECOND YEAR.

Literary Division.	*Science Division.*
Drummond, Michael.	Drury, H. D'Olier.
Henry, William E.	Glover, Ralph F.
Ievers, Robert W.	M'Kinney, Samuel B. G.
Drury, Richard J.	Lewis, W. Llewellyn.
Talbot, Bertram H.	Matthews, William.

FIRST YEAR.

Literary Division.	*Science Division.*
Thompson, David.	Harrison, John H.
Hart, Raphael.	Moran, John.
Foreman, William J.	* Clarke, John J.
Clarke, John J.	* Thompson, David.
	Patterson, William.
	O'Connor, P. Fenelon.

Faculty of Law.

THIRD YEAR.
M'Donald, Francis, B.A.

SECOND YEAR.
M'Swinney, Robert F., B.A.

FIRST YEAR.
Maguire, Thomas M., B.A.

---

* Ineligible, having obtained Scholarship in other division.

Faculty of Medicine.

FOURTH YEAR.
Saunderson, William H. | M'Auliffe, Thomas B.

THIRD YEAR.
M'Donnell, James O'M. | O'Brien, Daniel.

SECOND YEAR.
Pye, Joseph P. | Torrens, James.

FIRST YEAR.
Literary Division. | *Science Division.*
Simpson, William. | Hegarty, John.

School of Engineering.

THIRD YEAR.
Nightingale, Walter H.

SECOND YEAR.
Glover, R. Stephen. | Townsend, Thomas A.

FIRST YEAR.
Falkiner, George A. | Stratford, John.

SESSION 1868-69.

Faculty of Arts.

SENIOR SCHOLARSHIPS.

Ancient Classics, ...	M'Donald, Charles, B.A.
Modern Languages and Modern History,	Gillespie, Michael, B.A.
Mathematics, ...	Brooke, William, B.A.
Natural Philosophy, ...	Walsh, Michael, B.A.
Metaphysical and Economic Science, ..	Eaton, Thomas, B.A.
Chemistry, ...	Huey, John, B.A.

JUNIOR SCHOLARSHIPS.

THIRD YEAR.

Literary Division.	*Science Division.*
Drummond, Michael.	Drury, H. D'Olier.
Henry, William E.	Glover, Ralph F.
Ievers, Robert W.	M'Kinney, Samuel B. G.
Drury, Richard J.	Lewis, W. Llewellyn
Talbot, Bertram H.	Matthews, William.

SECOND YEAR.

Literary Division.	*Science Division.*
Mitchell, Robert,	Harrison, John H.
Thompson, David.	Concannon, Patrick.
Foreman, William J.	Moran, John.
	Patterson, William.
	O'Connor, P. Fenelon.
	Clarke, John J.

FIRST YEAR.

Literary Division.	*Science Division.*
Shiel, Joseph R.	Croke, J. O'Byrne.
Warren, William E.	Anderson, Adam.
Cullin, Henry C.	Mullally, Michael.
Moorhead, James.	Somerville, Richard N.
Milward, William H.	* Moorhead, James.
	Milward, George R.

* Ineligible, having obtained Scholarship in other division.

Faculty of Law.

SENIOR SCHOLARSHIP.

M'Donald, Francis, M.A.

THIRD YEAR.

M'Swinney, Robert F., M.A.

SECOND YEAR.

Maguire, Thomas M., B.A.

FIRST YEAR.

Mulligan, James.

Faculty of Medicine.

FOURTH YEAR.

O'Brien, Daniel. | M'Donnell, James O'M.

THIRD YEAR.

Pye, Joseph P. | Drury, H. D'Olier.
Colahan, William H. W. |

SECOND YEAR.

Blood, Robert. | Simpson, W.

FIRST YEAR.
Science Division.
Clements, Robert.

School of Engineering.

THIRD YEAR.

Glover, R. Stephen.

SECOND YEAR.

Falkiner, George A. | Stratford, John.

FIRST YEAR.

Holmes, Robert F. } *equal.*
Kain, Thomas.

Faculty of Arts.

SENIOR SCHOLARSHIPS.

Ancient Classics, ...	Henry, William E., B.A.
Modern Languages and Modern History,	Rentoul, James Alex., B.A.
Mathematics, ...	Glover, Ralph F., B.A.
Natural Philosophy, ...	Lewis, Walter L., B.A.
Metaphysical and Economic Science, ..	Mulligan, James, B.A.
Chemistry, ...	Griffin, Thomas, B.A.
Natural History, ...	*O'Donnell, Charles J., B.A.

JUNIOR SCHOLARSHIPS.

THIRD YEAR.

Literary Division.
Mitchell, Robert.
Thompson, David.
Foreman, William J.

Science Division.
Harrison, John H.
Concannon, Patrick.
Moran, John.
Patterson, William.
O'Connor, P. Fenelon.

SECOND YEAR.

Literary Division.
Cullin, Henry C.
Moorhead, James.
Shiel, Joseph R.
Warren, William E.
O'Shaughnessy, John F. A.

Science Division.
Croke, J. O'Byrne.
Anderson, Adam.
Mullally, Michael.
Somerville, Richard N.
Milward, George R.

FIRST YEAR.

Literary Division.
Maxwell, William H.
Lynam, James.
O'Callaghan, Matthew Q.
O'Neill, Peter J.
Byrne, Nicholas.

Science Division.
Freyer, P. Johnson.
Gorham, James J.
†Lynam, James.
Bourke, Palmer A.
M'Loughlin, James.
Joyce, Patrick K.

* Previously M'Donald.
† Ineligible, having obtained Scholarship in other division.

Faculty of Law.

SENIOR SCHOLARSHIP.

M'Swinney, Robert F., M.A.

THIRD YEAR.
Maguire, Thomas M., B.A.

SECOND YEAR.
Dooley, John L.

FIRST YEAR.
Todd, Robert H.

Faculty of Medicine.

FOURTH YEAR.

Colahan, William H. W.	Pye, Joseph P.

THIRD YEAR.

Walsh, Michael.	Colahan, Nicholas W.

SECOND YEAR.

Melville, Andrew S.	Brooke, William.

FIRST YEAR.

Literary Division.	*Science Division.*
Barker, Christopher F.	White, Michael.

School of Engineering.

THIRD YEAR.
Falkiner, George A.

SECOND YEAR.

Quinton, John H.	Holmes, Robert F.

FIRST YEAR

Lynam, Patrick.	Templeton, John W.

SESSION 1870-71.

Faculty of Arts.

SENIOR SCHOLARSHIPS.

Ancient Classics, ...	Mulligan, James, B.A.
Modern Languages and Modern History,	Moran, John, B.A.
Mathematics, ...	Harrison, John H., B.A.
Natural Philosophy, ...	Glover, Ralph F., B.A.
Metaphysical and Economic Science, ..	Todd, Robert H., B.A.
Chemistry, ...	Lewis, W. Llewellyn, B.A.
Natural History, ...	Brooke, William, B.A.

JUNIOR SCHOLARSHIPS.

THIRD YEAR.

Literary Division.	*Science Division.*
Moorhead, James.	Croke, J. O'Byrne.
Shiel, Joseph R.	Anderson, Adam.
Warren, William E.	Mullally, Michael.
O'Shaughnessy, John F. A.	Somerville, Richard N.
	Milward, George R.

SECOND YEAR.

Literary Division.	*Science Division.*
Lynam, James.	Freyer, P. Johnson.
Maxwell, William H.	*Lynam, J.
O'Neill, Peter.	Gorham, James J.
	Joyce, Patrick K.
	Ellison, James.
	Megarry, James.

FIRST YEAR.

Literary Division.	*Science Division.*
†Adams, David O.	†Adams, David O. } equal.
Milward, Edwin O.	Gordon, John.
M'Namara, John W.	Hickman, James.
Molony, Henry G.	Moylan, Michael J.
Dill, John.	Connolly, William E. S.

* Ineligible, having obtained Scholarship in other division.
† Having obtained *First* Place in both divisions, retains both Scholarships.

Faculty of Law.

SENIOR SCHOLARSHIP.

Maguire, Thomas M., B.A.

THIRD YEAR.
Drummond, Michael, M.A.

SECOND YEAR.
Rentoul, James Alex., B.A.

FIRST YEAR.
Concannon, Patrick.

Faculty of Medicine.

FOURTH YEAR.

Colahan, Nicholas W.	Fleming, William.

THIRD YEAR.

Holland, John J.	Gillespie, Michael.

SECOND YEAR.

White, Michael.	Morris, John J.

FIRST YEAR.

Literary Division.	*Science Division.*
Warren, J. Monteith.	Leitch, Josias.

School of Engineering.

THIRD YEAR.
Darcy, William E.

SECOND YEAR.

Lynam, Patrick.	Kain, Thomas.

FIRST YEAR.

Prendergast, Patrick J.	M'Auliffe, John.

SESSION 1871-72.

Faculty of Arts.

SENIOR SCHOLARSHIPS.

Ancient Classics, ...	Moorhead, James, B.A.
Modern Languages and Modern History,	Mullally, Michael, B.A.
Mathematics, ...	Concannon, Patrick, B.A.
Natural Philosophy, ...	Harrison, John H., B.A.
Metaphysical and Economic Science, ..	Moran, John, B.A.
Chemistry, ...	Brooke, William, B.A.

JUNIOR SCHOLARSHIPS.

THIRD YEAR.

Literary Division.	*Science Division.*
Lynam, James.	Freyer, P. Johnson.
Maxwell, William H.	* Lynam, James.
O'Neill, Peter.	Gorham, James J.
	Joyce, Patrick R.
	Ellison, James.
	Megarry, James.

SECOND YEAR.

Literary Division.	*Science Division.*
† Adams, David O.	† Adams, David O.
Milward, Edwin O.	Gordon, John.
M'Namara, John W.	Hickman, James. } *equal.*
Molony, Henry G.	Monroe, Samuel H.
M'Mordie, Elijah.	Moylan, Michael J. } *equal.*

FIRST YEAR.

Literary Division.	*Science Division.*
O'Connor, George.	O'Kinealy, Peter.
M'Namara, Joseph C.	Dundee, Isaac C.
Mullin, James.	Wallace, Hugh.
Ambrose, Robert.	Kelly, Michael.
Molony, John.	Hallowell, James.

---

* Ineligible, having obtained Scholarship in other division.

† Having obtained *First* Place in both divisions, retains both Scholarships.

Faculty of Law.

SENIOR SCHOLARSHIP.
Mulligan, James, M.A.

THIRD YEAR.
Rentoul, James Alex., B.A.

SECOND YEAR.
Shiel, Joseph R.

FIRST YEAR.
O'Neill, George F., M.A.

Faculty of Medicine.

FOURTH YEAR.
Holland, John J. | Gillespie, Michael J., B.A.

THIRD YEAR.
White, Michael. | Morris, John J.

SECOND YEAR.
Maguire, Daniel. | O'Connor, Peter F., B.A.

FIRST YEAR.

Literary Division. | *Science Division.*
O'Connor, Patrick. | Lynham, John I.

School of Engineering.

THIRD YEAR.
Lynam, Patrick.

SECOND YEAR.
Prendergast, Patrick J.

FIRST YEAR.
Kerin, John.

SESSION 1872-73.

Faculty of Arts.

SENIOR SCHOLARSHIPS.

Ancient Classics, ...	Maxwell, William H., B.A.
Mathematics, ...	Mullally, Michael, B.A.
Natural Philosophy, ...	Concannon, Patrick, M.A.
Metaphysical and Economic Science,	Shiel, Joseph R., B.A.
Chemistry, ...	Freyer, P. Johnson, B.A.
Natural History, `	Walsh, Michael, B.A.

JUNIOR SCHOLARSHIPS.

THIRD YEAR.

Literary Division.
* Adams, David O.
Milward, Edwin O.
M'Namara, John W.
Molony, Henry G.
M'Mordie, Elijah.

Science Division.
* Adams, David O.
Gordon, John.
Hickman, James. } *equal.*
Monroe, Samuel H. } *equal.*
Moylan, Michael J.

SECOND YEAR.

Literary Division.
O'Connor, George.
M'Namara, Joseph C.
Mullin, James.
Molony, John.
Watters, William.

Science Division.
O'Kinealy, Peter.
Fisher, John M.
Kelly, Michael.
Dundee, Isaac C.
Parker, John William.

FIRST YEAR.

Literary Division.
Geoghegan, Joseph.
M'Millan, John.
Lavertine, Charles.
M'Namara, William J. U.
Wilson, Samuel L.

Science Division.
Shore, Robert.
Kelly, William. } *equal.*
Lewis, John P.
Glassford, Charles O.
Goudy, James.

---

* Having obtained *First* Place in both divisions, retains both Scholarships.

Faculty of Law.

SENIOR SCHOLARSHIP.

Rentoul, James Alex., B.A.

THIRD YEAR.

O'Neill, Peter J., B.A.

SECOND YEAR.

Moran, John, B.A.

FIRST YEAR.

Hanna, James.

Faculty of Medicine.

FOURTH YEAR.

White, Michael.	Macauley, Roger.

THIRD YEAR.

Maguire, Daniel.	Dempsey, Alexander.

SECOND YEAR.

Lynham, John I.	Quirk, Martin.

FIRST YEAR.

Literary Division.	*Science Division.*
Hallowell, James.	Sheedy, John.

School of Engineering.

THIRD YEAR.

Prendergast, Patrick J.

SECOND YEAR.

Woods, Richard J.

FIRST YEAR.

FitzGerald, Henry.

SESSION 1873-74.

Faculty of Arts.

SENIOR SCHOLARSHIPS.

Ancient Classics, ...	Milward, Edwin O., B.A.
Modern Languages and Modern History,	Adams, David O., B.A.
Mathematics, ...	Gordon, John, B.A.
Natural Philosophy, ...	Freyer, P. Johnson, B.A.
Metaphysical and Economic Science, ..	Concannon, Patrick, B.A.
Chemistry, ...	Gorham, James J., B.A.
Natural History, ...	Joyce, Patrick K., B.A.

JUNIOR SCHOLARSHIPS.

THIRD YEAR.

Literary Division.	*Science Division.*
O'Connor, George.	O'Kinealy, Peter.
M'Namara, Joseph C.	Fisher, John M.
Mullin, James.	Kelly, Michael.
Molony, John.	Dundee, Isaac C.
Watters, William.	Parker, John William.

SECOND YEAR.

Literary Division.	*Science Division.*
Lavertine, Charles.	Shore, Robert.
Wilson, Samuel L.	M'Auliffe, Daniel.
Love, George C.	Goudy, James.
M'Millan, John.	Fisher, Joseph R.
M'Namara, William J. U.	

FIRST YEAR.

Literary Division.	*Science Division.*
Molohan, John P.	M'Master, James.
Kerr, Æneas.	M'Dermott, Cornelius.
Farrelly, Michael J.	Constable, Samuel. } *equal.*
Minniken, John.	Corry, Patrick.
Dripps, James T.	Horan, Timothy.

Faculty of Law.

SENIOR SCHOLARSHIP.

Mullally, Michael, B.A.

THIRD YEAR.

Shiel, Joseph R., B.A.

SECOND YEAR.

Hanna, James.

FIRST YEAR.

Greenfield, John K.

Faculty of Medicine.

FOURTH YEAR.

Freyer, P. Johnson, B.A. | Maguire, Daniel.

THIRD YEAR.

Lynham, John I. | O'Sullivan, Patrick J.

SECOND YEAR.

Stokes, William. | M'Afee, William.

FIRST YEAR.

Science Division.

Eakins, George R. | Delahunt, James J.

School of Engineering.

THIRD YEAR.

Woods, Richard J.

SECOND YEAR.

Mahon, Thomas.

FIRST YEAR.

Davern, John P.

SESSION 1874-75.

Faculty of Arts.

SENIOR SCHOLARSHIPS.

Modern Languages and Modern History,	Mullin, James, B.A.
Mathematics,	O'Kinealy, Peter, B.A.
Natural Philosophy,	Kelly, Michael, B.A.
Metaphysical and Economic Science,	Hanna, James, B.A.
Chemistry,	Molony, John S., B.A.
Natural History,	Milward, Edwin O., B.A.

JUNIOR SCHOLARSHIPS.

THIRD YEAR.

Literary Division.
Lavertine, Charles.
Wilson, Samuel L.
Love, George C.
M'Millan, John.
M'Namara, William J. U.

Science Division.
Shore, Robert.
M'Auliffe, Daniel.
Fisher, Joseph R.

SECOND YEAR.

Literary Division.
Kerr, Æneas.
Farrelly, Michael J.
Todd, Andrew.
Megaw, Robert T.

Science Division.
M'Master, James.
Constable, Samuel.
Smith, John.
Lewis, John P.
M'Dermott, Cornelius.
Morris, Richard H.

FIRST YEAR.

Literary Division.
* Henry, Augustine.
Hunter, Charles W.
Anderson, Joseph R.
Geoghegan, Alfred.

Science Division.
* Henry, Augustine.
Waterworth, Hugh.
Sheedy, Thomas. } *equal.*
Henderson, Thomas. }
Hackett, Robert I. Dalbey.
Gorham, John.

* Having obtained *First* Place in both divisions, retains both Scholarships.

Faculty of Law.

SENIOR SCHOLARSHIP.
Shiel, Joseph R., M.A.

THIRD YEAR.
Gordon, John, B.A.

SECOND YEAR.
Greenfield, John K.

Faculty of Medicine.

FOURTH YEAR.

| Lynham, John I. | O'Sullivan, Patrick J. |

THIRD YEAR.

| Beattie, Robert. | Stokes, William. |

SECOND YEAR.

| Love, Robert L. | Delahunt, James J. |

FIRST YEAR.

| *Literary Division.* | *Science Division.* |
| M'Kinlay, John. | Young, William J. |

School of Engineering.

THIRD YEAR.
Fisher, John M.

SECOND YEAR.

| Davern, John P. | Glassford, Charles O. |

FIRST YEAR.

| Barker, Alexander A. | Condon, Daniel E. |

Scholars. **175**

SESSION, 1875-76.

Faculty of Arts.

SENIOR SCHOLARSHIPS.

Ancient Classics,	O'Connor, George, M.A.
Modern Languages and Modern History,	Lavertine, Charles E., B.A.
Mathematics,	Kelly, Michael, B.A.
Natural Philosophy,	Shore, Robert, B.A.
Metaphysical and Economic Science,	Gordon, John, B.A.
Chemistry,	M'Namara, John W., B.A.
Natural History,	M'Namara, William J. U., B.A.

JUNIOR SCHOLARSHIPS.

THIRD YEAR.

Literary Division.	*Science Division.*
Kerr, Æneas.	M'Master, James.
Farrelly, Michael J.	Constable, Samuel.
Todd, Andrew.	Smith, John.
Megaw, Robert T.	Lewis, John P.
	Morris, Richard H.

SECOND YEAR.

Literary Division.	*Science Division.*
Hunter, Charles W.	Waterworth, Hugh.
Henry, Augustine.	Henderson, Thomas.
Condon, William O.	Hackett, Robert I. Dalbey.
	James, Arthur.
	Gorham, John.

FIRST YEAR.

Literary Division.	*Science Division.*
Dodds, Robert.	Henderson, John.
Thompson, George.	Sullivan, John.
Hume, George A.	Gahan, Garner.
Campbell, James A.	Andrews, James.
Watters, Francis O. M.	

Faculty of Law.

SENIOR SCHOLARSHIP.

O'Kinealy, Peter, M.A., LL.B.

FIRST YEAR.

Card, Thomas D., B.A.

K

Faculty of Medicine.

FOURTH YEAR.

Allen, William. | O'Connor, Patrick.

THIRD YEAR.

Mitchell, Robert. | O'Brien, Thomas M.

SECOND YEAR.

Riordan, Daniel. | M'Kinlay, John.

FIRST YEAR.

Science Division.

Martin, Hugh H. | Smith, John.

School of Engineering.

THIRD YEAR.

Molony, John S., B.A.

SECOND YEAR.

Barker, Alexander A. | Condon, Daniel E.

FIRST YEAR.

Gahan, Michael. | Lynam, Edward.

SESSION 1876-77.

Faculty of Arts.

SENIOR SCHOLARSHIPS.

Ancient Classics, ...	Farrelly, Michael J., B.A.
Modern Languages and Modern History,	M'Namara, Joseph C., B.A.
Mathematics, ...	Shore, Robert, B.A.
Natural Philosophy, ...	Hickman, James, B.A.
Metaphysical and Economic Science, ..	McGranahan, William, B.A.
Chemistry, ...	M'Namara, William J. U., B.A.

JUNIOR SCHOLARSHIPS.

THIRD YEAR.

Literary Division.	*Science Division.*
Hunter, Charles W.	Waterworth, Hugh.
Henry, Augustine.	Henderson, Thomas.
Condon, William O.	Hackett, Robert I. Dalbey.
	James, Arthur.
	Gorham, John.

SECOND YEAR.

Literary Division.	*Science Division.*
Dodds, Robert.	Sullivan, John.
Hume, George A.	Henderson, John.
Anderson, Joseph R.	Gahan, Garner.

FIRST YEAR.

Literary Division.	*Science Division.*
Brown, John I.	Anderson, Alexander.
Shine, Eugene.	Brown, William.
Gleeson, Edward J.	Moreland, Robert.
Nolan, Herbert, M.B.	Vance, Robert.
Hanly, John J.	Moorhead, John R.

Faculty of Law.

SENIOR SCHOLARSHIP.

Gordon, John, B.A.

SECOND YEAR.

Card, Thomas D., B.A.

FIRST YEAR.

Todd, Andrew, B.A.

N 2

Faculty of Medicine.

FOURTH YEAR.

Mitchell, Robert. | Delahunt, James J.

THIRD YEAR.

M'Kinlay, John. }
Riordan, Daniel. } *equal.*

SECOND YEAR.

Martin, John. | O'Malley, David J.

FIRST YEAR.

Literary Division. | *Science Division.*
Sheridan, Thomas M. | Elliott, John H.

School of Engineering.

THIRD YEAR.

Barker, Alexander A.

SECOND YEAR.

Lynam, Edward W. | Gahan, Michael.

FIRST YEAR.

M'Elrea, William.

SESSION 1877-78.

Faculty of Arts.

SENIOR SCHOLARSHIPS.

Ancient Classics, ...	Kerr, Æneas, B.A.
Modern Languages and History, ..	Todd, Andrew, B.A.
Natural Philosophy, ...	Henry, Augustine, B.A.
Metaphysical and Economic Science,	Henderson, Thomas, B.A.
Chemistry, ...	Shore, Robert, M.A.
Natural History, ...	Hackett, Robert I. Dalbey, B.A.

JUNIOR SCHOLARSHIPS.

THIRD YEAR.

Literary Division.	*Science Division.*
Dodds, Robert.	Sullivan, John.
Hume, George A.	Henderson, John.
Anderson, Joseph R.	Gahan, Garner.

SECOND YEAR.

Literary Scholarships.	*Science Scholarships.*
Brown, John I.	Vance, Robert.
Gleeson, Edward J.	Brown, William.
Shine, Eugene.	M'Dowell, Thomas H.
Hanly, John J.	Andrews, James.

FIRST YEAR.

Literary Division.	*Science Division.*
Jackson, William J.	Lowe, William J.
Morton, John H.	Eagar, Francis S.
Gillespie, James J.	Clarke, Samuel B.
Bain, John A.	Talbot, Thomas J.
Smyth, Thomas C.	* Jackson, William J.
	Mapother, Dillon E.

Faculty of Law.

FIRST YEAR.

England, William G.

* Ineligible, having obtained Scholarship in other division.

Faculty of Medicine.

FOURTH YEAR.

M'Kinlay, John. | Riordan, Daniel.

THIRD YEAR.

Reynolds, T. Taylor. | Martin, John.

SECOND YEAR.

O'Shaughnessy, Francis H. | Mullin, John F. L.

FIRST YEAR.

Literary Division. | *Science Division.*
Jackson, Joseph B. | Freyer, Samuel.

School of Engineering.

THIRD YEAR.

Lynam, Edward W.

SECOND YEAR.

M'Elrea, William. | Roseingrave, Thomas W.

FIRST YEAR.

Flatley, William P. | Horneck, Samuel.

SESSION, 1878-79.

Faculty of Arts.

SENIOR SCHOLARSHIPS.

Ancient Classics, ...	Dodds, Robert, B.A.
Modern Languages and Modern History,	Fisher, Joseph R., B.A.
Natural Philosophy, ...	Henderson, John, B.A.
Metaphysical and Economic Science,..	Hume, George A., B.A.
Chemistry, ...	Gahan, Garner, B.A.
Natural History, ...	Henry, Augustine, B.A.

JUNIOR SCHOLARSHIPS.

THIRD YEAR.

Literary Scholarships.
Brown, John 1.
Gleeson, Edward J.
Shine, Eugene.
Hanly, John J.

Science Scholarships.
Vance, Robert.
Brown, William.
M'Dowell, Thomas H.
Andrews, James.

SECOND YEAR.

Literary Division.
Jackson, William J.
Gillespie, James J.
Morton, John H.
Munro, William H.
Bain, John A.

Science Division.
Lowe, William J.
Anderson, Alexander.
Clarke, Samuel B.
Talbot, Thomas J.
Moorhead, John R.

FIRST YEAR.

Literary Division.
Kirker, H. Fitzwalter.
M'Laren, James B.
Millar, William J.
Morrow, Henry W.
O'Sullivan, Patrick.

Science Division.
Patterson, Samuel.
Rowney, George A. H.
Blackall, Patrick.
Gahan, Charles J.
Card, William.

Faculty of Law.

THIRD YEAR.
Todd, Andrew, B.A.

SECOND YEAR.
England, William G.

FIRST YEAR.
Donnell, William, B.A.

Faculty of Medicine.

FOURTH YEAR.

White, Sinclair. | Cochrane, Robert.

THIRD YEAR.

M'Loughlin, Francis. | Pritchard, Thomas.

SECOND YEAR.

Gibson, William W. | Fisher, Walter M.

FIRST YEAR.
Literary Division.

Copithorne, James G. | Farrelly, Thomas.

School of Engineering.

THIRD YEAR.

M'Elrea, William.

SECOND YEAR.

Hackett, Edward A. | Flatley, William P.

FIRST YEAR.

Mac Namara, Robert J.

SESSION 1879-80.

Faculty of Arts.
SENIOR SCHOLARSHIPS.

Ancient Classics, ...	Brown, John I., B.A.
Modern Languages and Modern History,	Campbell, James A., B.A.
Mathematics, ...	Vance, Robert, B.A.
Natural Philosophy, ...	Brown, William, B.A.
Metaphysical and Economic Science, ..	Currie, William S., B.A.
Natural History, ...	M'Farlane, Hugh, M.A.

JUNIOR SCHOLARSHIPS.
THIRD YEAR.

Literary Division.
Jackson, William J.
Gillespie, James J.
Morton, John H.
Munro, William H.
Bain, John A.

Science Division.
Lowe, William J.
Anderson, Alexander.
Clarke, Samuel B.
Talbot, Thomas J.
Moorhead, John R.

SECOND YEAR.

Literary Division.
M'Laren, James B.
Millar, William J.
Kirker, H. Fitzwalter.
M'Donagh, Redmond.
Molloy, Mark.

Science Division.
Patterson, Samuel.
Gahan, Charles J.
Foy, Alexander R.
M'Neill, David.
Rowney, George A. H.

FIRST YEAR.

Literary Division.
Shute, Charles C.
Newell, Peter.
M'Keague, Thomas M.
Watters, John.

Science Division.
Carroll, Henry.
Buckley, Thomas.
MacMillan, Robert.
Gillespie, Alexander P.
Freyer, John.
M'Dermott, James.

Faculty of Law.
SENIOR SCHOLARSHIP.
Todd, Andrew, LL.B.
THIRD YEAR.
Hume, George A., M.A.
SECOND YEAR.
Donnell, William, B.A.
FIRST YEAR.
Brown, James.

Faculty of Medicine.

FOURTH YEAR.

M'Laughlin, Francis. | Shore, Robert, M.A.

THIRD YEAR.

Gibson, William W. | O'Connell, David V.

SECOND YEAR.

Wise, Charles H. | Mitchell, William J.

FIRST YEAR.

Literary Division. | *Science Division.*
Clarke, Joseph J. | Thompson, William H.

School of Engineering.

THIRD YEAR.

Hackett, Edward A.

FIRST YEAR.

Hardy, Earle A. | Long, James L. S.

SESSION 1880-81.

Faculty of Arts.

SENIOR SCHOLARSHIPS.

Ancient Classics,	Jackson, William J., B.A.
Modern Languages and Modern History,	Bain, John A., B.A.
Mathematics,	Lowe, William J., B.A.
Natural Philosophy,	Anderson, Alexander, M.A.
Metaphysical and Economic Science,	Brown, John I., B.A.
Chemistry,	Clarke, Samuel B., B.A.
Natural History,	Munro, William H., B.A.

JUNIOR SCHOLARSHIPS.

THIRD YEAR.

Literary Division.
M'Laren, James B.
Millar, William J.
Kirker, H. Fitzwalter.
M'Donagh, Redmond.
Molloy, Mark.

Science Division.
Patterson, Samuel.
Gahan, Charles J.
Foy, Alexander R.
M'Neill, David.
Rowney, George A. H.

SECOND YEAR.

Literary Division.
Newell, Peter.
Moody, John.
Keating, William H.

Science Division.
Buckley, Thomas.
M'Dermott, James.
Card, William.
M'Granahan, James.
Freyer, John.

FIRST YEAR.

Literary Division.
Maxwell, Sydney L.
Hamilton, William.
Shannon, Owen J.
*Freyer, Samuel.
Hogg, T. Simpson.

Science Division.
Freyer, Samuel.
Kane, Hugh.
Morton, David.
M'Cune, Thomas H.
Stewart, John.
Waugh, Hugh.

---

* Ineligible, having obtained Scholarship in other division.

Faculty of Law.

SENIOR SCHOLARSHIP.
Hume, George A., M.A.

THIRD YEAR.
Donnell, William, B.A.

SECOND YEAR.
Brown, James.

Faculty of Medicine...

FOURTH YEAR.
Gibson, William W. | O'Connell, David V.

THIRD YEAR.
Mitchell, William J. | O'Gorman, Patrick.

SECOND YEAR.
Thompson, William H. | M'Glynn, John.

FIRST YEAR.
Literary Division. | *Science Division.*
Lennan, Vincent F. | Bartley, William.

School of Engineering.

SECOND YEAR.
Hardy, Earle A. | Thompson, William J.

FIRST YEAR.
Binns, Henry A.

SESSION 1881-82.

Faculty of Arts.

SENIOR SCHOLARSHIPS.

Ancient Classics, ...	M'Laren, James B., B.A.
Modern Languages and Modern History, ..	Jackson, William J., B.A.
Mathematics, ...	Anderson, Alexander, M.A.
Natural Philosophy, ...	Vance, Robert, M.A.
Metaphysical and Economic Science, ..	Millar, William J., B.A.
Chemistry, ...	Buchanan, Andrew, B.A.
Natural History, ...	Hanly, John J., B.A.

JUNIOR SCHOLARSHIPS.

THIRD YEAR.

Literary Division.	*Science Division.*
Newell, Peter.	Buckley, Thomas.
Moody, John.	M'Dermott, James.
Keating, William H.	Card, William.
	M'Granahan, James.
	Freyer, John.

SECOND YEAR.

Literary Division.	*Science Division.*
Shannon, Owen J.	Morton, David.
Thompson, James.	Freyer, Samuel.
Hamilton, Walter M.	M'Cune, Thomas H.
Hogg, T. Simpson.	Mahon, William.
Maxwell, Sydney L.	Kelly, Michael O.

FIRST YEAR.

Literary Division.	*Science Division.*
Evans, Isaac R.	Card, David.
M'Elwee, John.	Finucane, Thomas E.
Laing, John.	Frame, Arthur.
M'Farland, Andrew.	Gillespie, George.
Moody, William.	Atkinson, Hugh L.

Faculty of Law.

SENIOR SCHOLARSHIP.

Farrelly, Michael J., B.A.

FIRST YEAR.

Nelson, Thomas E., M.A.

Faculty of Medicine.

FOURTH YEAR.

Mitchell, William J. | O'Gorman, Patrick.

THIRD YEAR.

Thompson, William H. | Henderson, Robert W.

SECOND YEAR.

Bartley, William. | Munro, William H., B.A.

FIRST YEAR.

Literary Division. | *Science Division.*
Wade, Hugh E. | Condon, Richard T.

School of Engineering.

THIRD YEAR.
Thompson, William J.

SECOND YEAR.
Binns, Henry A.

FIRST YEAR.
Lynam, Francis J.

SESSION 1882-83.

Faculty of Arts.

SENIOR SCHOLARSHIPS.

Ancient Classics, ...	Keating, William H.
Modern Languages and Modern History,	Newell, Peter.
Natural Philosophy, ...	Patterson, Samuel, B.A.
Metaphysical and Economic Science, ..	Jackson, William J., M.A.
Chemistry, ...	Semple, Samuel, M.A.
Natural History, ...	Gahan, Charles J., M.A.

JUNIOR SCHOLARSHIPS.

THIRD YEAR.

Literary Division.	*Science Division.*
Shannon, Owen J.	Morton, David.
Thompson, James.	Freyer, Samuel.
Hamilton, Walter M.	M'Cune, Thomas H.
Hogg, T. Simpson.	Mahon, William.
Maxwell, Sydney L.	Kelly, Michael O.

SECOND YEAR.

Literary Division.	*Science Division.*
Evans, Isaac R.	Gillespie, George.
M'Elwee, John.	Finucane, Thomas E.
M'Coy, Daniel.	Carroll, Henry.
Gannon, William C.	M'Elney, Robert.
Davison, Robert H.	Frame, Arthur.

FIRST YEAR.

Literary Division.	*Science Division.*
Clarke, William A.	Martin, John.
M'Nulty, Thomas.	Humphreys, John.
* Benson, Arthur T.	Hopkins, Samuel.
M'Afee, Alexander.	Oldham, Thomas C. H.
Jordan, Michael J.	Benson, Arthur T.
Gregg, Andrew C.	

Faculty of Law.

THIRD YEAR.
Millar, William J., M.A.

SECOND YEAR.
Nelson, Thomas E.

FIRST YEAR.
M'Donagh, Redmond, B.A.

---

* Ineligible, having obtained Scholarship in other division.

Faculty of Medicine.

FOURTH YEAR.

Thompson, William H. | Henderson, Robert W.

THIRD YEAR.

Mahon, Ralph B. | MacNamara, Robert J.

SECOND YEAR.

Condon, Richard T. | Milligan, William.

FIRST YEAR.

Science Division.

Noble, William. | Reynolds, James S.

School of Engineering.

THIRD YEAR.

Rowney, George A. H., B.A.

SECOND YEAR.

Lynam, Francis J. | O'Shaughnessy, Michael M.

FIRST YEAR.

Allman, Alfred. } *equal.*
Joyce, Raoul.

SESSION 1883-84.

Faculty of Arts.

SENIOR SCHOLARSHIPS.

Ancient Classics, ...	Maxwell, Sydney L., B.A.
Modern Languages and Modern History, ..	Shannon, Owen J., B.A.
Mathematics, ·	Morton, David.
Natural Philosophy, ...	Freyer, Samuel.
Metaphysical and Economic Science, ..	Smith, Henry, B.A.
Chemistry, ...	M'Cune, Thomas H., B.A
Natural History, ...	Hogg, T. Simpson, B.A.

JUNIOR SCHOLARSHIPS.

THIRD YEAR.

Literary Division.	*Science Division.*
Evans, Isaac R.	Gillespie, George.
M'Elwee, John.	Finucane, Thomas E.
M'Coy, Daniel.	Carroll, Henry.
Gannon, William C.	M'Elney, Robert.
Davison, Robert H.	Frame, Arthur.

SECOND YEAR.

Literary Division.	*Science Division.*
Clarke, William A.	Humphreys, John.
Benson, Arthur J.	Martin, John.
Jordan, Michael J.	Card, David.
Gregg, Andrew C.	
M'Afee, Alexander.	

FIRST YEAR.

Literary Division.	*Science Division.*
Dugan, Charles W.	Keers, James.
Meeke, William M'E.	Dowd, Henry L.
Loftus, Joseph J.	Cowan, Moses H.
Hession, Nicholas J. M.	Keegan, James M.
Davidson, Andrew G.	Campbell, Richard J.

Faculty of Law.

JUNIOR SCHOLARSHIPS.

THIRD YEAR.	SECOND YEAR.	FIRST YEAR.
Nelson, Thomas E.	M'Donagh, Redmond.	Moorhead, John R.

Faculty of Medicine.

SENIOR SCHOLARSHIP.
Thompson, William H.

FOURTH YEAR.
MacNamara, Robert J. | Waters, George A.

THIRD YEAR.
Eagleton, John F.

SECOND YEAR.
Hamilton, James. | Waters, Eaton W.

FIRST YEAR.
Literary Division.
Stewart, Joseph. | M'Cormick, Edward.

School of Engineering.

THIRD YEAR.	FIRST YEAR.
O'Shaughnessy, Michael M.	Thompson, Atwell.

SESSION 1884-85.

Faculty of Arts.

SENIOR SCHOLARSHIPS.

Ancient Classics, ... Evans, Isaac R.
Modern Languages and Modern History .. Thompson, James, B.A.
Natural Philosophy, ... M'Cune, Thomas H., B.A.
Metaphysical and Economic Science, .. Sloane, George, B.A.
Chemistry, ... M'Elney, Robert, B.A.
Natural History, ... M'Elwee, John, B.A.

JUNIOR SCHOLARSHIPS.

THIRD YEAR.

Literary Division.

Clarke, William A.
Benson, Arthur J.
Jordan, Michael J.
Gregg, Andrew C.
M'Afee, Alexander.

Science Division.

Humphreys, John.
Martin, John.
Card, David.

SECOND YEAR.

Literary Division.

Davidson, Andrew G.
Dugan, Charles W.
Rusk, John.
Hession, Nicholas J. M.
Hegan, Edwin.

Science Division.

Henry, Moses.
Cowan, Moses H.
Keegan, James M.
Dowd, Henry L.
Keers, James M.

FIRST YEAR.

Literary Division.

Kennedy, William.
M'Kee, William J.
Adams, John A.
Cairnes, John E.
Bell, James.

Science Division.

M'Candless, Thomas.
Shore, Patrick B.
Farrington, Walter.
Charleton, Robert J.
Thompson, Cuthbert

Faculty of Law.

SCHOLARSHIPS.

THIRD YEAR.
M'Donagh, Redmond, M.A.

SECOND YEAR.
Moorhead, John R., B.A.

FIRST YEAR.
Malone, John.

Faculty of Medicine.

SENIOR SCHOLARSHIP.

Anatomy and Physiology,   ..   Macnamara, Robert J.

FOURTH YEAR.

Mahon, Ralph B. | Eagleton, John F.

THIRD YEAR.

Waters, Eaton W. | Hamilton, James.

SECOND YEAR.

Stewart, Joseph. | Pierse, Gerard J.

FIRST YEAR.

Literary Division. | *Science Division.*
Heaney, James H. | Foley, Thomas H.

School of Engineering.

SCHOLARSHIPS.

SECOND YEAR.

Thompson, Atwell.

FIRST YEAR.

Binns, William N. | Long, Samuel L.

SESSION 1885-86.

Faculty of Arts.

SENIOR SCHOLARSHIPS.

Ancient Classics, ...	.. Clarke, William A.
Metaphysical and Economic Science,	.. Gregg, Andrew C.
Chemistry, ...	.. Gillespie, George, B.A.
Natural History, ...	.. Martin, John.

JUNIOR SCHOLARSHIPS.

THIRD YEAR.

Literary Division.	*Science Division.*
Davidson, Andrew G.	Henry, Moses.
Dugan, Charles W.	Cowan, Moses H.
Rusk, John.	Keegan, James M.
Hession, Nicholas J. M.	Dowd, Henry L.
Hegan, Edwin.	Keers, James M.

SECOND YEAR.

Literary Division.	*Science Division.*
M'Kee, William J.	Thompson, Cuthbert.
Adams, John A.	Rentoul, Gervais C.
Hilton, Hugh.	Charleton, Robert J.
Hamilton, Samuel.	Farrington, Walter.
Cairnes, John E.	

FIRST YEAR.

Literary Division.	*Science Division.*
Maxwell, Michael T.	Bain, Alexander.
Irwin, Albert J.	* Semple, Robert J.
* Bain, Alexander.	M'Cay, Francis.
Semple, Robert J.	Keers, William.
Lydon, Martin F.	Freyer, Patrick W.

Faculty of Law.

JUNIOR SCHOLARSHIPS.

THIRD YEAR.

Moorhead, John R.

SECOND YEAR.

Smith, Henry.

FIRST YEAR.

Brown, William.

* Ineligible, having obtained Scholarship in other division.

Faculty of Medicine.

SENIOR SCHOLARSHIP.

Anatomy and Physiology, ... Mahon, Ralph B.

FOURTH YEAR.
Waters, Eaton W.

THIRD YEAR.

| Smith, Henry, B.A. | Stewart, Joseph. |

SECOND YEAR.

| Eldon, Joseph. | Loftus, Joseph J. |

FIRST YEAR.

| *Literary Division.* | *Science Division.* |
| Millea, William C. | Twomey, Michael. |

School of Engineering.

SCHOLARSHIPS.

THIRD YEAR.
Thompson, Atwell.

SECOND YEAR.

| Long, Samuel L. | Oldham, Thomas C. H. |

FIRST YEAR.

| Moon, Robert A. | Hall, Thomas A. |

SESSION 1886–87.

Faculty of Arts.

SENIOR SCHOLARSHIPS.

Ancient Classics, ...	Dugan, Charles W.
Modern Languages and Modern History, ..	Rusk, John, B.A.
Mathematics, ...	Thompson, Atwell, B.E.
Natural Philosophy, ...	Henry, Moses, B.A.
Metaphysical and Economic Science, ..	Humphreys, John.
Chemistry, ...	Keegan, James M., B.A.
Natural History, ...	M'Afee, Alexander, B.A.

JUNIOR SCHOLARSHIPS.

THIRD YEAR.

Literary Division.
M'Kee, William J.
Adams, John A.
Hilton, Hugh.
Hamilton, Samuel.
Cairnes, John E.

Science Division.
Thompson, Cuthbert.
Rentoul, Gervais C.
Charleton, Robert J.
Farrington, Walter.

SECOND YEAR.

Literary Division.
Kennedy, William.
Semple, Robert J.
Irwin, Albert J.
Maxwell, Michael T.

Science Division.
Bain, Alexander.
Millea, William C.
M'Cay, Francis.
Douglas, Charles.
Raddin, George H.

FIRST YEAR.

Literary Division.
O'Hara, Patrick J.
Clarke, Alexander F.
M'Askie, William J.
Gillespie, William H.
Donnan, William.

Science Division.
Gannon, William J.
Love, Robert.
Bunton, Christopher L. W.
Mangan, Denis.
Bradford, Herbert A.

Faculty of Law.

THIRD YEAR.
Smith, Joseph, B.A.

SECOND YEAR.
Brown, William, M.A.

FIRST YEAR.
Buckley, Thomas.

Faculty of Medicine.

SENIOR SCHOLARSHIP.

Anatomy and Physiology, ...   Waters, Eaton W.

FOURTH YEAR.

Smith, Henry, B.A. | Stewart, Joseph.

THIRD YEAR.

Pierse, Gerard J. | Taylor, William J.

SECOND YEAR.

Foley, Thomas H. | Laing, George M.

FIRST YEAR.

Literary Division. | *Science Division.*
O'Reilly, Henry W. H. | Connolly, Thomas J.

School of Engineering.

SCHOLARSHIPS.

THIRD YEAR.

Binns, William N..

SECOND YEAR.

Finucane, Thomas E. | Hall, Thomas A.

FIRST YEAR.

Thompson, John S.

SESSION 1887-88.

Faculty of Arts.
SENIOR SCHOLARSHIPS.

Ancient Classics, ... M'Kee, William J., B.A.
Modern Languages and Modern History, .. Hilton, Hugh.
Natural Philosophy, ... Keegan, James M., M.A.
Metaphysical and Economic Science, .. Davidson, Andrew G., B.A.
Chemistry, ... Farrington, Walter.

JUNIOR SCHOLARSHIPS.
THIRD YEAR.

Literary Division.
Kennedy, William.
Semple, Robert J.
Irwin, Albert J.
Maxwell, Michael T.

Science Division.
Bain, Alexander.
Millea, William C.
M'Cay, Francis.
Douglas, Charles.
Raddin, George H.

SECOND YEAR.

Literary Division.
Connolly, Thomas J.
Love, Robert.
Gillespie, William H.
O'Hara, Patrick J.
M'Askie, William J.
Gailey, Andrew.
Clarke, Alexander F.

Science Division.
Gannon, William J.
Bradford, Herbert A.
*Connolly, Thomas J.

FIRST YEAR.

Literary Division.
Browne, David.
Lee, William.
Morris, Patrick.

Science Division.
Paul, John.
Deans, John.
Harrison, Thomas J.
*Browne, David.
Keenan, John F.
Moran, John.
Cambbell, Henry.
Clements, Robert W.

Faculty of Law.
SECOND YEAR.
Buckley, Thomas.
FIRST YEAR.
O'Keeffe, James D.

---

* Ineligible, having obtained Scholarship in other Division.

Faculty of Medicine.

SENIOR SCHOLARSHIP.

Anatomy and Physiology, ... Stewart, Joseph, M.B.

FOURTH YEAR.

Pierse, Gerard J. | Taylor, William J.

THIRD YEAR.

Steen, James R. | Eldon, Joseph.

SECOND YEAR.

Heaney, James H. | Hamilton, Samuel.

FIRST YEAR.

Science Division.

Clements, Joseph E.

School of Engineering.

THIRD YEAR.

Finucane, Thomas E.

FIRST YEAR.

Binns, Edmund T. | Goodman, Charles W.

SESSION 1888-89.

Faculty of Arts.

SENIOR SCHOLARSHIPS.

Ancient Classics, ...	Kennedy, William, B.A.
Mathematics, ...	Bain, Alexander.
Natural Philosophy, ...	Hall, Thomas A., B.E.
Metaphysical and Economic Science,	Semple, Robert J., B.A.
Chemistry, ...	Thompson, Cuthbert.
Natural History, ...	Millea, William C.

JUNIOR SCHOLARSHIPS.

THIRD YEAR.

Literary Division.
Connolly, Thomas J.
Love, Robert.
Gillespie, William H.
O'Hara, Patrick J.
M'Askie, William J.
Gailey, Andrew.
Clarke, Alexander F.

Science Division.
Gannon, William J.
Bradford, Herbert A.

SECOND YEAR.

Literary Division.
Brown, David.
Mangan, Denis.
Downard, Thomas.
Deans, John.

Science Division.
Paul, John.
Harrison, Thomas J.
Clements, Robert W.
Hynes, Mortimer.
O'Dea, Martin.
Moran, John.

FIRST YEAR.

Literary Division.
Mahon, John S.
Beattie, Robert A.
Boyd, James.
Hunter, Charles H.
Glendenning, James P. C.

Science Division.
Deans, William.
Bain, Philander A.
Burkitt, James P.
Roe, Robert L.
Forbes, William J.

Faculty of Law.

THIRD YEAR.
Buckley, Thomas, B.A.

SECOND YEAR.
O'Connor, Francis J.

FIRST YEAR.
Jordan, Michael J., B.A.

Faculty of Medicine.

SENIOR SCHOLARSHIP.

Anatomy and Physiology, ... Taylor, William J.

FOURTH YEAR.

Steen, James R. | Eldon, Joseph.

THIRD YEAR.

Adams, John A., B.A. | Foley, Thomas H.

SECOND YEAR.

Martin, John. | Foley, Charles H.

FIRST YEAR.

Literary Division. | *Science Division.*
Campbell, Henry. | Robinson, James.

School of Engineering.

THIRD YEAR.
M'Cay, Francis.

FIRST YEAR.

Mahon, Arthur P. | Orpen, Richard T.

SESSION 1889-90.

Faculty of Arts.

SENIOR SCHOLARSHIPS.

Ancient Classics, ...	Gillespie, William H., B.A.
Modern Languages and Modern History,	O'Hara, Patrick J.
Mathematics, ...	M'Cay, Francis, B.A.
Metaphysical and Economic Science, ..	Gailey, Andrew, B.A.
Chemistry, ...	Gannon, William J., B.A.

THIRD YEAR.

Literary Division.	*Science Division.*
Brown, David.	Paul, John.
Mangan, Denis.	Harrison, Thomas J.
Downard, Thomas.	Clements, Robert W.
Deans, John.	Hynes, Mortimer.
	O'Dea, Martin.
	Moran, John.

SECOND YEAR.

Literary Division.	*Science Division.*
Mahon, John S.	Kane, Thomas.
Beattie, Robert A.	Burkitt, James P.
Boyd, James.	Keenan, John F.
Hunter, Charles H.	Forbes, William J.
Gilchrist, Andrew.	Deans, William.

FIRST YEAR.

Literary Division.	*Science Division.*
O'Hara, Charles H.	M'Clelland, John A.
Rooney, John W.	Bright, James.
Walker, William.	Hayes, John C.
Caldwell, John.	M'Hugh, Patrick.
Keegan, David M.	Keillor, William R.

Faculty of Law.

THIRD YEAR.
Muldoon, John.

SECOND YEAR.
M'Connell, John K., B.A.

FIRST YEAR.
Leitch, Andrew C.

Faculty of Medicine.

SENIOR SCHOLARSHIP.

Anatomy and Physiology, ... Adams, John A., B.A.

FOURTH YEAR.

Kelly, Thomas B. | Heaney, James H.

THIRD YEAR.

Foley, Charles H. | Costello, Michael J. B.

SECOND YEAR.

Connolly, Thomas J. | Clements, Joseph A.

FIRST YEAR.

Literary Division. | *Science Division.*
Boyd, William. | Moran, Michael.

School of Engineering.

THIRD YEAR.

Raddin, George H.

SECOND YEAR.

Mahon, Arthur P. | Binns, Edmund T.

FIRST YEAR.

Emerson, Thomas. | Stuart, William.

SESSION 1890-91.

Faculty of Arts.

SENIOR SCHOLARSHIPS.

Ancient Classics, ...	Mangan, Denis, B.A.
Modern Languages and Modern History, ..	Moran, John.
Mathematics, ...	Paul, John, B.A.
Natural Philosophy, ...	Gannon, William J., B.A.
Metaphysical and Economic Science, ..	Downard, Thomas, B.A.
Chemistry, ...	Hynes, Mortimer.
Natural History, ...	Connolly, Thomas J.

SENIOR EXHIBITION.

Ancient Classics, ...	Browne, David.

JUNIOR SCHOLARSHIPS.

THIRD YEAR.

Literary Division.	*Science Division.*
Mahon, John S.	Kane, Thomas.
Beattie, Robert A.	Burkitt, James P.
Boyd, James.	Keenan, John F.
Hunter, Charles H.	Forbes, William J.
Gilchrist, Andrew.	Deans, William.

SECOND YEAR.

Literary Division.	*Science Division.*
O'Hara, Charles H.	M'Clelland, John A.
Keegan, David M.	Hayes, John C.
Beatty, John.	Rutledge, Andrew.
Stuart, James.	M'Cay, Daniel.
	Lundy, Joseph.

FIRST YEAR.

Literary Division.	*Science Division.*
Mac Gregor, William.	Anderson, Henry.
Barniville, Richard T.	Burke, William.
Sloane, John.	Stewart, John.
M'Ilwaine, Robert.	Henry, John.
Walker, Andrew J.	Ewing, William H.

Faculty of Law.

THIRD YEAR.
M'Connell, John K., B.A.

SECOND YEAR.
Leitch, Andrew C.

FIRST YEAR.
Conroy, John C.

Faculty of Medicine.

SENIOR SCHOLARSHIP.

Anatomy and Physiology, ... Kelly, Thomas B.

FOURTH YEAR.

Costello, Michael J. B. | Foley, Charles H.

THIRD YEAR.

Allen, Robert. | Baile, Richard.

SECOND YEAR.

Clements, Robert W. | M'Donnell, Edward De M.

FIRST YEAR.

Literary Division. | *Science Division.*
Turkington, Humphrey. | Daly, John J.

School of Engineering.

THIRD YEAR.

Mahon, Arthur P.

SECOND YEAR.

Emerson, Thomas.

FIRST YEAR.

Brady, Thomas T. | Thornton, Martin.

SESSION 1891-92.

Faculty of Arts.
SENIOR SCHOLARSHIPS.

Ancient Classics, ... Mahon, John S., B.A.
Modern Languages and Modern History, .. Emerson, Thomas, B.A.
Mathematics, ... Burkitt, James P., B.A.
Metaphysical and Economic Science, ... Gilchrist, Andrew, B.A.
Chemistry, ... Keenan, John F.
Natural History, ... Downard, Thomas, B.A.

JUNIOR SCHOLARSHIPS.
THIRD YEAR.

Literary Division.
O'Hara, Charles H.
Keegan, David M.
Beatty, John.
Stuart, James.

Science Division.
M'Clelland, John A.
Hayes, John C.
Rutledge, Andrew.
M'Cay, Daniel.
Lundy, Joseph.

SECOND YEAR.

Literary Division.
Mac Gregor, William.
Walker, William.
M'Ilwaine, Robert.
Barniville, Richard T.
Sloane, John.
Rutledge, John G.
Walker, Andrew J.

Science Division.
Henry, John.
Ewing, William H.
Wilson, David.

FIRST YEAR.

Literary Division.
Flack, William T.
Hanna, Robert K.
Bell, William H.
Naughton, Owen.
M'Cay, Charles.

Science Division.
Stuart, Thomas.
Montgomery, Alexander W.
Bright, John S.
Henry, Moses.
Mallagh, Joseph.

Faculty of Law.
THIRD YEAR.
Leitch, Andrew C.
SECOND YEAR.
Conroy, John C.
FIRST YEAR.
Macnamara, Michael A.

Faculty of Medicine.

SENIOR SCHOLARSHIP.

Anatomy and Physiology,   ..   Bunton, Christopher L. W., M.B.

FOURTH YEAR.
Allen, Robert.

THIRD YEAR.
Clements, Joseph A. | Hynes, Mortimer.

SECOND YEAR.
Carroll, William S. | Moran, Michael.

FIRST YEAR.
Literary Division. | *Science Division.*
Kirwan, James St. L. | Rooney, John W.

School of Engineering.

THIRD YEAR.
Binns, Edmund T.

SECOND YEAR
Stewart, William. | Gallagher, Stephen G.

FIRST YEAR.
Clements, Samuel D., B.A.

SESSION 1892–93.

Faculty of Arts.

SENIOR SCHOLARSHIPS.

Ancient Classics, ...	Hunter, Charles H.
Modern Languages and Modern History,	O'Hara, Charles H.
Mathematics, ...	Hayes, John C., B.A.
Natural Philosophy, ...	M'Clelland, John A., B.A.
Metaphysical and Economic Science,	Glendenning, James P.C., B.A.
Natural History, ...	Clements, Robert W., B.A.

JUNIOR SCHOLARSHIPS.

THIRD YEAR.

Literary Division.

Mac Gregor, William.
Walker, William.
M'Ilwaine, Robert.
Barniville, Richard T.
Sloane, John.
Rutledge, John G.
Walker, Andrew J.

Science Division.

Henry, John.
Ewing, William H.
Wilson, David.

SECOND YEAR.

Literary Division.

Entrican, Samuel W.
Flack, William T.
Hanna, Robert K.
Scott, Frederick S.
M'Cay, Charles.

Science Division.

Bright, John S.
Thompson, William L.
Thornton, Martin.

FIRST YEAR.

Literary Division.

Mills, John A.
Kernaghan, Thomas W.
Neilson, Robert A.
M'Elfatrick, Thomas A.
Hewitt, Alfred G.

Science Division.

Johnston, James.
Maybin, Hugh.
Ryan, Hugh.

Faculty of Law.

THIRD YEAR.
Conroy, John C.

SECOND YEAR.
Macnamara, Michael A.

FIRST YEAR.
Caldwell, John.

Faculty of Medicine.

SENIOR SCHOLARSHIP.

Anatomy and Physiology, ... Connolly, Thomas J., B.A.

FOURTH YEAR.

Clements, Joseph A. | Lyden, Martin F.

THIRD YEAR.

Downard, Thomas, B.A. | Nixon, John C.

SECOND YEAR.

Kirwan, James St. L. | Threlfall, Richard B.

FIRST YEAR.

Literary Division. | *Science Division.*
Montgomery, Alexander W. Nicholson, William.

School of Engineering.

THIRD YEAR.

M'Cay, Daniel.

SECOND YEAR.

Slade, Cecil A.

FIRST YEAR.

Vance, James W. | Howley, Richard J.

SESSION 1893-94.

Faculty of Arts.

SENIOR SCHOLARSHIPS.

Ancient Classics, ...	MacGregor, William, B.A.
Modern Languages and Modern History, ..	M'Ilwaine, Robert, B.A.
Mathematics, ...	M'Clelland, John A., M.A.
Natural Philosophy, ...	Henry, John, B.A.
Metaphysical and Economic Science, ..	Curry, Samuel, B.A.
Chemistry, ...	Walker, Andrew J.
Natural History, ...	Nixon, John C., B.A.

JUNIOR SCHOLARSHIPS.

THIRD YEAR.

Literary Division.
Entrican, Samuel W.
Flack, William T.
Hanna, Robert K.
Scott, Frederick S.
M'Cay, Charles.

Science Division.
Bright, John S.
Thompson, William L.
Thornton, Martin.

SECOND YEAR.

Literary Division.
Johnston, James.
Mills, John A.
Neilson, Robert A.
Kernaghan, Thomas W.
Bell, William H.

Science Division.
Stuart, Thomas.
Ryan, Hugh.
Burke, William.
Maybin, Hugh.

FIRST YEAR.

Literary Division.
Reid, John.
Norris, Joseph.
Brown, Henry.
Strain, James K. C.
Roberts, Joseph A.

Science Division.
Moody, James.
Watt, George.
Lyons, Frederick W.
M'Kinley, David.
Orr, William R.

Faculty of Law.

THIRD YEAR.
Macnamara, Michael A.

SECOND YEAR.
Rice, James P.

FIRST YEAR.
M'Auliffe, Michael J.

Faculty of Medicine.

SENIOR SCHOLARSHIP.

Anatomy and Physiology, ...   Allen, Robert, M.B.

FOURTH YEAR.
Downard, Thomas, B.A.

THIRD YEAR.
O'Malley, John F. | M'Manus, Michael.

SECOND YEAR.
Montgomery, Alexander W. | M'Kelvey, Thomas.

FIRST YEAR.
Literary Division. | *Science Division.*
Waters, Joseph J. | Paisley, William.

School of Engineering.

THIRD YEAR.
Walker, William.

SECOND YEAR.
Wilson, David. | Howley, Richard.

FIRST YEAR.
Carmichael, John S.

SESSION 1894-95.

Faculty of Arts.

SENIOR SCHOLARSHIPS.

Ancient Classics, ...	Entrican, Samuel W., B.A.
Special Prize, ..	Flack, William T., B.A.
Modern Languages and Modern History,	Hanna, Robert K., B.A.
Natural Philosophy, ...	Walker, William, B.A.
Metaphysical and Economic Science, ..	Keegan, David M., B.A.
Special Prize, ...	Mac Gregor, William, M.A
Chemistry, ...	Nixon, John C., B.A.
Natural History, ...	Montgomery, Alexander W

JUNIOR SCHOLARSHIPS.

THIRD YEAR.

Literary Division.	*Science Division.*
Johnston, James.	Stuart, Thomas.
Mills, John A.	Ryan, Hugh.
Neilson, Robert A.	Burke, William.
Kernaghan, Thomas W.	Maybin, Hugh.
Bell, William H.	

SECOND YEAR.

Literary Division.	*Science Division.*
Reid, John.	Carmichael, John S.
Brown, Henry.	Lyons, Frederick W.
Strain, James K. C.	Moody, James.
M'Lean, Robert J.	Watt, George.
Farley, William J.	

FIRST YEAR.

Literary Division.	*Science Division.*
Hezlett, James M.	Rishworth, Frank S.
Curry, David S.	Hallidy, Robert J.
Fleming, George H.	Mills, William S.
Walker, Cuthbert F.	O'Dea, Simon.
Scott, Ernest F.	O'Flaherty, John F. M.

Faculty of Law.

SECOND YEAR.

Rutledge, John G., M.A.

FIRST YEAR.

M'Ilwaine, Robert, M.A.

Faculty of Medicine.

SENIOR SCHOLARSHIP.

Anatomy and Physiology, ... Allen, Robert, M.B.

FOURTH YEAR.

O'Malley, John F. | M'Manus, Michael.

THIRD YEAR.

Henry, Moses. | Corry, John G. } *equal.*
Keenan, John F., B.A. } *equal.*

SECOND YEAR.

Paisley, William. | Hewitt, Alfred J.

FIRST YEAR.

Literary Division. | *Science Division.*
Keogh, William M. P. | Kerans, George C. L.

School of Engineering.

THIRD YEAR.
Wilson, David.

FIRST YEAR.
Gaston, James.

The Blayney Exhibition.

In Classics.

Johnston, James. | Mills, John A. (*proxime accessit*).

SESSION 1895-96.

Faculty of Arts.

SENIOR SCHOLARSHIPS.

Ancient Classics, ...	Mills, John A.
Mathematics, ...	Stuart, Thomas, B.A.
Natural Philosophy, ...	Maybin, Hugh, B.A.
Metaphysical and Economic Science, ...	*Johnston, James, B.A.
Chemistry, ...	Ryan, Hugh, B.A.
Natural History, ...	Neilson, Robert A.
Special Prize, ...	Clarke, John Andrew.

JUNIOR SCHOLARSHIPS.

THIRD YEAR.

Literary Division.	*Science Division.*
Reid, John.	Carmichael, John S.
Brown, Henry.	Lyons, Frederick W.
Strain, James K. C.	Moody, James.
M'Lean, Robert J.	Watt, George.
Farley, William J.	

SECOND YEAR.

Literary Division.	*Science Division.*
Hezlett, James M.	Rishworth, Frank S.
Watson, John.	†Hezlett, James M.
Walker, Cuthbert F.	Mills, William S.
Curry, David S.	Gaston, James.
Scott, Ernest F.	

FIRST YEAR.

Literary Division.	*Science Division.*
Booth, Samuel.	M'Lean, Andrew H.
Bailey, Alexander T.	Ebbitt, Richard.
Best, Robert.	Whitton, Joseph.
O'Hara, Valentine.	

Faculty of Law.

SENIOR EXHIBITION.
M'Namara, Michael J.

JUNIOR SCHOLARSHIPS.

THIRD YEAR.	SECOND YEAR.	FIRST YEAR.
Rutledge, John G., M.A.	MacGregor, William, M.A.	Jones, James, M.A.

---

* Has gained an open Exhibition in Modern History at Merton Coll., Oxford.

† Ineligible, having obtained Scholarship in other division. Awarded a Special Prize.

Faculty of Medicine.

SENIOR SCHOLARSHIP.

Anatomy and Physiology, .. Montgomery, Alexander W., B.A.

JUNIOR SCHOLARSHIPS.

FOURTH YEAR.
Carbery, Edward O. B.

SECOND YEAR.

Keogh, William M. P. | Kerans, George C. L.

FIRST YEAR.
Science Division.

Cawley, Patrick T. | Anderson, Joseph G.

School of Engineering.

SECOND YEAR.
Pearson, James D.

FIRST YEAR.
Fleming, George H.

The Blayney Exhibition.

In Classics. | *In Science.*
Reid, John. | Carmichael, John S.

SESSION 1896–97.

Faculty of Arts.

SENIOR SCHOLARSHIPS.

Ancient Classics, ...	Reid, John.
Special Prize, ...	Kernaghan, Thomas W., B.A.
Mathematics, ...	Lyons, Frederick W., B.A.
Natural Philosophy, ...	Ryan, Hugh, B.A.
Metaphysical and Economic Science, ..	Strain, James K. C., B.A.
Natural History, ...	Mills, John A.

JUNIOR SCHOLARSHIPS.

THIRD YEAR.

Literary Division.	*Science Division.*
Hezlett, James M.	‡ Rishworth, Frank S.
Watson, John.	† Hezlett, James.
Walker, Cuthbert F.	Mills, William S.
Currie, David S.	Gaston, James.
Scott, Ernest F.	

SECOND YEAR.

Literary Division.	*Science Division.*
Booth, Samuel.	Hallidy, Robert J.
Barr, Andrew.	M'Lean, Andrew H.
Best, Robert.	
Bailey, Alexander T.	
O'Hara, Valentine.	

FIRST YEAR.

Literary Division.	*Science Division.*
* Warnock, William.	* Warnock, William.
Clarke, Margaret.	Perry, Samuel.
Simpson, William A.	Renshaw, John W.
Aimers, Margaret M.	Moore, William I.
† Renshaw, John W.	Brennan, Thomas. } equal.
Bodkin, Leo F.	Mann, Samuel. } equal.

Faculty of Law.

SENIOR EXHIBITION.
Rutledge, John G., M.A.

---

* Having obtained *First* place in both divisions, retains both Scholarships.
† Ineligible, having obtained Scholarship in other division.
‡ Resigned.

Faculty of Law—*continued.*

JUNIOR SCHOLARSHIPS.

THIRD YEAR.
Mac Gregor, William, M.A.

SECOND YEAR.
Jones, James, M.A.

FIRST YEAR.
Kernaghan, Thomas W., B.A.

Faculty of Medicine.

SENIOR SCHOLARSHIP.

Anatomy and Physiology, ... Paisley, William.

JUNIOR SCHOLARSHIPS.

FOURTH YEAR.

* Paisley, William.	Hewitt, Alfred J.

THIRD YEAR.

Keogh, William M. P.	Neilson, Robert A.

SECOND YEAR.

Cawley, Patrick T.	Anderson, Joseph G.

FIRST YEAR.

Literary Division.	*Science Division.*
Walsh, Thomas.	Sandys, William A. } *equal.* Clements, John.

School of Engineering.

THIRD YEAR.
Carmichael, John S.

SECOND YEAR.

Fleming, George H.	Rishworth, Frank S.

The Blayney Exhibition.

Classics, ... Hezlett, James.

* Resigned.

SESSION 1897-98.

Faculty of Arts.

SENIOR SCHOLARSHIPS.

Ancient Classics, ...	Farley, William J., B.A.
Modern Languages, } .. .. .. Modern History,	Watson, John, B.A.
Natural Philosophy, ...	Hezlett, James M., B.A.
Metaphysical and Economic Science, ..	Curry, David S.
Chemistry, ...	Mills, William S.
Natural History, ...	Scott, Ernest F.

SENIOR EXHIBITION.

Modern Language and Modern History, .. Walker, Cuthbert F., B.A.

JUNIOR SCHOLARSHIPS.

THIRD YEAR.

Literary Division.	*Science Division.*
Barr, Andrew.	Walsh, Thomas.
Booth, Samuel.	Hallidy, Robert J.
Bailey, Alexander T.	McLean, Andrew H.
Clarke, John A.	

SECOND YEAR.

Literary Division.	*Science Division.*
* Warnock, William.	* Warnock, William.
Clarke, Margaret.	Moore, William I.
Aimers, Margaret M.	Mann, Samuel.
Simpson, William A.	Renshaw, John W.
Bodkin, Leo F.	

FIRST YEAR.

Literary Division.	*Science Division.*
* Strain, Thomas G.	* Strain, Thomas G.
Williams, William J.	Cummins, Robert J.
McCausland, Joseph.	Hall, John.
O'Gorman, Andrew.	Bailey, Robert.
O'Flynn, Michael J.	

SCHOLARS.

Faculty of Law.

SENIOR EXHIBITION.

MacGregor, William, M.A., LL.B.

---

* Having obtained *First* place in both divisions, retains both Scholarships.

JUNIOR SCHOLARSHIPS.

SECOND YEAR.

John T. Monahan.

Faculty of Medicine.

SENIOR EXHIBITION.

Anatomy and Physiology, ... Hewitt, Alfred J.

JUNIOR SCHOLARSHIPS.

FOURTH YEAR.

Kerans, George C. L.

THIRD YEAR.

Cawley, Patrick T. | Anderson, Joseph G.

SECOND YEAR.

* Walsh, Thomas. | Sandys, William A.
Richards, Henry E. S. |

FIRST YEAR.

Literary Division. | *Science Division.*
† Forde, Dudley. | Forde, Dudley.
Dee, James. |

School of Engineering.

JUNIOR SCHOLARSHIPS.

THIRD YEAR.
Rishworth, Frank S.

SECOND YEAR..
Whitton, Joseph.

FIRST YEAR.
Emerson, Richard G.
Hamilton, Thomas.

The Blayney Exhibition.

Science, ... McLean, Andrew H.

---

* Ineligible, having obtained an Arts Scholarship of the Third Year
Science Division.
† Ineligible, having obtained a Scholarship in the Science Division.

SESSION 1898–99.

Faculty of Arts.

SENIOR SCHOLARSHIPS.

Ancient Classics, ... Booth, Samuel.
Natural Philosophy, ... M'Lean, Andrew H.
Natural History, ... Walsh, Thomas.

JUNIOR SCHOLARSHIPS.

THIRD YEAR.

Literary Division.	*Science Division.*
Rea, Thomas.	Moore, William I.
Clarke, Margaret.	Whitton, Joseph.
Aimers, Margaret M.	
* Simpson, William A.	

SECOND YEAR.

Literary Division.	*Science Division.*
†Strain, Thomas G.	†Strain, Thomas G.
M'Causland, Joseph.	Perry, Samuel.
Williams, William J.	Hall, John.
M'Grath, Edward H.	
O'Gorman, Andrew.	
O'Flynn, Michael J.	

FIRST YEAR.

Literary Division.	*Science Division.*
Warnock, James.	Cole, James A.
Porterfield, Samuel. } *equal.*	‡ Warnock, James.
O'Neill, Joseph J.	M'Lachlan, Robert B.
Lydon, Patrick J.	
M'Feeters, Robert J.	
Daly, Emily D. M.	
M'Conaghy, John.	
Gailey, William.	

Faculty of Law.

JUNIOR SCHOLARSHIPS.

FIRST YEAR.

Bodkin, Leo F.

---

* Ineligible, having obtained a Medical Scholarship of the First Year —Science Division.

† Having obtained *First* place in both divisions, retains both Scholarships.

‡ Ineligible, having obtained a Scholarship in the Literary Division.

Faculty of Medicine.

SENIOR SCHOLARSHIP.

Anatomy and Physiology, ... Anderson, Joseph G.

JUNIOR SCHOLARSHIPS.

FOURTH YEAR.

* Anderson, Joseph G. | Mills, John A., B.A.

THIRD YEAR.

Richards, Henry E. S. | Scott, Ernest F.

SECOND YEAR.

Warnock, William. | Best, Robert.

FIRST YEAR.

Literary Division. | *Science Division.*
Burke, Henry J. | Simpson, William A.

School of Engineering.

SENIOR SCHOLARSHIP.

Hall, Arthur A., B.A.

JUNIOR SCHOLARSHIPS.

THIRD YEAR.
Mills, William S., B.A.

SECOND YEAR.

Cummins, Robert J. | Burden, William M'C.

The Blayney Exhibition.

Classics, ... Williams, William J.

---

* Ineligible, having obtained the Senior Scholarship in Anatomy and Physiology.

SESSION 1899-1900.

Faculty of Arts.

SENIOR SCHOLARSHIPS.

Modern Languages and Modern History, ..	Aimers, Margaret M.
Natural Philosophy, ...	Moore, William Irwin, B.A.
Metaphysical and Economic Science, ..	Bodkin, Leo F.
Chemistry, ...	Walsh, Thomas, B.A.
Natural History, ...	Best, Robert.

SENIOR EXHIBITION.

Modern Languages and Modern History, ..	Clarke, Margaret.

JUNIOR SCHOLARSHIPS.

THIRD YEAR.

Literary Division.	*Science Division.*
M'Grath, Edward H.	Strain, Thomas G.
Williams, William J.	Cummins, Robert J.
O'Gorman, Andrew.	

SECOND YEAR.

Literary Division.	*Science Division.*
O'Neill, Joseph J.	Warnock, James.
Porterfield, Samuel.	Cole, James A.
* Warnock, James.	Walsh, Peter.
Lydon, Patrick J.	M'Lachlan, John S.
Lyons, James A.	Ebbitt, Richard W.
Reid, Patrick.	

FIRST YEAR.

Literary Division.	*Science Division.*
Heaslett, George H.	Bell, Gilmore.
Morrison, William J.	Maxwell, George.
Kenny, Patrick J.	Rutherford, Robert G.
Steinberger, Cecil L. M.	* Kenny, Patrick J.
Perry, Margaret.	* Morrison, William J.
	Mullery, Edward W.
	Angus, Samuel.

Faculty of Law.

JUNIOR SCHOLARSHIP.

FIRST YEAR.

M'Mullan, Hugh S., M.A.

---

* Ineligible, having obtained Scholarship in other division.

M

Faculty of Medicine.

SENIOR SCHOLARSHIP IN ANATOMY AND PHYSIOLOGY.
Richards, Henry E. S.

SENIOR EXHIBITION.
Sandys, William A.

JUNIOR SCHOLARSHIPS.

FOURTH YEAR.

*Sandys, William A.	Clements, John.

THIRD YEAR.

Warnock, William.	Forde, Dudley.

SECOND YEAR.

Simpson, William A.	O'Flynn, Michael J.

FIRST YEAR.

Literary Division.	*Science Division.*
Byrne, James.	Flack, James.

School of Engineering.

SENIOR SCHOLARSHIP.
Whitton, Joseph, B.E.

SENIOR EXHIBITION.
Hardiman, James C.

JUNIOR SCHOLARSHIPS.

THIRD YEAR.

†Cummins, Robert J.	Mann, Samuel.

SECOND YEAR.

O'Hara, Donald J.	Mairs, William C.

FIRST YEAR.

Roseingrave, Thomas W.	Rutledge, Patrick V.

The "Blayney" Exhibition.
Science, ... Strain, Thomas G.

The "Dr. and Mrs. W. A. Browne" Scholarship.
Steinberger, Cecil L. M

The answering of Mr. Edward H. M'Grath was very favourably reported on by the Examiner.

---

* Ineligible, having obtained a Senior Exhibition.
† Ineligible, having obtained a Scholarship in Arts of the Third Year (Science Division).

SESSION 1900-1901.

Faculty of Arts.

SENIOR SCHOLARSHIPS.

English, Modern Languages, and Modern History, ...	Rea, Thomas, M.A.
Metaphysics and Political Science, ..	Williams, William J.
Natural History, ...	M'Causland, Joseph.

SENIOR EXHIBITIONS.

Ancient Classics, ...	O'Gorman, Andrew.
English, Modern Languages, and Modern History, ...	M'Grath, Edward H.

JUNIOR SCHOLARSHIPS.

THIRD YEAR.

Literary Division.	*Science Division.*
O'Neill, Joseph J.	Warnock, James.
Lydon, Patrick J.	M'Lachlan, Robert B.
Reid, Patrick.	Flack, James. ⎱ equal.
	Hall, John. ⎰
	Cole, James A.

SECOND YEAR.

Literary Division.	*Science Division.*
Angus, Samuel.	Bell, Gilmore.
Steinberger, Cecil L. M.	Rutherford, Robert J.
Kenny, Patrick J.	
Perry, Margaret.	
Brash, Robert.	
Morrison, William J.	

FIRST YEAR.

Literary Division.	*Science Division.*
Thompson, Frances L.	Perry, Agnes M.
Minnis, Samuel.	Clarke, Rosalind.
*Clarke, Rosalind.	Compton, Arthur J. W.
O'Brien, Michael.	Philpott, Nicholas C.
Walsh, Patrick M.	*O'Brien, Michael.
	Duncan, Robert M.

---

* Ineligible, having obtained Scholarship in other division.

M 2

Faculty of Law.

JUNIOR SCHOLARSHIP.

FIRST YEAR.

Turner, Alexander K.

Faculty of Medicine.

SENIOR SCHOLARSHIP.

Anatomy and Physiology.—Walsh, Thomas, B.A.

JUNIOR SCHOLARSHIPS.

THIRD YEAR.

Simpson, William A.	O'Flynn, Michael J.

SECOND YEAR.

Porterfield, Samuel.	Shanklin, John G.

FIRST YEAR.

Literary Division.	*Science Division.*
Cusack, Patrick J.	Byrne, Francis P.

School of Engineering.

SENIOR SCHOLARSHIP.

Cummins, Robert J., B.E.

JUNIOR SCHOLARSHIPS.

THIRD YEAR.

Mairs, William C.

SECOND YEAR.

M'Lachlan, John S.	Moore, John A.

FIRST YEAR.

Watson, Edwin.

The "Blayney" Exhibition.

O'Neill, Joseph J.

The "Dr. and Mrs. W. A. Browne" Scholarship.

Steinberger, Cecil L. M.

SESSION 1901–1902.

Faculty of Arts.

SENIOR SCHOLARSHIPS.

English and Modern Languages, ..	O'Neill, Joseph J., B.A.
Mathematics, ...	Cole, James A., B.A.
Natural Philosophy, ...	Warnock, James, B.A.
Chemistry, ...	M'Causland, Joseph, B.A.
Natural History, ...	Byrne, James.

SENIOR EXHIBITION.

English and Modern Languages, .. Lydon, Patrick J.

JUNIOR SCHOLARSHIPS.

THIRD YEAR.

Literary Division.
Angus, Samuel.
Steinberger, Cecil L. M.
Perry, Margaret.
Lyons, James A.
Kenny, Patrick J.

Science Division.
Walsh, Peter.
Brash, Robert.
Maxwell, George.
Bell, Gilmore.

SECOND YEAR.

Literary Division.
Minnis, Samuel.
Thompson, Frances L.

Science Division.
Perry, Agnes M.
Clarke, Rosalind.
Compton, Arthur J. W.
Duncan, Robert M.

FIRST YEAR.

Literary Division.
May, Thomas.
M'Clean, Louis T. L.
Brash, Janet W.
*Lynham, John E. A.
Moon, Katie.

Science Division.
Lynham, John E. A.
Compton, Samuel J. M.
Forsythe, John.

* Ineligible, having obtained Scholarship in other division.

Faculty of Law.
JUNIOR SCHOLARSHIPS.
SECOND YEAR.
Turner, Alexander K.

FIRST YEAR.
Cusack, Patrick J.

Faculty of Medicine.
JUNIOR SCHOLARSHIPS.
FOURTH YEAR.
Simpson, William A.
THIRD YEAR.

Porterfield, Samuel.	Flack, James.

SECOND YEAR.

Dowling, John.	Flack, Isaac.

FIRST YEAR.

Literary Division.	*Science Division.*
Dunlop, John L.	Carson, William F. A.

School of Engineering.
SENIOR SCHOLARSHIP.
Mairs, William C.
JUNIOR SCHOLARSHIP.
THIRD YEAR.
M'Lachlan, John S.
SECOND YEAR.

Watson, Edwin.	M'Lachlan, Robert B.

FIRST YEAR.

Montagu, Cuthbert F.	Smith, Henry W. S.

The "Blayney" Exhibition.
Perry, Agnes M.

The "Dr and Mrs. W. A. Browne" Scholarships.
Steinberger, Cecil L. M.

SESSION 1902-1908.

Faculty of Arts.

SENIOR SCHOLARSHIPS.

Ancient Classics, ...	Angus, Samuel, B.A.
English and Modern Languages, ...	Steinberger, Cecilia L. M., B.A.
Mathematics, ...	Maxwell, George.
Metaphysics, Political Science, and History,	Lydon, Patrick J., B.A.
Chemistry, ...	Brash, Robert.

SENIOR PRIZE.

Ancient Classics, ...	Kenny, Patrick J.

JUNIOR SCHOLARSHIPS.

THIRD YEAR.

Literary Division.	*Science Division.*
Minnis, Samuel.	Perry, Agnes M.
Thompson, Frances L.	Clarke, Rosalind.
Eakin, Mary D.	M'Crea, Robert A. M. L.

SECOND YEAR.

Literary Division.	*Science Division.*
Brash, Janet W.	Lynham, John E. A.
O'Brien, Michael.	Watson, Edwin.
M'Clean, Louis T. L.	Harrison, Alexander L.
Forsythe, John.	Hannigan, James J.
* Harrison, Alexander L.	

FIRST YEAR.

Literary Division.	*Science Division.*
Matthews, William D. W.	Fogarty, Philip C.
* M'Donagh, Stephen J.	M'Donagh, Stephen J.
Perry, Janet H.	Perry, Alice J.
Rentoul, Gervais S. C.	Brash, George T.
Henry, Rachel J. L.	M'Cleery, Ernest F.
Lynham, Lilian E. M.	

Faculty of Law.

JUNIOR SCHOLARSHIPS.

SECOND YEAR.

Cusack, Patrick J.

FIRST YEAR.

Lynch, John B.

---

* Ineligible, having obtained Scholarship in other division.

Faculty of Medicine.

SENIOR SCHOLARSHIP.

Anatomy and Physiology, ... Porterfield, Samuel, B.A.

JUNIOR SCHOLARSHIPS.

FOURTH YEAR.

Shanklin, John G. | Flack, James.

THIRD YEAR.

Flack, Isaac. | Dowling, John.

SECOND YEAR.

Gannon, James J. A. | Dunlop, John L.

FIRST YEAR.

Literary Division. | *Science Division.*
Dagg, Christina M. C. | Garry, John W.

School of Engineering.

SENIOR SCHOLARSHIP.

M'Lachlan, John S., B.A.

JUNIOR SCHOLARSHIPS.

THIRD YEAR.

M'Lachlan, Robert B.

SECOND YEAR.

Duncan, Robert M. | Montagu, Cuthbert F. } *equal.*
| Smith, Henry W. S. }

FIRST YEAR.

May, Thomas. | Hickson, Robert C.

The "Blayney" Exhibition.

Thompson, Frances L.

The "Dr. and Mrs. W. A. Browne" Scholarship.

Minnis, Samuel.

LIST OF PRIZES AWARDED AT THE SESSIONAL EXAMINATIONS IN THE SESSION 1901–1902.

Faculty of Arts.

FIRST YEAR.

Latin,	..	..	..	First Rank { Thomas May. / Louis T. L. M'Clean.
,,	..	..	..	Second Rank Janet W. Brash.
,,	..	..	..	,, ,, John E. A. Lynham.
Greek,	..	..	..	First Rank Louis T. L. M'Clean.
,,	..	..	..	Second Rank John Forsythe.
French,	..	..	..	First Rank Janet W. Brash.
,,	..	..	..	Second Rank John A. E. Lynham.
German,	..	..	..	First Rank Janet W. Brash.
English,	..	..	..	,, ,, John E. A. Lynham.
,,	..	..	..	,, ,, Thomas May.
,,	..	..	..	Second Rank Louis T. L. M'Clean.
Matematics,	..	..		First Rank John E. A. Lynham.
,,	..	..	•	,, ,, Samuel J. M. Compton.
Experimental Physics,	..			,, ,, Thomas May.
,,	,,	..		Second Rank Samuel J. M. Compton.

SECOND YEAR.

Latin,	..	..	..	First Rank Samuel Minnis.
,,	..	..	..	,, ,, Frances L. Thompson.
Greek,	..	..	..	,, ,, Frances L. Thompson.
French,	..	..	..	,, ,, Samuel Minnis.
,,	..	..	..	Second Rank Agnes M. Perry.
,,	..	..	..	,, ,, Rosalind Clarke.
German,	..	..	..	First Rank Samuel Minnis.
English,	..	..	..	,, ,, Samuel Minnis.
,,	..	..	..	,, ,, Frances L. Thompson.
Mathematics,	..	..		,, ,, Agnes M. Perry.
,,	..	..		Second Rank Rosalind Clarke.
Experimental Physics,	..			First Rank Arthur J. W. Compton.
,,	,,	..		Second Rank Agnes M. Perry.
,,	,,	..		,, ,, Rosalind Clarke.
Logic,	..	..	..	First Rank Samuel Minnis.
,,	..	..	..	Second Rank James Z. Sloan.
Practical Physics,	..			First Rank) Agnes M. Perry.
,,	,,	..		Second Rank Arthur J. W. Compton.
Chemistry,	..	..	..	First Rank Rosalind Clarke.
,,	..	..	..	,, ,, { Robert A. M. L. M'Crea. / Robert M. Duncan.
,,	(Laboratory Class),	..		,, ,, Rosalind Clarke.
,,	,,	,,		Second Rank Agnes M. Perry.
Mathematical Physics,	..			First Rank Agnes M. Perry.

Third Year.

Latin,	.. .. ..	First Rank	Samuel Angus.
Greek,	.. .. ..	,, ,,	Samuel Angus.
French,	.. .. ..	,, ,,	Margaret Perry.
German,	.. .. ..	,, ,,	Margaret Perry.
English,	.. .. ..	Second Rank	Margaret Perry.
Mathematics,	.. ..	,, ,,	Robert Brash.
,,	.. .. ..	,, ,,	Peter Walsh.
Experimental Physics,	..	,, ,,	Robert Brash.
Physiology,	.. ..	,, ,,	Peter Walsh.
Natural History,	.. ..	First Rank	Peter Walsh.
Practical Biology,	..	Second Rank	Peter Walsh.

Postgraduate.

French,	.. .. ..	First Rank	{ Edward H. M'Grath. / Joseph J. O'Neill.
German,	.. .. ..	,, ,,	Edward H. M'Grath.
English,	.. .. ..	,, ,,	Joseph J. O'Neill.
,,	.. .. ..	Second Rank	Edward H. M'Grath.
Mathematical Physics,	..	First Rank	James A. Cole.

Faculty of Law.

First Year.

English Law,	.. ..	Second Rank	Henry G. Connolly.

Second Year.

English Law,	.. ..	First Rank	Alex. K. Turner.
Civil Law,	.. ..	Second Rank	Alex. K. Turner.

Faculty of Medicine.

First Year.

Chemistry,	.. ..	First Rank	James J. A. Gannon.
,,	.. .. ..	,, ,,	William F. A. Carson.
,,	.. .. ..	Second Rank	Joseph M. A. Costello.
,,	.. .. ..	,, ,,	William T. Henderson.
Anatomy,	.. .. ..	First Rank	John L. Dunlop.
,,	.. .. ..	Second Rank	William F. A. Carson.
Natural Philosophy,	..	,, ,,	James J. A. Gannon.
Practical Biology,	..	First Rank	Joseph M. A. Costello.
,, ,,	..	Second Rank	John L. Dunlop.
Zoology,	.. ..	,, ,,	{ James J. A. Gannon. / John L. Dunlop.
French,	.. .. ..	First Rank	Richd. G. C. M. Kinkead.
,,	.. .. ..	Second Rank	William F. A. Carson.

SECOND YEAR.

Chemistry,	.. ..	First Rank	{ Patrick Reid.
			James Warnock.
	.. ..	Second Rank	John Dowling.
Materia Medica,	.. ..	,, ,,	Paul J. O'Flynn.
Anatomy, ..	.. ..	First Rank	Patrick Reid.
,,	.. ..	,, ,,	Paul J. O'Flynn.
Physiology,	.. ..	,, ,,	James Warnock.
,,	.. ..	Second Rank	John Dowling.

THIRD YEAR.

Medicine, ..	.. ..	First Rank	Samuel Porterfield.
,,	.. .. ..	Second Rank	James Flack.
,,	.. .. ..	,, ,,	John G. Shanklin.
Surgery, ..	.. ..	,, ,,	James Byrne.
,,	.. .. ..	,, ,,	Samuel Porterfield.
Anatomy, ..	.. ..	,, ,,	John G. Shanklin.
Physiology,	.. ..	,, ,,	Samuel Porterfield.
Medical Jurisprudence,	..	First Rank	Frederick J. Cairns.

FOURTH YEAR.

Midwifery,	.. ..	First Rank	William A. Simpson
Medical Jurisprudence,	..	,, ,,	William A. Simpson.

School of Engineering.

FIRST YEAR.

Engineering,	.. ..	First Rank	Henry W. S. Smith.
,,	.. .. ..	,, ,,	Cuthbert F. Montagu.
,,	.. .. ..	,, ,,	Robert C. Dick.
,,	.. .. ..	,, ,,	Robert M. Duncan.
Drawing, ..	.. ..	,, ,,	Cuthbert F. Montagu.
,,	.. .. ..	Second Rank	Robert M. Duncan.
,,	. .. ..	,, ,,	Robert C. Dick.
Chemistry,	.. ..	First Rank	{ Cuthbert F. Montagu.
			Robert C. Dick.
,,	.. ..	Second Rank	Henry W. S. Smith.
Mathematics,	.. ..	First Rank	Cuthbert F. Montagu.
Practical Physics,	..	,, ,,	Robert M. Duncan.
,, ,, ..	..	Second Rank	Henry W. S. Smith.
Experimental Physics,	..	First Rank	Henry W. S. Smith.
,, ,,	..	Second Rank	Robert C. Dick.

Second Year.

Engineering,	..	..	First Rank	Robert B. M'Lachlan.
,,	..	..	,, ,,	Edwin Watson.
Drawing, ..	..	..	,, ,,	Robert B. M'Lachlan.
,,	..	..	,, ,,	Edwin Watson.
Chemistry,	..	..	,, ,,	Robert B. M'Lachlan.
,,	..	..	,, ,,	Edwin Watson.
Mathematics,	..	..	,, ,,	Edwin Watson.
,,	..	..	Second Rank	Robert B. M'Lachlan.
Mathematical Physics,	..		,, ,,	Edwin Watson.
,, ,,	..		,, ,,	Robert B. M'Lachlan.

Third Year.

Engineering,	..	..	Second Rank	William C. Mairs.
Drawing, ..	..	..	First Rank	William C. Mairs.
,,	..	..	,, ,,	John S. M'Lachlan.
Mineralogy and Geology,			,, ,,	William C. Mairs.

DEGREES, EXHIBITIONS, HONOURS, &c., OB-
TAINED BY STUDENTS OF THE COLLEGE
AT THE EXAMINATIONS OF THE ROYAL
UNIVERSITY OF IRELAND IN 1902.

AUTUMN.

Faculty of Arts.

JUNIOR FELLOWSHIP IN MATHEMATICAL SCIENCE.

Stuart, Thomas, M.A., D.SC.

THE "DR. AND MRS. W. A. BROWNE" GOLD MEDAL AND PRIZE.

Steinberger, Cecilia L. M., B.A. (Sch.).

M.A. DEGREE EXAMINATION.

Honours in Modern Literature.

O'Neill, Joseph J., B.A., ... Second Class.

PASS.

M'Grath, Edward H., B.A.

B.A. DEGREE EXAMINATION.

SUMMER.

PASS.

Curran, Anthony.	M'Lachlan, John S.
Hall, John.	Porterfield, Samuel.
Lyons, James A.	

AUTUMN.

EXHIBITIONS.

Angus, Samuel (Sch.), ... First Class (£42).
Steinberger, Cecilia L. M. (Sch.), .. First Class (£42).

Honours in Ancient Classics.

Angus, Samuel (Sch.), ... First Class.

Honours in Modern Literature.

Steinberger, Cecilia L. M. (Sch.), ... First Class.

PASS.

Lydon, Patrick J.

SECOND UNIVERSITY EXAMINATION.

SUMMER.

EXHIBITIONS.

Minnis, Samuel (Sch.),	.. ..	First Class (£36).
Perry, Agnes M. (Sch.),	... ..	Second Class (£18).

Honours in Latin.

Minnis, Samuel (Sch.), ...   Second Class.

Honours in English.

Minnis, Samuel (Sch.), ...   First Class.

Honours in French.

Minnis, Samuel (Sch.), ...   First Class (First Place).

Honours in German.

Minnis, Samuel (Sch.), ...   First Class (First Place).

Honours in Mathematics.

Perry, Agnes M. (Sch.), ...   Second Class.

Honours in Mathematical Physics.

Perry, Agnes M. (Sch.), ...   Second Class.

PASS.

Clarke, Rosalind.	M'Lachlan, Robert B.
Compton, Arthur J. W.	Moore, John A.
Hannigan, James J.	Thompson, Frances L.
M'Crea, Robert A. M. L.	Walsh, Peter.
M'Farland, William J.	

FIRST UNIVERSITY EXAMINATION.

SUMMER.

EXHIBITIONS.

Lynham, John E. A.,	.. ..	Second Class (£15).
May, Thomas, ..	.. .. ..	Second Class (£15).
Brash, Janet W.,	.. .. ..	Second Class (£15).

Honours in Latin.

May, Thomas,	.. .. ..	Second Class.
Brash, Janet W.,	.. .. ..	Second Class.

Honours in English.

May, Thomas, ...   Second Class.

Honours in German.

Brash, Janet W., ...   First Class.

Honours in Mathematics.

Lynham, John E. A., ...   Second Class.

French.

May, Thomas.

Declared qualified to compete, but did not present himself for the Oral Examination.

PASS.

Compton, Samuel J. M.	Macaulay, John C.
Costello, Joseph M. A.	M'Clean, Louis T. L.
Forsythe, John.	M'Gillycuddy, Henry A.
Hughes, John.	Moon, Katie.
Johnston, Georgina.	O'Sullivan, Christopher F. X.

AUTUMN.

PASS.

Burke, Joseph D. G.

Faculty of Medicine.

M.B., B.CH., B.A.O. DEGREE EXAMINATION.

SPRING.

PASS.

Clements, John.

AUTUMN.

UPPER PASS.

Warnock, William.

PASS.

Best, Robert.

THIRD EXAMINATION IN MEDICINE.
PASS.
SPRING.

Shanklin, John G.

SECOND EXAMINATION IN MEDICINE.

Spring.

Pass.

Flack, James. | Warnock, James, B.A.

FIRST EXAMINATION IN MEDICINE.

Summer.

Pass.

Dunlop, John L. | Grogan, Patrick J.
Gannon, James A. |

Autumn.

Pass.

Costello, Joseph M. A. | M'Crea, Robert A. M. L.
Henderson, William T. |

School of Engineering.

Summer.

B.E. DEGREE EXAMINATION.

Honours.

Fleming, Samuel H., B.A., ... Second Class.

Pass.

Mairs, William C.

SECOND PROFESSIONAL EXAMINATION.

Exhibition.

M'Lachlan, John S., ... Second Class (£18).

Honours.

M'Lachlan, John S., ... Second Class.

Pass.

Brash, Robert. | Watson, Edwin.
M'Lachlan, Robert B. |

FIRST PROFESSIONAL EXAMINATION.

PASS.

Dale, William.
Dick, Robert C.
Duncan, Robert M.
Hannigan, James J.

Montagu, Cuthbert F.
Moore, John A.
Smith, Henry W. S.

OTHER DISTINCTIONS.

Under-Secretaryship to the Lord Lieutenant of Ireland.

Mac Donnell, Sir Anthony P., D.LIT., K.C.S.I.

An Instructorship in Engineering under the Egyptian Ministry of Education.

Rishworth, Frank S., B.E., B.A.

Assistant County Surveyorship.

Hamilton, Thomas.

O'Hara, Donald J.

Renewal of Science Research Scholarship by H. M. Exhibition (1851) Commissioners.

Mills, William S., M.A.

APPENDIX.

FOR the information of Students, abstracts are here given of the regulations of the Royal University of Ireland; of the University of London, as well as of the Licensing Corporations in Medicine, and of the Honourable Society of King's Inns. The conditions of admission to the Competitive Examinations for certain Home and Foreign appointments are added.

At the end of each abstract, reference is made to the source from which full information may be obtained. Students are reminded that these regulations are subject to frequent change. Care should be taken to consult the latest official rules. These may be referred to in the College Library.

I. Royal University of Ireland.
II. University of London.
III. Royal Colleges of Physicians and Surgeons in Ireland, England, and Scotland.
IV. Regulations prescribed by General Medical Council.
V. Regulations for admission to the Bar.
VI. Inspectorships of National Schools.
VII. County Surveyorships.
VIII. Army, Navy, and Indian Medical Services.
IX. Home Civil Service, Class 1.
X. Civil Service of India, Eastern Cadetships, etc., etc.

I.—ROYAL UNIVERSITY OF IRELAND.

GENERAL REGULATIONS.

The following Degrees and Diplomas are conferred by the University :—

Arts—
Bachelor of Arts, . B.A.
Master of Arts, . M.A.
Doctor of Literature, D.Lit.

Mental and Moral Philosophy—
Doctor of Philosophy, D.Ph.

Science—
Bachelor of Science, . B.Sc.
Doctor of Science, . D.Sc.

Engineering—
A Special Diploma, Dip. in Eng.
Bachelor of Engineering, B.E.
Master of Engineering, M.E.

Music—
Bachelor of Music, . B.Mus.
Doctor of Music, . D.Mus.

Medicine—
Bachelor of Medicine, M.B.
Doctor of Medicine, . M.D.

Surgery—
Bachelor of Surgery, . B.Ch.
Master of Surgery, . M.Ch.

Obstetrics—
Bachelor of Obstetrics, B.A.O.
Master of Obstetrics, M.A.O.

Sanitary Science—
A Special Diploma.

Mental Diseases—
A Special Diploma.

Law—
Bachelor of Laws, . LL.B.
Doctor of Laws, . . LL.D.

Agriculture—
A Special Diploma.

Teaching—
A Special Diploma.

All Degrees, Honours, Exhibitions, Prizes, Scholarships, Studentships, and Junior Fellowships in this University shall be open to Students of either sex.

Candidates for any Degree in this University must have passed the Matriculation Examination. Students from other Universities and Colleges are included in this rule.

MATRICULATION.

(Dublin and Local* Centres.)

Subjects.

I. Latin.
II. Any one of the following Languages:—Greek, French, German, Italian, Spanish, Celtic, Sanskrit, Hebrew, Arabic.
III. English Language and Literature.
IV. Elementary Mathematics.
V. Natural Philosophy.

THE FIRST UNIVERSITY EXAMINATION.

One Academical Year after Matriculation. (Dublin and Local* Centres.)

Subjects.

I. Latin.
II. Any one of the following Languages:—Greek, French, German, Italian, Spanish, Celtic, Sanskrit, Hebrew, Arabic.
III. English Language and Literature.
IV. Mathematics.
V. Natural Philosophy.

---

* There is a Centre in Queen's College, Galway.

Faculty of Arts.

Second University Examination in Arts.

One Academical Year after First University Examination.
(Dublin and Local* Centres).

Subjects.

I. Latin.
II. Greek.
III. English Language and Literature.
IV. Any one of the following Languages:—French, German, Italian, Spanish, Celtic, Sanskrit, Hebrew, Arabic.
V. Logic.
VI. Civil and Constitutional History.
VII. Mathematics.
VIII. Mathematical Physics.
IX. Experimental Physics.
X. Chemistry.
XI. Botany and Zoology.
XII. Geology (including Mineralogy and Physical Geography).

N.B.—Candidates at this Examination must answer in four of the foregoing subjects, one of which must be Latin or Mathematics; but candidates entering for Honours in any subject may, if they choose, present as a fifth subject the Honour Course in any of the remaining eight of the foregoing subjects.

Candidates entering for Honours in any subject and presenting a Modern Language as one of the four obligatory subjects, will be at liberty to present, as a fifth subject, the Honour Course in any other of the Languages mentioned under head IV.

B.A. Degree Examination.

One Academical Year after Second University Examination; held in Dublin only.

Subjects.

I. Latin.
II. Greek.
† III. English and History: or either English or History with any one of the following Languages:—French, German, Italian, Spanish, Celtic, Sanskrit, Hebrew, Arabic.
IV. Logic, and any one of the following:—Metaphysics, Ethics, History of Philosophy, Political Economy.
V. Mathematics.
VI. Mathematical Physics.
VII. Experimental Physics.
VIII. Chemistry.
IX. Physiology.
X. Zoology and Botany.
XI. Geology, including Mineralogy and Physical Geography.

* There is a Centre in Queen's College, Galway.
† Attention is directed to the fact that, to constitute a subject, both English and History require to be supplemented as set forth in III.

Pass.—Candidates who desire a Pass Degree only, must answer in any one of the following groups of subjects, to be selected by them when entering for the Examination:—

A. (1) Latin, (2) Greek, and (3) any one other of the above subjects.*
B. (1) Latin, (2) Logic, Metaphysics, with History of Philosophy, and (3) either Ethics or Political Economy.
C. (1) Mathematics, and (2) (3) two others of the above subjects, one of which must be one of those enumerated under heads VI. to XI.

Honours.—Candidates may obtain the B.A. Degree with Honours in the Honour Courses of any one of the following groups of subjects:—

I. Latin and Greek Languages and Literature.
II. English, and any two of the following Languages:—French, German, Italian, Spanish, Celtic, Sanskrit, Hebrew, Arabic.
III. Logic, Metaphysics, Ethics, and History of Philosophy.
IV. Civil and Constitutional History, Political Economy, and General Jurisprudence.
V. Mathematics and Mathematical Physics.
VI. Mathematical Physics and Experimental Physics.
VII. Any two of the following subjects:—

i. Experimental Physics. iii. Botany and Zoology.
ii. Chemistry. iv. Physiology *or* Geology.

Any Candidate selecting Group III. will be at liberty to substitute for *Ethics* any one of the three subjects included in Group IV.

Any Candidate selecting Group IV. will be at liberty to substitute English for either Political Economy or General Jurisprudence; but only three-fourths of the marks obtained in English will be counted towards Honours and Exhibitions.

At the Examination in Honour groups for the B.A. Degree, Candidates who fail to obtain Honours may be adjudged to have passed the examination for the B.A. Degree, provided their answering nearly approaches the standard at which Honours are awarded.

M.A. DEGREE EXAMINATION.

One Academical Year after B.A.

Candidates at this Examination will be required to answer in any one of the following groups of subjects:—

I. Latin and Greek Languages and Literature.
II. English, and any two of the following Languages:—French, German, Italian, Spanish, Celtic, Sanskrit, Hebrew, Arabic.

* See last foot-note on previous page.

III. Logic, Metaphysics, Ethics, and History of Philosophy.
IV. Civil and Constitutional History, Political Economy, and Political Philosophy.
V. Mathematics and Mathematical Physics.*
VI. Mathematical Physics and Experimental Physics.*
VII. Any two of the following subjects:—

i. Experimental Physics.*   iii. Botany and Zoology.*
ii. Chemistry.*   iv. Physiology *or* Geology.*

Any Candidate selecting Group III. shall be at liberty to substitute for *Ethics* any one of the three subjects included in Group IV.

Any Candidate selecting Group IV. will be at liberty to substitute English, for either Political Economy or Political Philosophy; but only three-fourths of the marks gained in English will be counted towards Honours.

D.Lit. Degree.

Final Examination, three Academical years after B.A.

D.Ph. Degree.

Examination, three Academical years from the time of obtaining the B.A. Degree.

B. Sc. Degree.

Examination, one Academical year from the time of graduating in any Faculty in the University.

D.Sc. Degree.

Examination, three Academical years after Graduation in any Faculty in the University.

Diploma in Teaching.

The Diploma is conferred only on Graduates in Arts of the Royal University,

The Examination consists of two parts : the first part to be passed by Candidates not less than one Academical Year after graduation, and the second part not less than one Academical Year after passing the first part.

---

* All candidates who present themselves at the M.A. Degree Examination in any group of subjects included in the First Part of the Examination for the D.Sc. Degree, shall, if eligible for both the B.Sc. Degree and for the M.A. Degree, specify for which of these Degrees they desire to present themselves ; and they shall be entitled to obtain the Degree only which they so specify.

A. Subjects for the First Part of the Examination :—
  I. Methods of Teaching, School Management and Organisation.
  II. The History of Education ; the Lives and Works of Eminent
    Teachers ; and the Systems of Instruction adopted in
    different Countries.

B. Subjects for the Second Part of the Examination :—
  I. Mental and Moral Science in relation to the work of Teaching.
  II. Practical Skill in Teaching.

Faculty of Law.

There are three Examinations in Law :—
  1. The First Examination in Law.
  2. The Examination for LL.B. Degree.
  3. The Examination for LL.D. Degree.

Candidates in Law must be Graduates in Arts of the University.

Faculty of Medicine.

The Course for the Degrees in Medicine, Surgery, and Obstetrics, shall be of at least five Medical years duration; but Graduates in Arts or Science who shall have spent a year in the study of Physics, Chemistry, and Biology, and have passed an Examination in these subjects for the Degrees in question, shall be held to have completed the first of the five years of Medical Study.

Candidates for Medical Degrees, who began their Medical Studies after January 1st, 1892, must have been registered by Medical Council for 57 months, and must be fully 21 years of age.

All Candidates for these Degrees, in addition to attending the lectures and complying with other conditions prescribed, must pass the following Examinations :—

  The Matriculation Examination.
  The First University Examination.
  The First Examination in Medicine.
  The Second Examination in Medicine.
  The Third Examination in Medicine.
  The M.B., B.Ch., B.A.O. Degrees Examination.

Medical Curriculum.

First Year.

The First Year Course of Medical studies consists of :—

(a) Natural Philosophy, taught experimentally—

Either a Six Months' Course with Lectures (illustrated experimentally) on three days in the week;

Or, a Three Months' Course with Lectures (illustrated experimentally) on at least five days in the week.

(b) Chemistry, a Six Months' Systematic Course.

(c) Biology—

Botany, a three Months' Course with Lectures and Demonstrations on at least three days in the week.

Zoology, a Three Months' Course with Lectures and Demonstrations on at least three days in the week.

(d) Anatomy, a Six Months' Systematic Course (Optional).

(e) Practical Anatomy (Dissections), a Six Months' Course (Optional).

The Systematic Course in Anatomy and Dissections should enable the Student to acquire a good knowledge of the bones, joints, and muscles, and such knowledge of the vessels and viscera and of the larger nerves, as he may reasonably be supposed to have acquired at this period of his Medical Studies.

(f) Practical Chemistry, a Three Months' Course (Optional).

This attendance must not be simultaneous with attendance at the Systematic Course.

Students who have taken the B.A. Degree in any of the subjects named for the First Year Course of Medical Studies shall, upon the production of certificates of attendance in recognised institutions at proper courses of instruction in such subject or subjects, be exempted from attending any further lectures or passing examinations in such subject or subjects.

But, to entitle a Candidate to any of the privileges here conceded, he must have obtained, at the B.A. Examination in the subject or subjects in which he now claims exemption, Honours, 50 per cent. of the Pass Marks, or the equivalent of this percentage on Honour Papers.

In addition, any Student who may have passed the Second University Examination in Arts, and at such Examination shall have obtained in Biology, either Honours, or 50 per cent. of the Pass Marks, may be exempted from presenting Biology at the First Examination in Medicine; he must, however, lodge the necessary certificates.

Certificates of attendance upon a Course of Lectures on Natural Philosophy, taught experimentally, will be accepted, although such attendance may have taken place prior to the Candidate's first year of Medical Studies, provided such course fulfilled the conditions prescribed for the first year of Medical Studies in this subject.

Second Year.

The studies assigned to the Second Year must not be entered upon until the completion of the course assigned to the First Year, that is, until the completion of such a course of study as would qualify a Candidate for admission to the First Examination in Medicine.

The Second Year Course of Medical Studies consists of :—

(a) Anatomy, a Six Months' Systematic Course (if not attended during the First Year).

(b) Practical Anatomy [Dissections], a Six Months' Course (if not attended during the First Year).

    Students who in the First Year have attended the courses of Anatomy prescribed for the Second Year, may in the Second Year attend the course of Anatomy prescribed for the Third Year.

(c) Practical Chemistry, a Three Months' Course (if not attended during First Year).

(d) Physiology, a Six Months' Systematic Course.

    The Systematic Course in Physiology should enable the Student to acquire a good knowledge of Physiological Chemistry, and of the following:—Development of tissues; the Physiology of muscle, nerve-fibres, and nerve-cells (but not of the brain and spinal cord) ; also, the Physiology of blood, lymph, and lymphoid organs, digestion, circulation, respiration, animal heat, secretion and excretion (including the functions of the skin and kidneys). The advanced portions of the subject, *e.g.*, Embryology, the Histology and Physiology of the central nervous system and of the organs of special sense, of voice, and of reproduction, are comprised in the Advanced Systematic Course of Physiology prescribed for the Third Year.

(e) Materia Medica, Pharmacology and Therapeutics, a Three Months' Course (optional). This subject may be studied in either the Second or Third Year of Medical Studies; but it will be included in the subjects of the Third Examination in Medicine.

(f) Practical Physiology and Histology (optional), a Three Months' Laboratory Course of at least two hours three times a week. One third, at least, of the time shall be devoted to Practical Physiology, and this shall be stated explicitly in the certificate or certificates of attendance. This Course may be taken either in the Second or in the Third Year.

(g) Hospital Attendance for the Second Year. Attendance during a *Winter* Session of Six Months. (The total Hospital attendance will be as heretofore, *i.e.* Attendance during thirty-three months.)

N

Third Year.

No certificate of attendance at instruction in any of the branches of study assigned to the Third Year will be accepted where such attendance appears to have taken place prior to the completion of the Second Year of Medical Studies, except as herein provided.

The Third Year Course of Medical Studies consists of :—

(*a*) Anatomy, a Six Months' Advanced Systematic Course (if not attended during the Second Year).

(*b*) Practical Anatomy [Dissections], a Six Months' Course (if not attended during the Second Year).

> The Course of Advanced Systematic Anatomy should be such as to enable Students to perfect their knowledge of the branches of Anatomy prescribed for the Second Examination in Medicine, and also of the whole nervous system and the organs of sense.

(*c*) Physiology, a Six Months' Advanced Systematic Course.

> The Course of Physiology must be distinct from the Course in the Second Year of Medical Studies. It shall deal expressly with those parts of the subject which are not prescribed for the Second Year's Course, and shall comprise Embryology, the Histology and Physiology of the central nervous system, and of the organs of special sense, of voice, and of reproduction.

(*d*) Practical Physiology and Histology (if not attended during the Second Year).

(*e*) Any *one* or *two* of the following :—

> 1. Medicine, a Six Months' Course.
>
> 2. Surgery, a Six Months' Course.
>
> 3. Midwifery, and Diseases of Women and Children.

> This may be attended either as one complete course of at least six months, embracing both branches of the subject, or as two courses of three months each, one in Midwifery, the other in Diseases of Women and Children. These two courses must not be simultaneous.

(*f*) Materia Medica, Pharmacology, and Therapeutics, a Three Months' Course (if not attended during Second Year).

(*g*) Practical Pharmacy,* a Three Months' Course, with Lectures on at least two days in the week, given in a recognised School in a properly equipped Laboratory by a duly appointed Lecturer on Pharmacy.

(This Course may be attended before, at the same time as, or after that on Materia Medica, but must be attended in the Third Year.)

(*h*) Hospital Attendance.

Attendance during a *Winter* Session of Six Months, and a *Summer* Session of Three Months at a General Hospital recognised by the University, and at the Clinical Lectures delivered therein.

(*i*) Fever Hospital.

Attendance during a period of *Three* consecutive months at a Fever Hospital of repute, or in the Fever Wards of a General Hospital. If the attendance takes place during a regular Winter or Summer Session, it may be reckoned as a portion of the prescribed total Hospital attendance of thirty-three months.

But neither attendance at a Fever Hospital, nor the "Personal Charge" of Fever cases, can be recognised, where it takes place prior to attendance at the course of Lectures on the Theory and Practice of Medicine.

(*j*) Attendance on at least six *post-mortem* examinations.

(*k*) Attendance for at least three consecutive months in a General Hospital as Clinical Clerk, and three consecutive months as Dresser; such attendances not to be simultaneous.

Any of these attendances may take place at any time during the Third, Fourth, or Fifth Year.

Fourth Year.

No certificate of attendance at instruction in any of the branches of study assigned to the Fourth Year will be accepted, where such attendance appears to have taken place prior to the completion of the Third Year of Medical Studies, except as herein provided.

The Fourth Year Course comprises the following subjects at least :—

(*a*) Such of the following as may not have been attended during the Third Year of Medical Studies:—

1. Medicine, a Six Months' Course.
2. Surgery, a Six Months' Course.
3. Midwifery, and Diseases of Women and Children, a Six Months' Course.

---

* *All* Candidates are required to lodge Certificates of having attended this Course in accordance with these regulations.

(*b*) Operative Surgery.

The course of instruction must be given in a recognised Medical School by a duly appointed Lecturer in Surgery. The Certificate of attendance must show that the Candidate has attended at least three-fourths of the whole period of the Course, such attendances not to be under any circumstances less than on twenty-four distinct days; and that the Candidate himself has, during such Course, performed at least four major operations on the dead subject under the direction of the Lecturer.

Printed forms for this Certificate may be had on application.

(*c*) Medical Jurisprudence, a Three Months' Course.

(*d*) Pathology, a Three Months' Systematic Course of at least two lectures per week in a recognised Medical School.

Practical Pathology, a Three Months' Laboratory Course of at least three days per week in a recognised Medical School.

These Courses may be taken simultaneously.

(*e*) Ophthalmology and Otology, a Three Months' Systematic Course in a recognised Medical School. This course may be attended either before or the same time as, but not after, the Hospital attendance in these subjects.

(*f*) Hospital attendance.

Attendance during a *Winter* Session of Six Months and a *Summer* Session of Three Months at a General Hospital recognised by the University, and at the Clinical Lectures delivered therein.

(*g*) Fever Hospital.

Attendance during a period of *Three* consecutive months at a Fever Hospital of repute, or in the Fever Wards of a General Hospital, if not attended during Third Year.

(*h*) Attendance on at least six *post-mortem* examinations, if not attended during Third Year.

(*i*) Attendance for at least three months in a General Hospital as Clinical Clerk, and three months as Dresser; such attendance not to be simultaneous (if not attended during Third Year).

Fourth and Fifth Years.

Attendance on the remaining parts of the Medical Curriculum may take place during either the Fourth or the Fifth Year. These parts are—

(*a*) Sanitary Science. A Three Months' Systematic Course in a recognised school. This course shall include practical demonstrations on Hygienic Apparatus and Models, and visits to Institutions and Buildings where Sanitary Appliances may be inspected.

(*b*) Mental Diseases.

> A Three Months' Course in a recognised Institution where Clinical Instruction on Mental Diseases is given.

(*c*) Practical Midwifery.

> Attendance for a period of six months at a recognised Midwifery Hospital, containing not less than fifteen beds in regular occupation where Clinical Instruction in Midwifery and Diseases of Women and Children is given, or for six months at a Midwifery Dispensary recognised by the Senate, where similar Clinical Instruction is given. During this period the Candidate is required to attend at least *twenty* Labours, of *ten* of which at least he must have had personal charge.

(*d*) Ophthalmology and Otology. Attendance for a period of three months at a recognised Hospital, having at least ten beds devoted to diseases of the Eye and Ear.

(*e*) Fever Hospital.

> Attendance during a period of *three* consecutive months at a Fever Hospital of repute, or in the Fever Wards of a General Hospital if not already attended.

(*f*) Attendance on at least six complete *post-mortem* examinations, if not already attended.

(*g*) Attendance for at least three months in a General Hospital as Clinical Clerk, and three months as Dresser; such attendance not to be simultaneous, if not already attended.

(*h*) Personal charge of at least ten Fever cases.

> Printed Forms of Certificate of "Personal charge" of cases may be had on application.

> N.B.—The expression *personal charge* implies that the student fulfils towards the case the duties commonly assigned to a Clinical Clerk.

> Attendance in a Fever Hospital, or on Fever Cases, must not take place during the period of attendance on Practical Midwifery and Gynæcology.

Vaccination.

> A course of practical instruction under a Public Vaccinator, including attendance on at least ten distinct days at a Dispensary when vaccination is being performed.
> Printed Forms for this Certificate may be had on application.

Fifth Year.

Hospital Attendance. Attendance during a *Winter* Session of Six Months at a recognised General Hospital, and at the Clinical Lectures delivered therein.

APPENDIX.

For the information of Students, abstracts are here given of the regulations of the Royal University of Ireland; of the University of London, as well as of the Licensing Corporations in Medicine, and of the Honourable Society of King's Inns. The conditions of admission to the Competitive Examinations for certain Home and Foreign appointments are added.

At the end of each abstract, reference is made to the source from which full information may be obtained. Students are reminded that these regulations are subject to frequent change. Care should be taken to consult the latest official rules. These may be referred to in the College Library.

  I. Royal University of Ireland.
  II. University of London.
 III. Royal Colleges of Physicians and Surgeons in Ireland, England, and Scotland.
 IV. Regulations prescribed by General Medical Council.
  V. Regulations for admission to the Bar.
 VI. Inspectorships of National Schools.
 VII. County Surveyorships.
VIII. Army, Navy, and Indian Medical Services.
 IX. Home Civil Service, Class 1.
  X. Civil Service of India, Eastern Cadetships, etc., etc.

I.—ROYAL UNIVERSITY OF IRELAND.

General Regulations.

The following Degrees and Diplomas are conferred by the University :—

Arts—
 Bachelor of Arts, . B.A.
 Master of Arts, . M.A.
 Doctor of Literature, D.Lit.
Mental and Moral Philosophy—
 Doctor of Philosophy, D.Ph.
Science—
 Bachelor of Science, . B.Sc.
 Doctor of Science, . D.Sc.
Engineering—
 A Special Diploma, Dip. in Eng.
 Bachelor of Engineering, B.E.
 Master of Engineering, M.E.
Music—
 Bachelor of Music, . B.Mus.
 Doctor of Music, . D.Mus.
Medicine—
 Bachelor of Medicine, M.B.
 Doctor of Medicine, . M.D.

Surgery—
 Bachelor of Surgery, . B.Ch.
 Master of Surgery, . M.Ch.
Obstetrics—
 Bachelor of Obstetrics, B.A.O.
 Master of Obstetrics, M.A.O.
Sanitary Science—
 A Special Diploma.
Mental Diseases—
 A Special Diploma.
Law—
 Bachelor of Laws, . LL.B.
 Doctor of Laws, . . LL.D.
Agriculture—
 A Special Diploma.
Teaching—
 A Special Diploma.

All Degrees, Honours, Exhibitions, Prizes, Scholarships, Studentships, and Junior Fellowships in this University shall be open to Students of either sex.

Candidates for any Degree in this University must have passed the Matriculation Examination. Students from other Universities and Colleges are included in this rule.

MATRICULATION.

(Dublin and Local* Centres.)

Subjects.

I. Latin.
II. Any one of the following Languages:—Greek, French, German, Italian, Spanish, Celtic, Sanskrit, Hebrew, Arabic.
III. English Language and Literature.
IV. Elementary Mathematics.
V. Natural Philosophy.

THE FIRST UNIVERSITY EXAMINATION.

One Academical Year after Matriculation. (Dublin and Local* Centres.)

Subjects.

I. Latin.
II. Any one of the following Languages:—Greek, French, German, Italian, Spanish, Celtic, Sanskrit, Hebrew, Arabic.
III. English Language and Literature.
IV. Mathematics.
V. Natural Philosophy.

---

* There is a Centre in Queen's College, Galway.

First Professional Examination.

One Academical Year after Matriculation.

No Candidate can be adjudged to have passed this Examination with a view to proceeding to a Degree in Engineering unless he shall have previously passed the First University Examination, or unless he shall pass it in the same calendar year in which he passes this Examination.

Subjects, and Schedule of Marks:*

1. Mathematics, ... 200.
2. Experimental Physics, . . . 100.
3. Systematic Chemistry, . . . 100.
4. Drawing and Descriptive Architecture, 200.

Second Professional Examination.

One Academical Year after First Professional Examination.

Subjects, and Schedule of Marks:*

1. Mathematics, ... 200.
2. Mathematical Physics, . . . 100.
3. Practical Chemistry, ... 100.
4. Practical Engineering, . . . 200.

B.E. Degree.

One Academical Year after Second Professional Examination.

Subjects, and Schedule of Marks:*

1. Mathematical Physics, . . 200.
2. Geology, including Physical Geography, 100.
3. Civil Engineering, ... 500.
4. Drawing, ... 100.

For this Examination, in addition to Mathematical Physics and Geology (including Physical Geography) there shall be a group of compulsory subjects, and also a group of optional subjects, as follows:—

COMPULSORY GROUP.

1. Strength of Materials, Stresses and Strains.
2. Surveying, Levelling, and Mensuration.
3. Drawing.
4. An Elementary knowledge of the Structure of Railways and Roads.

---

* At all Professional Examinations 35 per cent. of the maximum number of marks assigned to a subject will be the general Pass Standard.

Any two of the following :—

1. Railway Engineering, including Stations and Appliances and a general knowledge of the structure and working of the Locomotive.
2. Harbours, Docks, Rivers, and Canals.
3. Waterworks, including a general knowledge of pumping machinery.
4. County and Municipal work, including Building Construction ; Sanitary Engineering, Sewerage and Refuse Disposal.
5. Electrical Engineering, including Tramways, and the distribution of light and power.

Each of these branches of Engineering shall include the subject of Bridges, Foundations, and Tunnels, so far as these necessarily enter into the construction of the works belonging to that branch.

Diploma in Engineering.

A Diploma in Engineering will be granted to any Candidate who, without having passed the Matriculation and First University Examination, passes the Two Professional and the Degree Examinations.

M.E. Degree.

One Academical Year after B.E.
Candidates must furnish evidence of having spent one year at least under an Engineer in practice after having obtained the Degree of B.E.

Subjects :

1. Applied Natural Philosophy.
2. Engineering.

Diploma in Agriculture.

Candidates for this Diploma must pass the following examinations :—

1. The Matriculation *or* the Preliminary Examination.
2. The First Examination in Agriculture.
3. The Second Examination in Agriculture.
4. The Diploma Examination.

1. For the Matriculation Examination, see page 90.

For the Preliminary Examination the subjects are:—

    i. English.
    ii. Mathematics.
    iii. Natural Philosophy.

2. For the First Examination in Agriculture the subjects are:—

    i. Book-keeping.
    ii. Mathematics.
    iii. Natural Philosophy.
    iv. Chemistry.
    v. Botany and Zoology.
    vi. Land Surveying.

3. For the second Examination in Agriculture the subjects are:—

    i. Chemistry applied to Agriculture.
    ii. Botany and Zoology.
    iii. Physiology.
    iv. Land Surveying.

4. For the Diploma Examination in Agriculture the subjects are:—

    i. Geology.
    ii. Veterinary Hygiene.
    iii. Economic Science as applied to Agriculture.
    iv. Agriculture, Horticulture, and Forestry.

Degrees in Music.

B.Mus. Degree.

All Candidates for the Degree must pass the following Examinations:—

    The Matriculation Examination.
    The First University Examination.
    The First Examination in Music.
    The Degree Examination.

D.Mus. Degree.

Three Academical Years after B.Mus.

The detailed accounts of the subjects of Royal University Examinations (which may vary from year to year) are to be found in the University Calendar.

Table of University Fees.

	£ s. d.	£ s. d.
For the Matriculation Examination,		1 0 0
,, First University Examination,		1 0 0
,, Second University Examination in Arts,		1 0 0
,, B.A. Degree Examination,	1 0 0 ⎫	3 0 0
Upon admission to Degree,	2 0 0 ⎭	
For the M.A. Degree Examination,	2 0 0 ⎫	4 0 0
Upon admission to Degree,	2 0 0 ⎭	
For the D.Lit. Degree Examination,	2 0 0 ⎫	5 0 0
Upon admission to Degree,	3 0 0 ⎭	
For the D.Ph. Degree Examination,	2 0 0 ⎫	5 0 0
Upon admission to Degree,	3 0 0 ⎭	
For the B.Sc. Degree Examination,	1 0 0 ⎫	4 0 0
Upon admission to Degree,	3 0 0 ⎭	
For the D.Sc. Degree Examination,	2 0 0 ⎫	5 0 0
Upon admission to Degree,	3 0 0 ⎭	
For the Studentship Examination,		2 0 0
,, Junior Fellowship Examination,		2 0 0
,, First Professional Examination in Engineering,		1 0 0
,, Second Professional Examination in Engineering,		1 0 0
,, B.E. Degree Examination,	1 0 0 ⎫	3 0 0
Upon admission to Degree,	2 0 0 ⎭	
Upon admission to the Diploma in Engineering,		2 0 0
For the M.E. Degree Examination,	2 0 0 ⎫	4 0 0
Upon admission to Degree,	2 0 0 ⎭	
For the First Examination in Music,		1 0 0
,, B. Mus. Degree Examination,	1 0 0 ⎫	3 0 0
Upon admission to Degree,	2 0 0 ⎭	
For the D. Mus. Degree Examination,	2 0 0 ⎫	5 0 0
Upon admission to Degree,	3 0 0 ⎭	
For the First Examination in Medicine,		1 0 0
,, Second Examination in Medicine,		1 0 0
,, Third Examination in Medicine,		1 0 0
,, Examination for the M.B., B.Ch., B.A.O. Degrees,		2 0 0
,, Qualifying Certificate,		10 0 0
,, M.D. Degree Examination,	2 0 0 ⎫	5 0 0
Upon admission to Degree,	3 0 0 ⎭	
For the M.Ch. Degree Examination,	2 0 0 ⎫	5 0 0
Upon admission to Degree,	3 0 0 ⎭	
For the M.A.O. Degree Examination,	2 0 0 ⎫	5 0 0
Upon admission to Degree,	3 0 0 ⎭	
For the Diploma in San. Science Examination,	2 0 0 ⎫	5 0 0
Upon admission to Diploma,	3 0 0 ⎭	
For the Examination for Hutchinson Stewart Mental Diseases Scholarship, and Diploma for Mental Diseases,	2 0 0 ⎫	5 0 0
Upon admission to the Diploma,	3 0 0 ⎭	
For the Medical Studentship Examination,		2 0 0
For the First Examination in Law,		1 0 0

TABLE OF UNIVERSITY FEES—*continued.*

	£	s.	d.	£	s.	d.
For the LL.B. Degree Examination, . .	1	0	0	4	0	0
Upon admission to Degree, . . .	3	0	0			
For the LL.D. Degree Examination, . .	2	0	0	5	0	0
Upon admission to Degree, . . .	3	0	0			
For the Preliminary Examination in Agriculture, . .				1	0	0
,, First Examination in Agriculture, . . .				1	0	0
,, Second Examination in Agriculture, . . .				1	0	0
,, Diploma in Agriculture Examination,	1	0	0	3	0	0
Upon admission to Diploma, . . .	2	0	0			
For the Diploma in Teaching Examination (First Part), ...	1	0	0	5	0	0
,, Diploma in Teaching Examination (Second Part), ...	1	0	0			
Upon admission to Diploma, . . .	3	0	0			
Fee chargeable for late entry for any Examination, ...				0	10	0

N.B.—A Fee paid for any Examination cannot under any circumstances be returned, or made available for any Examination subsequent to or other than that for which it was paid.

The attention of Students is particularly directed to the notices specifying the last days for sending in notices of intention to be present at Examinations. (Within fourteen days after the date aforesaid, Candidates may enter on paying a late fee of ten shillings additional.)

These dates will be found in the University Calendar.

Exhibitions, Medals, Scholarships, Studentships, and Fellowships in Arts.

1. The following *Exhibitions* may be awarded annually, in Arts, by the Senate :—

    At *Matriculation*—Ten First Class of £24 each, and twenty Second Class of £12 each.

    At *First University Examination*—Ten First Class of £30 each, and twenty Second Class of £15 each.

    At *Second University Examination*—Eight First Class of £36 each, and sixteen Second Class of £18 each.

    At *B.A. Degree Examination*—Seven First Class of £42 each, and fourteen Second Class of £21 each.

2. *Dr. Henry Hutchinson Stewart Scholarship in Arts.*

Value £30 annually, tenable for 3 years, awarded in connection with Summer Examinations, on combined Honour marks, at Second University Examination in Arts in the year, and First University Examination in the year immediately preceding, in English and in a Modern language.

3. *Chancellor's Gold Medal for English Prose Composition.*

Subject for 1903—"Grattan." Limited to Graduates of not more than three years' standing.

4. *The Dr. and Mrs. W. A. Browne Gold Medal and Prize.*

A Gold Medal (value £10) and a Prize of £5 shall be offered each year for competition amongst the candidates for the B.A. Degree Examination (Honours) in Modern Literature, for a colloquial knowledge of the French and German Languages. The Gold Medal will be awarded to the first candidate and the Prize to the second candidate in order of merit.

5. *Medals.*

The Senate may award Gold Medals to those who take first place in any of the Courses appointed for M.A. Degree.

6. *English and Latin Verse Compositions.*

Two Gold Medals are offered annually for competition— the one for the best English Verse Composition, and the other for the best Latin Verse Composition. Each competitor must be either an Undergraduate or a Graduate of not more than one year's standing.

Subjects for 1903.—

> *English*—Death of Byron.
> *Latin*—Thermopylæ.

In and after 1903 all Prose and Verse Compositions must be type-written or printed, and will not be returnable.

7. *Scholarships.*

The Senate offer for competition in October, 1903, ten Scholarships, tenable for three consecutive years, viz. :—Five First Class at £40 per annum each, and five Second Class at £20 per annum each.

Of these Scholarships two First Class and two Second Class are offered for proficiency in Ancient Classics, two First

Class and two Second Class for proficiency in Mathematical Science, and one First Class and one Second Class for proficiency in Modern Literature.

They are open to Matriculated Students of the University from the time of their Matriculation up to and including the Scholarship Examination held next after they shall have passed the First University Examination, subject to the following conditions :—

1. That the Candidate shall be under twenty-one years of age on the first day of January of the year in which the Scholarship Examination is held.

2. That the Candidate shall have obtained Honours either at the Matriculation Examination or at the First University Examination in the subject of the Scholarship for which he is a Candidate, or in one of the subjects if there be more than one.

3. That the Candidate shall not be a Matriculated Student of any other University.

4. That in the case of the Scholarships in Modern Literature the Candidate shall be a natural-born subject of the Crown.

These Scholarships may be held together with the Exhibitions awarded at the various University Examinations, but no person shall hold more than one Scholarship, and if the answering of any Candidate be such as to qualify for two or more, the Senate shall determine in which subject the Candidate shall be elected a Scholar.

It shall be in the power of the Senate to substitute Second Class Scholarships in any cases in which in their opinion the answering was not sufficient to merit First Class Scholarships, and whenever the Senate shall consider it necessary to withhold one or more of the Scholarships offered in any subject, they may award such Scholarships as additional Scholarships in either of the other subjects, if in their opinion the answering in such subject is deserving thereof.

7. *Studentships.*

Five are offered annually for competition, value £100 per annum each, tenable for three consecutive years. They are awarded in connection with M.A. Examinations.

Candidates must be under 26 years of age on the first day of January of the year in which the Studentship Examination is held.

8. *Junior Fellowships.*

In October, 1903, there will be offered for competition among the Graduates in Arts of the University of not less than two years standing, three Junior Fellowships. Such Fellowships shall be tenable for four consecutive years, and shall be of the annual value of £200 each. Junior Fellows shall be bound to take part in the conduct of University Examinations.

The subjects in which these Fellowships will be awarded will be :—

    I. Natural Philosophy.
    II. Chemistry, with Experimental Physics.
    III. Natural Science.

Faculty of Law Exhibitions.

The Senate may award the following :—

One First Class Exhibition of £20, and one Second Class Exhibition of £10, at First Examination in Law.

One First Class Exhibition of £42, and one Second Class Exhibition of £21, at LL.B. Degree Examination.

Engineering Exhibitions.

The following may be awarded annually by the Senate :—

One First Class Exhibition of £30, and one Second Class of £15, at First Professional Examination.

One First Class of £36, and one Second Class of £18, at Second Professional Examination.

At B.E. Degree Examination, one First Class of £42, and one Second Class of £21.

Agricultural Exhibitions.

The following Exhibitions may be awarded annually by the Senate :—

At the First Examination in Agriculture, one First Class of £30, and one Second Class of £15.

At the Second Examination in Agriculture, one First Class of £36, and one Second Class of £18.

At the Diploma Examination, one First Class of £42, and one Second Class of £21.

Faculty of Medicine.

The following Exhibitions may be awarded annually by the Senate :—

At *First Examination in Medicine*—Two First Class of £20 each ; two Second Class of £10 each.

At *Second Examination in Medicine*—Two First Class of £25 each ; two Second Class of £15 each.

At *Third Examination in Medicine*—Two First Class of £30 each ; two Second Class of £20 each.

At the *M.B., B.Ch., B.A.O. Degrees Examination*—Two First Class of £40 each ; two Second Class of £25 each.

Travelling Medical Scholarship.

An Examination for this Scholarship, value £100, is held in October. The subjects are in rotation :—

Anatomy and Histology (1902).
Physiology (1903).

Dr. Henry Hutchinson Stewart's Medical Scholarships.

One, value £10, tenable for three years in subjects of the Autumn Second Examination in Medicine.

One, value £50, tenable for three years, for competition among Medical Graduates of not more than two years' standing, for proficiency in the knowledge of Mental Diseases.

Medical Studentship.

A Studentship in Medicine, value £200, tenable for two years, will be offered for competition among Graduates in Medicine of the University in October, 1903.

Subjects of Examination :—

1. Physiology.
2. Physiological Chemistry.

II.—UNIVERSITY OF LONDON.

Candidates for Degrees in the University of London are required to pass the General Matriculation Examination.

DEGREES IN THE FACULTY OF ARTS.

Candidates for the Degree of B.A. are required to pass the Intermediate Examination in Arts.

No Candidate will be admitted to the Intermediate Examination within one Academical Year of the time of his passing the Matriculation Examination.

No Candidate will be admitted to the B.A. Examination within one Academical Year of the time of his passing the Intermediate Examination in Arts, nor within three years of his Matriculation.

Candidates for the Degree of M.A. are admitted to the Examination after the lapse of an Academic year from the date of obtaining B.A., provided they have attained the age of twenty.

Candidates for the Degree of D. Lit. must have obtained the Degree of M.A. in the University, and will be admitted to the Examination for the Degree of D.Lit., at an interval of at least one Academical year from the date of the M.A. Examination.

Candidates for the Degree of Bachelor of Science must pass the Matriculation Examination, the Intermediate Examination in Science, and the B.Sc. Examination. One year must elapse between the Matriculation Examination and the Intermediate Examination in Science, one year between the B.Sc. Examination and the Intermediate Examination in Science, and three years between the B.Sc. Examination and the Matriculation Examination. Two Academical years must elapse from date of the B.Sc. Examination before the Candidate can be admitted to the Examination for the Degree of D.Sc.

DEGREES IN THE FACULTY OF LAW.

No Candidate will be admitted to the Intermediate in Laws within nine months from the date of his Matriculation Examination, nor to the LL.B. Degree Examination within less than two years from the date of his Intermediate Examinations in Laws, nor within three years of passing the Matriculation Examination, unless he have already graduated in one of the Faculties of the University, in which case he may be admitted after the lapse of one year.

No Candidate under the age of thirty will be admitted to the Examination for the Degree of LL.D. until after the expiration of two Academical years from the date of his passing the LL.B. Examination.

MEDICINE.

Bachelor of Medicine (M.B.).

Every Candidate for the Degree of Bachelor of Medicine shall be required :—

1. To have passed the Matriculation Examination in this University not less than five years previously.
2. To have passed the Preliminary Scientific (M.B.) Examination not less than four years previously.
3. To have been engaged in his Professional Studies during five years subsequent to Matriculation, and four years subsequent to passing the Preliminary Scientific Examination, at one or more of the Medical Institutions or Schools recognized by this University; one year, at least, of the four to have been spent in one or more of the recognized Institutions or Schools of the United Kingdom.
4. To pass two Examinations in Medicine.

Preliminary Scientific (M.B.) Examination.

No Candidate shall be admitted to this Examination unless he has passed the Matriculation Examination.

Intermediate Examination in Medicine.

No Candidate shall be admitted to this Examination unless he has passed the Preliminary Scientific Examination at least two years previously.

Degrees of M.B., B.S., M.S., and M.D.

No Candidate shall be admitted to the Examination for M.B. within twenty-one months of the time of his passing the Intermediate Examinations.

A Candidate for the Degree of B.S. (Bachelor of Surgery) must have passed the Examination for the Degree of M.B., and produce certain required certificates. Candidates for the Degree of M.S. (Master in Surgery) must have taken the Degree of B.S. at least two years previously, and produce certain required certificates. Candidates for the Degree of M.D. must have taken the Degree of M.B. at least two years previously, and must produce certain required certificates.

Candidates for the Degree of M.D. in *State Medicine* must have taken the Degree of M.B. at least two years previously, and must produce certain required Certificates.

For further information see the Calendar of the University of London, which may be consulted in the College Library.

III.—ROYAL COLLEGES OF PHYSICIANS AND SURGEONS OF IRELAND, ENGLAND, AND SCOTLAND.

A.—*Conjoint Examinations in Ireland by the Royal College of Physicians and Royal College of Surgeons.*

1. Every Student must be registered in the books of the General Medical Council. No credit will be given for study, unless registration shall have been effected within fifteen days of its commencement.

Five years' Course (obligatory on all Candidates commencing their studies on or after 1st January, 1892).

First Professional Examination.

Subjects.

1. Chemistry and Physics.
2. Biology.

Fee, £15 15s.

Second Professional Examination.

Subjects.

1. Anatomy.
2. Physiology and Histology.

Fee, £10 10s.

Third Professional Examination.

Subjects.

1. Pathology.
2. Materia Medica, Pharmacy, and Therapeutics.
3. Forensic Medicine and Public Health.

Final Examination.

Subjects.

1. Medicine, including Fevers, Mental Diseases, and Diseases of Children.
2. Surgery, including Operative and Ophthalmic Surgery.
3. Midwifery and Gynæcology, Vaccination, and Diseases of New-born Children.

Fee, £6 6s.

Full information may be had on application to the Secretary of Committee of Management, Royal College of Physicians, Kildare-street, Dublin.

B.—*Regulations of the Examining Board in England (Royal College of Physicians of London and Royal College of Surgeons of England), for Candidates who commenced their Professional Studies on or after 1st January, 1892.*

PROFESSIONAL EXAMINATIONS.

First Examination.

1. Chemistry and Physics.   2. Practical Pharmacy.   3. Elementary Biology.

This Examination may be taken in three parts at different times, or the whole may be taken at one time.   Fee, £10 10s.

Second Examination.

1. Anatomy.   2. Physiology.   Fee, £10 10s.

Third or Final Examination.

PART I.—Medicine, including Medical Anatomy, Pathology, Practical Pharmacy (if not previously passed), Therapeutics, Forensic Medicine, and Public Health.

PART II.—Surgery, including Pathology, Surgical Anatomy, and the use of Surgical Appliances.

PART III.—Midwifery and Diseases of Women.
Fee (for whole Examination), £21.

Synopses indicating the range of subjects in the several examinations, and full information as to the course of study required, and certificates prescribed, may be obtained of the Secretary, Examination Hall, Victoria Embankment, London, W.C

C.—*Conjoint Examinations in Scotland of the Royal College of Surgeons and Royal College of Physicians, Edinburgh, and Faculty of Physicians and Surgeons, Glasgow (Triple Qualification), for Candidates who began study on or after 1st January,* 1892.

First Examination.

Elementary Biology, Physics, Chemistry. Fee, £5.

Second Examination.

Anatomy and Physiology, including Histology. Fee, £5.

Third Examination.

Pathology, Materia Medica, and Pharmacy. Fee, £5.

Final Examination.

1. Medicine, including Therapeutics, Medical Anatomy, and Clinical Medicine ;
2. Surgery, including Surgical Anatomy, Clinical Surgery, and Diseases and Injuries of the Eye ;
3. Midwifery, and Diseases of Women and of New-born Children ;
4. Medical Jurisprudence and Public Health. Fee £15.

Secretaries for Edinburgh are :—
    R. W. Philip, M.D., F.R.C.P.E., R.C.P. EDIN.
    Francis Cadell, M.B., F.R.C.S.E., R.C.S. EDIN.

Secretary for Glasgow is :—
    Alexander Duncan, B.A., LL.D., F.P. & S. GLAS.

IV.—REGULATIONS PRESCRIBED BY GENERAL MEDICAL COUNCIL RESPECTING MEDICAL COURSES IN AND AFTER 1892.

With regard to the Course of Study and Examinations which persons desirous of qualifying for the Medical Profession shall go through in order that they may become possessed of the requisite knowledge and skill for the efficient practice of the Profession, the General Medical Council have resolved that the following conditions ought to be enforced without exception on *all* who commence their Medical Studies at any time after January 1, 1892 :—

(*a*) With the exception provided below, the period of Professional Studies between the date of Registration as a Medical

Student and the date of Final Examination for any Diploma which entitles its bearer to be registered under the *Medical Acts*, must be a period of *bonâ fide* study during not less than five years.

The first four of the five years of Medical Study should be passed at a School or Schools of Medicine recognised by any of the Licensing Bodies, provided that the First Year may be passed at a University, or Teaching Institution, recognised by any of the Licensing Bodies, where the subjects of Physics, Chemistry, and Biology are taught.

The Examination in the Elements of Physics, Chemistry, and Biology should be passed before the beginning of the Second Winter Season.

The exception referred to above in (*a*) is as follows :—

Graduates in Arts or Science of any University recognised by the Medical Council, who shall have spent a year in the Study of Physics, Chemistry, and Biology, and have passed an Examination in these subjects for the Degrees in question, should be held to have completed the first of the five years of Medical Study.

V.—THE BAR.

Extract from Educational Regulations of the Honourable Society of King's Inns :—

XX. Graduates of the Queen's University in Ireland, Royal University of Ireland, Oxford, Cambridge, and London Universities, may qualify for call to the Bar by attending two continuous Courses of the Lectures of the two Professors at the King's Inns, and in the case of all such Graduates, except Graduates of the Royal University of Ireland, or of the London University, by attending for a year the Lectures of two of the Professors of Law in their respective Universities, and passing the Examinations (if any) held by the Professors at the end of each Course ; and in the case of Graduates of the Royal University of Ireland, by attending for one year the Lectures of two of the Professors of Law in one of the Queen's Colleges at Belfast, Cork, or Galway, and passing the like Examinations, if such be held, and in the case of Graduates of the University of London, by attending for one year the Lectures of two of the Professors of Law in University College, and passing the like Examinations if such be held.

VI.—APPOINTMENT OF COUNTY SURVEYORS.

A candidate for the position of County Surveyor, if not existing County Surveyor,

(*a.*) must on the last day fixed by the County Council for receiving applications be not less than twenty-six years of age and not more than forty years:

(*b.*) must show that he has been regularly trained as a Civil Engineer and engaged in the practice of his profession in a responsible position in charge of important works for not less than four years: and

(*c.*) must present himself to the Civil Service Commissioners for literary examination under the Scheme set forth in the Schedule annexed.

It will be necessary for all candidates, if not existing County Surveyors in Ireland, to satisfy the Local Government Board as to age, health, character, and the possession of the necessary practical and professional qualifications, and to satisfy the Civil Service Commissioners as to competency.

Candidates who are existing County Surveyors in Ireland, and have already been certified by the Civil Service Commissioners, will be obliged to satisfy the Commissioners that they have retained their professional knowledge and skill, and the Local Government Board as to age, health, and character.

All Candidates must submit their applications to the County Council within the time fixed by the Council in their advertisement of the vacancy.

A list of applicants will then be forwarded to the Local Government Board, and the Board, after the necessary inquiries have been made, will notify the names to the Civil Service Commissioners.

The result of the examination will be notified by the Board to the County Council, by whom the final selection will be made.

LOCAL GOVERNMENT BOARD,
DUBLIN, *August*, 1899.

SCHEDULE.

EXAMINATIONS FOR COUNTY SURVEYORSHIPS IN IRELAND.

The Examination consists of two parts, and will be in the following subjects, viz. :—

PART I.

MATHEMATICS—including Geometry, Trigonometry, Algebra, Differential and Integral Calculus, and Geometrical Optics.

MECHANICAL PHILOSOPHY—Including Statics and Dynamics, Hydrostatics and Hydraulics, Pneumatics, and Heat regarded as a source of Power.

EXPERIMENTAL SCIENCE — Including Inorganic Chemistry, Heat, Electricity, and Magnetism.

GEOLOGY AND MINERALOGY.

PART II.

Strength and other properties of Materials, and the Calculation of Stresses and Strains.

(A.) RAILWAY AND CANAL ENGINEERING.

(B.) MARINE ENGINEERING—Including Harbour, Dock, Sea, and Reclamation Works.

(C.) HYDRAULIC ENGINEERING—Including Water Supply, Sewerage, and Irrigation.

(D.) COUNTY WORKS—Including Architecture, Roads, Drainage, and River Works.

Each of the groups lettered (A), (B), (C), (D) to include Designs, Estimates, Specifications, and the mechanical contrivances connected with it.

Candidates must pass in one subject in Part I., and must attain such a standard of proficiency in Parts I. and II. combined as shall satisfy the Civil Service Commissioners.

CIVIL SERVICE COMMISSION,
June, 1899.

Appointment of Assistant Surveyors for Counties in Ireland.

1. Every person who is appointed an Assistant Surveyor in any County in Ireland must produce satisfactory evidence to the Local Government Board for Ireland that his health and character are good, and, except in the case of an existing Assistant Surveyor within the meaning of section 109 (1) of the Local Government (Ireland) Act, 1898, that at the date of the resolution of the County Council appointing him his age was not less than 21 years, or more than 45 years.

2. Every person appointed as aforesaid who

   (*a*) has a diploma or degree in Engineering from a University or College of Science in the United Kingdom, or a certificate from His Majesty's Civil Service Commissioners, that he is qualified to act as a deputy for a County Surveyor; or

   (*b*) is an Associate Member of the Institution of Civil Engineers, London, or an Associate Member of the Institution of Civil Engineers, Ireland, or has a certificate of having passed the Voluntary Examination for candidates for Surveyorships held by the Incorporated Association of Municipal and County Engineers;

   (*c*) was on the first day of April, 1899, an Assistant Surveyor in a county in Ireland, or if appointed in any such county between the first day of April, 1899, and the date of this Order, satisfies the Local Government Board for Ireland that he is fully qualified to discharge the duties of his office,

shall be deemed qualified for the position of Assistant County Surveyor without further examination.

3. Every person appointed as aforesaid who is not qualified under the provisions of the foregoing Article of this Order must produce to the Local Government Board for Ireland satisfactory evidence that he has profited by training in one of the two following ways, that is to say, either

o

(1) By service with a County Surveyor, Civil Engineer, or Architect for not less than two years; or

(2) By attendance at an Engineering School of some University or College of Science in the United Kingdom for not less than one year, and by having been engaged in practical work in connection with Civil Engineering or Building for one year at the least.

4. Every person appointed as aforesaid who is not qualified under the provisions of Article 2 of this Order must, in addition to possessing one of the qualifications specified in Article 3, also pass a qualifying examination to the satisfaction of the Local Government Board for Ireland in the following subjects :—

(1) English Composition as tested by writing a business letter from rough notes, or a short essay on some subject connected with his profession.
(2) Arithmetic.
(3) Mensuration.
(4) Building construction.
(5) Construction and maintenance of roads.
(6) Chain surveying and levelling.

VII.—REGULATIONS FOR THE ENTRY OF CANDIDATES FOR COMMISSIONS IN THE MEDICAL DEPARTMENT OF THE ROYAL NAVY.

Limits of Age, 21–28 *at date of Examination.*

Candidates must be registered under the Medical Act in force, as qualified to practice Medicine and Surgery in Great Britain and Ireland.

Candidates will be examined by the Examining Board in the following compulsory subjects, and the highest number of marks attainable will be distributed as follows :—

	Marks.
(a) Medicine, Materia Medica, Therapeutics, and General Hygiene, ...	1200
(b) Surgery and Surgical Anatomy, . . .	1200

The Examination in Medicine and Surgery will be in part practical, and will include, beyond papers, the examination of patients, the examination of Pathological specimens, a knowledge of Bacteriology, the performance of operations on the dead body, and the application of Surgical apparatus.

The attention of Candidates is specially drawn to the importance of the section of Operative Surgery, as a competent knowledge in this subject is essential in order to qualify for a Commission.

No Candidate shall be considered eligible who shall not have obtained, at least, one-third of the maximum marks in each of the above *compulsory subjects.*

Candidates may be examined in the following voluntary subjects, for which the maximum number of marks obtainable will be :—

Natural Sciences—

	Marks.
Chemistry (300) ; Physiology (300) ; Zoology (300) ; Botany (300) ; Geology and Physical Geography (300), ...	600
No candidate will be allowed to present himself for examination in more than two of these subjects.	
French and German (300) each, ...	600

A number less than one-third of the marks attainable in each of these voluntary subjects will not be allowed to count in favour of the Candidate who has qualified in the compulsory subjects.

The knowledge of Modern Languages being considered of great importance, all intending competitors are urged to qualify in French and German.

Further information may be had from :—

DIRECTOR-GENERAL,

Medical Department,

Admiralty,

Northumberland Avenue,

London, W.C.

26th *March*, 1902.

o 2

REGULATIONS FOR ADMISSION TO THE ROYAL ARMY MEDICAL CORPS.

Limits of Age, 21–28 *at date of Examination.*

Candidates must possess, under the Medical Acts in force in the United Kingdom at the time of their appointments, a registrable qualification to practice.

SUBJECTS FOR THE ENTRANCE EXAMINATION.

Candidates will be examined by the examining board in medicine and surgery. The examination will be of a clinical and practical character, partly written and partly oral, marks being allotted under the following scheme :—

MEDICINE (*written*).

	Maximum Marks.
A. Examination and Report upon a medical case in the wards of a hospital, ...	125
B. Commentary upon a case in medicine, . . .	125

[Three hours allowed for A and B together.]

MEDICINE (*oral*).

A. Clinical cases ; Clinical Pathology, ...	75
B. Morbid Anatomy and Morbid Histology, . . .	75

[One quarter of an hour allowed for each table.]

SURGERY (*written*).

A. Examination and report upon a surgical case in the wards of a hospital, ...	125
B. Commentary upon a case in surgery, ...	125

[Three hours allowed for A and B together.]

SURGERY (*oral*).

A. Clinical cases, including diseases of the eye ; surgical instruments and appliances, ...	75

[One quarter of an hour allowed for this table.]

B. Operative surgery and surgical anatomy, . . .	75

Total marks, .	800

The following headings are published as a guide to Candidates in drawing up their reports on cases :—

(*a*) A brief history of the case as given by the patient, including such points only (if any) in the family or personal history as have a distinct bearing upon the present illness or incapacity.

(*b*) A detailed account of the subjective symptoms and physical signs elicited by the candidate's personal examination of the patient, noting the absence of any which might be expected to be present in a similar case.

(*c*) Where there is any reasonable doubt in the mind of the candidate as to an exact diagnosis, he is to give the alternatives, with his reasons for making the selection.

(*d*) A commentary upon the case as a whole, pointing out the symptoms which may be considered typical, and those which appear to be unusual or only accidental complications.

(*e*) Suggestions as to treatment, both immediate and possibly necessary at a later date.

(*f*) A forecast of the progress and probable termination of the case.

Similarly the commentary on the report of a case submitted to the Candidate should discuss :—

(*a*) The family and personal history and other conditions preceding the development of the condition described.

(*b*) The relative significance of the physical signs' symptoms, other indications of disease noted, and the general clinical aspects of the case.

(*c*) The diagnosis, with reasons for selection of the most probable, when a positive diagnosis cannot be attained.

(*d*) The treatment, dietectic, medicinal, operative, &c., including a criticism of the plan adopted, and alternative schemes of treatment in case of disagreement.

(*e*) The morbid appearances, and an account of the *post-mortem* examination (if any).

The examination will be held in London, and will occupy about four days.

The appointments announced for competition will be filled up from the list of qualified Candidates arranged in the order of merit, as determined by the total number of marks each has obtained.

Having gained a place in this entrance examination, the successful candidates will undergo 2 months' instruction in hygiene and bacteriology, after which they will be examined in these subjects. The maximum number of marks obtainable at this examination will be 100.

On completion of the above course lieutenants on probation will be ordered to proceed to the Depôt of the Royal Army Medical Corps at Aldershot for a 3 months' course of instruction in the technical duties of the Corps, and at the end of the course will be examined in the subjects taught. The maximum number of marks obtainable at this examination will be 100.

A lieutenant on probation who fails to qualify in either of these examinations will be allowed a second trial, and, should he qualify, will be placed at the bottom of the list. Should he again fail in either examination, his commission will not be confirmed.

Further information may be had from—

ADJUTANT-GENERAL TO THE FORCES,

Horse Guards, War Office,

Pall Mall,

London, S.W.

1st *May*, 1902.

REGULATIONS FOR THE EXAMINATION OF CAN-
DIDATES FOR ADMISSION TO HIS MAJESTY'S
INDIAN MEDICAL SERVICE.

Limits of Age, 21–28, *at date of Examination.*

Candidates must possess a diploma, or diplomas, entitling them, under the Medical Acts, to practise both Medicine and Surgery in Great Britain and Ireland.

The following Certificates must be produced :—

(*a*) A Certificate of Registration, under the Medical Acts, of the degrees, diplomas, and licenses possessed by the candidate.

(*b*) A Certificate of having attended a course of instruction for not less than three months at an Ophthalmic Hospital, or the Ophthalmic Department of a General Hospital, which course shall include instruction in the errors of refraction.

SUBJECTS OF EXAMINATION.

Candidates will be examined by the Examining Board in the following subjects, and the highest number of marks obtainable will be distributed as follows :—

	Marks.
1. Medicine, including Therapeutics,	1,200
2. Surgery, including Diseases of the Eye,	1,200
3. Surgical Anatomy and Physiology,	600
4. Pathology and Bacteriology,	600
5. Midwifery, and Diseases of Women and Children,	600
6. Chemistry, Pharmacy, and either Botany or Zoology,	600

N.B.—The Examination in Medicine and Surgery will be in part practical, and will include operations on the dead body, the application of Surgical apparatus, and the examination of Medical and Surgical patients at the bedside. The examination in Chemistry will be limited to the elements of the science, and to its application to Medicine, Pharmacy, and Practical Hygiene.

No candidate shall be considered eligible who shall not have obtained at least one-third of the marks obtainable in each of the above subjects, and one-half of the aggregate marks for all the subjects.

Further information may be obtained from—

THE MILITARY SECRETARY,

India Office,

London, S.W.

October, 1902.

VIII.—HOME CIVIL SERVICE.

CLERKSHIPS (CLASS I.).—REGULATIONS.

1. Candidates must have attained the age of 22, and must not have attained the age of 24 on the first day of the Competitive Examination.

EXTRACT FROM THE REGULATIONS RESPECTING OPEN COMPETITIVE EXAMINATIONS FOR CLERKSHIPS (CLASS I.) IN THE CIVIL SERVICE.

Out of the list resulting from each Examination will be filled (provided there be Candidates duly qualified) :—

(*a*) All the vacancies in Class I. which may have been reported to the Civil Service Commissioners up to the date of the announcement of the result of the Examination.

(*b*) Any additional vacancies occurring within six months from the date of the announcement of the result of the Examination, which the Head of the Department may desire to have so filled.

Candidates will be allowed to choose, according to their place on the list, among the vacancies (*a*) for which they are duly qualified; or they may elect to wait for the chance of a vacancy (*b*). When vacancies (*b*) occur, they will be offered in rotation to the qualified Candidates then on the list, who will be free to decline them without forfeiting their claim to subsequent vacancies (*b*).

The subjects of Examination for the Home Civil Service are substantially the same as those prescribed for the Indian Civil Service.

Further information with regard to appointments in the Post Office, War Office, and Admiralty, may be obtained on application to the Secretary, Civil Service Commission, London, S.W.

SPECIAL REGULATIONS RESPECTING OPEN COMPETITIVE EXAMINATIONS FOR THE SITUATION OF ASSISTANT EXAMINER IN THE PATENT OFFICE.

1. The limits of age for this situation are 21 and 24, and candidates must be of the prescribed age on the first day of the Examination.

2. At the Examination, exercises will be set in the following subjects only :—

1. English Composition.
2. Arithmetic (including Vulgar and Decimal Fractions).
3. Précis.
4. Geometry (Elementary and Practical).
5. Mechanical Drawing.
6. Mechanics and Mechanism.
7. Chemistry.
8. Electricity and Magnetism.
9. Hydrostatics, Hydraulics, and Pneumatics.

Candidates must pass to the satisfaction of the Civil Service Commissioners in one of the subjects numbered 6, 7, and 8, according to the nature of the situation vacant, *i.e.*, according as the duties to be performed render a knowledge of Mechanics and Mechanism, of Chemistry, or of Electricity and Magnetism, absolutely necessary. The remaining subjects are optional.

CIVIL SERVICE COMMISSION, S.W.,
28th June, 1898.

SPECIAL REGULATIONS RESPECTING OPEN COMPETITIVE EXAMINATIONS FOR JUNIOR APPOINTMENTS IN THE SUPPLY AND ACCOUNTING DEPARTMENTS OF THE ADMIRALTY.

The limits of age for these situations are 18 and 20, and candidates must be of the prescribed age on the first day of the Examination.

The Examination will be in the following subjects :—

CLASS I.

1. Mathematics I. (Elementary, including Arithmetic).
2. Latin.
3. French or German.
4. English Composition.
5. Geography.

CLASS II.

6. Mathematics II. (Advanced).
7. German or French.
8. Greek.
9. English History.
10. Chemistry and Heat.
11. Physics.
12. Physiography and Geology.

All the subjects of Class I. may be taken up. Only two of the subjects of Class II. may be taken up, and if one of these be a Modern Language it must be different from the Modern Language selected in Class I. No Candidate will be eligible who fails to pass a qualifying examination in Arithmetic and English Composition.

CIVIL SERVICE COMMISSION,
4th October, 1898.

SPECIAL REGULATIONS* RESPECTING OPEN COMPETITIVE EXAMINATIONS FOR THE SITUATION OF ASSISTANT CIVIL ENGINEER (2ND GRADE) IN THE DEPARTMENT OF THE DIRECTOR OF ENGINEERING AND ARCHITECTURAL WORKS IN THE ADMIRALTY, AT THE HEAD OFFICE AND THE OUTPOSTS.

(*Supplementary to the General Regulations respecting Open Competitive Examinations for Situations in the Civil Service included in Schedule A of the Order in Council of 4th June, 1870.*)

I. The limits of age for this situation are 23 and 28. Candidates must be of the prescribed age on the first day of the Examination.

II. Candidates will be required to show what technical education and practical training they have undergone to qualify themselves for a situation of this nature. They must show to the satisfaction of the Civil Service Commissioners (1) that they have served, for at least three years, in a public or private office, under a Civil Engineer or Architect in good general practice, or a Superintending Engineer of one of His Majesty's Dockyards, or a Commanding Royal Engineer; or (2) that they have in some other capacity acquired a three

---

* *These Regulations are liable to alterations for future Examinations.*

years' practical experience on important works; and (3) that they have fully profited by their practical training, and possess the necessary qualifications and experience. Evidence on these points must be sent in at such times and in such manner as the Civil Service Commissioners may appoint. If it prove *primâ facie* satisfactory, the Candidate will be admitted to Examination, subject to such further inquiry as may be necessary.

III. The Examination consists of two parts, and will be in the following subjects, viz.:—

PART I.

Maximum Marks.

Mathematics, including Geometry, Trigonometry, and Algebra, ‥ ‥ ‥ ‥ ‥ ‥	200
Mechanical Philosophy, including Statics and Dynamics, Hydrostatics and Hydraulics, Pneumatics, and Heat regarded as a Source of Power, ‥ ‥	200
Experimental Science, including Inorganic Chemistry, Heat, Electricity, and Magnetism, ‥ ‥ ‥	200

PART II.

†Drawing.—(a) Drawing and Design of Engineering Works, ‥ ‥ ‥ ‥	300
(b) Details of Construction (including Theory of Construction) in Engineering Works, ‥ ‥ ‥	300
(c) Drawing and Design of Architectural Works, ‥ ‥ ‥ ‥	150
(d) Details of Construction (including Theory of Construction) in Architectural Works, ‥ ‥ ‥	150

} 900

Quantities: Squaring dimensions, preparation and examination of builders' accounts, abstracting, getting into bill, and pricing, ‥ ‥ ‥ ‥	100
Estimates and Specifications, ‥ ‥ ‥ ‥	100
†Use and Properties of Materials, ‥ ‥ ‥	200
†Surveying and Levelling, ‥ ‥ ‥ ‥	150
Sanitary Engineering, ‥ ‥ ‥ ‥ ‥	200

There will be an Oral Examination in subjects marked thus †. The Oral Examination in Drawing will be chiefly on the work sent in by the Candidate in the Written Examination.

No Candidate will be eligible who does not pass in one at least of the heads included in Part I., and in each of the subjects in Part II.

IV. A fee of £6 will be required from each Candidate attending Examination.

V. Applications for permission to attend an Examination must be made at such times and in such manner as the Commissioners may appoint.

CIVIL SERVICE COMMISSION,
24th May, 1898.

A MEMORANDUM *as to the Salary and Prospects, &c., of the situation is printed below.*

Each successful Candidate will accept his appointment subject to the express condition that the Staff of the Department is liable to re-organization from time to time, as the interests of the public service may require, and that no claim to compensation on his behalf can be admitted if such re-organization shall in effect reduce the number, or alter the conditions of superior appointments in the department. Promotion to higher grades depends on merit, and on the occurrence of vacancies, but no right of promotion to higher classes or grades is recognized.

MEMORANDUM.

The Civil Service Commissioners are authorized by the Lords Commissioners of the Admiralty to make the following announcements :—

1. Assistant Civil Engineers (2nd Grade) will enter the Admiralty Service on the express understanding that they are liable to serve as required at any of His Majesty's Naval Establishments at home or abroad. No Candidate will be accepted by the Admiralty who fails to satisfy the Medical Director-General of the Navy as to his physical fitness for service abroad.

2. An Assistant Civil Engineer (2nd Grade) on first entry will be on probation for two years. During probation a salary of £180 per annum will be paid, then if the period of probation is satisfactorily passed, the salary will be £200 for the third year, and will progress by annual increments of £10 to a maximum of £300.

3. Assistant Civil Engineers (2nd Grade) are eligible for promotion without further examination (if selected) through the successive grades of—

Assistant Civil Engineer (1st Grade)—(minimum £300, annual increment £15, maximum £400).

Civil Engineer—(minimum £400, annual increment £20, maximum £500).

Superintending Civil Engineer—(minimum £600, annual increment £25, maximum £700) :—

to that of Assistant Director of Works—(minimum £850, annual increment £50, maximum £1000, with an allowance of £200 per annum to the Senior Assistant).

4. Whilst serving in London or at a Foreign Station salaries (except that of Assistant Director of Works) are further augmented by local allowances to meet increased expense of living, and Unfurnished Official Residences (or allowances in lieu) are granted in the higher ranks both at Home and Foreign Stations.

5. The Engineer Staff of the Admiralty will be interchangeable with the staff at the Ports, the same prospect of promotion to the higher posts being open to all. It should be clearly understood, however, that promotion will in all cases be governed by merit and not by seniority, and that annual increments of pay are conditional on service being satisfactory.

6. The numbers of the Establishment of each rank are at the present time as follows :—

2 Assistant Directors of Works.
11 Superintending Civil Engineers.
12 Civil Engineers.
22 Assistant Civil Engineers (First Grade).
21   ,,   ,,   ,, (Second Grade).

20th May, 1902.

IX.—CIVIL SERVICE OF INDIA.

No person will be deemed qualified who shall not satisfy the Civil Service Commissioners :—(i.) That he is a natural-born subject of His Majesty. (ii.) That his age will be above twenty-one years and under twenty-three years on the 1st day of the year in which the Examination is held. (iii.) That he has no disease, constitutional affection, or bodily infirmity unfitting him, or likely to unfit him, for the Civil Service of India. (iv.) That he is of good moral character.

For the Examination commencing on the 1st August, 1902, application must be made on the prescribed form on or before the 1st July, 1902, accompanied by a list of the subjects in which the Candidate desires to be examined. Further information with regard to appointments in the Post Office, War Office, and Admiralty, may be obtained on application to the Secretary, Civil Service Commission, London, S.W.

Should the evidence upon the above points be *prima facie* satisfactory to the Civil Service Commissioners, the Candidate, on payment of the prescribed fee, will be admitted to the examination.

The Open Competitive Examination will take place only in the following branches of knowledge :—

			Marks.
English Composition,	. . . . . .	.	500
Sanskrit Language and Literature,	. . .	.	500
Arabic do. do.	. . . .	.	500
Greek do. do.	. . . .	.	750
Latin do. do.	. . . .	.	750
English do. do. (including special period named by the Commissioners), *	. . .	.	500
French Language and Literature,	. . . .	.	500
German do. do.	. . . .	.	500
Mathematics (pure and applied),	. . . .	.	900
Advanced Mathematical subjects (pure and applied),		.	900

Natural Science, *i.e.* any number not exceeding *three* of the following subjects :—

Chemistry,	. . . . . . ⎫
Physics,	. . . . . . ⎪
Geology,	. . . . . . ⎬ 600 each = 1800
Botany,	. . . . . . ⎪
Zoology,	. . . . . . ⎪
Animal Physiology,	. . . . ⎭

* A Syllabus, defining in general terms the character of the Examination in the various subjects, may be obtained on application to the Secretary, Civil Service Commission.

Greek History (Ancient, including Constitution), . .	400
Roman History (ditto, ditto), ...	400
English History, ...	500
General Modern History (period to be selected by Candidates from list in the Syllabus issued by the Commissioners), *	500
Logic and Mental Philosophy (Ancient and Modern), .	400
Moral Philosophy (Ancient and Modern), . . .	400
Political Economy and Economic History, . . .	500
Political Science (including Analytical Jurisprudence, the Early History of Institutions, and Theory of Legislation), ...	500
Roman Law, ...	500

English Law. Under the head of " English Law " shall be included the following subjects, viz. :—

(1) Law of Contract; (2) Law of Evidence; (3) Law of the Constitution; (4) Criminal Law; (5) Law of Real Property ; and of these five subjects Candidates shall be at liberty to offer any four, but not more than four, ... 500

Candidates are at liberty to name any or all of these branches of knowledge. None is obligatory.

The marks assigned to Candidates in each branch will be subject to such deduction as the Civil Service Commissioners may deem necessary, in order to secure that "no credit be allowed for merely superficial knowledge." Marks assigned in English Composition and Mathematics will be subject to no deduction. The Examination will be conducted on paper and *vivâ voce*.

The Candidates who obtain the greatest aggregate number of marks will be deemed to be selected Candidates for the Civil Service of India, provided they appear to be in other respects duly qualified.

Should any of the selected Candidates become disqualified, the Secretary of State for India will determine whether the vacancy shall be filled up or not. In the former case, the Candidate next in order of merit, and in other respects duly qualified, shall be deemed to be a selected Candidate.

---

* A Syllabus, defining in general terms the character of the Examination in the various subjects, may be obtained on application to the Secretary, Civil Service Commission.

Examinations for Eastern Cadetships, viz.:

FOR CADETSHIPS IN THE CIVIL SERVICES OF CEYLON AND OF HONG KONG, THE STRAITS SETTLEMENTS AND THE PROTECTED STATES OF THE MALAY PENINSULA.

[The next Examination for Eastern Cadetships will be held under these Regulations. Alterations may be made for any subsequent Examination.]

1. The Cadets, who must be natural-born British subjects, are selected by open competitive examination held by the Civil Service Commissioners, to whom all inquiries on the subject should be addressed.

The examinations for these appointments will, as a rule, be held in the month of August of those years in which vacancies have occurred in the Civil Service of Ceylon or in that of Hong Kong, the Straits Settlements, and the Protected States of the Malay Peninsula ; and the successful Candidates will be allotted, as and when opportunity offers, to the various Colonies or States in which vacancies may exist, upon a consideration of all the circumstances, including their own wishes; but the requirements of the Public Service will rank before every other consideration, and the Secretary of State retains full discretion to allot as he thinks fit.

2. Candidates must be between the ages of 21 and 24 on the first day of August in the year in which the Examination is held, and must satisfy the Civil Service Commissioners that they are duly qualified in respect of health and character. They must be of sound constitution, possessed of good sight, and physically qualified for service in tropical climates, and they will be called upon to undergo a strict medical examination to test these points.

3. The subjects of the Examination are the same as those prescribed for the Indian Civil Service.

4. Application for permission to attend one of these Examinations must be made in the writing of the Candidate, at such times and in such manner as may be fixed by the Commissioners.

CIVIL SERVICE COMMISSION, LONDON, S.W.,
10th March, 1902.

X.—OPEN COMPETITIVE EXAMINATIONS.

FOR THE SITUATION OF STUDENT INTERPRETER FOR THE OTTOMAN DOMINIONS, PERSIA, GREECE, AND MOROCCO.

1. Candidates will be required to satisfy the Civil Service Commissioners : —

> (*a*) That they are natural-born subjects of His Majesty.
>
> (*b*) That their age on the first day of the Examination is not less than 18 or more than 24.
>
> (*c*) That they are duly qualified in respect of health and character.
>
> (*d*) That they are unmarried.

2. The Examination will be in the following subjects :—

Obligatory.

  I. Handwriting and Orthography.
  II. Arithmetic (including Vulgar and Decimal Fractions).
  III. English Composition.
  IV. French. (Translation from and into, writing from dictation, writing a letter in French on ordinary subjects, and conversation, paying particular attention to accents, genders, and tenses.)
  V. Latin.

Optional.

  I. Ancient Greek.
  II. Italian.
  III. German.
  IV. Spanish.

3. A fee of £4 will be required from every Candidate attending the Examination.

CIVIL SERVICE COMMISSION,
  7th November, 1901.

XI.—EXAMINATIONS FOR THE SITUATION OF STUDENT INTERPRETER IN CHINA, JAPAN, OR SIAM.

The Regulations are similar to those under which the foregoing Examinations are held ; but the subjects of Examination are as follows :—

Obligatory.

I. Handwriting and Orthography.
II. Arithmetic (including Vulgar and Decimal Fractions).
III. English Composition.

Optional.

IV. Précis.
V. Geography.
VI. Euclid (Books I. to IV.).
VII. Latin.
VIII. French.
IX. German.
X. (*a*) The Elements of Criminal Law ;
   (*b*) The principles of British Mercantile and Commercial Law relating to (1) Shipping, (2) Negotiable Instruments, Bills of Exchange, and Promissory Notes, (3) Contracts for the Carriage of Goods, (4) Contracts for Marine Insurance, Bottomry, and Respondentia, (5) Contracts with Seamen, (6) The Doctrines of stoppage *in transitu* and lien.

Notice of these Examinations is given by advertisement in the *London Gazette*, and some other papers.

CIVIL SERVICE COMMISSION,
  7th November, 1901.

EXAMINATION PAPERS, 1902-1903.

MATRICULATION.

LATIN.

Examiner—PROFESSOR SANDFORD.

1. Translate into English :—

(*a*) Nulla enim virtus aliam mercedem laborum desiderat praeter hanc laudis : qua quidem *detracta*, iudices, quid est quod in hoc tam exiguo vitae curriculo tantis nos in laboribus *exerceamus* ?

(*b*) Cognosce ex me, quoniam hoc primum tempus discendi *nactus es*, quam multa esse oporteat in eo, qui alterum accuset : ex quibus si unum aliquod in te *cognoveris*, ego iam tibi ipse *istuc* quod expetis concedam.

(*c*) Quid *faciat* laetas segetes, quo *sidere* terram
Vertere, Maecenas, ulmisque adiungere vites
Conveniat, quae cura boum, qui cultus *habendo*
Sit pecori, apibus quanta experientia *parcis*,
Hinc canere incipiam.

2. Parse *fully* the words italicised.

3. Translate into Latin :—

(*a*) I believe this one point—that you could have been known by none if not by Sicilians.

(*b*) Choose which you will of the two alternatives—that this was done or was not, was true or was false.

(*c*) Since this is so, what reason have you to doubt about his citizenship ?

(*d*) He came to Rome in the consulship of Marius and Catulus ; one of whom could supply great subjects for writing, the other not only achievements but appreciative taste.

4. (*a*) Give, with dates, some account of the career of Pyrrhus in Italy.

(*b*) What were the changes Caius Gracchus sought to introduce at Rome ?

(*c*) Who were the leaders in the First Civil war ? What were its causes ? When and how was it concluded ?

FRENCH.

Examiner—PROFESSOR STEINBERGER.

1. Translate into French :—

He was quite worthy of receiving such a reward for having saved his brother's life.

I cannot be persuaded that you were right in abandoning the study of the law without consulting your father.

I am ashamed of my former laziness.

Would that I had been with you at that time of danger.

I am persuaded that he will not be able to finish this business before the first of May.

It cannot be denied that he has erred in entrusting to that slave so important an affair.

If I had known that you had resolved to go to Athens, I should have asked my brother to accompany you.

He told me why his brother had done this.

When Cæsar arrived in Gaul, he found the country in a great commotion and in fear, lest the Germans should cross the Rhine and make themselves masters of the country.

2. Oral Examination in French Grammar and Authors prescribed.

ENGLISH.

Examiner—PROFESSOR TRENCH.

1. Distinguish strong verbs and weak verbs.
   Classify pronouns.
   Explain and illustrate the term ' simile.'

2. Narrate the final incidents in the story of Waverley and his friends.
   Describe the metre of *Paradise Lost*.

3. Narrate the first day's battle in *Paradise Lost*, vi.

SUBJECT FOR ESSAY.

Patriotism.

MATHEMATICS.

ARITHMETIC AND ALGEBRA.

Examiner—PROFESSOR BROMWICH.

1. Multiply 1·4286 by ·85714, giving your answer correctly to three places of decimals. Verify your work by dividing the answer by 1·4286.

2. Extract the square root of 17 to four places of decimals and compare its value with that of $4\frac{1}{8}\frac{8}{7}$.

3. Find to the nearest shilling the amount of £500 in 3 years at 4 per cent., at compound interest.

4. Simplify

$$(p + q)(p - q)(p^2 - q^2)(p^2 + q^2)^2 - (p^2 - q^2)^4.$$

5. Solve

$$\frac{1}{x + 1} - \frac{1}{x + 2} = \frac{1}{x + 3} - \frac{1}{x + 4}.$$

6. How long will an up and a down train take to pass each other, each being 55 yards long, and each travelling at 45 miles an hour?

7. If in two triangles ABC, PQR, we have $AB = PQ$ and the angles A, C equal to the angles P, R, respectively, prove that the triangles are equal in all respects.

8. Find the longest and the shortest chords that can be drawn through a given point within a given circle.

9. If $ABCD$ is a quadrilateral inscribed in a circle, prove that the sum of the angles A, C is equal to the sum of the angles B, D, and that each sum is equal to two right angles.

———

EXPERIMENTAL PHYSICS.

Examiner—PRESIDENT ANDERSON.

1. Define *acceleration*. A falling body describes the last 50 feet of its descent in 1½ seconds. From what height did it fall, and with what speed does it reach the ground?

2. One particle, moving with a speed of 15, overtakes another, moving in the same direction, with speed 10. After collision they move together with speed 12. Compare their masses.

3. Define *stable, unstable*, and *neutral equilibrium*, and give examples.

4. What is meant by the pressure of a fluid at a point? How would you measure the atmospheric pressure at a given point?

5. A body floats with one-tenth of its volume above the surface of water. What fraction of its volume would project above the surface if it were floating in liquid of density 1·25?

6. Describe. the construction of a pump suitable for condensing a gas.

LITERARY SCHOLARSHIPS OF THE FIRST YEAR.

LATIN.

FIRST PAPER.

Examiner—PROFESSOR SANDFORD.

1. Translate, with short notes :—

(*a*) Insuber eques (Ducario nomen erat) facie quoque noscitans, Consul, en, inquit, hic est, popularibus suis, qui legiones nostras cecidit, agrosque et urbem est depopulatus. Iam ego hanc victimam Manibus peremptorum foede civium dabo : subditisque calcaribus equo, per confertissimam hostium turbam impetum facit : obtruncatoque prius armigero, qui se infesto venienti obiecerat, consulem lancea transfixit. Spoliare cupientem triarii obiectis scutis arcuere. Magnae partis fuga inde primum coepit : et iam nec lacus nec montes obstabant pavori. Per omnia arta praeruptaque velut caeci evadunt : armaque et viri super alium alii praecipitantur.—LIVY xxii.

(*b*) Illud etiam in tali consilio vobis animadvertendum, Patres conscripti, censeam (si tamen duriores esse velitis, quod nullo nostro merito faciatis) cui nos hosti relicturi sitis : Pyrrho videlicet, qui nos hospitum numero habuit captivos, an barbaro ac Poeno, qui utrum avarior an crudelior sit, vix existimari potest. Si videatis catenas, squalorem, deformitatem civium vestrorum, non minus profecto vos ea species moveat, quam si ex altera parte cernatis stratas Cannensibus campis legiones vestras. Intueri potestis sollicitudinem et lacrimas in vestibulo curiae stantium cognatorum nostrorum, exspectantiumque responsum vestrum.—*Ibid.*

(c) Ea cum Ciceroni nuntiarentur, ancipiti malo permotus, quod neque urbem ab insidiis privato consilio longius tueri poterat, neque exercitus Manli quantus aut quo consilio foret satis conpertum habebat, rem ad senatum refert, iam antea volgi rumoribus exagitatum. Itaque, quod plerumque in atroci negotio solet, senatus decrevit, darent operam consules ne quid res publica detrimenti caperet.—SALLUST, *Cat.*

(d) Longe mihi alia mens est, patres conscripti, cum res atque pericula nostra considero, et cum sententias nonnullorum ipse mecum reputo. Illi mihi disseruisse videntur de poena eorum, qui patriae parentibus, aris atque focis suis bellum paravere : res autem monet cavere ab illis magis quam quid in illos statuamus consultare. Nam cetera malificia tum persequare, ubi facta sunt : hoc, nisi provideris ne accidat, ubi evenit, frustra iudicia inplores : capta urbe nihil fit relicui victis.—*Ibid.*

(e) Missi legati renuntiarunt L. Cornelium ad magistratus subrogandos Romam venturum. De litteris L. Corneli, quas scripserat secundum proelium cum Bois factum, disceptatio in senatu fuit, quia privatim plerisque senatoribus legatus M. Claudius scripserat fortunae populi Romani et militum virtuti gratiam habendam, quod res bene gesta esset ; consulis opera et militum aliquantum amissum et hostium exercitum cuius delendi oblata fortuna fuerit, elapsum : milites eo plures perisse, quod tardius ex subsidiis, qui laborantibus opem ferrent, successissent ; hostes e manibus emissos, quod equitibus legionariis et tardius datum signum esset et persequi fugientes non licuisset.

2. Translate into Latin :—

Metellus now appeared before Corinth. Animated by a feeling of humanity, he wished to spare the city. Such a magnificent ancient city was indeed something venerable to many a Roman, and the idea of destroying it was terrible to Metellus. It is also possible that he grudged the Consul Mummius, who was already advancing in quick marches, the honour of bringing the war to a close. Once more Metellus sent some Greeks to the army, offering, according to Roman notions, fair terms if they would but lay down their arms. What else could he have done? But Diaeus, who knew that his life was forfeited, goaded the poor people to madness.—NIEBUHR.

8. (*a*) Give an account of the war with the Cimbri and Teutones. What other war were the Romans waging at the same time?

(*b*) Trace the internal history of Rome between 100 B.C. and 90 B.C.

(*c*) Sketch the career of Pompey up to the year 65 B.C.

LATIN.

SECOND PAPER.

Examiner—PROFESSOR SANDFORD.

Translate, parsing fully the words italicised :—

(*a*) Sis licet felix, ubicunque mavis,
Et memor *nostri*, Galatea, vivas :
Teque nec laevus vetet ire picus,
    Nec vaga cornix.

Sed vides, quanto trepidet tumultu
Pronus Orion. Ego quid sit ater
Adriae novi sinus, et quid albus
    Peccet Iapyx.

Hostium uxores puerique caecos
Sentiant motus orientis Austri, et
Aequoris nigri fremitum, et trementes
    Verbere ripas.

                  HORACE.

(b) Dicunt in tenero gramine pinguium
    Custodes ovium carmina fistula,
    Delectantque deum, cui pecus et nigri
        Colles Arcadiae placent.

Adduxere sitim tempora, Virgili:
Sed pressum Calibus ducere Liberum
Si *gestis*, iuvenum nobilium cliens,
    Nardo vina mereberis.

Nardi parvus onyx eliciet cadum,
Qui nunc Sulpiciis accubat horreis
Spes donare novas largus, amaraque
    Curarum *eluere* efficax.

ID.

Scan the first stanza in each of these two passages:—

(c) Mancipiis locuples eget aeris Cappadocum rex:
    Ne *fueris* hic tu.   Chlamydes Lucullus, ut aiunt,
    Si posset centum scenae praebere rogatus,
    ' Qui possum tot ? ' ait : ' tamen et, quaeram et, quot
        habebo,'
    ' Mittam ' : post paulo scribit, sibi milia quinque
    Esse domi chlamydum ; partem, vel *tolleret* omnes.
    Exilis domus est, ubi non et multa supersunt,
    Et dominum fallunt, et prosunt furibus.   Ergo
    Si res sola potest facere et servare beatum,
    Hoc primus repetas opus, hoc postremus omittas.
    Si fortunatum species et gratia praestat ;
    Mercemur servum, qui *dictet* nomina, laevum
    Qui fodicet latus, et cogat trans pondera dextram
    Porrigere : ' Hic multum in Fabia valet, ille Velina ;
    Cui libet is fasces dabit, eripietque curule,
    Cui volet, importunus, ebur ' : ' Frater, Pater,' adde ;
    Ut cuique est aetas, ita quemque facetus adopta.

ID.

(d) Sed tuus hic populus, sapiens et iustus in uno,
    Te nostris ducibus, te Graiis anteferendo,
    Cetera nequaquam simili ratione modoque
    Aestimat, et, nisi quae terris semota suisque
    Temporibus defuncta videt, fastidit et odit :
    Sic fautor veterum, ut tabulas peccare vetantes,

Quas bis quinque viri sanxerunt, foedera regum
Vel *Gabiis*, vel cum rigidis aequata Sabinis,
Pontificum libros, annosa volumina vatum,
Dictitet Albano Musas in monte locutas.
Si, quia Graecorum sunt antiquissima quaeque
Scripta vel optima Romani pensantur eadem
Scriptores trutina; non est, quod multa loquamur:
Nil intra est *olea*, nil extra est in nuce duri.
Venimus ad summum fortunae; pingimus, atque
Psallimus et luctamur Achivis doctius unctis.

Id.

2. (*a*) How does Horace express?—Take care that no one reaches the harbour before you. You live well if you take pains to be really what you are said to be. He will praise your sport enthusiastically, if he believes that you sympathise with his pursuits.

(*b*) Carmine tu gaudes, hic delectatur iambis,
    Ille Bioneis sermonibus et sale nigro.
Explain fully the allusions.

8. (*a*) Conjugate the Latin verbs with which the following English words are connected:—revert, fossil, dejected, pendant, express, allude, separate, fixture, fiction, victor, vision.

(*b*) Give the Latin for:—Tell me which of your two letters I am to believe. It is of great importance to you as well as to Caesar, who complained that you had kept him in the dark about this subject. Whether Cicero intercedes or no, I will ask him whether he can pardon you.

GREEK.

First Paper.

Examiner—Professor McElderry.

1. Translate:—

δᾶερ ἐμεῖο, κυνὸς κακομηχάνου ὀκρυοέσσης,
ὥς μ᾽ ὄφελ᾽ ἤματι τῷ, ὅτε με πρῶτον τέκε μήτηρ,
οἴχεσθαι προφέρουσα κακὴ ἀνέμοιο θύελλα
εἰς ὄρος ἢ εἰς κῦμα πολυφλοίσβοιο θαλάσσης,

ἔνθα με κῦμ᾽ ἀπόερσε πάρος τάδε ἔργα γενέσθαι.
αὐτὰρ ἐπεὶ τάδε γ᾽ ὧδε θεοὶ κακὰ τεκμήραντο,
ἀνδρὸς ἔπειτ᾽ ὤφελλον ἀμείνονος εἶναι ἄκοιτις,
ὃς ᾔδη νέμεσίν τε καὶ αἴσχεα πόλλ᾽ ἀνθρώπων.
τούτῳ δ᾽ οὔτ᾽ ἀρ νῦν φρένες ἔμπεδοι οὔτ᾽ ἄρ᾽ ὀπίσσω
ἔσσονται· τῷ καί μιν ἐπαυρήσεσθαι ὀίω.
ἀλλ᾽ ἄγε νῦν εἴσελθε καὶ ἕζεο τῷδ᾽ ἐπὶ δίφρῳ,
δᾶερ, ἐπεί σε μάλιστα πόνος φρένας ἀμφιβέβηκεν
εἵνεκ᾽ ἐμεῖο κυνὸς καὶ Ἀλεξάνδρου ἔνεκ᾽ ἄτης,
οἷσιν ἐπὶ Ζεὺς θῆκε κακὸν μόρον, ὡς καὶ ὀπίσσω
ἀνθρώποισι πελώμεθ᾽ ἀοίδιμοι ἐσσομένοισιν.

HOMER.

Comment on the syntax of ἀπόερσε in above extract.

Annotate : ἀνοπαῖα, ἀργειφόντης; κρητῆρας ἐπεστέψαντο ποτοῖο (with reference to Virgil's rendering); πόρεν δ᾽ ὅ γε σήματα λυγρά. How is this clause important in the Homeric controversy?

2. Translate :—

Θαυμάζω δὲ τῶν δυναστευόντων ἐν ταῖς πόλεσιν, εἰ προσήκειν αὑτοῖς ἡγοῦνται μέγα φρονεῖν, μηδὲν πώποθ᾽ ὑπὲρ τηλικούτων πραγμάτων μήτ᾽ εἰπεῖν μήτ᾽ ἐνθυμηθῆναι δυνηθέντες. ἐχρῆν γὰρ αὐτούς, εἴπερ ἦσαν ἄξιοι τῆς παρούσης δόξης, ἁπάντων ἀφεμένους τῶν ἄλλων περὶ τοῦ πολέμου τοῦ πρὸς τοὺς βαρβάρους εἰσηγεῖσθαι καὶ συμβουλεύειν. τυχὸν μὲν γὰρ ἄν τι συνεπέραναν· εἰ δὲ καὶ προαπεῖπον, ἀλλ᾽ οὖν τούς γε λόγους ὥσπερ χρησμοὺς εἰς τὸν ἐπιόντα χρόνον ἂν κατέλιπον. νῦν δ᾽ οἱ μὲν ἐν ταῖς μεγίσταις δόξαις ὄντες ἐπὶ μικροῖς σπουδάζουσιν, ἡμῖν δὲ τοῖς τῶν πολιτικῶν ἐξεστηκόσι περὶ τηλικούτων πραγμάτων συμβουλεύειν παραλελοίπασιν.—ISOCRATES.

Write a short note upon the career of Isocrates, with special reference to his political ideas as shown in the *Panegyricus.*

3. Translate :—

Ἀκούεις, Αἰσχίνη, τοῦ νόμου λέγοντος σαφῶς, πλὴν ἐάν τινας ὁ δῆμος ἢ ἡ βουλὴ ψηφίσηται· τούτους δὲ ἀναγορευέτω. τί οὖν, ὦ ταλαίπωρε, συκοφαντεῖς; τί λόγους πλάττεις; τί

σαυτὸν οὐκ ἐλλεβορίζεις ἐπὶ τούτοις; ἀλλ' οὐδ' αἰσχύνει φθόνου
δίκην εἰσάγων, οὐκ ἀδικήματος οὐδενός, καὶ νόμους τοὺς μὲν
μεταποιῶν, τῶν δ' ἀφαιρῶν μέρη, οὓς ὅλους δίκαιον ἦν ἀναγι-
γνώσκεσθαι τοῖς γε ὀμωμοκόσι κατὰ τοὺς νόμους ψηφιεῖσθαι;
ἔπειτα τοιαῦτα ποιῶν λέγεις ἃ δεῖ προσεῖναι τῷ δημοτικῷ, ὥσπερ
ἀνδριάντα ἐκδεδωκὼς κατὰ συγγραφήν, εἶτ' οὐκ ἔχοντα ἃ προσῆκεν
ἐκ τῆς συγγραφῆς κομιζόμενος, ἢ λόγῳ τοὺς δημοτικούς, ἀλλ'
οὐ τοῖς πράγμασι καὶ τοῖς πολιτεύμασι γιγνωσκομένους. καὶ
βοᾷς ῥητὰ καὶ ἄρρητα ὀνομάζων, ὥσπερ ἐξ ἀμάξης, ἃ σοὶ καὶ
τῷ σῷ γένει πρόσεστιν, οὐκ ἐμοί.—Demosthenes.

Annotate fully the construction of the clause beginning
ἢ λόγῳ down to γιγνωσκομένους.

Explain : ὑπωμοσία, συμμορία, ἀρχιτέκτων, ἀποστολεύς,
ἑωλοκρασία.

UNPRESCRIBED PASSAGE.

4. Translate :—

καὶ τὸ γ' εἰς τὸν Ἑλλήσποντον ἐκπέμπειν ἕτερον στρατηγὸν
τοῦτ' ἐστίν. εἰ γὰρ δεινὰ ποιεῖ Διοπείθης καὶ κατάγει τὰ
πλοῖα, μικρόν, ὦ ἄνδρες Ἀθηναῖοι, μικρὸν πινάκιον ταῦτα πάντα
κωλῦσαι δύναιτ' ἄν, καὶ λέγουσιν οἱ νόμοι ταῦτα τοὺς ἀδικοῦντας
εἰσαγγέλλειν, οὐ μὰ Δία δαπάναις καὶ τριήρεσι τοσαύταις ἡμᾶς
αὐτοὺς φυλάττειν, ἐπεὶ τοῦτό γ' ἐστὶν ὑπερβολὴ μανίας· ἀλλ'
ἐπὶ μὲν τοὺς ἐχθρούς, οὓς οὐκ ἔστι λαβεῖν ὑπὸ τοῖς νόμοις,
καὶ στρατιώτας τρέφειν καὶ τριήρεις ἐκπέμπειν καὶ χρήματα
εἰσφέρειν δεῖ καὶ ἀναγκαῖόν ἐστιν, ἐπὶ δ' ἡμᾶς αὐτοὺς ψήφισμα,
εἰσαγγελία, πάραλος, ταῦτ' ἐστὶν ἱκανά. ταῦτ' ἦν εὖ φρονούντων
ἀνθρώπων, ἐπηρεαζόντων δὲ καὶ διαφθειρόντων τὰ πράγματα, ἃ
νῦν οὗτοι ποιοῦσιν.—Demosthenes.

GREEK.
Second Paper.
Examiner—Professor McElderry.

1. Translate into Greek :—

But with respect to the present crisis I should wish to
offer suitable advice.   Before we begin the struggle we must
clearly consider, while it is still in our power to maintain the

peace, what are our hopes and resources for the war. We must measure our abilities both by sea and land, and the strength and position of the enemy whom we are about to engage. If you are guided by me, either you will endure patiently whatever the stronger may command, or, if you determine rather to die than to desert the cause of liberty, you will silently collect your forces and by a sudden attack anticipate the designs of the king.

GRAMMAR.

2. (*a*) Contrast the uses of οὐ and μή.

(*b*) Explain the use of the 'optative of indefinite frequency.'

(*c*) Give the principal parts of γιγνώσκω, ἀκούω, τρέχω, τιτρώσκω, ἵημι.

HISTORY AND LITERATURE.

3. (*a*) Give a summary of the causes which led up to the Peloponnesian war.

(*b*) Indicate the position in Greek history of Sphodrias, Histiaeus, Phokion, Timoleon. Give dates.

(*c*) Write a note on the poets of the Lesbian school.

(*d*) Give some account of the old, middle, and new comedy. Whence is derived our knowledge of the last?

UNPRESCRIBED PASSAGE.

4. Translate into English:—

> Ὦ πόποι, ὡς ὅδε πᾶσι φίλος καὶ τίμιός ἐστιν
> ἀνθρώποις, ὁτεών τε πόλιν καὶ γαῖαν ἵκηται!
> πολλὰ μὲν ἐκ Τροίης ἄγεται κειμήλια καλὰ
> ληίδος· ἡμεῖς δ' αὖτε ὁμὴν ὁδὸν ἐκτελέσαντες
> οἴκαδε νισσόμεθα κενεὰς σὺν χεῖρας ἔχοντες.
> καὶ νῦν οἱ τάδ' ἔδωκε χαριζόμενος φιλότητι
> Αἴολος· ἀλλ' ἄγε θᾶσσον ἰδώμεθα, ὅττι τάδ' ἐστίν,
> ὅσσος τις χρυσός τε καὶ ἄργυρος ἀσκῷ ἔνεστιν·
>
> Ὣς ἔφασαν· βουλὴ δὲ κακὴ νίκησεν ἑταίρων·
> ἀσκὸν μὲν λῦσαν, ἄνεμοι δ' ἐκ πάντες ὄρουσαν.

τοὺς δ' αἶψ' ἁρπάξασα φέρεν πόντονδε θύελλα
κλαίοντας, γαίης ἄπο πατρίδος· αὐτὰρ ἔγωγε
ἐγρόμενος, κατὰ θυμὸν ἀμύμονα μερμήριξα,
ἠὲ πεσὼν ἐκ νηὸς ἀποφθίμην ἐνὶ πόντῳ,
ἦ ἀκέων τλαίην, καὶ ἔτι ζωοῖσι μετείην.

HOMER.

FRENCH.

Examiner—PROFESSOR STEINBERGER.

COMPOSITION.

1. Translate into French :—

Francis Drake was the first Englishman who sailed round the world. He did not intend to do this, but to attack and plunder Spanish ships. It was in the time of Elizabeth, Queen of England. With one ship Drake attacked the Spaniards where he could find them. His ship was full of gold and silver, which had been destined for Spain. He wished to return to England. As, however, many Spanish ships were trying to capture him, he sailed to the East Indies, crossed the Indian Ocean, rounded the Cape of Good Hope, and so returned to England. His voyage had lasted nearly three years, from 1577 to 1580. The Queen was proud of him, and knighted him on board the ship which had sailed round the world.

GRAMMAR.

2. Give a list of the neuter verbs that are always conjugated with *être*. Form sentences (with translation) with the verbs *convenir* and *descendre*, showing their differences of meaning when construed with *être* and when with *avoir*.

3. Translate :—Listen to him; think of it; think of them; offer him some; I have applied to him; trust her; they have surrendered to them; we complain of you; we expected to hear from you; if you go to the concert, take me with you.

4. Account for the use of the subjunctive in the sentences that follow, and translate them :—

Attendez patiemment qu'on vienne vous chercher.
Je trouve étrange que vous ayez fait cette démarche.
Si je croyais qu'il arrivât demain, je l'attendrais.
Il n'y a personne qui le sache.
C'est la moindre récompense qu'on lui doive.
                          Formons un traité
Qui mette pour jamais mes droits en sûreté.

5. Translate : I was busy writing. What is to be done? That is nothing to me. How is that? There is going to be a fight. One would take him to be eighty years of age. It is now ten years since he went. It being four o'clock we left the place. Your life is at stake. He bears us a grudge. It is in vain for you to try.

6. Describe, *in French*, any character or incident that you remember from any of the prescribed books (about 15 lines).

UNPRESCRIBED PASSAGE.

7. Translate into English :—

UN CHEMIN EN PROVENCE.

Ce chemin plein de méandres, traversé en maint endroit par le ruisseau qui saute d'un bord à l'autre, tantôt serré entre des bancs de rochers, tantôt élargi par le caprice des piétons dans les herbes, est ridé et vallonné, mais nulle part il n'est difficile, et il offre une des rares promenades poétiques qu'on puisse faire sans danger dans ce pays. Le ruisselet a si peu d'eau que, quand il lui plaît de changer de lit, il couvre le sable du chemin d'une gaze argentée qu'on verrait à peine, si son frissonnement ne la trahissait pas. Des herbes folles, des plantes aromatiques se pressent sur ses marges, comme si elles voulaient se hâter de tout boire avant l'été, qui dessèche tout. Les pins sont beaux pour des pins de Provence : protégé par la falaise qui forme autour de la forêt un amphithéâtre assez majestueux, ils ont pu grandir sans se tordre.—GEORGE SAND.

8. Oral Examination.

GERMAN.

Examiner—Professor Steinberger.

Composition.

1. Translate into German :—

(*a*) How fond these people are of dinner parties; I think they have one every day; last week I was asked to one, and I have just received another invitation for Thursday.

(*b*) It takes from five to six days now to go to America; you can spend part of your summer holidays in New York.

(*c*) No one knows where he resides; he gets his letters addressed to him ' Post-office, Dublin'; but he does not call for them himself.

(*d*) One of his friends asks for his letters, and, as soon as he has got them, sends them to him.

(*e*) Pray, do not imagine that a penny of your money will be touched by me, or any other person.

(*f*) She has a great liking for sweetmeats, however unwholesome they may be.

Grammar.

2. Construct two German sentences to illustrate the use of Was für ein and was für einer, and two others, showing the difference between Mal and Zeit.

3. Mention the case governed by each of the following prepositions, and give the English meaning — laut, gemäß, unweit, binnen, wegen, ohne, nebst, zuwider, gegen.

4. Translate into German:—Twice three are six; for the third time; once for all; thirdly; during the last three weeks; to catch a cold; my head aches.

5. Give the English meaning of each of the following substantives:—Der Leiter, die Leiter; der Heide, die Heide; die Mark, das Mark; der Thor, das Thor; der Gehalt, das Gehalt.

P 8

AUTHORS.

6. Translate into English :—

I.

Balb erschien Gustav Adolph am Ufer, den baierischen Verschanzungen gegenüber, nachdem er sich das ganze Augsburgische Gebiet dießseits des Lechs unterworfen und seinen Truppen eine reiche Zufuhr aus diesem Landstrich geöffnet hatte. Es war im Märzmonat, wo dieser Strom von häufigen Regengüssen und von dem Schnee der tyrolischen Gebirge zu einer ungewöhnlichen Höhe schwillt, und zwischen steilen Ufern mit reißender Schnelligkeit fluthet. Ein gewisses Grab öffnete sich dem waghälsigen Stürmer in seinen Wellen, und am entgegenstehenden Ufer zeigten ihm die feindlichen Kanonen ihre mörderischen Schlünde. Ertrotzte er dennoch mitten durch die Wuth des Wassers und des Feuers den fast unmöglichen Uebergang, so erwartet die ermatteten Truppen ein frischer und muthiger Feind in einem unüberwindlichen Lager, und nach Erholung schmachtend, finden sie eine Schlacht. Mit erschöpfter Kraft müssen sie die feindlichen Schanzen ersteigen, deren Festigkeit jedes Angriffs zu spotten scheint. Eine Niederlage, an diesem Ufer erlitten, führt sie unvermeidlich zum Untergang; denn derselbe Strom, der ihnen die Bahn zum Siege erschwert, versperrt ihnen alle Wege zur Flucht, wenn das Glück sie verlassen sollte.— Schiller.

II.

König Friedrich Wilhelm I. war, wie bekannt, kein Fürst von einnehmender Art. Er war durch und durch Despot, in seinem Hause, seinem Heere, seinem Staate, und dabei zwar gutmüthig, aber jähzornig und ungebildet. Jedoch hatte er zwei Eigenschaften, die seinen Despotismus selbst zum Vortheil seines Landes machten, einen unbedingten Trieb zur Selbständigkeit und einen unerschütterlichen rechtschaffenen Willen. Unaufhörlich vermehrte er mit einem ganz hervorragenden Organisationstalente sein Heer, übte es mit eisernem, genauem, kleinlichem Fleiße; „ein Fürst," sagte er, „der keine Soldaten hat, findet keine Achtung in der Welt."— Sybel.

7. Oral Examination, Monday, November 8, at 10 o'clock.

ENGLISH.

Examiner—PROFESSOR TRENCH.

1. Describe the scene that takes place in Brutus's tent (*Jul. Cæs.* ACT. IV. Sc. iii.).

2. Explain the following terms and phrases from *Coriolanus* :—

(*a*) bisson conspectuities.

(*b*) this is clean kam.

(*c*) the one side must have bale.

(*d*) I would not have been so fidiused.

(*e*) You have made good work . . . You that stood so much upon the voice of occupation.

3. Give some examples from Bacon (*a*) of metaphors, and (*b*) of similes.

4. Reproduce some of Bacon's remarks *either* on Friendship, *or* on Studies.

ESSAY.

Write a short Essay on "Shakespeare's Roman Women."

CELTIC.

Examiner—JOHN MAC NEILL, B.A.

1. Translate into English :—

Do bí ceann Condín corgarta ó ingnib na cailliǵe, ⁊ an cnoiceann an liobannaiǵ anuan an a plucaib. Téiö Dianmaiö amaċ ⁊ do ṫeangṁuiǵ póing caonaċ ain. Do ṁanb Dianmaiö an póing ⁊ do ċongain í, ⁊ ċuɡ an cnoiceann inteaċ, ⁊ do öeanuiǵ an ceann Condín ó, ⁊ do öeann ⁊ do blátuiǵ é, ionnur gun ɡab lein an geneiö úin aṁail cnoiceann náöúnta, go nöubaint Dianmaiö : 'Dan liom, a Condín, ir maiċ do ċuaiö coṁnac na caillige öuit, óin ir maiċ tagann do caipín öuit, ⁊ go maini ö tú é.'—*Eachtra Lomnochtain.*

2. Translate into English :—

1. Ɗo ʓaɓ ꞃé ꝺo ꞃʓιúꞃꞃaιɓ aιꞃ. 2. Ní ꝺéaꞃnaιɓ mé a ɓeaʓ ꝺ'euʓcoιꞃ aιꞃ. 3. Maꞃ ꝺo ʓꞃáɓuιʓ ꞃé eaꞃʓaιne, cιʓeaɓ ꞃí aιꞃ. 4. Sʓꞃíɓneoιꞃ naċ ꝺcuʓann ꝺ'a aιꞃe aċc aoιꞃ, aʓ aṁuꞃꝺꞃaιʓ aṁaιl maꝺaιʓ. 5. Iꞃ ꞃó-ṁóꞃ ꝺo ʓoιlleaꞃ aꞃ mo ċꞃoιꝺe ꝼeaꞃʓ ꝺo ċuꞃ oꞃc.—*Irish Phrase-Book.*

6. Ní ɓꞃuaꞃaꝺaꞃ caoι aꞃ a ċaɓaιꞃc ιꞃceaċ. 7. Iꞃ ꝺeacaιꞃ a ċuꞃ a ʓcéιll ꝺ' ιomaꝺ a ꝺcaιꞃɓe ꝼéιn ꝺo leanṁuιn. 8. Ɗo ꝼeaꞃaꝺ ꝼáιlce ꞃιu aʓ maιċιɓ an ɓaιle. 9. Ιonann lιcꞃeaċa ꝺo na h-Éιꞃeannaċaιɓ aʓuꞃ ꝺo na Laιꝺneoꞃaιɓ, ꝼóꞃ ní ɓíonn aca *x, y, z.* 10. Ɑcá ꞃé céιllιꝺe aʓaꝺ-ꞃa ꞃιn ꝺo ꝺeunaṁ.—*Handbook of Irish Idioms.*

GRAMMAR.

3. Show, with examples, what are the chief uses of the subjunctive (or optative) mood, present and past, in Irish.

4. Write a note on the usage of the verb-forms called passive (also called indefinite and autonomous) in Irish, having especial regard to intransitive verbs. Give examples.

5. How is the function of the infinitive and present participle expressed in Irish ? The infinitive and present participle can govern a direct object in English, Latin, etc. In what case is a noun in Irish corresponding to this direct object ? What is the Irish usage when the object in English or Latin is a personal pronoun ? Give examples.

6. Translate into Irish :—

Isbeirne is this country in which thou art, O son of the king of Africa. There came a serpent to us, which devoured our heavy flocks, and slew all our people, and made a slaughter of our armies, so that none are alive but those who are here. And our ancients had left it to us as a prophecy, that when the ball of fire would blaze up, the son of the king of Africa would come to us and relieve us from the distress in which we are, and would slay that wonderful serpent.

7. Translate into English :—

baoi baoiṗṙi aṙuṙ boċṙuiḃe móṙ aṙ a h-aiċle ṙin ṗoṙ
cloinn Neiṁioḃ aṙ Ṗoṁóṙċaiḃ aṙ ḃioṙailc na ṙcaċ bo
ḃṙiṙ Neiṁiḃ oṙṙa. Moṙc, iomoṙṙo, ṁac Ḃeilioḃ, aṙuṙ
Conainṙ ṁac Ṗaoḃaiṙ ó n-ṙoiṗċioṙ Cop Conoinṙ a
n-imiol Éiṙionn ċuaiḃ, aṙa ṙaiḃe loinṙioṙ, aṙuṙ iab 'n
a ṙ-coṁnuiḃe a b-Cop Conuinṙ, ba 'n-ṙoiṗċioṙ Coiṙiniṙ,
aṙ caḃaċ óíoṙa aṙ clannaiḃ Neiṁeaḃ ; aṙuṙ ba h-é
méb an óíoṙa ṙoin bá b-cṙian cloinne, aṙuṙ eaċa, aṙuṙ
bleaċca, ṗeaṙ n-Éiṙionn bo ċioḃlacaḃ óóiḃ ṙaċa bliaḃna
Oiḃċe Shaṁna ṙo Maṙ ṙ-Céiḃne iḃiṙ Ḃhṙoḃaoiṙ aṙuṙ
Éiṙne.—*Keating's History.*

8. Translate into English :—

Iaṙ ṙin b'ṗiaṙṙuiṙ Coḃ be'n ċailliṙ cṙéaḃ ṗab
b'aimṙiṙ ó ṗuaiṙ a haċaiṙ báṙ, 'nó ca hainm acá oṙc
ṗéin ?' 'beċuine iṙ ainm baṁṙa,' aṙ ṙí, 'aṙuṙ cá cṙí
ċéaḃ bliaḃan ó ṗuaiṙ m'aċaiṙ báṙ.' 'Cṙéaḃ bo ḃeiṙ
beó ṙiḃ an ṗab ṙin ?' aṙ Coḃ. 'Ḋn bcuṙaiṙ ṗo beaṙa
an coṙn aṙ a bcuṙaṙ an beoċ ḋuic ó ċiainiḃ ?' 'Ḃo
ċonnaiṙc mé,' aṙ Coḃ. 'Maiṙeaḃ,' aṙ ṙí, 'ṙiḃ bé neaċ
ólṗaṙ beoċ aṙ ṙaċ lá, ní luiṙeann aoiṙ nó úṙ-cṙáḃ aiṙ,
cṙé ḃiċ ṙíoṙ, aṙuṙ cáiḃ ṙeóiḃ eile aṙainn aṙ a ḃṗuiliḃ
iomaḃ buaḃ maṙ ṙúḃ.'

SCIENCE SCHOLARSHIPS OF THE FIRST YEAR.
[Arts, Medicine, and Engineering.]

First Paper.
ARITHMETIC AND ALGEBRA.
Examiner—Professor Bromwich.

1. Find the value of

$$(2\sqrt{7} - 3\sqrt{3} + \tfrac{1}{4}\sqrt{6})^2$$

to two places of decimals.

2. If A is less than B, and if q, r are the quotient and remainder when B is divided by A, and s, t the quotient and remainder when B is divided by r, prove that

$$\frac{A}{B} = \frac{1}{q} - \frac{1}{qs} + F,$$

where F is less than $\dfrac{1}{qs}$.

3. Solve the equation

$$(x+1)(x+2)(x+3) = (x-3)(x+4)(x+5).$$

4. A takes m times as long to do a piece of work as B and C together; B n times as long as C and A together; C x times as long as A and B together. Find x in terms of m, n.

5. Solve the equations

$$x + y = 1, \quad ax + by = c,$$

and prove that

$$a^2x + b^2y = c^2 - (c - a)(c - b).$$

6. If the sum of m terms of an Arithmetical Progression is to the sum of n terms in the ratio $m^2 : n^2$, prove that the mth term will be to the nth term as $2m - 1 : 2n - 1$.

7. Find p, q, so that

$$x^4 + x^2y^2 + y^4 = (x^2 + pxy + y^2)(x^2 + qxy + y^2).$$

Factorize $\quad 4b^2c^2 - (b^2 + c^2 - a^2)^2.$

8. Solve the equations

$$\frac{1}{x} + \frac{1}{1-y} = \frac{1}{1-x} + \frac{1}{y} = c$$

in the cases (i) $c = 2$, (ii) $c = 4$.

9. In how many different ways can a bracelet be made of 12 blue and 3 red beads, no two red beads being together?

10. If $\binom{n}{r}$ denotes the number of combinations of n things, r at a time, prove that

$$\binom{n+1}{r} = \binom{n}{r} + \binom{n}{r-1}.$$

Use this to prove the binomial theorem for a positive index, by the method of induction.

SECOND PAPER.

GEOMETRY AND TRIGONOMETRY.

Examiner—PROFESSOR BROMWICH.

1. A, B, C, D are the angular points of a square whose side is a and whose centre is O; prove that
$$AP^2 + BP^2 + CP^2 + DP^2 = 4 \cdot OP^2 + 2a^2,$$
P being any point in the plane of the square.

2. AB, XY are parallel chords of a circle; prove that the arcs AX, BY are equal.

$ABCDEF$ are the angular points of a hexagon inscribed in a circle; AB is parallel to DE, BC to EF, prove that CD is parallel to FA.

[N.B.—The hexagon must not be assumed to be *regular*.]

3. Divide a given straight line into two parts so that the difference of the squares on the two parts may be double the rectangle contained by them.

4. OM, ON are two fixed lines; from a point P perpendiculars PM, PN are let fall on the fixed lines, prove that if the length MN is constant, the locus of P is a circle, with centre O.

5. If A, B are fixed points, and the ratio $AP : BP$ is fixed, prove that P lies on a certain circle which passes between the two points A, B.

6. Find $\sin 18°$, and prove that if $a = 18°$,
$$\sec 2a = 4 \sin a = \operatorname{cosec} a - 2,$$
$$\sin^2 2a = \tfrac{1}{4} + \sin^2 a.$$

7. If $A + B + C = 180°$, and $\cos A = \cos B \cos C$, then $\tan B \tan C = 2$.

8. Solve the equation for x
$$\tan^{-1}\left[(1 - x)/(1 + x)\right] = \tfrac{1}{2}\tan^{-1}x.$$

9. The sides of a triangle are proportional to 4, 7, 9, find the two smallest angles, given

$\log 2 = \cdot 30103$, $\log \tan 12° 36' = \bar{1} \cdot 34933$,

$\log \tan 24° 5' = \bar{1} \cdot 65028$, $\log \tan 12° 37' = \bar{1} \cdot 34992$,

$\log \tan 24° 6' = \bar{1} \cdot 65062$.

10. Find the radius of a circle inscribed in a sector of a circle of radius a, the angle of the sector being $60°$.

LITERARY SCHOLARSHIPS OF THE SECOND YEAR.

LATIN.

First Paper.

Examiner—Professor Sandford.

1. Translate, with short notes :—

I.

Quinctius ex timore hostium plus, quam ex re ipsa, spei nactus, per triduum insequens territavit eos ; nunc proeliis lacessendo, nunc operibus intersaepiendo quaedam, ne exitus ad fugam esset.   His comminationibus compulsus tyrannus Pythagoram rursus oratorem misit, quem Quinctius primo aspernatum excedere castris iussit : deinde suppliciter orantem, advolutumque genibus, tandem audivit. Prima oratio fuit omnia permittentis arbitrio Romanorum : deinde, quum ea velut vana et sine effectu nihil proficerent, eo deductae res, ut his conditionibus, quae ex scripto paucis ante diebus editae erant, indutiae fierent : pecuniaque et obsides accepti.   Dum oppugnatur tyrannus, Argivi, nuntiis aliis prope super aliis afferentibus, tantum non iam captam Lacedaemonem esse, erecti et ipsi, simul eo quod Pythagoras cum parte validissima praesidii excesserat, contempta paucitate eorum, qui in arce erant, duce Archippo quodam, praesidium expulerunt.   Timocratem Pellenensem, quia clementer praefuerat, vivum fide data emiserunt.   Huic laetitiae Quinctius supervenit, pace data tyranno, dimissisque ab Lacedaemone Eumene et Rhodiis et L. Quinctio fratre ad classem.—Livy.

II.

Sed haec vetera, illud vero recens, Caesarem meo consilio interfectum.   Iam vereor, patres conscripti, ne, quod turpissimum est, praevaricatorem mihi apposuisse videar, qui me non solum meis laudibus ornaret, sed etiam oneraret alienis.   Quis enim meum in ista societate gloriosissimi facti nomen audivit ?   Cuius autem, qui in eo numero fuisset, nomen est occultatum ?   Occultatum dico ?   cuius non statim divulgatum? Citius dixerim iactasse se aliquos, ut fuisse in ea societate viderentur, quum conscii non fuissent, quam ut quisquam celari vellet qui fuisset. Quam veri simile porro est in tot hominibus partim obscuris partim adolescentibus neminem occultantibus meum nomen latere potuisse? Etenim si auctores ad liberandam patriam desiderarentur illis actoribus, Brutos ego impellerem, quorum uterque L. Bruti imaginem cotidie videret, alter etiam Ahalae.—CICERO.

III.

Nam quod aiunt plerosque consolationibus nihil levari adiunguntque consolatores ipsos confiteri se miseros, cum ad eos impetum suum fortuna converterit, utrumque dissolvitur. Sunt enim ista non naturae vitia, sed culpae. Stultitiam autem accusare quamvis copiose licet. Nam et qui non levantur, ipsi se ad miseriam invitant, et qui suos casus aliter ferunt, atque ut auctores aliis ipsi fuerunt, non sunt vitiosiores quam fere plerique, qui avari avaros, gloriae cupidos gloriosi reprehendunt. Est enim proprium stultitiae aliorum vitia cernere, oblivisci suorum. Sed nimirum hoc maxumum est experimentum, cum constet aegritudinem vetustate tolli, hanc vim non esse in die positam, sed in cogitatione diuturna. Nam si et eadem res est et idem est homo, qui potest quicquam de dolore mutari, si neque de eo, propter quod dolet, quicquam est mutatum neque de eo, qui dolet? Cogitatio igitur diuturna nihil esse in re mali dolori medetur, non ipsa diuturnitas.—ID.

2. Translate into Latin :—

I will likewise do justice—I ought to do it—to the honourable gentleman who led us in this house. Far from the duplicity wickedly charged upon him, he acted his part with alacrity and resolution. We all felt inspired by the example he gave us, even down to myself, the weakest in that phalanx. I declare, for one, I knew well enough (it could not be concealed from anybody) the true state of things; but in my life I never came with so much spirits into this house. It was a time for a *man* to act in. We had powerful enemies; but we had faithful and determined friends, and a glorious cause. We had a great battle to fight! but we had the means of fighting: not as now when our arms are tied behind us.—BURKE.

8. (*a*) How has Philology been freed from the reproach that, "Etymology is a science in which the vowels count for nothing and the consonants for very little "?

(*b*) What are the meanings of the following technical terms :— velar, analogy, ablaut, rhotacism? Give examples.

(*c*) Classify the uses of the ablative in Latin, giving examples.

LATIN.

SECOND PAPER.

Examiner—PROFESSOR SANDFORD.

1. Translate, with short notes :—

(*a*) Ac iam olim, seras posuit quum vinea frondes,
Frigidus et silvis Aquilo decussit honorem ;
Iam tum acer curas venientem extendit in annum
Rusticus, et curvo Saturni dente relictam
Persequitur vitem attondens, fingitque putando.
Primus humum fodito, primus devecta cremato
Sarmenta, et vallos primus sub tecta referto ;
Postremus metito.   Bis vitibus ingruit umbra ;
Bis segetem densis obducunt sentibus herbae ;
Durus uterque labor.   Laudato ingentia rura,
Exiguum colito.   Nec non etiam aspera rusci
Vimina per silvam, et ripis fluvialis arundo
Caeditur, incultique exercet cura salicti.
Iam vinctae vites, iam falcem arbusta reponunt,
Iam canit effectos extremus vinitor antes.

VIRGIL.

(*b*) Cuncta equidem tibi, Rex, fuerit quodcumque, fatebor
Vera, inquit : ' neque me Argolica de gente negabo :
Hoc primum ; nec, si miserum fortuna Sinonem
Finxit, vanum etiam mendacemque improba finget.
Fando aliquod si forte tuas pervenit ad aures
Belidae nomen Palamedis et inclyta fama
Gloria : quem falsa sub proditione Pelasgi
Insontem, infando indicio, quia bella vetabat,
Demisere neci ; nunc cassum lumine lugent

Illi me comitem et consanguinitate propinquum
Pauper in arma pater primis huc misit ab annis :
Dum stabat regno incolumis, regumque vigebat
Consiliis, et nos aliquod nomenque decusque
Gessimus.   Invidia postquam pellacis Ulixi
(Haud ignota loquor) superis concessit ab oris :
Afflictus vitam in tenebris luctuque trahebam,
Et casum insontis mecum indignabar amici.

ID.

(*c*) Hic et Aloïdas geminos, immania vidi
Corpora : qui manibus magnum rescindere caelum
Aggressi, superisque Iovem detrudere regnis.
Vidi et crudeles dantem Salmonea poenas,
Dum flammas Iovis et sonitus imitatur Olympi.
Quatuor hic invectus equis et lampada quassans,
Per Graium populos mediaeque per Elidis urbem
Ibat ovans, divumque sibi poscebat honorem,
Demens ! qui nimbos et non imitabile fulmen
Aere et cornipedum pulsu simularat equorum.
At pater omnipotens densa inter nubila telum
Contorsit ; non ille faces, nec fumea taedis
Lumina ; praecipitemque immani turbine adegit.

ID.

(*d*)   Festo quid potius die
Neptuni faciam ? Prome reconditum,
Lyde strenua Caecubum,
Munitaeque adhibe vim sapientiae.

Inclinare meridiem
Sentis, ac veluti stet volucris dies,
Parcis deripere horreo
Cessantem Bibuli Consulis amphoram ?

Nos cantabimus invicem
Neptunum, et virides Nereïdum comas :
Tu curva recines lyra
Latonam, et celeris spicula Cynthiae :

Summo carmine, quae Cnidon
Fulgentesque tenet Cycladas, et Paphon
Iunctis visit oloribus :
Dicetur merita Nox quoque naenia.

HORACE.

2. (*a*) 'The positive excellences of the *Aeneid* are so numerous and splendid that the claim of its author to be the Roman Homer is not unreasonable.' Discuss this statement.

(*b*) What, according to Mackail, was 'the great work of Horace's life'? On what grounds does he justify his view?

(*c*) Compare the three elegiac poets of Rome.

3. (*a*) Give an account of the achievements which caused Cato to say that 'no king was worthy to be named by the side of Hamilcar Barcas.'

(*b*) Sketch the career of the man of whom Mommsen writes, 'no single man contributed more to the success of the common enterprise' [after Cannae].

(*c*) What causes does Mommsen suggest for the weakness shown by Philip during the Second Punic war?

(*d*) Give an account of the battle of Cynoscephalae.

GREEK.
First Paper.
Examiner—Professor McElderry.

1. Translate :—

(*a*) Ἥλιον μαρτυρόμεσθα δρῶσ' ἃ δρᾶν οὐ βούλομαι.
εἰ δὲ δή μ' Ἥρα θ' ὑπουργεῖν σοί τ' ἀναγκαίως ἔχει
τάχος ἐπιρροίβδην θ' ὁμαρτεῖν ὡς κυνηγέτῃ κύνας,
εἶμί γ'· οὔτε πόντος οὕτω κύμασι στένων λάβρος
οὔτε γῆς σεισμὸς κεραυνοῦ τ' οἶστρος ὠδῖνας πνέων,
οἷ' ἐγὼ στάδια δραμοῦμαι στέρνον εἰς Ἡρακλέους
καὶ καταρρήξω μέλαθρα καὶ δόμους ἐπεμβαλῶ,
τέκν' ἀποκτείνασα πρῶτον· ὁ δὲ κανὼν οὐκ εἴσεται
παῖδας οὓς ἔτικτ' ἐναίρων, πρὶν ἂν ἐμῆς λύσσης ὑφῇ.
ἢν ἰδοὺ καὶ δὴ τινάσσει κρᾶτα βαλβίδων ἄπο
καὶ διαστρόφους ἑλίσσει σῖγα γοργωποὺς κόρας.
ἀμπνοὰς δ' οὐ σωφρονίζει, ταῦρος ὣς ἐς ἐμβολήν,
δεινὰ μυκᾶται δὲ Κῆρας ἀνακαλῶν τὰς Ταρτάρου.

EURIPIDES.

(*b*)   ἔκτοσθεν δ' αὐλῆς μέγας ὄρχατος ἄγχι θυράων
τετράγυος· περὶ δ' ἕρκος ἐλήλαται ἀμφοτέρωθεν.
ἔνθα δὲ δένδρεα μακρὰ πεφύκει τηλεθόωντα,
ὄγχναι καὶ ῥοιαὶ καὶ μηλέαι ἀγλαόκαρποι
συκέαι τε γλυκεραὶ καὶ ἐλαῖαι τηλεθόωσαι.
τάων οὔ ποτε καρπὸς ἀπόλλυται οὐδ' ἀπολείπει
χείματος οὐδὲ θέρευς, ἐπετήσιος· ἀλλὰ μάλ' αἰεὶ
ζεφυρίη πνείουσα τὰ μὲν φύει, ἄλλα δὲ πέσσει.
ὄγχνη ἐπ' ὄγχνῃ γηράσκει, μῆλον δ' ἐπὶ μήλῳ,
αὐτὰρ ἐπὶ σταφυλῇ σταφυλή, σῦκον δ' ἐπὶ σύκῳ.
ἔνθα δέ οἱ πολύκαρπος ἀλωὴ ἐρρίζωται,
τῆς ἕτερον μὲν θειλόπεδον λευρῷ ἐνὶ χώρῳ
τέρσεται ἠελίῳ, ἑτέρας δ' ἄρα τε τρυγόωσιν,
ἄλλας δὲ τραπέουσι· πάροιθε δέ τ' ὄμφακές εἰσιν
ἄνθος ἀφιεῖσαι, ἕτεραι δ' ὑποπερκάζουσιν.

HOMER.

(*c*)   τὸ μὲν δεῖσαι Λακεδαιμονίους μὴ ὁμολογήσωμεν τῷ
βαρβάρῳ κάρτα ἀνθρωπήϊον ἦν. ἀτὰρ αἰσχρῶς γε οἴκατε
ἐξεπιστάμενοι τὸ Ἀθηναίων φρόνημα ἀρρωδῆσαι, ὅτι οὔτε
χρυσός ἐστι γῆς οὐδαμόθι τοσοῦτος, οὔτε χώρη κάλλεϊ καὶ ἀρετῇ
μέγα ὑπερφέρουσα, τὰ ἡμεῖς δεξάμενοι ἐθέλοιμεν ἂν μηδίσαντες
καταδουλῶσαι τὴν Ἑλλάδα. πολλά τε γὰρ καὶ μεγάλα ἐστὶ τὰ
διακωλύοντα ταῦτα μὴ ποιέειν, μηδ' ἢν ἐθέλωμεν· πρῶτα μὲν
καὶ μέγιστα τῶν θεῶν τὰ ἀγάλματα καὶ τὰ οἰκήματα ἐμπε·
πρησμένα τε καὶ συγκεχωσμένα, τοῖσι ἡμέας ἀναγκαίως ἔχει
τιμωρέειν ἐς τὰ μέγιστα μᾶλλον ἤπερ ὁμολογέειν τῷ ταῦτα
ἐργασαμένῳ, αὖτις δὲ τὸ Ἑλληνικὸν ἐὸν ὅμαιμόν τε καὶ
ὁμόγλωσσον, καὶ θεῶν ἱδρύματά τε κοινὰ καὶ θυσίαι ἤθεά τε
ὁμότροπα, τῶν προδότας γενέσθαι Ἀθηναίους οὐκ ἂν εὖ ἔχοι.
ἐπίστασθέ τε οὕτω, εἰ μὴ πρότερον ἐτυγχάνετε ἐπιστάμενοι,
ἔστ' ἂν καὶ εἷς περιῇ Ἀθηναίων, μηδαμὰ ὁμολογήσοντας ἡμέας
Ξέρξῃ.—HERODOTUS.

(*d*)   πῶς λέγεις, ὦ Ἄνυτε; οὗτοι ἄρα μόνοι τῶν ἀντιποιουμένων
τι ἐπίστασθαι εὐεργετεῖν τοσοῦτον τῶν ἄλλων διαφέρουσιν, ὅσον
οὐ μόνον οὐκ ὠφελοῦσιν, ὥσπερ οἱ ἄλλοι, ὅ τι ἄν τις αὐτοῖς
παραδῷ, ἀλλὰ καὶ τὸ ἐναντίον διαφθείρουσι; καὶ τούτων φανερῶς

χρήματα ἀξιοῦσι πράττεσθαι; ἐγὼ μὲν οὖν οὐκ ἔχω ὅπως σοι πιστεύσω· οἶδα γὰρ ἄνδρα ἕνα Πρωταγόραν πλείω χρήματα κτησάμενον ἀπὸ ταύτης τῆς σοφίας ἢ Φειδίαν τε, ὃς οὕτω περιφανῶς καλὰ ἔργα εἰργάζετο, καὶ ἄλλους δέκα τῶν ἀνδριαντοποιῶν· καίτοι τέρας λέγεις, εἰ οἱ μὲν τὰ ὑποδήματα ἐργαζόμενοι τὰ παλαιὰ καὶ τὰ ἱμάτια ἐξακούμενοι οὐκ ἂν δύναιντο λαθεῖν τριάκονθ᾽ ἡμέρας μοχθηρότερα ἀποδιδόντες ἢ παρέλαβον τὰ ἱμάτιά τε καὶ ὑποδήματα, ἀλλ᾽ εἰ τοιαῦτα ποιοῖεν, ταχὺ ἂν τῷ λιμῷ ἀποθάνοιεν, Πρωταγόρας δὲ ἄρα ὅλην τὴν Ἑλλάδα ἐλάνθανε διαφθείρων τοὺς συγγιγνομένους καὶ μοχθηροτέρους ἀποπέμπων ἢ παρελάμβανε πλέον ἢ τετταράκοντα ἔτη.—PLATO, *Meno.*

(e) εἰ τοίνυν τις ὑμῶν ἐνοκεῖ πέπεισται, πολὺ τοῦ δεηθῆναί τινος τοιούτου νῦν ἀπέχειν τὴν πόλιν, ταῦτα μὲν εὐχέσθω τοῖς θεοῖς, κἀγὼ συνεύχομαι, λογιζέσθω δὲ πρῶτον μὲν ὅτι περὶ νόμου μέλλει φέρειν τὴν ψῆφον, ᾧ μὴ λυθέντι δεήσει χρῆσθαι, δεύτερον δ᾽ ὅτι βλάπτουσιν οἱ πονηροὶ νόμοι καὶ τὰς ἀσφαλῶς οἰκεῖν οἰομένας πόλεις. οὐ γὰρ ἂν μετέπιπτε τὰ πράγματ᾽ ἐπ᾽ ἀμφότερ᾽, εἰ μὴ τοὺς μὲν ἐν κινδύνῳ καθεστηκότας καὶ πράξεις χρησταὶ καὶ νόμοι καὶ ἄνδρες χρηστοὶ καὶ πάντ᾽ ἐξητασμέν᾽ ἐπὶ τὸ βέλτιον προῆγε, τοὺς δ᾽ ἐν ἁπάσῃ καθεστάναι δοκοῦντας εὐδαιμονίᾳ πάντα ταῦτ᾽ ἀμελούμενα ὑπέρρει κατὰ μικρόν.— DEMOSTHENES.

2. (a) In the first extract, name metre and scan first line,

(b) Annotate : ἀτρύγετος, ἀμφιέλισσαι, διερός, πίσυρες.

(c) Give Herodotean forms for πῶς, ἀποκρίνομαι, ἀποληφθεὶς ἐνταῦθα, οὖν·

(d) How does Socrates in the *Meno* define figure and colour ? Give the Greek if possible.

(e) Explain ἔνδειξις, ἀπαγωγή, ἀγχιστεία; and write a note upon the process of legislation at Athens.

UNPRESCRIBED PASSAGE.

3. Translate :—

καὶ ταῦτα μὲν δὴ ταῦτα·
οἷον δ᾽ αὖ τόδ᾽ ἔρεξε καὶ ἔτλη καρτερὸς ἀνὴρ
ἐκεῖ ποτε ἐπὶ στρατείας, ἄξιον ἀκοῦσαι. ξυννοήσας γὰρ αὐτόθι

ἑωθέν τι εἱστήκει σκοπῶν, καὶ ἐπειδὴ οὐ προύχώρει αὐτῷ, οὐκ ἀνίει ἀλλὰ εἱστήκει ζητῶν. καὶ ἤδη ἦν μεσημβρία, καὶ ἄνθρωποι ᾐσθάνοντο, καὶ θαυμάζοντες ἄλλος ἄλλῳ ἔλεγεν ὅτι Σωκράτης ἐξ ἑωθινοῦ φροντίζων τι ἔστηκε. τελευτῶντες δέ τινες τῶν νέων, ἐπειδὴ ἐσπέρα ἦν, δειπνήσαντες (καὶ γὰρ θέρος τότε γ᾽ ἦν) χαμεύνια ἐξενεγκάμενοι ἅμα μὲν ἐν τῷ φύχει καθηῦδον ἅμα δ᾽ ἐφύλαττον αὐτὸν εἰ καὶ τὴν νύκτα ἑστήξοι. ὁ δὲ εἱστήκει μέχρι ἕως ἐγένετο καὶ ἥλιος ἄνεσχεν· ἔπειτ᾽ ᾤχετο ἀπιὼν προσευξάμενος τῷ ἡλίῳ.—PLATO.

GREEK.

SECOND PAPER.

Examiner—PROFESSOR McELDERRY.

1. Translate into Greek :—

I hear people say : ' We will take Sebastopol and then we will treat for peace.' I am not going to say that you cannot take Sebastopol. I am not going to argue against the power of England and France. I might admit, for the sake of argument, that you can take Sebastopol. You may occupy ten miles of territory in the Crimea for any time ; you may build a town there ; you may carry provisions and reinforcements there, for you have the command of the sea ; but while you do all this you will have no peace with Russia. Nobody who knows the history of Russia can think for a moment that you are going permanently to occupy any portion of her territory and at the same time be at peace with that Empire.— R. COBDEN.

2. (*a*) What is known of the organization of the Athenian Empire, and from what sources?

(*b*) Write notes upon—τὸ τῶν Μεγαρέων ψήφισμα, ὀστρακισμός, ἡλιαία, πολέμαρχος.

3. (*a*) What is ablaut? Illustrate fully by examples.

(*b*) Enumerate, with examples, the different forms used for the expression of wish.

(*o*) Classify the uses of ἄν.

4. Translate into English :—

ΑΓΓ. ὠή, τίς ἐν πύλαισι δωμάτων κυρεῖ ;
      ἀνοίγετ᾽, ἐκπορεύετ᾽ Ἰοκάστην δόμων.
      ὠὴ μάλ᾽ αὖθις· διὰ μακροῦ μέν, ἀλλ᾽ ὅμως
      ἔξελθ᾽, ἄκουσον, Οἰδίπου κλεινὴ δάμαρ,
      λήξασ᾽ ὀδυρμῶν πενθίμων τε δακρύων.

IO.   ὦ φίλτατ᾽, ἦ που ξυμφορὰν ἥκεις φέρων
      Ἐτεοκλέους θανόντος, οὗ παρ᾽ ἀσπίδα
      βέβηκας ἀεί, πολεμίων εἴργων βέλη ;
      τί μοί ποθ᾽ ἥκεις καινὸν ἀγγελῶν ἔπος ;
      τέθνηκεν ἢ ζῇ παῖς ἐμός ; σήμαινέ μοι.

ΑΓΓ. ζῇ, μὴ τρέσῃς τόδ᾽, ὥς σ᾽ ἀπαλλάξω φόβου.

IO.   τί δ᾽, ἑπτάπυργοι πῶς ἔχουσι περιβολαί ;

ΑΓΓ. ἑστᾶσ᾽ ἄθραυστοι, κοὐκ ἀνήρπασται πόλις.

IO.   ἦλθον δὲ πρὸς κίνδυνον Ἀργείου δορός ;

ΑΓΓ. ἀκμήν γ᾽ ἐπ᾽ αὐτήν· ἀλλ᾽ ὁ Καδμείων Ἄρης
      κρείσσων κατέστη τοῦ Μυκηναίου δορός.

EURIPIDES.

Arts, Medicine, and Engineering.

FRENCH.

Examiner—PROFESSOR STEINBERGER.

COMPOSITION.

1. Translate into French :—

The great mistake which most people make about travelling is that that they travel without any other object except that of doing what other people do. They think they must follow certain routes, adhere to a certain routine, and see certain things, even if they do not interest them in the least. Those who never care to look at a picture at home spend days in wearily dragging themselves through interminable picture galleries. They may be seen standing bored to death before the masterpieces of Tintoret and Veronese.

Those who do not know whether their own parish church is Norman or Tudor spend weeks in rushing from one cathedral town to another, vainly trying to remember which had a campanile and which a baptistery, so that they may have some new dinner talk when they return from abroad. Those who can barely distinguish a manuscript from a printed book will take the greatest trouble to obtain introductions to all the principal librarians in Europe, who will be expected to waste valuable time in showing them treasures they can neither appreciate nor understand. All this is very foolish and a useless waste of time and money. Almost every one has some taste, and is capable of enjoying something which travelling can procure him.—*Saturday Review.*

UNPRESCRIBED PASSAGES.

2. Translate into English :—

(*a*) C'est la haute mer. L'eau y est très-profonde. Un écueil absolument isolé comme le rocher Douvres attire et abrite les bêtes qui ont besoin de l'éloignement des hommes. Il y a là, à une profondeur où les plongeurs atteignent difficilement, des antres, des caves, des repaires, des entre-croisements de rues ténébreuses. Les espèces monstrueuses y pullulent. On s'entre-dévore. Des formes épouvantables, faites pour n'être pas vues par l'œil humain, errent dans cette obscurité, vivantes. De vagues linéaments de gueules, de nageoires, de mâchoires ouvertes, d'écailles, de griffes, y flottent, y tremblent, y grossissent, s'y décomposent et s'y effacent dans la transparence sinistre.

Voir le dedans de la mer, c'est voir l'imagination de l'Inconnu. C'est la voir du côté terrible. Le gouffre est analogue à la nuit. Là s'accomplissent en pleine sécurité les crimes de l'irresponsable. Là, dans une paix affreuse, les ébauches de la vie, presque fantômes, tout à fait démons, vaquent aux farouches occupations de l'ombre.—VICTOR HUGO.

(*b*) Les cris de la corneille ont annoncé l'orage,
  Le bélier effrayé veut rentrer au hameau.
  Une sombre fureur agite le taureau,
  Qui respire avec force, et, relevant la tête,
  Par ses mugissements appelle la tempête.

Q

On voit à l'horizon, de deux points opposés,
Des nuages monter dans les airs embrasés ;
On les voit s'épaissir, s'élever et s'étendre.
D'un tonnerre éloigné le bruit s'est fait entendre :
Les flots en ont frémi, l'air en est ébranlé,
Et le long du vallon le feuillage a tremblé.
Les monts ont prolongé le lugubre murmure
Dont le son lent et sourd attriste la nature.
Il succède à ce bruit un calme plein d'horreur,
Et la terre en silence attend dans la terreur.
Des monts et des rochers le vaste amphithéâtre
Disparaît tout à coup sous un voile grisâtre ;
Le nuage élargi les couvre de ses flancs ;
Il pèse sur les airs tranquilles et brûlants,
Mais des traits enflammés ont sillonné la nue,
Et la foudre, en grondant, roule dans l'étendue :
Elle redouble, vole, éclate dans les airs.

SAINT-LAMBERT.

8. Epreuve orale sur les auteurs préscrits.

GERMAN.

Examiner—PROFESSOR STEINBERGER.

COMPOSITION.

1. Translate into German :—

In the month of June, in the year fifteen hundred and fifty-nine, the French nation was afflicted by an accident equally sad and sudden. A marriage had just been celebrated at the court; the king of Spain had espoused the Princess Elisabeth ; but being unable to be present at the wedding, he had, according to the customs of the age, sent the Duke of Alba as his representative. The festivities were to end with a great tournament, and King Henry II., who prided himself on his skill as a knight, was going to break three lances against three adversaries of his choice. The two first courses had ended without accident, and the third adversary was going to start. He was a son of the Count of Lorges, and belonged to the Scottish guard ; his name was Montgomery. As he was very tall and strong, he upset the king in his saddle by the blow of his lance, and Henry II. rolled to the ground. The three courses being now over, some other knights ought to have continued the tournament. But the king, annoyed at having been unhorsed, bade them retire, and ordered Montgomery to recommence the combat.

UNPRESCRIBED PASSAGES.

2. Translate into English :—

I.

Der Mensch hat wohl täglich Gelegenheit, über den Unbestand aller irdischen Dinge Betrachtungen anzustellen, wenn er will, und mit seinem Schicksale zufrieden zu werden, wenn auch nicht viele gebratene Tauben für ihn in der Luft herumfliegen. Aber auf dem seltsamsten Wege kam ein deutscher Handwerksbursche in Amsterdam durch den Irrthum zur Wahrheit. Denn als er in diese große und reiche Handelsstadt voll prächtiger Häuser, wogender Schiffe und geschäftiger Kaufleute gekommen war, fiel ihm sogleich ein großes und schönes Haus in die Augen, wie er auf seiner ganzen Wanderschaft von Tuttlingen bis nach Amsterdam noch keines gesehen hatte. Lange betrachtete er mit Bewunderung dieses kostbare Gebäude, die sechs Kamine auf dem Dache, die schönen Gesimse und die hohen Fenster, größer als an des Vaters Hause die Thür.—J. P. Hebel.

II.

Die Quelle.

Du liebliche Quelle, du wandelst dahin
In duftigen Schattengeweben,
Und weckest den sanftern, melodischen Sinn
In meinem umnachteten Leben.

Wie krachend auch durch den vernichteten Wald
Der rasende Donnersturm wüthe;
Du wandelst, von ruhigen Tönen umwallt,
Bewegt von der rostigen Blüthe.

Q 2

Ich trat aus des Lebens Vernichtung hervor
In deine geheiligten Schauer;
Da schwang das Gemüth sich begeistert empor
Aus Nächten der dunkleren Trauer.

Und drunten verhallte der kleinliche Laut
Der Erd', im Gewölke verborgen;
Den Sohn der Begeistrung, mit Göttern vertraut,
Erreichen nicht irdische Sorgen.

Du ließest auf deiner umdämmerten Bahn
Das Leben im Bilde mich sehen;
Ein Wellenspiel ist es, ein ewiges Nahn
Und Fernen, und Kommen und Gehen.

Und ob auch der Schatten des Ufers hinein
In deine Verklärungen falle;
So trägst du die Bläue des Himmels doch rein
Im tönenden, lichten Krystalle.

Dir gleiche, von Geniusblitzen erhellt,
Der Zögling der heiligen Musen;
Sein hoher Beruf ist: er trägt für die Welt
Den Himmel im tönenden Busen.

Tiedge.

3. Oral examination on the Prescribed Authors.

ENGLISH.

FIRST PAPER.

*Examiner—*PROFESSOR TRENCH.

1. Discuss the influence of the Witches upon Macbeth. Describe his interviews with them, with this object before you.

2. What evidence have we with regard to the date at which the play (Macbeth) was written?

3. In what context does Pope speak of human life as a 'middle state'? Consider whether other portions of the Essay on Man also deal with it as a middle state.

4. Show, by an analysis of the poem, how Gray treats the subject of the Progress of Poesy.

5. Discuss the grounds of Addison's appreciation of the old ballad. Do you know of any others in the prescribed period of literature who cared for ballads?

ENGLISH.

SECOND PAPER.

Examiner—PROFESSOR TRENCH.

1. Consider Johnson's criticism of Pope's *Homer*.

2. What is Johnson's object in writing *Rasselas*? Has he attained it?

ESSAY.

Literature in the reign of Queen Anne.

Or,

Pope's Philosophy.

SCIENCE SCHOLARSHIPS OF THE SECOND YEAR.

MATHEMATICS.

FIRST PAPER.

Examiner—PROFESSOR BROMWICH.

1. Solve the equations for x, y, z, t,

$$ax + by + cz = 0, \quad bz - cy = p - at, \quad cx - az = q - bt,$$
$$ay - bx = r - ct.$$

Consider what happens if $ap + bq + cr = 0$.

2. If x_m denotes the product
$$x(x - 1)(x - 2) \ldots (x - m + 1),$$
prove that

    (i) $(x - m)x_m = x_{m+1}$;

    (ii) $(x + y - n)x_m y_{n-m} = x_{m+1} y_{n-m} + x_m y_{n-m+1}.$

Deduce Vandermonde's theorem (by the method of induction)

$$(x + y)_n = x_n + n x_{n-1} y_1 + \ldots + \binom{n}{m} x_{n-m} y_m + \ldots + y_n,$$

where $\binom{n}{m}$ is the number of combinations of n things, m at a time.

3. If the equations
$$lx + my = 1, \qquad ax^2 + by^2 = 1,$$
have only one solution, then $l^2/a + m^2/b = 1$, and the solution is $x = l/a$, $y = m/b$. Give a geometrical interpretation, if you can.

4. If
$$\tan \beta \, \cot \tfrac{1}{2}(a + \gamma) = \tan \gamma \, \cot \tfrac{1}{2}(a + \beta),$$
and $\beta \neq \gamma$, prove that
$$bc + ca + ab = (a + b + c)/abc,$$
where $a = \tan \tfrac{1}{2}a$, $b = \tan \tfrac{1}{2}\beta$, $c = \tan \tfrac{1}{2}\gamma$.

5. The internal bisector of the angle A of a triangle ABC meets BC in D; and the radius of the circumcircle drawn through C meets AD in E. Show that the length of DE is
$$ab \cos A/(b + c) \cos (\tfrac{1}{2}A - B).$$

6. In a triangle the sides are as $5 : 6 : 7$: find the angles, each to the nearest minute.

7. Trace the graphs of
$$y = x^2 - 5x + 6, \qquad xy = x^2 - 5x + 6, \qquad y^2 = x^2 - 5x + 6.$$

8. Differentiate with respect to x,
$$\left[\frac{x - (x^2 - 1)^{\frac{1}{2}}}{x + (x^2 - 1)^{\frac{1}{2}}} \right]^{\frac{1}{2}}, \qquad \log (\cot \tfrac{1}{2}x).$$

9. Find the tangent to each of the curves in question 7 at their points of intersection with the line $x = 2$.

10. Show that the logarithmic curve $y = \log x$ has its hollow downwards at all points of its length. Deduce that a logarithm found by the ordinary method of 'proportional parts' is a little less than its true value.

Taking $\log_{10} 2 = {\cdot}301$, $\log_{10} 3 = {\cdot}477$, find $\log_{10} 2{\cdot}5$, both accurately and by 'proportional parts.'

MATHEMATICS.

SECOND PAPER.

Examiner—PROFESSOR BROMWICH.

1. PL, PM, PN are the perpendiculars drawn from P on the sides BC, CA, AB of a given triangle; prove that, if the ratio $LM : LN$ is given, the locus of P is a circle with respect to which B and C are inverse points.

2. A circle touches AB, AC at B, C, respectively; show that the square of the perpendicular from any point P of the circle upon the chord BC is equal to the rectangle contained by the perpendiculars from P on the sides AB, AC.

3. A sphere passes through two fixed points and touches a fixed plane; prove that the point of contact lies on a fixed circle.

4. A, B, C, D are four points not in one plane; prove that if the mid-points of AB, BC, CD, DA lie on a circle then the lines AC, BD are perpendicular.

5. Show that the determinant

$$\begin{vmatrix} 1 + a, & 1, & 1, \\ 1, & 1 + \beta, & 1, \\ 1, & 1, & 1 + \gamma, \end{vmatrix} = \beta\gamma + \gamma a + a\beta + a\beta\gamma.$$

What would be the value if the diagonal were replaced by

$$(1 + a)^2, (1 + \beta)^2, (1 + \gamma)^2 ?$$

Express your result in terms of

$$p = a + \beta + \gamma, \quad q = \beta\gamma + \gamma a + a\beta, \quad r = a\beta\gamma.$$

6. A, B, C, D are four points in order on a straight line such that

$$AB = BC = CD,$$

and the angles subtended by AB, BC, CD at any point P are θ, ϕ, ψ : prove that

$$(\cot \theta + \cot \phi)(\cot \psi + \cot \phi) = 4 \csc^2 \phi.$$

7. Write down the expression for the area of a triangle when the coordinates of the angular points are given. Prove that the area of the triangle formed by the three lines

$$x = a, \quad y = b, \quad x/b + y/a = 1 \quad \text{is} \quad \tfrac{1}{2}(a^2 - ab + b^2)^2/ab.$$

8. PQ, PR are chords of the circle $x^2 + y^2 = 1$, and pass through the points $(\tfrac{1}{2}, 0)$, $(-\tfrac{1}{2}, 0)$, respectively. Show that the equation to QR is

$$x \cos \theta + \tfrac{4}{3}y \sin \theta + 1 = 0,$$

if the coordinates of P are $(\cos \theta, \sin \theta)$.

9. Prove that the parabolas $y^2 = ax$, $x^2 = by$, intersect at the point $x = (ab^2)^{\frac{1}{3}}$, $y = (a^2b)^{\frac{1}{3}}$. Write down the equations to the tangents to the curves at this point, and prove the angle between them is θ, where

$$\tan \theta = \tfrac{3}{2} a^{\frac{1}{3}}b^{\frac{1}{3}}/(a^{\frac{2}{3}} + b^{\frac{2}{3}}).$$

10. Find the equation to the normal at the point $(at, a/t)$ of the rectangular hyperbola $xy = a^2$; and prove that the perpendicular from the centre on the normal does not cut the curve in real points.

EXPERIMENTAL PHYSICS.

[*Arts, Medicine, and Engineering.*]

Examiner—PRESIDENT ANDERSON.

1. Define *momentum* and *kinetic energy*. Show that if two masses have equal momenta, the smaller has the greater kinetic energy.

2. Two spherical shells, one of gold and the other of silver, have the same weight, size, and surface. When allowed to roll down an inclined plane, the silver shell moves the faster. Why?

3. Show how the height of a mountain may be deduced from barometric observations. The pressure at sea-level being 31 inches, that at the summit of one mountain is found to be 25 inches, and that at the summit of another 20·16 inches : show that, neglecting corrections for temperature, the height of the former is about half that of the latter.

4. Define *specific heat.* What volumes of water and mercury should be mixed together so that the final temperature may be the arithmetic mean of the original temperature, the density of mercury being 13·6, and its specific heat ·033 ?

5. Describe any form of compensation pendulum, and explain the principle on which it is constructed.

6. Water, if kept very still, can be cooled below its freezing point without the formation of ice. Let a quantity of water be in this way cooled down to – 10° C., and then shaken, so that it begins to freeze. How much of it will become ice ?

7. Describe an experiment illustrating the refraction of sound. Explain why sounds are heard more distinctly when travelling in the direction of the wind than when travelling in the opposite direction.

8. The inner coating of a Leyden jar is connected by a wire with the prime conductor of an electric machine and with a gold-leaf electroscope. If the jar is insulated, a fraction of a turn produces a large divergence, but if uninsulated, it requires several turns to produce an equal divergence. Explain this.

9. A current of electricity flows through a wire which is thicker at one end than the other. State what differences you would expect to observe at the two ends.

10. Explain how to graduate an ammeter by an electrolytic method.

11. How is a lens constructed so as to produce a colourless image ?

———

There was also a Practical Examination in the Laboratory for Candidates in Medicine and Engineering.

LITERARY SCHOLARSHIPS OF THE THIRD YEAR.

LATIN.

FIRST PAPER.

Examiner—PROFESSOR SANDFORD.

1. Translate, with short notes :—

(*a*) Non nimis in Niptris ille sapientissimus Graeciae
saucius lamentatur vel modice potius :

> Pedetemptim, inquit, et sedato nisu,
> Ne succussu arripiat maior
> Dolor.

Pacuvius hoc melius quam Sophocles (apud illum enim
perquam flebiliter Ulixes lamentatur in volnere) ; tamen
huic leviter gementi illi ipsi, qui ferunt saucium, personae
gravitatem intuentes non dubitant dicere :

> Tu quoque, Ulixes, quamquam graviter
> Cernimus ictum, nimis paene animo es
> Molli, qui consuetus in armis
> Aevom agere. . . .

Intellegit poëta prudens ferendi doloris consuetudinem esse
non contemnendam magistram.—CICERO.

(*b*) Quod ita esse dies declarat, quae procedens ita mitigat,
ut isdem malis manentibus non modo leniatur aegritudo,
sed in plerisque tollatur. Karthaginienses multi Romae
servierunt, Macedones rege Perse capto ; vidi etiam in
Peloponneso, cum essem adulescens, quosdam Corinthios.
Hi poterant omnes eadem illa de Andromacha deplorare :

> Haec omnia vidi . . .,

sed iam decantaverant fortasse. Eo enim erant voltu, ora-
tione, omni reliquo motu et statu, ut eos Argivos aut Sicy-
onios diceres, magisque me moverant Corinthi subito
aspectae parietinae quam ipsos Corinthios, quorum animis
diuturna cogitatio callum vetustatis obduxerat.—*Ibid.*

(c) Sed tamen ipse Caesar habet peracre iudicium, et, ut Servius, frater tuus, quem litteratissimum fuisse iudico, facile diceret, ' hic versus Plauti non est, hic est,' quod tritas aures haberet notandis generibus poëtarum et consuetudine legendi, sic audio Caesarem, cum volumina iam confecerit ἀποφθεγμάτων, si quod adferatur ad eum pro meo, quod meum non sit, reicere solere : quod eo nunc magis facit, quia vivunt mecum fere cotidie illius familiares.   Incidunt autem in sermone vario multa, quae fortasse illis cum dixi nec illitterata nec insulsa esse videantur.   Haec ad illum cum reliquis actis perferuntur : ita enim ipse mandavit.   Sic fit ut, si quid praeterea de me audiat, non audiendum putet.   Quam ob rem Oenomao tuo nihil utor : etsi posuisti loco versus Accianos.—Cicero.

(d) Ex Asia rediens cum ab Aegina Megaram versus navigarem, coepi regiones circumcirca prospicere.   Post me erat Aegina, ante me Megara, dextra Piraeeus, sinistra Corinthus : quae oppida quodam tempore florentissima fuerunt, nunc prostrata et diruta ante oculos iacent.   Coepi egomet mecum sic cogitare : ' Hem! nos homunculi indignamur, si quis nostrum interiit aut occisus est, quorum vita brevior esse debet, cum uno loco tot oppidum cadavera proiecta iacent ?   Visne tu te, Servi, cohibere et meminisse hominem te esse natum ? '—*Ibid.*

(e) Igitur ut Batavi miscere ictus, ferire umbonibus, ora fodere, et stratis qui in aequo adstiterant, erigere in colles aciem coepere, ceterae cohortes aemulatione et impetu conisae proximos quosque caedere : ac plerique semineces aut integri festinatione victoriae relinquebantur.   Interim equitum turmae, ut fugere covinnarii, peditum se proelio miscuere.   Et quamquam recentem terrorem intulerant, densis tamen hostium agminibus et inaequalibus locis haerebant; minimeque aequa nostris iam pugnae facies erat, cum aegre clivo instantes simul equorum corporibus impellerentur ; ac saepe vagi currus, exterriti sine rectoribus equi, ut quemque formido tulerat, transversos aut obvios incursabant.—Tacitus.

2. Translate into Latin :—

I will likewise do justice—I ought to do it—to the honourable gentleman who led us in this House.   Far from the duplicity wickedly charged upon him, he acted his part with alacrity and resolution. We all felt inspired by the example he gave us, even down to myself, the weakest in that phalanx. I declare, for one, I knew well enough (it could not be concealed from anybody) the true state of things; but in my life I never came with so much spirits into this House. It was a time for a *man* to act in. We had powerful enemies; but we had faithful and determined friends, and a glorious cause. We had a great battle to fight; but we had the means of fighting: not as now when our arms are tied behind us.—BURKE.

8. (*a*) How has Philology been freed from the reproach that, 'Etymology is a science in which the vowels count for nothing, and the consonants for very little' ?

(*b*) What are the meanings of the following technical terms :—velar, analogy, ablaut, rhotacism? Give examples.

(*c*) Classify the uses of the ablative in Latin, giving examples.

LATIN.

SECOND PAPER.

Examiner—PROFESSOR SANDFORD.

1. Translate with notes :—

(*a*) Grande et conspicuum nostro quoque tempore monstrum,
Caecus adulator dirusque a ponte satelles,
Dignus Aricinos qui mendicaret ad axes,
Blandaque devexae iactaret basia rhedae.
Nemo magis rhombum stupuit; nam plurima dixit
In laevam conversus; at illi dextra iacebat
Belua. Sic pugnas Cilicis laudabat, et ictus,
Et pegma, et pueros inde ad velaria raptos.
Non cedit Veiento, sed, ut fanaticus, oestro
Percussus, Bellona, tuo, divinat et, Ingens
Omen habes, inquit, magni clarique triumphi :
Regem aliquem capies, aut de temone Britanno

Excidet Arviragus : peregrina est belua : cernis
Erectas in terga sudes ?   Hoc defuit unum
Fabricio, patriam ut rhombi memoraret et annos.
' Quidnam igitur censes ? Conciditur ?' Absit ab illo
Dedecus hoc, Montanus ait.   Testa alta paretur
Quae tenui muro spatiosum colligat orbem.
Debetur magnus patinae subitusque Prometheus.

JUVENAL.

(*b*) Contentus fama iaceat Lucanus in hortis
Marmoreis : at Serrano tenuique Saleio
Gloria quantalibet quid erit, si gloria tantum est ?
Curritur ad vocem iucundam et carmen amicae
Thebaidos, laetam quum fecit Statius urbem
Promisitque diem : tanta dulcedine captos
Afficit ille animos, tantaque libidine vulgi
Auditur ; sed, quum fregit subsellia versu,
Esurit, intactam Paridi nisi vendat Agaven.
Ille et militiae multis lagitur honorem,
Semestri vatum digitos circumligat auro.
Quod non dant proceres, dabit histrio.   Tu Camerinos
Et Bareas, tu nobilium magna atria curas ?

Ibid.

(*c*) Hic, ubi sidereus propius videt astra colossus,
    Et crescunt media pegmata celsa via,
Invidiosa feri radiabant atria regis,
    Unaque iam tota stabat in urbe domus.
Hic, ubi conspicui venerabilis amphitheatri
    Erigitur moles, stagna Neronis erant.
Hic, ubi miramur velocia munera thermas,
    Abstulerat miseris tecta superbus ager.
Claudia diffusas ubi porticus explicat umbras,
    Ultima pars aulae deficientis erat.
Reddita Roma sibi est, et sunt, te praeside, Caesar,
    Deliciae populi, quae fuerant domini.

MARTIAL.

(*d*)   Cuius vis fieri, libelle, munus ?
    Festina tibi vindicem parare,
    Ne nigram cito raptus in culinam
    Cordyllas madida tegas papyro,
    Vel turis piperisque sis cucullus.

Faustini fugis in sinum ?   Sapisti.
Cedro nunc licet ambules perunctus,
Et frontis gemino decens honore
Pictis luxurieris umbilicis ;
Et te purpura delicata velet,
Et cocco rubeat superbus index.
Illo vindice nec Probum timeto.

Ibid.

(e)   Non usitata, non tenui ferar
Penna biformis per liquidum aethera
    Vates : neque in terris morabor
        Longius : invidiaque maior

Urbes relinquam.   Non ego pauperum
Sanguis parentum, non ego, quem vocas
    Dilecte, Maecenas, obibo,
        Nec Stygia cohibebor unda.

Iam iam residunt cruribus asperae
Pelles ; et album mutor in alitem
    Superne : nascunturque leves
        Per digitos humerosque plumae.

HORACE.

2. (a) Give the substance of Mackail's appreciation of Lucretius.   What curious parallelism does he notice between Lucretius and Milton ?

(b) On what grounds does Sellar disbelieve in any golden age of Roman poetry before the time of Ennius ?   To what does he attribute the origin of the legendary tales of Roman History ?

(c) Give a list of the Roman writers you would class as belonging to the ' Augustan age.'

(d) The constitutional position of the Emperor rested on three bases.   Name them.   In one important respect the Principate differed from other magistracies ?

(e) State what you know of the *Augustales.*

(f) Give an account of ' the part of the policy of Tiberius which did most to render him disliked both by contemporaries and posterity.'

(g) Who was it that first called Cassius ' the last of the Romans ' ?   What was the effect on his own fortunes ?

GREEK.

First Paper.

Examiner—Professor McElderry.

1. Translate into English :—

(*a*) λόγῳ μὲν ἐξήκουσ᾽, ὄπωπα δ᾽ οὐ μάλα,
τὸν πελάταν λέκτρων ποτὲ τῶν Διὸς
Ἰξίον᾽ ἀν᾽ ἄμπυκα δὴ δρομάδ᾽ ὡς ἔβαλ᾽ ὁ παγκρατὴς Κρόνου παῖς.
ἄλλον δ᾽ οὔτιν᾽ ἔγωγ᾽ οἶδα κλύων οὐδ᾽ ἐσιδὼν μοίρᾳ
τοῦδ᾽ ἐχθίονι συντυχόντα θνατῶν,
ὃς οὔτ᾽ ἔρξας τιν᾽ οὔτε νοσφίσας,
ἀλλ᾽ ἴσος ὢν ἴσοις ἀνήρ,
ὠλέκεθ᾽ ὧδ᾽ ἀτίμως. τόδε τοι θαῦμά μ᾽ ἔχει.
πῶς ποτε πῶς ποτ᾽ ἀμφιπλάκτων ῥοθίων μόνος κλύων,
πῶς ἄρα πανδάκρυτον οὕτω βιοτὰν κατέσχεν.

Sophocles.

(*b*)   ὣς ἔφατο, Τρῶας δὲ κατὰ κρῆθεν λάβε πένθος
ἄσχετον, οὐκ ἐπιεικτόν, ἐπεί σφισιν ἕρμα πόληος
ἔσκε καὶ ἀλλοδαπός περ ἐών· πολέες γὰρ ἅμ᾽ αὐτῷ
λαοὶ ἕποντ᾽, ἐν δ᾽ αὐτὸς ἀριστεύεσκε μάχεσθαι.
βὰν δ᾽ ἰθὺς Δαναῶν λελιημένοι· ἦρχε δ᾽ ἄρα σφιν
Ἕκτωρ χωόμενος Σαρπηδόνος. αὐτὰρ Ἀχαιοὺς
ὦρσε Μενοιτιάδεω Πατροκλῆος λάσιον κῆρ.
Αἴαντε πρώτω προσέφη, μεμαῶτε καὶ αὐτώ·
" Αἴαντε, νῦν σφῶϊν ἀμύνεσθαι φίλον ἔστω,
οἷοί περ πάρος ἦτε μετ᾽ ἀνδράσιν, ἢ καὶ ἀρείους.
κεῖται ἀνὴρ ὃς πρῶτος ἐσήλατο τεῖχος Ἀχαιῶν,
Σαρπηδών. ἀλλ᾽ εἴ μιν ἀεικισσαίμεθ᾽ ἑλόντες,
τεύχεά τ᾽ ὤμοιϊν ἀφελοίμεθα, καί τιν᾽ ἑταίρων
αὐτοῦ ἀμυνομένων δαμασαίμεθα νηλέϊ χαλκῷ."

Homer.

(*c*) διὸ δὴ καὶ ὁ μέν τις δίνην περιτιθεὶς τῇ γῇ ὑπὸ τοῦ οὐρα-
νοῦ μένειν δὴ ποιεῖ τὴν γῆν, ὁ δὲ ὥσπερ καρδόπῳ πλατείᾳ βάθρον
τὸν ἀέρα ὑπερείδει· τὴν δὲ τοῦ ὡς οἷόν τε βέλτιστα αὐτὰ τεθῆναι
δύναμιν οὕτω νῦν κεῖσθαι, ταύτην οὔτε ζητοῦσιν οὔτε τινὰ οἴονται
δαιμονίαν ἰσχὺν ἔχειν, ἀλλὰ ἡγοῦνται τούτου Ἄτλαντα ἄν ποτε ἰσ-
χυρότερον καὶ ἀθανατώτερον καὶ μᾶλλον ἅπαντα ξυνέχοντα ἐξευρεῖν,

καὶ ὡς ἀληθῶς τἀγαθὸν καὶ δέον ξυνδεῖν καὶ ξυνέχειν οὐδὲν οἴονται. ἐγὼ μὲν οὖν τοιαύτης αἰτίας, ὅπη ποτὲ ἔχει, μαθητὴς ὁτουοῦν ἥδιστ᾽ ἂν γενοίμην· ἐπειδὴ δὲ ταύτης ἐστερήθην καὶ οὔτ᾽ αὐτὸς εὑρεῖν οὔτε παρ᾽ ἄλλου μαθεῖν οἷός τε ἐγενόμην, τὸν δεύτερον πλοῦν ἐπὶ τὴν τῆς αἰτίας ζήτησιν ᾗ πεπραγμάτευμαι, βούλει σοι, ἔφη, ἐπίδειξιν ποιήσωμαι, ὦ Κέβης ;—Plato.

(d) καὶ ὑμεῖς μήθ᾽ ὡς δικασταὶ γενόμενοι τῶν ἡμῖν ποιουμένων μήθ᾽ ὡς σωφρονισταί, ὃ χαλεπὸν ἤδη, ἀποτρέπειν πειρᾶσθε, καθ᾽ ὅσον δέ τι ὑμῖν τῆς ἡμετέρας πολυπραγμοσύνης καὶ τρόπου τὸ αὐτὸ ξυμφέρει, τούτῳ ἀπολαβόντες χρήσασθε, καὶ νομίσατε μὴ πάντας ἐν ἴσῳ βλάπτειν αὐτά, πολὺ δὲ πλείους τῶν Ἑλλήνων καὶ ὠφελεῖν. ἐν παντὶ γὰρ πᾶς χωρίῳ, καὶ ᾧ μὴ ὑπάρχομεν, ὅ τε οἰόμενος ἀδικήσεσθαι καὶ ὁ ἐπιβουλεύων διὰ τὸ ἑτοίμην ὑπεῖ- ναι ἐλπίδα τῷ μὲν ἀντιτυχεῖν ἐπικουρίας ἀφ᾽ ἡμῶν, τῷ δὲ, εἰ ἥξομεν, μὴ ἀδεεῖ εἶναι κινδυνεύειν, ἀμφότεροι ἀναγκάζονται ὁ μὲν ἄκων σωφρονεῖν, ὁ δ᾽ ἀπραγμόνως σώζεσθαι. ταύτην οὖν τὴν κοινὴν τῷ τε δεομένῳ καὶ ὑμῖν νῦν παροῦσαν ἀσφάλειαν μὴ ἀπώσησθε, ἀλλ᾽ ἐξισώσαντες τοῖς ἄλλοις μεθ᾽ ἡμῶν τοῖς Συρα- κοσίοις, ἀντὶ τοῦ ἀεὶ φυλάσσεσθαι αὐτούς, καὶ ἀντεπιβουλεῦσαί ποτε ἐκ τοῦ ὁμοίου μεταλάβετε.—Thucydides.

2. (a) Write a note on the character of Neoptolemus.

(b) Is Patroclus' equipment in the arms of Achilles likely to have been part of the original story?

(c) What was the δεύτερος πλοῦς as explained in the sequel to the above passage from the *Phaedo*?

Explain ἀνταπόδοσις (ἀνταποδιδόναι) and ἀνάμνησις.

Wherein do they fail to afford the complete proof desired?

(d) In the passage from Thucydides discuss any differences of reading and interpretation.

Annotate—

καὶ σύ, ὦ Πρύτανι, ταῦτα εἴπερ ἡγεῖ σοι προσήκειν κήδεσθαί τε τῆς πόλεως, καὶ βούλει γενέσθαι πολίτης ἀγαθός, ἐπιψήφιζε, καὶ γνώμας προτίθει αὖθις Ἀθηναίοις, νομίσας, εἰ ὀρρωδεῖς τὸ ἀναψηφίσαι, τὸ μὲν λύειν τοὺς νόμους μὴ μετὰ τοσῶνδ᾽ ἂν μαρτύρων αἰτίαν σχεῖν.

παρασκευὴ γὰρ αὕτη πρώτη ἐκπλεύσασα μιᾶς πόλεως δυνάμει Ἑλληνικῇ πολυτελεστάτη δὴ καὶ εὐπρεπεστάτη τῶν εἰς ἐκεῖνον τὸν χρόνον ἐγένετο.

UNPRESCRIBED PASSAGE.

3. Translate into English :—

ἐκ παίδων σμικρῶν ἀρξάμενοι, μέχρι οὗπερ ἂν ζῶσι, καὶ διδάσκουσι καὶ νουθετοῦσιν. ἐπειδὰν θᾶττον συνιῇ τις τὰ λεγόμενα, καὶ τροφὸς καὶ μήτηρ καὶ παιδαγωγὸς καὶ αὐτὸς ὁ πατὴρ περὶ τούτου διαμάχονται, ὅπως βέλτιστος ἔσται ὁ παῖς, παρ' ἕκαστον καὶ ἔργον καὶ λόγον διδάσκοντες καὶ ἐνδεικνύμενοι ὅτι τὸ μὲν δίκαιον, τὸ δὲ ἄδικον, καὶ τόδε μὲν καλόν, τόδε δὲ αἰσχρόν, καὶ τόδε μὲν ὅσιον, τόδε δὲ ἀνόσιον, καὶ τὰ μὲν ποίει, τὰ δὲ μὴ ποίει· καὶ ἐὰν μὲν ἑκὼν πείθηται· εἰ δὲ μή, ὥσπερ ξύλον διαστρεφόμενον καὶ καμπτόμενον εὐθύνουσιν ἀπειλαῖς καὶ πληγαῖς· μετὰ δὲ ταῦτα εἰς διδασκάλων πέμποντες πολὺ μᾶλλον ἐντέλλονται ἐπιμελεῖσθαι εὐκοσμίας τῶν παίδων ἢ γραμμάτων τε καὶ κιθαρίσεως· οἱ δὲ διδάσκαλοι τούτων τε ἐπιμελοῦνται, καὶ ἐπειδὰν αὖ γράμματα μάθωσι καὶ μέλλωσι συνήσειν τὰ γεγραμμένα, ὥσπερ τότε τὴν φωνήν, παρατιθέασιν αὐτοῖς ἐπὶ τῶν βάθρων ἀναγιγνώσκειν ποιητῶν ἀγαθῶν ποιήματα καὶ ἐκμανθάνειν ἀναγκάζουσιν, ἐν οἷς πολλαὶ μὲν νουθετήσεις ἔνεισι, πολλαὶ δὲ διέξοδοι καὶ ἔπαινοι καὶ ἐγκώμια παλαιῶν ἀνδρῶν ἀγαθῶν, ἵνα ὁ παῖς ζηλῶν μιμῆται καὶ ὀρέγηται τοιοῦτος γενέσθαι.—PLATO.

GREEK.

SECOND PAPER.

Examiner—PROFESSOR McELDERRY.

1. Translate into Greek :—

To this the Athenians, by the advice of Themistocles, replied that they would send an embassy of their own to discuss the matter, and so got rid of the Spartan envoys. He then proposed that he should himself start at once for Sparta, and that they should give him colleagues who were not to go immediately, but were to wait until the wall reached the lowest height which could possibly be defended. The whole people, men, women, and children, should join in the work, and they must spare no building, private or public, which could be of use, but demolish them all. Having given these instructions, and intimated that he would manage affairs at Sparta, he departed. On his arrival he did not at once present himself officially to the magistrates, but delayed and made excuses; and when any of them asked him why he did not appear before the assembly, he said that he was waiting for his colleagues, who had been detained by some engagement; he was daily expecting them and wondered that they had not appeared.—JOWETT.

2. (*a*) Explain fully the constructions of πρίν.

(*b*) Write a note on the accusative absolute. Is it ever used personally?

(*c*) How are diminutives of Greek nouns formed? · Give examples.

(*d*) What is meant by 'Attic future,' and 'Attic reduplication'?

(*e*) Compare the following words with their Latin equivalents :—ἀστήρ, δαήρ, δάκρυ, ἕπομαι, θεός, ἵππος, ἧπαρ, οἶκος, πέντε, ὕπνος.

UNPRESCRIBED PASSAGE.

3. Translate into English :—

ὦ παῖδες, ὧδ' ἕπεσθ'. ἐγὼ γὰρ ἡγεμὼν
σφῷν αὖ πέφασμαι καινός, ὥσπερ σφὼ πατρί.
χωρεῖτε, καὶ μὴ ψαύετ', ἀλλ' ἐᾶτέ με
αὐτὸν τὸν ἱρὸν τύμβον ἐξευρεῖν, ἵνα
μοῖρ' ἀνδρὶ τῷδε τῇδε κρυφθῆναι χθονί.
τῇδ', ὧδε, τῇδε βᾶτε· τῇδε γάρ μ' ἄγει
Ἑρμῆς ὁ πομπὸς ἥ τε νερτέρα θεός.
ὦ φῶς ἀφεγγές, πρόσθε πού ποτ' ἦσθ' ἐμὸν,
νῦν δ' ἔσχατόν σου τοὐμὸν ἅπτεται δέμας.
ἤδη γὰρ ἕρπω τὸν τελευταῖον βίον
κρύψων παρ' Ἅιδην. ἀλλὰ, φίλτατε ξένων,
αὐτός τε χώρα θ' ἥδε πρόσπολοί τε σοὶ
εὐδαίμονες γένοισθε, κἀπ' εὐπραξίᾳ
μέμνησθέ μου θανόντος εὐτυχεῖς ἀεί.

SOPHOCLES.

FRENCH.

COMPOSITION.

Examiner—PROFESSOR STEINBERGER.

1. Translate into French :—

Anyone who visited Regent's Park, about fifty years ago, must have seen at the east side an imposing detached villa, proudly built in the midst of a parklike ground. It was called Holford House, because its proprietor was a Mr. Holford. He was a most mysterious gentleman, who rose as suddenly in metropolitan society as he disappeared from it, after an interval of about ten years. To all appearances he was possessed of an enormous fortune, but no one ever knew how he had acquired his wealth. Some spoke of his luck at the stock exchange ; others said he came from the Colonies ; a few took him for an American ; and a newspaper once asserted he was the chief director of a company trading in Australian meat. A man with large means in London is soon surrounded by friends, and as Mr. Holford had neither an occupation, nor a family, nor any other relations, but entertained splendidly, and was a most agreeable host, his drawing-room, his garden, and his green-house were always crowded with visitors. He spoke little, and there was always an air of mystery in his ways. Once every three months he disappeared for a week or two without telling anyone where he went.

UNPRESCRIBED PASSAGES.

2. Translate into English :—

I.

Au milieu d'un taillis peu épais, et à travers lequel on peut apercevoir les objets à une assez grande distance, s'élevait d'un seul jet une haute futaie composée presque en totalité de pins et de chênes. Obligé de croître sur un terrain très circonscrit et privé des rayons du soleil, chacun de ces arbres monte rapidement pour chercher l'air et la lumière. Aussi droit que le mât d'un vaisseau, il s'élance au-dessus de tout ce qui l'environne. C'est seulement quand il est parvenu à une région supérieure, qu'il étend tranquillement ses branches et s'enveloppe de leur ombre.

D'autres le suivent bientôt dans cette sphère élevée, et

tous, entrelaçant leurs rameaux, forment comme un dais immense. Au-dessous de cette voûte humide et immobile l'aspect change et prend un caractère nouveau.

Un ordre majestueux règne au-dessus de votre tête. Près du sol, au contraire, tout offre l'image de la confusion et du chaos : des troncs incapables de supporter plus long-temps leurs branches se sont fendus dans la moitié de leur hauteur et ne présentent plus à l'œil qu'un sommet aigu et déchiré. D'autres, longtemps ébranlés par le vent, ont été précipités d'une seule pièce sur la terre. Arrachées du sol, leurs racines forment comme autant de remparts naturels derrière lesquels plusieurs hommes pourraient facilement se mettre à couvert. Des arbres immenses, retenus par les branches qui les environnent, restent suspendus dans les airs et tombent en poussière sans toucher le sol.—A. DE TOCQUEVILLE.

II.

Enfant, j'ai quelquefois passé des jours entiers
Au jardin, dans les prés, dans quelques verts sentiers,
Creusés sur les coteaux par les bœufs du village,
Tout voilés d'aubépine et de mûre sauvage ;
Mon chien auprès de moi, mon livre dans la main,
M'arrêtant sans fatigue, et marchant sans chemin,
Tantôt lisant, tantôt ecorçant quelque tige,
Suivant d'un œil distrait l'insecte qui voltige,
L'eau qui coule au soleil en petits diamants,
Ou l'oreille clouée à des bourdonnements.
Puis, choisissant un gîte à l'abri d'une haie
Comme un lièvre tapi qu'un aboiement effraie,
Je reprenais de l'œil et du cœur ma lecture.

A. DE LAMARTINE.

8. Epreuve orale sur les auteurs préscrits.

GERMAN.

Examiner—PROFESSOR STEINBERGER.

COMPOSITION.

1. Translate into German :—

The town was strongly placed at the foot of a mountain, not far from the banks of the Severn, and was of great extent. Its walls inclosed a space more than double that of Roman London, while the remains of its forum, its theatre and amphitheatre, as well as the broad streets which contrast with the narrow alleys of other British towns, show its wealth and importance. But with its storm by the West-Saxons, the very existence of the city came to an end. Its ruins show that the place was plundered and burned, while the bones which lie scattered among them tell their tale of the flight and massacre of its inhabitants, of women and children hewn down in the streets, and wretched fugitives stifled in the hidden places whither they had fled with their little savings for shelter. A British poet, in verses still left to us, sings piteously the death-song of Uriconium, the white town in the valley.—J. R. GREEN.

UNPRESCRIBED PASSAGES.

2. Translate into English :—

i.

Das flache Land, das wir vor uns hatten, stimmte schlecht zu der Vorstellung, die wir uns von der Insel Margarita gemacht. Während man beschäftigt war, die Angaben der Karten zu vergleichen, ohne sie in Uebereinstimmung bringen zu können, signalisirte man vom Mast einige kleine Fischerboote. Der Capitän des Pizarro rief sie durch einen Kanonenschuß herbei; aber ein solches Zeichen dient zu nichts in den Ländern, wo der Schwache, wenn er dem Starken begegnet, glaubt sich nur auf Vergewaltigungen gefaßt machen zu müssen. Die Boote ergriffen die Flucht nach Westen zu, und wir sahen uns hier in derselben Verlegenheit, wie bei unserer Ankunft auf den Canarien vor der kleinen Insel Graciosa. Niemand an Bord war je in der Gegend am Land gewesen. So ruhig die See war, so schien doch die Nähe eines kaum ein paar Fuß hohen Eilands Vorsichtsmaßregeln zu erheischen. Man steuerte nicht weiter dem Lande zu, und da das Senkblei nur drei bis vier Faden Wasser anzeigte, warf man eilends den Anker aus. — A. v. Humboldt.

II.

Der Spaziergang.

Sei mir gegrüßt, mein Berg mit dem röthlich strahlenden Gipfel!
  Sei mir, Sonne, gegrüßt, die ihn so lieblich bescheint!
Dich auch grüß' ich, belebte Flur, euch, säuselnde Linden,
  Und den fröhlichen Chor, der auf den Aesten sich wiegt;
Ruhige Bläue, dich auch, die unermeßlich sich ausgießt
  Um das braune Gebirg, über den grünenden Wald,
Auch um mich, der, endlich entflohn des Zimmers Gefängniß
  Und dem engen Gespräch, freudig sich rettet zu dir.
Deiner Lüfte balsamischer Strom durchrinnt mich erquickend,
  Und den durstigen Blick labt das energische Licht.
Kräftig auf blühender Au erglänzen die wechselnden Farben,
  Aber der reizende Streit löset in Anmuth sich auf.
Frei empfängt mich die Wiese mit weithin verbreitetem Teppich:
  Durch ihr freundliches Grün schlingt sich der ländliche Pfad.
Um mich summt die geschäftige Bien', mit zweifelndem Flügel
  Wiegt der Schmetterling sich über dem röthlichen Klee.
Glühend trifft mich der Sonne Pfeil, still liegen die Weste,
  Nur der Lerche Gesang wirbelt in heiterer Luft.

Schiller.

3. Mündliche Prüfung über vorgeschriebene Schriftsteller.

ENGLISH.

First Paper.

Examiner—Professor Trench.

1. Does Shakespeare bring out Hamlet's character by contrasting it with that of other persons in the play?

2. Consider whether the *Merchant of Venice* is rightly designated a comedy.
Compare Antonio and Bassanio, or Portia and Jessica.

3. Describe the Red Cross Knight's meeting with Despair.

4. Refer to passages in *Paradise Lost*, i., ii., which specially illustrate Milton's several excellences, showing why you select them.

5. What is Lyrical Poetry? Give a short account of Lyrical Poetry 1579 to 1616.

ENGLISH.

SECOND PAPER.

Examiner—PROFESSOR TRENCH.

1. Consider Sidney's view of the poets as moralists.
2. Examine Bacon's use of quotation.

SUBJECT FOR ESSAY.

Spenser.

Or,

The death of Ophelia.

LOGIC.

Examiner—PROFESSOR TRENCH.

1. What do you understand by—general notion; predicables; mediate inference; analytic proposition.

2. State or discuss the logical characteristics of—metropolis; consciousness; brilliance; national; Edward VII.

3. Construct a syllogism in camenes, and a syllogism in datisi, and explain how Aristotle's dictum is applicable to them.

4. Test the following arguments—(*a*) plants alone have flowers; zoophytes have no flowers; therefore they are not plants.

(*b*) If a conclusion is more certain to be wrong where the reasoning is correct from premises that are false, will not the best logician be the worst guide in subjects where no certainty is attainable?

5. Why is IEO never valid and EIO always valid, if the only difference is in the order of the premises?

HISTORY.

Examiner—PROFESSOR TRENCH.

1. Relate the chief incidents in the constitutional disputes which led to Civil War in England.

2. Narrate the career of Hugh O'Neill. Explain Wentworth's Irish policy and methods.

3. Consider the growth of royal authority in France.

4. Discuss—(*a*) the causes, and (*b*) the results of the Thirty Years' War.

SCIENCE SCHOLARSHIPS OF THE THIRD YEAR.

MATHEMATICS.

FIRST PAPER.

Examiner—PROFESSOR BROMWICH.

1. Prove that the equation $y = (ax + b)/(cx + d)$ can be put in the form $\mu\eta = \lambda\xi$, where λ, μ are the roots of the equation in t, $(a - t)(d - t) - bc = 0$, and

$$\xi = (x - a)/(x - \beta), \qquad \eta = (y - a)/(y - \beta),$$
$$a = (a - \lambda)/c = b/(d - \lambda), \qquad \beta = (a - \mu)/c = b/(d - \mu).$$

Deduce that four equations of this type between (y, x), (z, y), (w, z), $(x, w,)$ lead to

$$x = y = z = w = a \text{ or } \beta,$$

unless $\qquad a^2 + d^2 + 2bc = 0,$

when the four equations are equivalent to three only.

2. If the coefficients of an infinite series $\Sigma a_n x^n$ are real, and such that (for large values of n) we have

$$\frac{a_n}{a_{n+1}} = p + \frac{q}{n} + \frac{r}{n^2} + \dots,$$

prove that the series converges for all real values of x between the limits $\pm p$; and that it converges for $x = -p$ if $q/p > 0$, for $x = +p$ if $q/p > 1$.

3. Evaluate

$$\begin{vmatrix} 1, & a, & 0, & 0, & 0, \\ a, & 1, & a, & 0, & 0, \\ 0, & a, & 1, & a, & 0, \\ 0, & 0, & a, & 1, & a, \\ 0, & 0, & 0, & a, & 1, \end{vmatrix}.$$

4. Show that the number of different ways in which a given number $6n$ can be divided into three parts (each part being a positive integer greater than 2) is $3(n-1)^2$. What will be the number of ways if the positive integers are not restricted to be greater than 2?

5. Find an expression for $\tan 7\theta$ in terms of $\tan \theta$, and deduce the equation with roots

$$\tan^2(\tfrac{1}{7}\pi), \quad \tan^2(\tfrac{2}{7}\pi), \quad \tan^2(\tfrac{3}{7}\pi).$$

Prove that

$$\sec^2(\tfrac{1}{7}\pi) + \sec^2(\tfrac{2}{7}\pi) + \sec^2(\tfrac{3}{7}\pi) = 24$$
$$= 3[\operatorname{cosec}^2(\tfrac{1}{7}\pi) + \operatorname{cosec}^2(\tfrac{2}{7}\pi) + \operatorname{cosec}^2(\tfrac{3}{7}\pi)].$$

6. Two perpendicular lines in an inclined plane make angles a, $\beta \,(< \tfrac{1}{2}\pi)$ with the horizontal: find θ, the angle of slope of the plane. Prove that $(a + \beta)$ cannot exceed $\tfrac{1}{2}\pi$, and that θ cannot be greater than $(a + \beta)$.

7. Prove that the sum of the infinite series

$$\frac{1}{1.2.3} + \frac{1}{3.4.5} + \frac{1}{5.6.7} + \dots = \log 2 - \tfrac{1}{2}.$$

Discuss the validity of the transformations you employ.

8. If x is numerically less than unity, prove that

$$(1 - x^2)/(1 - 2x \cos \theta + x^2) = 1 + 2x \cos \theta + 2x^2 \cos 2\theta$$
$$+ 2x^3 \cos 3\theta + \dots$$

and find an expression for $\cos n\theta$ in terms of $\cos \theta$.

R

344 Science Scholarships of the Third Year.

9. If θ is the angle subtended by the edge of a regular dodecahedron at its centre, prove that

$$3 \cos \theta = \sqrt{5},$$

and that the length of the edge is $(\sqrt{5} - 1)/\sqrt{3}$ times the radius of the circumscribing sphere.

10. A, B, C, D are four points not in the same plane. Points P, Q, R, S are taken on AB, BC, CD, DA respectively, in such a way that

$$\frac{AP}{PB} = \frac{DR}{RC}, \quad \frac{BQ}{QC} = \frac{AS}{SD},$$

prove that the lines PR and QS intersect.

———

MATHEMATICS.

SECOND PAPER.

Examiner—PROFESSOR BROMWICH.

1. Define the continuity of a one-valued function of a real variable; and prove that the function

$$\frac{1}{\log(1+x)} - \frac{1}{x}$$

is continuous for values $-1 < x < \infty$, and has a continually diminishing positive fractional value.

2. If $x + y + z = 3$, prove that (with certain restrictions) the product $f(x) . f(y) . f(z)$ is a maximum or minimum for $x = y = z = 1$, according as $f''(1)$ is less or greater than $[f'(1)]^2/f(1)$.

3. Find the equation to the tangent at any point of the curve

$$x/a = (1 + t^2)/(1 - t^2), \quad y/b = (1 + t^2)/2t.$$

Find also the radius of curvature, and trace the curve.

4. Prove that four normals can be drawn from any point (x_0, y_0) to the conic $x^2/a^2 + y^2/b^2 = 1$; and that if all the normals are real, then of their intersections with $x = 0$ three are on one side of the centre, and one on the other side.

5. Integrate

$$\int (\sin^{-1}x)\, dx, \quad \int \frac{dx}{1 + e^x}, \quad \int \frac{\sec^2 x\, dx}{1 + \sin^2 x}.$$

6. Show that

$$\int_{-\infty}^{+\infty} \frac{(px^2 + 2qx + r)\, dx}{(ax^2 + 2bx + c)^2} = \frac{(ar - 2bq + cp)\,\pi}{2\,(ac - b^2)^{\frac{3}{2}}},$$

and

$$\int_{-\infty}^{+\infty} \frac{dx}{ax^4 + 2bx^2 + c} = \frac{\pi}{[2c\,(b + \sqrt{ac})]^{\frac{1}{2}}},$$

where, in the first, $ac > b^2$, and a, c are positive; while, in the second, a, b, c are all positive, with $b^2 > ac$.

7. Prove that the centre of gravity of the area contained between a parabola and any chord, divides the diameter bisecting the chord in the ratio $3 : 2$.

8. Trace the curve

$$4a^2 y^2\,(x^2/a^2 + y^2/b^2 - 1) + b^2\,(a^2 - x^2) = 0,$$

and prove that the area bounded by the curve and the two lines

$$x = a, \quad x = 3a/2\sqrt{2}$$

is

$$\tfrac{1}{16}\,(10 - 3\pi)\,ab.$$

9. Verify that if

$$a^2 + ad + d^2 + bc = 0,$$

the expression

$$x + \frac{ax + b}{cx + d} + \frac{-dx + b}{cx - a}$$

is not altered by writing in place of x either of the two fractions

$$\frac{ax + b}{cx + d}, \quad \frac{-dx + b}{cx - a}.$$

10. Prove (by using question 9, or in any other way) that if a is one root of the cubic

$$\frac{c^2x^3 + 3bcx + b\,(d - a)}{(cx + d)\,(cx - a)} = \lambda,$$

then the other two roots are

$$\frac{aa + b}{ca + d}, \quad \frac{-da + b}{ca - a},$$

provided that

$$a^2 + ad + d^2 + bc = 0.$$

MATHEMATICAL PHYSICS.

(*For Arts and Engineering.*)

Examiner—PRESIDENT ANDERSON.

1. Find the centre of mass of a pyramid on a triangular base, and show that it coincides with that of four equal particles at its corners.

2. At any number of points of a parabola, forces are applied represented by the tangents and normals at these points: show that the parabola will remain at rest if the focus is fixed.

8. Prove that the path of a projectile is a parabola, and that the angular velocity of the projectile about the focus of its path varies inversely as its distance from the focus.

4. A ball is dropped from a height h on to a horizontal plane. Show that the whole distance through which it moves before coming to rest is $h\,\dfrac{1 + e^2}{1 - e^2}$, where e is the coefficient of restitution.

5. Find the acceleration of a particle moving with uniform speed in a circle.

A circular string, of radius a, is rotating in its own plane about its centre with uniform angular velocity w: find its tension, the mass per unit length being m.

6. Two particles of masses m and m' are suspended by a string over a smooth pulley: find the acceleration of their centre of mass.

7. A triangle is immersed in a homogeneous liquid with its base in the surface. Prove that a horizontal line drawn through the centre of pressure divides it into two portions on which the thrusts are equal.

8. A uniform rod rests in a position inclined to the vertical, with half its length immersed in water, and can turn about a point in it at a distance equal to one-sixth of the length of the rod from the end below the water. Find the specific gravity of the rod.

9. Prove that, if the minimum deviation for rays incident on a prism be a, the refractive index cannot be less than $\sec \frac{a}{2}$.

10. Find when Venus appears brightest, assuming the orbits of the Earth and Venus to be circles.

EXPERIMENTAL PHYSICS.

Examiner—PRESIDENT ANDERSON.

1. State what you know regarding the effect of air-resistance on the path of a projectile, and on the motion of a falling body. Why is the first part of the path of a golf-ball sometimes concave upwards?

2. Define 'Young's modulus.' Young's modulus for steel being $18.4 \times 10''$ dynes per square centimetre, calculate the work done in increasing the length of a steel bar, 10 centimetres long and 1 square centimetre section, by 1 millimetre.

3. Find the overtones of a stretched string, and show that they are harmonics. Find also the first three overtones of a stretched string having at its middle point a particle whose mass is great compared with that of the string.

4. Describe Joly's steam calorimeter, and his method of finding the specific heat of a gas at constant volume.

5. Explain Bottomley's experiment in which a loaded wire cuts its way through a block of ice and leaves the block whole after its passage.

6. Explain the thermal effect produced by compressing suddenly (*a*) a gas, and (*b*) water at a temperature between 0° and 4° C.

7. Explain why it is that the brightness of the flame of a lamp is independent of its distance. When a telescope is used to view an object of sensible apparent diameter, show that the brightness of the image observed may be either equal to or less than that of the object, and distinguish the two cases.

8. Show how the results of spectrum analysis may be used in determining the constitution and motions of the stars, and explain the principles underlying these applications.

9. How would you prove, by experiment, that the surface of the Earth at any place is charged with electricity ?

10. Show how temperatures may be measured by currents produced by thermo-electric couples. Is the current produced proportional to the difference of temperature of the junctions ?

There was also a Practical Examination in the Laboratory.

———

CHEMISTRY.

Examiner—PROFESSOR SENIER.

[*Formulæ, equations, and diagrams to be used whenever possible.*]

1. Explain (*a*) the meaning of the terms 'molecule' and 'atom'; (*b*) the evidence leading to the molecular and atomic hypotheses ; (*c*) the importance of these hypotheses in the development of chemistry.

2. (*a*) How may the changes that sulphur undergoes when heated be observed experimentally? (*b*) What explanation of these changes has been suggested?

3. State (*a*) how hydrochloric acid is obtained in the Le Blanc soda manufacture ; (*b*) how chlorine is prepared from it, including an explanation of Weldon's improvements; (*c*) how chlorine is made use of in the manufacture of ' bleaching powder '; (*d*) how the last substance is valued for commercial purposes.

4. (*a*) What is meant by 'ignition points' ? (*b*) Illustrate by those of hydrogen and oxygen, carbon disulphide and oxygen, phosphorus and oxygen, methane and oxygen, nitrogen and oxygen. (*c*) Explain the use of the Davy lamp in preventing explosions in coal-mines.

5. Describe and explain how the chlorides of the following elements may be obtained experimentally:—iron, mercury, silver, barium, phosphorus, oxygen.

6. (*a*) What acids result from the combination of water with phosphorus pentoxide? Explain (*b*) how these acids may be distinguished; (*c*) their behaviour when heated; (*d*) their supposed constitution.

ZOOLOGY AND BOTANY.

Examiner—PROFESSOR RICHARD J. ANDERSON.

1. Classify the Echinodermata. Refer to the chief distinctive marks in each order.

2. Write an account of the structure of a fresh-water Mussel.

3. Describe the respiratory apparatus in Fishes, and note the varieties.

4. What are the distinctive peculiarities of the Primate and Marsupial Orders?

5. Write an account of the anatomy and physiology of the Leaf.

6. Define the Scrophulariaceæ, Geraniaceæ, and Caryophyllaceæ.

7. Give a list of orders in which the stamens are adherent to the Corolla.

8. How do light and heat influence or affect plants?

GEOLOGY AND MINERALOGY.

Examiner—Professor Richard J. Anderson.

1. Give an account of the rainfall in Europe.

2. Write a brief account of the physical features of Australia.

3. Enumerate the minerals which contain phosphorus, referring to their most striking physical features.

4. Give the chemical composition, crystalline system, hardness, specific gravity, and colour of :—Spodumene, Rhodonite, Leucite, Heulandite, Hornblende, Labradorite, Anhydrite, Sphene, Lapis Lazuli, and Siderite.

5. Give an account of the Monoclinic System.

6. Enumerate the most characteristic fossils of Leassic Rocks, assigning each to its proper zoological position. Where a type existed before or after Liassic times. This fact should be noted.

7. Enumerate the divisions of the Carboniferous system. Refer especially to the varieties of rocks found in the Lower Carboniferous in the British Isles.

8. Locate in their zoological position and give the geological horizon of :—Aviculo-pecten, Phacops, Phragmoceras, Cidaris, Hippopodium, Voltzia, Walchia, and Dadoxylom.

SENIOR SCHOLARSHIP—ANCIENT CLASSICS.

GREEK.

First Paper.

Examiner—Professor McElderry.

1. Translate into English :—

ἄλλοισι δ᾽ ἅλικες ἄλλοι·
τὰ δ᾽ αὐτὸς ἄν τις ἴδῃ,
ἔλπεταί τις ἕκαστος ἐξοχώτατα φάσθαι.

οἶον αἰνέων κε Μελησίαν ἔριδα στρέφοι,
ῥήματα πλέκων, ἀπάλαιστος ἐν λόγῳ ἕλκειν,
μαλακὰ μὲν φρονέων ἐσλοῖς,
τραχὺς δὲ παλιγκότοις ἔφεδρος.

PINDAR.

Explain :—(*a*) πολλῶν ἐπέβαν καιρὸν οὐ ψεύδει βαλών.
(*b*) ἔστι δ' ἐοικὸς ὀρειᾶν γε Πελειάδων μὴ τηλόθεν 'Ωαρίωνα
νεῖσθαι.   (*c*) ἴυγγι δ' ἕλκομαι ἦτορ νεομηνίᾳ θιγέμεν.

2. Translate into English :—

(*a*) ἡ μὲν οὖν ἐποποιία τῇ τραγῳδίᾳ μέχρι μόνου μέτρου
μεγάλου, μίμησις εἶναι σπουδαίων, ἠκολούθησεν· τῷ δὲ τὸ
μέτρον ἁπλοῦν ἔχειν καὶ ἀπαγγελίαν εἶναι, ταύτῃ διαφέρουσιν·
ἔτι δὲ τῷ μήκει ἡ μὲν ὅτι μάλιστα πειρᾶται ὑπὸ μίαν περίοδον
ἡλίου εἶναι ἢ μικρὸν ἐξαλλάττειν, ἡ δὲ ἐποποιία ἀόριστος τῷ
χρόνῳ· καὶ τούτῳ διαφέρει, καίτοι τὸ πρῶτον ὁμοίως ἐν ταῖς
τραγῳδίαις τοῦτο ἐποίουν καὶ ἐν τοῖς ἔπεσιν.—ARISTOTLE.

You may emend if necessary.

(*b*) εἴδη δὲ ἀναγνωρίσεως, πρώτη μὲν ἡ ἀτεχνοτάτη καὶ ᾗ
πλείστῃ χρῶνται δι' ἀπορίαν, ἡ διὰ τῶν σημείων. τούτων δὲ
τὰ μὲν σύμφυτα, οἶον " λόγχην ἣν φοροῦσι Γηγενεῖς," ἢ ἀστέρας
οἵους ἐν τῷ Θυέστῃ Καρκίνος· τὰ δὲ ἐπίκτητα, καὶ τούτων τὰ
μὲν ἐν τῷ σώματι, οἶον οὐλαί, τὰ δὲ ἐκτός, τὰ περιδέρρεα, καὶ
οἶον ἐν τῇ Τυροῖ διὰ τῆς σκάφης.—ID.

State the gist of Aristotle's criticisms on Sophocles and
Euripides.

3. Translate into English :—

(*a*)   πόθῳ δ' ὑπερποντίας
φάσμα δόξει δόμων ἀνάσσειν·
εὐμόρφων δὲ κολοσσῶν
ἔχθεται χάρις ἀνδρί·
ὀμμάτων δ' ἐν ἀχηνίαις
ἔρρει πᾶσ' 'Αφροδίτα.
ὀνειρόφαντοι δὲ πενθήμονες
πάρεισιν δόξαι φέρουσαι χάριν ματαίαν.

B 8

μάταν γὰρ εὖτ᾽ ἂν ἐσθλά τις δοκῶν ὁρᾶν,
παραλλάξασα διὰ χερῶν,
βέβακεν ὄψις οὐ μεθύστερον
πτεροῖς ὀπαδοῖς ὕπνου κελεύθοις.

AESCHYLUS.

(b) ἐπεὶ δ᾽ ἐπεμνησάμεσθ᾽ ἀμειλίχων
πόνων, ἀκαίρως δὲ δυσφιλὲς γαμή-
λευμ᾽, ἀπεύχετον δόμοις,
γυναικοβούλους τε μήτιδας φρενῶν
ἐπ᾽ ἀνδρὶ τευχεσφόρῳ,
ἐπ᾽ ἀνδρὶ δῄοισιν ἐπικότῳ σέβας·
τίων δ᾽ ἀθέρμαντον ἑστίαν δόμων
γυναικείαν ἄτολμον αἰχμάν.
κακῶν δὲ πρεσβεύεται τὸ Λήμνιον
λόγῳ· γοᾶται δὲ δήποθεν κατά-
πτυστον· εἴκασεν δέ τις
τὸ δεινὸν αὖ Λημνίοισι πήμασιν.

ID.

The traditional view of the plot of the *Agamemnon* has been criticised ?

In (b) you are at liberty to adopt and defend any other readings or arrangement.

4. Translate into English :—

(a) Δεῦρο, Μοῦσ᾽,
ἐλθέ, φλεγυρὸν πυρὸς ἔχουσα μένος,
ἔντονος Ἀχαρνική·
οἷον ἐξ ἀνθράκων πρινίνων
φέψαλος ἀνήλατ᾽ ἐρεθιζόμενος οὐρίᾳ ῥιπίδι,
ἡνίκ᾽ ἂν ἐπανθρακίδες ὦσι παρακείμεναι·
οἱ δὲ Θασίαν ἀνακυκῶσι λιπαράμπυκα
οἱ δὲ μάττωσιν· οὕ-
τω σοβαρὸν ἐλθὲ μέλος εὔτονον, ἀγροικότερον,
ὡς ἐμὲ λαβοῦσα τὸν δημότην.

ARISTOPHANES.

(b) καὶ πρῶτον μὲν λόγισαι φαύλως, μὴ ψήφοις, ἀλλ' ἀπὸ
    χειρός,
    τὸν φόρον ἡμῖν ἀπὸ τῶν πόλεων ξυλλήβδην τὸν
    προσιόντα·
    κᾆξω τούτου τὰ τέλη χωρίς, καὶ τὰς πολλὰς ἑκατοστάς,
    πρυτανεῖα, μέταλλ', ἀγοράς, λιμένας, μισθούς, καὶ
    δημιόπρατα·
    τούτων πλήρωμα, τάλαντ' ἐγγὺς δισχίλια γίγνεται ἡμῖν.
    ἀπὸ τούτων νυν μισθὸν κατάθες τοῖσι δικασταῖς ἐνιαυτοῦ,
    ἓξ χιλιάσιν, κοὔπω πλείους ἐν τῇ χώρᾳ κατένασθεν,
    γίγνεται ἡμῖν ἑκατὸν δήπου καὶ πεντήκοντα τάλαντα.

                              Id.

Annotate (b) where needful. The passage bears upon a disputed question in history ?

5. Translate into English :—

τοσοῦτον δὲ διενήνοχεν ἀναισχυντίᾳ τῶν ἁπάντων ἀνθρώπων, ὥστε ὑμᾶς πειρᾶται πείθειν, τοσούτους ὄντας εἷς ὤν, ὡς οὐκ εἰμὶ τῶν ἀδυνάτων ἐγώ. καίτοι εἰ τοῦτο πείσει τινὰς ὑμῶν, ὦ βουλή, τί με κωλύει κληροῦσθαι τῶν ἐννέα ἀρχόντων, καὶ ὑμᾶς ἐμοῦ μὲν ἀφελέσθαι τὸν ὀβολὸν ὡς ὑγιαίνοντος, τούτῳ δὲ ψηφίσασθαι πάντας ὡς ἀναπήρῳ; οὐ γὰρ δήπου τὸν αὐτὸν ὑμεῖς μὲν ὡς δυνάμενον ἀφαιρήσεσθε τὸ διδόμενον, οἱ δὲ ὡς ἀδύνατον ὄντα κληροῦσθαι κωλύσουσιν. ἀλλὰ γὰρ οὔτε ὑμεῖς τούτῳ τὴν αὐτὴν ἔχετε γνώμην, οὔθ' οὗτος εὔλογα δοκεῖ ποιεῖν. ὁ μὲν γὰρ ὥσπερ ἐπικλήρου τῆς συμφορᾶς οὔσης ἀμφισβητήσων ἥκει καὶ πειρᾶται πείθειν ὑμᾶς ὡς οὐκ εἰμὶ τοιοῦτος οἷον ὑμεῖς ὁρᾶτε πάντες· ὑμεῖς δὲ (ὃ τῶν εὖ φρονούντων ἔργον ἐστί) μᾶλλον πιστεύετε τοῖς ὑμετέροις αὐτῶν ὀφθαλμοῖς ἢ τοῖς τούτου λόγοις.—Lysias.

Explain where needful. Annotate τὸ 'Ανάκειον, προθεσμία, ἀντωμοσία.

6. Translate into English :—

Ἅπας ὁ τῶν ἀνθρώπων βίος, ὦ ἄνδρες 'Αθηναῖοι, κἂν μεγάλην πόλιν οἰκῶσι κἂν μικράν, φύσει καὶ νόμοις διοικεῖται. τούτων δ' ἡ μὲν φύσις ἐστὶν ἄτακτον καὶ ἀνώμαλον καὶ κατ' ἄνδρα ἴδιον τοῦ ἔχοντος, οἱ δὲ νόμοι κοινὸν καὶ τεταγμένον καὶ ταὐτὸ πᾶσιν. ἡ μὲν οὖν φύσις, ἂν ᾖ πονηρά, πολλάκις φαῦλα βούλεται· διόπερ τοὺς τοιούτους ἐξαμαρτάνοντας εὑρήσετε. οἱ δὲ νόμοι τὸ δίκαιον καὶ τὸ καλὸν καὶ τὸ συμφέρον βούλονται, καὶ τοῦτο ζητοῦσι, καὶ ἐπειδὰν εὑρεθῇ, κοινὸν τοῦτο πρόσταγμα ἀπεδείχθη, πᾶσιν ἴσον καὶ ὅμοιον, καὶ τοῦτ' ἔστι νόμος, ᾧ πάντας πείθεσθαι προσήκει διὰ πολλά, καὶ μάλισθ' ὅτι πᾶς ἐστι νόμος εὕρημα μὲν καὶ δῶρον θεῶν, δόγμα δ' ἀνθρώπων φρονίμων, ἐπανόρθωμα δὲ τῶν ἑκουσίων καὶ ἀκουσίων ἁμαρτημάτων, πόλεως δὲ συνθήκη κοινή, καθ' ἣν πᾶσι προσήκει ζῆν τοῖς ἐν τῇ πόλει.— DEMOSTHENES.

GREEK.

SECOND PAPER.

Examiner—PROFESSOR McELDERRY.

1. Translate into Greek :—

And therefore I must confess it seemed strange to me when I came home, and heard our people say such fine things of the power, riches, glory, magnificence, and trade of the Chinese, because I saw and knew that they were a contemptible herd, or crowd of ignorant, sordid slaves, subjected to a government qualified only to rule such a people ; and, in a word, for I am now launched quite beside my design, I say, in a word, were not its distance inconceivably great from Muscovy, and was not the Muscovite empire almost as rude, impotent, and ill-governed a crowd of slaves as they, the Czar of Muscovy might, with much ease, drive them all out of their country, and conquer them in one campaign ; and had the Czar, who I since hear is a growing prince, and begins to appear formidable in the world, fallen this way, instead of attacking the warlike Swedes, in which attempt none of the powers of Europe would have ended or interrupted him ; he might by this time have been Emperor of China, instead of being beaten by the King of Sweden at Narva, when the latter was not one to six in number.—DEFOE.

UNPRESCRIBED PASSAGE.

2. Translate into English :—

ὦ σοφώτατοι θεαταί, δεῦρο τὸν νοῦν πρόσχετε.
ἠδικημέναι γὰρ ὑμῖν μεμφόμεσθ' ἐναντίον·
πλεῖστα γὰρ θεῶν ἁπάντων ὠφελούσαις τὴν πόλιν,
δαιμόνων ἡμῖν μόναις οὐ θύετ' οὐδὲ σπένδετε·
αἵτινες τηροῦμεν ὑμᾶς. ἢν γὰρ ᾖ τις ἔξοδος
μηδενὶ ξὺν νῷ, τότ' ἢ βροντῶμεν ἢ ψεκάζομεν.
εἶτα τὸν θεοῖσιν ἐχθρὸν βυρσοδέψην Παφλαγόνα
ἡνίχ' ᾑρεῖσθε στρατηγόν, τὰς ὀφρῦς ξυνήγομεν,
κἀποιοῦμεν δεινά· βροντὴ δ' ἐρράγη δι' ἀστραπῆς·
ἡ σελήνη δ' ἐξέλειπε τὰς ὁδούς· ὁ δ' ἥλιος,
τὴν θρυαλλίδ' εἰς ἑαυτὸν εὐθέως ξυνελκύσας,
οὐ φανεῖν ἔφασκεν ὑμῖν, εἰ στρατηγήσει Κλέων.
ἀλλ' ὅμως, εἵλεσθε τοῦτον· φασὶ γὰρ δυσβουλίαν
τῇδε τῇ πόλει προσεῖναι· ταῦτα μέντοι τοὺς θεούς,
ἅττ' ἂν ὑμεῖς ἐξαμάρτητ', ἐπὶ τὸ βέλτιον τρέπειν.

ARISTOPHANES.

3. (*a*) Give a brief account of Xenophon's public career and historical works.

(*b*) Explain: σεισάχθεια, δοκιμασία, περιοικος, προβού-λευμα.

4. (*a*) Examine the formation of :—ἑώρων, κρεισσων, βλώσκω, ἅπαξ.

(*b*) What are the chief peculiarities of *either* the Aeolic dialect *or* the Ionic of Herodotus?

LATIN.

FIRST PAPER.

Examiner—PROFESSOR SANDFORD.

1. For Latin Composition and Grammar, see the paper set at the same time for Literary Scholarship of the Third Year.

2. Translate and annotate the following passages :—

(a) Igitur senatus consultum si erit factum, scribes ad me : sin minus, rem tamen conficies. Mihi enim attribui oportebit, item Bibulo. Sed non dubito, quin senatus consultum expeditum sit, in quo praesertim sit compendium populi. De Torquato, probe. De Masone et Ligure, quum venerint. De illo, quod Chaerippus : quoniam hic quoque πρόσνευσιν sustulisti ; o provincia ! etiamne hic mihi curandus est ? Curandus autem hactenus, ne quid ad senatum, consule, aut numera. Nam de ceteris—. Sed tamen commode, quod cum Scrofa. De Pomptinio, recte scribis. Est enim ita, ut, si ante Kalend. Iun. Brundisii futurus sit, minus urgendi fuerint M. Annius et Tullius. Quae de Sicinio audisti, ea mihi probantur : modo ne illa exceptio in aliquem incurrat bene de nobis meritum.—CICERO, *ad Att.* v. 4.

(b) Is igitur Gavius, quum Apameae me nuper vidisset Romam proficiscens, me ita appellavit : (Culleolum vix auderem :) unde, inquit, me iubes petere cibaria praefecti ? Respondi lenius, quam putabant oportuisse, qui aderant ; me non instituisse iis dare cibaria, quorum opera non essem usus. Abiit iratus. Huius nebulonis obiratione si Brutus moveri potest, licebit eum solis ames ; me aemulum non habebis. Sed illum eum futurum esse puto, qui esse debet. Tibi tamen caussam notam esse volui : et ad ipsum haec perscripsi diligentissime. Omnino (soli enim sumus) nullas umquam ad me litteras misit Brutus, ne proxime quidem de Appio, in quibus non inesset arrogans, ἀκοινώνητον aliquid. Tibi autem valde solet in ore esse,

Granius autem
non contemnere se et reges odisse superbos :

in quo tamen ille mihi risum magis, quam stomachum
movere solet.—Id., *ib.* vi 8.

(*c*) Venio ad Piraeea, in quo magis reprehendendus sum,
quod homo Romanus Piraeea scripserim, non Piraeeum
(sic enim omnes nostri locuti sunt), quam quod in addi-
derim. Non enim hoc ut oppido praeposui, sed ut loco : et
tamen Dionysius noster, qui est nobiscum, et Nicias Cous
non rebatur, oppidum esse Piraeea. Sed de re videro.
Nostrum quidem si est peccatum, in eo est, quod non ut
de oppido locutus sum, sed ut de loco, secutusque sum, non
dico Caecilium,

'. . . Mane ut ex portu in Piraeeum,'
(malus enim auctor Latinitatis est), sed Terentium, cuius
fabellae, propter elegantiam sermonis, putabantur a C.
Laelio scribi :
'Heri aliquot adolescentuli coimus in Piraeeum.'
Et idem :

'Mercator hoc addebat. . . .
. . . captam e Sunio.'
Quod si δήμους oppida volumus esse ; tam est oppidum
Sunium, quam Piraeeus. Sed, quoniam Grammaticus es,
si hoc mihi ζήτημα persolveris, magna me molestia
liberaris.—Id., *ib.* 7.

(*d*) Mox iter L. Lucullo quondam penetratum, apertis quae
vetustas obsaepserat, pergit. Et venientes Tiridatis Volo
gesisque de pace legatos haud aspernatus, adiungit iis cen
turiones cum mandatis non inmitibus : nec enim adhuc eo
ventum, ut certamine extremo opus esset. Multa Romanis
secunda, quaedam Parthis evenisse, documento adversus
superbiam. Proinde et Tiridati conducere intactum vasta-
tionibus regnum dono accipere, et Vologesen melius societate Romana quam damnis mutuis genti Parthorum
consulturum. Scire quantum intus discordiarum quamque
indomitas et praeferoces nationes regeret : contra impera·
tori suo immotam ubique pacem et unum id bellum esse.
Simul consilio terrorem adicere, et megistanas Armenios,
qui primi a nobis defecerant, pellit sedibus, castella eorum
excindit, plana edita, validos invalidosque pari metu
complet.—Tacitus, *Ann.*, xv. 17.

(*e*) Trucidatis tot insignibus viris, ad postremum Nero virtutem ipsam excindere concupivit interfecto Thrasea Paeto et Barea Sorano, olim utrisque infensus, et accedentibus causis in Thraseam, quod senatu egressus est, cum de Agrippina referretur, ut memoravi, quodque iuvenalium ludicro parum spectabilem operam praebuerat ; eaque offensio altius penetrabat, quia idem Thrasea Patavi, unde ortus erat, ludis cetastis a Troiano Antenore institutis habitu tragico cecinerat. Die quoque, quo praetor Antistius ob probra in Neronem composita ad mortem damnabatur, mitiora censuit obtinuitque ; et cum deum honores Poppaeae decernuntur, sponte absens, funeri non interfuerat. Quae obliterari non sinebat Capito Cossutianus, praeter animum ad flagitia praecipitem iniquus Thraseae, quod auctoritate eius concidisset, iuvantis Cilicum legatos, dum Capitonem repetundarum interrogant.—Id., *Ib.*, xvi. 21.

LATIN.

Second Paper.

Examiner—Professor Sandford.

1. Translate and annotate the following passages :—

(*a*) Tum, quorum attonitae Baccho nemora avia matres
Insultant thiasis, neque enim leve nomen Amatae,
Undique collecti coëunt, Martemque fatigant.
Ilicet infandum cuncti contra omina bellum,
Contra fata deum, perverso numine poscunt :
Certatim regis circumstant tecta Latini.
Ille, velut pelagi rupes immota, resistit ;
[Ut pelagi rupes, magno veniente fragore,]
Quae sese, multis circum latrantibus undis,
Mole tenet ; scopuli nequidquam et spumea circum
Saxa fremunt, laterique illisa refunditur alga.
Verum ubi nulla datur caecum exsuperare potestas
Consilium, et saevae nutu Junonis eunt res ;

Multa deos aurasque pater testatus inanes,
' Frangimur heu fatis,' inquit, ferimurque procella !
Ipsi has sacrilego pendetis sanguine poenas,
O miseri.   Te, Turne, nefas, te triste manebit
Supplicium ; votisque deos venerabere seris :
Nam mihi parta quies, omnisque in limine portus ;
Funere felici spolior.'   Nec plura locutus
Sepsit se tectis, rerumque reliquit habenas.

VIRGIL, *Aen.* vii.

(*b*)   At procul in sola secretae Troades acta
Amissum Anchisen flebant, cunctaeque profundum
Pontum aspectabant flentes : ' Heu, tot vada fessis,
Et tantum superesse maris ! ' vox omnibus una.
Urbem orant ; taedet pelagi perferre laborem.
Ergo inter medias sese haud ignara nocendi
Conjicit, et faciemque deae vestemque reponit :
Fit Beroë, Tmarii conjux longaeva Dorycli,
Cui genus et quondam nomen natique fuissent ;
Ac sic Dardanidum mediam se matribus infert :
O miserae, quas non manus, inquit, ' Achaïca bello
Traxerit ad letum patriae sub moenibus ! o gens
Infelix ! cui te exitio fortuna reservat ?
Septima post Trojae excidium jam vertitur aestas,
Quum freta, quum terras omnes, tot inhospita saxa
Sideraque emensae ferimur ; dum per mare magnum
Italiam sequimur fugientem, et volvimur undis.

ID., *ib.* v.

(c)   Omne quod est igitur nulla regione viarum
Finitumpst : namque extremum debebat habere :
Extremum porro nullius posse videtur
Esse, nisi ultra sit quod finiat ; ut videatur
Quo non longius haec sensus natura sequatur.
Nunc extra summam quoniam nil esse fatendum,
Non habet extremum, caret ergo fine modoque.
Nec refert quibus adsistas regionibus eius :
Usque adeo, quem quisque locum possedit, in omnis
Tantundem partis infinitum omne relinquit.
Praeterea si iam finitum constituatur
Omne quod est spatium, siquis procurrat ad oras
Ultimus extremas iaciatque volatile telum,

Id validis utrum contortum viribus ire
Quo fuerit missum mavis longeque volare,
An prohibere aliquid censes obstareque posse ?
Alterutrum fatearis enim sumasque necessest.
Quorum utrumque tibi effugium praecludit et omne
Cogit ut exempta concedas fine patere.
Nam sive est aliquid quod probeat efficiatque
Quo minu' quo missum est veniat finique locet se,
Sive foras fertur, non est a fine profectum.
Hoc pacto sequar atque, oras ubicumque locaris
Extremas, quaeram quid telo denique fiat.
Fiet uti nusquam possit consistere finis,
Effugiumque fugae prolatet copia semper.

LUCRETIUS, Bk. i.

(*d*) Ecquid agis ? Siccas insana canicula messes
Iamdudum coquit, et patula pecus omne sub ulmo est :
Unus ait comitum.—Verumne ? itane ? Ocius adsit
Huc aliquis !—Nemon ?—Turgescit vitrea bilis :
Finditur : Arcadiae pecuria rudere dicas.—
    Iam liber et bicolor positis membrana capillis,
Inque manus chartae nodosaque venit arundo.
Tunc queritur, crassus calamo quod pendeat humor,
Nigra quod infusa vanescat sepia lympha ;
Dilutas queritur geminet quod fistula guttas.—
O miser inque dies ultra miser ! Huccine rerum
Venimus ? At cur non potius, teneroque palumbo
Et similis regum pueris, pappare minutum
Poscis, et iratus mammae lallare recusas ?—
An tali studeam calamo ?—Cui verba ? Quid istas
Succinis ambages ? Tibi luditur : effluis amens.
Contemnere : sonat vitium, percussa maligne
Respondet viridi non cocta fidelia limo.
Udum et molle lutum es, nunc nunc properandus et acri
Fingendus sine fine rota.

PERSIUS, *Sat.* iii.

DA. Aliquando osculando meliust, uxor, pausam fieri ;
Atque adorna, ut rem divinam faciam, quom intro advenero,
Laribus familiaribus, quom auxerunt nostram familiam.
Sunt domi agni et porci sacres. Sed quid istum remo-
    ramini,
Mulieres, Trachalionem ? Atque optume, eccum, exit foras.

Tr. Ubiubi erit, iam investigabo, et mecum ad te adducam
  simul
Pleusidippum. Da. Eloquere, ut haec res obtigit de filia.
Eum rogato, ut linquat alias res et huc veniat. Tr. Licet.
Da. Dicito, daturum meam illi filiam uxorem... Tr. Licet.
Da. Et patrem eius me novisse, et mi esse cognatum.
  Tr. Licet.
Da. Sed propera. Tr. Licet. Da. Iam hic fac sit, coena,
  ut curetur. Tr. Licet.
Da. Omnian' licet? Tr. Licet. Sed scin', quid est, quod
  te volo?
Quod promisisti, ut memineris, hodie ut liber sim. Da. Licet.
Tr. Fac, ut exores Pleusidippum, ut me emittat manu...
  Da. Licet.
Tr. Et tua filia facito oret; facile exorabit; Da. Licet.
Tr. Atque ut mi Ampelisca nubat, ubi ego sim liber...
  Da. Licet.
Tr. Atque ut gratum mihi beneficium factis experiar.
  Da. Licet.
Tr. Omnian' licet? Da. Licet : tibi rursum refero gratiam.
Sed propera ire in urbem actutum, et recipe te huc rursum.
  Tr. Licet.
Iam hic ero : tu interibi adorna ceterum, quod opus est.
  Da. Licet.
Hercules istum infelicet cum sua licentia :
Ita meas replevit auris. Quidquid memorabam, licet.

Plautus, Rudens.

2.—(*a*) Give an account of the lives and works of the
two Senecas.

(*b*) What is meant by *Satira Menippea*? ˙ What examples
of it are still extant?

(*c*) Summarise Sellar's appreciation of Ennius.

(*d*) Write etymological notes on—luna, filius, soror.

(*e*) Give five instances of the influence of " *analogy* " in
Latin.

SENIOR SCHOLARSHIP IN ENGLISH AND MODERN LANGUAGES.

ENGLISH.

FIRST PAPER.

Examiner—PROFESSOR TRENCH.

1. Write notes on—sowninge ; y-chaped ; hindreste ; algate ; catel ; yeldhalle ; it thoughte me ; han.

2. Estimate the dramatic value of the changes which Shakespeare made in the story of Lear.

3. Describe the scene in *Richard III.* where Richard ascends the throne.

4. Summarize the contents of Wordsworth's preface to *The Excursion.*

5. Consider Byron's capacity for description.

ENGLISH.

SECOND PAPER.

Examiner—PROFESSOR TRENCH.

1. Consider Coleridge's critical method and principles, comparing them with those of other critics.

2. Write an Essay on English lyrical poetry 1800–1850.

FRENCH.

Examiner—PROFESSOR CADIC.

I. ESSAI.

Le candidat traitera le sujet suivant :—

Ronsard et son école.

II. Faire l'historique des sons nasals et de l'*e* féminin.

III. Traduisez en français :—

He had, from the commencement of his reign, applied himself to public business after a fashion unknown among kings. Lewis the Fourteenth, indeed, had been his own

prime minister, and had exercised a general superintendence over all the departments of the government ; but
this was not sufficient for Frederic.   He was not content
with being his own prime minister ; he would be his own
sole minister.   Under him there was no room, not merely
for a Richelieu or a Mazarin, but for a Colbert, a Louvois,
or a Torcy.   A love of labour for its own sake, a restless
and insatiable longing to dictate, to intermeddle, to make
his power felt, a profound scorn and distrust of his fellow-
creatures, made him unwilling to ask counsel, to confide
important secrets, to delegate ample powers.

GERMAN.

Examiner—Professor Cadic.

I. Auffaß.

Der Kandidat wird den folgenden Gegenstand behandeln :
Freytag und seine Werke.

II. Erklären und erläutern Sie Verners Geset und den
grammatischen Wechsel.

III. Übersetzen Sie ins Deutsche :—

Meanwhile the Parliament met.   The ministers, more
hated by the people than ever, were secure of a majority,
and they had also reason to hope that they would have the
advantage in the debates as well as in the divisions ; for
Pitt was confined to his chamber by a severe attack of gout.
His friends moved to defer the consideration of the treaty
till he should be able to attend ; but the motion was rejected.
The great day arrived.   The discussion had lasted some time,
when a loud huzza was heard in Palace Yard.   The noise
same nearer and nearer, up the stairs, through the lobby,
the door opened, and from the midst of a shouting multitude.
came forth Pitt, born in the arms of his attendants.   His
face was thin and ghastly, his limbs swathed in flannel, his
crutch in his hand.

SENIOR SCHOLARSHIP IN MATHEMATICS.

Examiner—PROFESSOR BROMWICH.

1. Find the result of replacing x by

(i) $(ay + b)/(cy + d)$,

(ii) $(-dy + b)/(cy - a)$

in the expression

$$x + \frac{ax+b}{cx+d} + \frac{-dx+b}{cx-a}.$$

Examine the special form of the result, in case we have

$$a^2 + ad + d^2 + bc = 0.$$

2. From the result of question 1 deduce (or otherwise prove) that if one root of the cubic

$$c^2x^3 + 3bcx + b(d-a) = 0$$

is a, then the other two roots are

$$(aa + b)/(ca + d), \quad \text{and} \quad (-da + b)/(ca - a),$$

provided that

$$a^2 + ad + d^2 + bc = 0.$$

3. If $x = a + h\phi(x)$ is an equation for x, such that $\phi'(a)$ is not infinite, and if $f(x)$ can be expanded in a series

$$f(a) + A_1 h + \ldots + A_n h^n + \ldots,$$

prove that nA_n is the coefficient of $1/(x - a)$ in the expansion of

$$f'(x)\left[\phi(x)/(x - a)\right]^n$$

in powers of $(x - a)$.

Taking the case $x = 1 + h(1 - 1/kx)$,

show that $\log x = A_1 h + \ldots + A_n h^n + \ldots,$

where

$$A_n = (-1)^{n-1}\frac{1}{n}\left[1 - \frac{n^2}{1^2.k} + \frac{n^2(n^2-1^2)}{1^2.2^2.k^2}\right.$$
$$\left. - \frac{n^2(n^2-1^2)(n^2-2^2)}{1^2.2^2.3^2.k^3} + \ldots\right].$$

4. Trace the curve
$$x^m + y + xy^m = 0$$
for the values $m = 3$, $m = 4$.

5. A parabola is drawn to osculate the circle $x^2 + y^2 = 1$ at the point $(\cos a, \sin a)$, and with its axis parallel to Ox; show that its vertex is given by
$$x = \tfrac{1}{2}(3 \cos a - \cos^3 a), \quad y = \sin^3 a,$$
and that its latus rectum is $2 \cos^3 a$.

6. If $y^2 = x^2 - 2px + 1$, where p is a positive proper fraction, prove that
$$\int_0^1 \frac{x^2}{y^3}\, dx + \int_1^\infty \left(\frac{x^2}{y^3} - \frac{1}{x}\right) dx = \frac{2p-1}{1-p} + \log \frac{2}{1-p}.$$

7. If $c \sin \theta = \sin(2\phi - \theta)$, prove that
$$\int_0^\theta \frac{d\theta}{(1 - c^2 \sin^2 \theta)^{\frac{3}{2}}} = \int_0^\phi \frac{2\,d\phi}{\left[(1+c)^2 - 4c^2 \sin^2 \phi\right]^{\frac{3}{2}}}.$$

8. The length of the curve
$$y = \tfrac{1}{8}(x^4 + 6x^2),$$
measured from the origin, is $\tfrac{1}{6}x(x^2 + 4)^{\frac{3}{2}}$.

9. If x, y are connected by the equation
$$x^2 - 2cxy + y^2 = 1 - c^2,$$
then
$$\left(\frac{dy}{dx}\right)^2 = \frac{y^2 - 1}{x^2 - 1}.$$

10. Find the length of and the equations to the perpendicular from the point (a, b, c) on the line (for which $lp + mq + nr = 0$)
$$ny - mz = p, \quad lz - nx = q, \quad mx - ly = r,$$
the coordinates being rectangular Cartesians in space.

SENIOR SCHOLARSHIP—METAPHYSICS, POLITICAL SCIENCE, AND HISTORY.

METAPHYSICS.

Examiner—PROFESSOR TRENCH.

1. Distinguish the terms *Philosophy*, *Metaphysics*, *Psychology*.

2. Write some account of *Idealism*.

8. Consider any three of the following :—

 (a) ' The true *thing in itself*, the *being*, as distinguished from the phenomenon, is not the object of such as we conceive it, but the object out of all relation to our faculties; and as such it is manifestly unknowable.'

 (b) ' It is only through *Touch* that we have any direct perception of an external world.'

 (c) ' The note of *Sense* is *receptivity*, that of *Intellect* is *spontaneity*.'

 (d) ' If a man who is asleep believes he is awake, a man who is awake has no way of conclusively deciding that he is not asleep.'

POLITICAL SCIENCE.

Examiner—PROFESSOR BASTABLE.

[*Not more than* SIX *questions to be answered.*]

1. Consider the influence of the theory of natural law on the development of (a) jurisprudence, (b) economics.

2. What subjects are, properly speaking, included under the title ' Political Science ' ?
Illustrate your answer by reference to the authors that you have studied.

3. Show clearly the services rendered to society by a monetary system. Give a short account of the development of money.

4. Give a full analysis of the term 'right.'
Notice the chief (*a*) jural, (*b*) political difficulties encountered in this process.

5. 'The movement of progressive societies has hitherto been from status to contract.'
Examine this proposition critically.

6. How is the rate of interest determined under the conditions of free competition?
Apply your answer to the question of the expediency of usury laws.

7. What is a 'village community'?
Notice the chief points in dispute respecting the nature and historical position of this institution.

8. Consider the changes in the relative importance of land and capital at different historical periods.

9. Give a short historical sketch of the agencies by which Roman law was developed.

10. Discuss the advantages and disadvantages of a flexible,' as contrasted with a 'rigid,' constitution.

11. What are the chief causes that affect the foreign exchanges?
How do exchange movements influence domestic trade?

12. Compare 'direct' with 'indirect' taxation, giving illustrations of the working of each form.

HISTORY.

Examiner—PROFESSOR TRENCH.

1. Relate the career and show the influence of Frederick the Great.

2. Consider the rise, and explain the causes of the downfall, of royal authority in France.

3. Narrate the career and discuss the policy of R. Walpole.

4. Sketch the course of events in Ireland from 1780 to 1800.

SENIOR SCHOLARSHIP—CHEMISTRY.

CHEMISTRY.

FIRST DAY'S EXAMINATION.

Examiner—PROFESSOR SENIER.

[*Formulæ, equations, and diagrams are to be used whenever possible.*]

1. Explain (*a*) the meaning of the terms 'molecule' and 'atom'; (*b*) the evidence leading to the molecular and atomic hypotheses; (*c*) the importance of these hypotheses in the development of chemistry.

2. Give an account of the researches of Pasteur on the tartaric acids, and the 'stereo' explanation subsequently suggested by Van't Hoff and others.

3. If a solution of hydrogen peroxide containing one gram of that compound is treated with an excess of chromic acid, what volume of oxygen would be liberated measured at 17° and 754 mm. ?

4. (*a*) What is the action of potassium hydroxide on chloroform and on carbon tetrachloride, respectively? (*b*) Of what use are these reactions in the solution of synthetical problems ?

5. (*a*) Explain the action of phenylhydrazine on aldehydes and ketones; and (*b*) show the importance of these reactions in the study of aldehydic and ketonic hexol derivatives.

6. Explain (*a*) the interaction of aceto-acetic ester, and its mono- and di-alkyl derivatives, with alkalies, and (*b*) the application of these reactions to ketone and acid syntheses.

SECOND AND THIRD DAYS' EXAMINATION.

Examiner—PROFESSOR SENIER.

1. Make a complete qualitative examination of the powders marked respectively (*a*) and (*b*).

[(*a*) Hydroxycarbonate of lead mixed with sodium iodide; (*b*) ferrous phosphate.]

2. Determine the proportion of the acidic radicle in the crystals given you. [Potassium dichromate.]

BLAYNEY EXHIBITION—CLASSICS.

GREEK.

FIRST PAPER.

Examiner—PROFESSOR MCELDERRY.

For Greek Prose :—

Of course a man is not bound to be a politician any more than he is bound to be a soldier ; and there are perfectly honourable ways of quitting both politics and the military profession. But neither in the one way of life nor the other, is a man entitled to take all the sweet and leave all the sour. A man who belongs to the army only in time of peace, who appears at reviews in Hyde Park, escorts the sovereign with the utmost valour and fidelity to and from the House of Lords, and retires as soon as he thinks it likely that he may be ordered on an expedition, is justly thought to have disgraced himself. Some portion of the censure due to such a holiday-soldier may justly fall on the mere holiday-politician, who flinches from his duties as soon as those duties become difficult and disagreeable, that is to say, as soon as it becomes peculiarly important that he should resolutely perform them.

GREEK.

Examiner—PROFESSOR MCELDERRY.

SECOND PAPER.

A. UNPRESCRIBED PASSAGES.

1. Translate into English :—

(*a*) νὺξ μὲν ἔπειτ᾽ ἐπὶ γαῖαν ἄγεν κνέφας· οἱ δ᾽ ἐνὶ πόντῳ
ναῦται εἰς Ἑλίκην τε καὶ ἀστέρας Ὠρίωνος
ἔδρακον ἐκ νηῶν· ὕπνοιο δὲ καί τις ὁδίτης
ἤδη καὶ πυλαωρὸς ἐέλδετο· καί τινα παίδων
μητέρα τεθνεώτων ἀδινὸν περὶ κῶμ᾽ ἐκάλυπτεν·
οὐ δὲ κυνῶν ὑλακὴ ἔτ᾽ ἀνὰ πτόλιν, οὐ θρόος ἦεν
ἠχήεις· σιγὴ δὲ μελαινομένην ἔχεν ὄρφνην.
ἀλλὰ μάλ᾽ οὐ Μήδειαν ἐπὶ γλυκεροῦ λάβεν ὕπνος.
πολλὰ γὰρ Αἰσονίδαο πόθῳ μελεδήματ᾽ ἔγειρεν

s 2

δειδυῖαν ταύρων κρατερὸν μένος, οἷσιν ἔμελλεν
φθίσθαι ἀεικελίῃ μοίρῃ κατὰ νειὸν Ἄρηος.
πυκνὰ δέ οἱ κραδίη στηθέων ἔντοσθεν ἔθυιεν,
ἠελίου ὡς τίς τε δόμοις ἐνιπάλλεται αἴγλη
ὕδατος ἐξανιοῦσα, τὸ δὴ νέον ἠὲ λέβητι,
ἠέ που ἐν γαυλῷ κέχυται· ἡ δ' ἔνθα καὶ ἔνθα
ὠκείῃ στροφάλιγγι τινάσσεται ἀίσσουσα·
ὣς δὲ καὶ ἐν στήθεσσι κέαρ ἐλελίζετο κούρης.

APOLLONIUS RHODIUS.

(*b*) οἱ δ' Ἀθηναῖοι γνόντες καθ' ἑκάτερον τὸν ἔσπλουν ὥρμη-
σαν ἐπ' αὐτούς, καὶ τὰς μὲν πλείους καὶ μετεώρους ἤδη τῶν νεῶν
καὶ ἀντιπρρους προῴσπεσόντες ἐς φυγὴν κατέστησαν, καὶ ἐπι-
διώκοντες ὡς διὰ βραχέος ἔτρωσαν μὲν πολλάς, πέντε δ' ἔλαβον,
καὶ μίαν τούτων αὐτοῖς ἀνδράσι· ταῖς δὲ λοιπαῖς ἐν τῇ γῇ κατα-
πεφευγυίαις ἐνέβαλλον. αἱ δὲ καὶ πληρούμεναι ἔτι, πρὶν ἀνά-
γεσθαι, ἐκόπτοντο· καί τινας καὶ ἀναδούμενοι κενὰς εἷλκον, τῶν
ἀνδρῶν ἐς φυγὴν ὡρμημένων. ἃ ὁρῶντες οἱ Λακεδαιμόνιοι, καὶ
περιαλγοῦντες τῷ πάθει, ὅτι περ αὐτῶν οἱ ἄνδρες ἀπελαμβάνοντο
ἐν τῇ νήσῳ, παρεβοήθουν, καὶ ἐπεσβαίνοντες ἐς τὴν θάλασσαν
ξὺν τοῖς ὅπλοις ἀνθεῖλκον ἐπιλαμβανόμενοι τῶν νεῶν, καὶ ἐν
τούτῳ κεκωλῦσθαι ἐδόκει ἕκαστος, ᾧ μή τινι καὶ αὐτὸς ἔργῳ
παρῆν. ἐγένετό τε θόρυβος μέγας καὶ ἀντηλλαγμένος τοῦ
ἑκατέρων τρόπου περὶ τὰς ναῦς· οἵ τε γὰρ Λακεδαιμόνιοι ὑπὸ
προθυμίας καὶ ἐκπλήξεως, ὡς εἰπεῖν, ἄλλο οὐδὲν ἢ ἐκ γῆς
ἐναυμάχουν, οἵ τε Ἀθηναῖοι κρατοῦντες, καὶ βουλόμενοι τῇ
παρούσῃ τύχῃ ὡς ἐπὶ πλεῖστον ἐπεξελθεῖν, ἀπὸ νεῶν ἐπεζομά-
χουν.—THUCYDIDES.

B. PRESCRIBED AUTHORS.

2. Translate into English :—

(*a*) ἁρμονίᾳ μὲν καὶ ῥυθμῷ χρώμεναι μόνον ἥ τε αὐλτικὴ καὶ
ἡ κιθαριστικὴ, κἂν εἴ τινες ἕτεραι τυγχάνουσιν οὖσαι τοιαῦται
τὴν δύναμιν, οἷον ἡ τῶν συρίγγων. Αὐτῷ δὲ τῷ ῥυθμῷ μιμεῖται
χωρὶς ἁρμονίας ἡ τῶν ὀρχηστῶν, καὶ γὰρ οὗτοι διὰ τῶν σχηματι-
ζομένων ῥυθμῶν μιμοῦνται καὶ ἤθη καὶ πάθη καὶ πράξεις. Ἡ δὲ
[ἐποποιΐα] μόνον τοῖς λόγοις ψιλοῖς ἢ τοῖς μέτροις· καὶ τούτοις

εἴτε μιγνῦσα μετ' ἀλλήλων, εἴθ' ἑνί τινιγένει χρωμένη τῶν μέτρων, <ἀνώνυμος> τυγχάνουσα μέχρι τοῦ νῦν. οὐδὲν γὰρ ἂν ἔχοιμεν ὀνομάσαι κοινὸν τοὺς Σώφρονος καὶ Ξενάρχου μίμους, καὶ τοὺς Σωκρατικοὺς λόγους· οὐδὲ εἴ τις διὰ τριμέτρων ἢ ἐλεγείων ἢ τῶν ἄλλων τινῶν τοιούτων ποιοῖτο τὴν μίμησιν.—ARISTOTLE, *De Poetica.*

Justify the omission of ἐποποιία, and the insertion of ἀνώνυμος ; and write a note on Sophron.

(*b*) δεῖ μὲν οὖν ἐν ταῖς τραγῳδίαις ποιεῖν τὸ θαυμαστόν· μᾶλλον δ' ἐνδέχεται ἐν τῇ ἐποποιίᾳ τὸ ἄλογον, (δι' ὃ συμβαίνει μάλιστα τὸ θαυμαστόν,) διὰ τὸ μὴ ὁρᾶν εἰς τὸν πράττοντα. ἐπεὶ τὰ περὶ τὴν Ἕκτορος δίωξιν ἐπὶ σκηνῆς ὄντα, γελοῖα ἂν φανείη· οἱ μὲν ἑστῶτες καὶ οὐ διώκοντες, ὁ δὲ ἀνανεύων. ἐν δὲ τοῖς ἔπεσι λανθάνει. τὸ δὲ θαυμαστὸν ἡδύ. σημεῖον δέ· πάντες γὰρ προστιθέντες ἀπαγγέλλουσιν, ὡς χαριζόμενοι. δεδίδαχε δὲ μάλιστα Ὅμηρος καὶ τοὺς ἄλλους ψευδῆ λέγειν ὡς δεῖ. ἔστι δὲ τοῦτο παραλογισμός. οἴονται γὰρ ἄνθρωποι, ὅταν τουδὶ ὄντος τοδὶ ᾖ, ἢ γινομένου γίνηται, εἰ τὸ ὕστερόν ἐστι, καὶ τὸ πρότερον εἶναι ἢ γίνεσθαι. τοῦτο δέ ἐστι ψεῦδος. δι' ὃ εἴη ἂν τὸ πρῶτον ψεῦδος. ἀλλ' οὐδὲ τούτου ὄντος, ἀνάγκη εἶναι ἢ γενέσθαι ἢ προσθεῖναι. διὰ γὰρ τὸ τοῦτο εἰδέναι ἀληθὲς ὄν, παραλογίζεται ἡμῶν ἡ ψυχὴ καὶ τὸ πρῶτον ὡς ὄν. παράδειγμα δὲ τούτου ἐκ τῶν Νίπτρων.—*Ibid.*

You may adopt and defend any variants you prefer. How does Aristotle classify metaphor ? Give an example of each kind.

3. In the *Acharnians*, translate with notes where needful :—

(*a*)　ἐμέλλετ' ἄρ' ἅπαντες ἀνασείειν βοήν,
ὀλίγου τ' ἀπέθανον ἄνθρακες Παρνήσιοι,
καὶ ταῦτα διὰ τὴν ἀτοπίαν τῶν δημοτῶν.
ὑπὸ τοῦ δέους δὲ τῆς μαρίλης μοι συχνὴν
ὁ λάρκος ἐνετίλησεν ὥσπερ σηπία.
δεινὸν γὰρ οὕτως ὀμφακίαν πεφυκέναι
τὸν θυμὸν ἀνδρῶν, ὥστε βάλλειν καὶ βοᾶν,
ἐθέλειν τ' ἀκοῦσαι μηδὲν ἴσον ἴσῳ φέρον.

(b)   οἱ γέροντες οἱ παλαιοί μεμφόμεσθα τῇ πόλει·
οὐ γὰρ ἀξίως ἐκείνων ὧν ἐναυμαχήσαμεν
γηροβοσκούμεσθ᾽ ὑφ᾽ ὑμῶν, ἀλλὰ δεινὰ πάσχομεν,
οἵτινες γέροντας ἄνδρας ἐμβαλόντες ἐς γραφάς,
ὑπὸ νεανίσκων ἐᾶτε καταγελᾶσθαι ῥητόρων,
οὐδὲν ὄντας, ἀλλὰ κωφούς, καὶ παρεξηυλημένους,
οἷς Ποσειδῶν ἀσφάλειός ἐστιν ἡ βακτηρία·
τονθορύζοντες δὲ γήρᾳ τῷ λίθῳ προσέσταμεν,
οὐχ ὁρῶντες οὐδέν, εἰ μὴ τῆς δίκης τὴν ἠλύγην.

4. In the *Wasps*, translate with short notes if required :—

ξυλλεγέντες γὰρ καθ᾽ ἑσμούς, ὡσπερεὶ τἀνθρήνια,
οἱ μὲν ἡμῶν οὗπερ ἄρχων, οἱ δὲ παρὰ τοὺς Ἕνδεκα,
οἱ δ᾽ ἐν Ὠιδείῳ δικάζουσ᾽, οἱ δὲ πρὸς τοῖς τειχίοις
ξυμβεβυσμένοι πυκνόν, νεύοντες εἰς τὴν γῆν, μόλις,
ὥσπερ οἱ σκώληκες, ἐν τοῖς κυττάροις κινούμενοι.
ἔς τε τὴν ἄλλην δίαιταν ἐσμὲν εὐπορώτατοι.
πάντα γὰρ κεντοῦμεν ἄνδρα, κἀκπορίζομεν βίον.
ἀλλὰ γὰρ κηφῆνες ἡμῖν εἰσὶν ἐγκαθήμενοι,
οὐκ ἔχοντες κέντρον· οἳ μένοντες ἡμῶν τοῦ φόρου
τὸν γόνον κατεσθίουσιν, οὐ ταλαιπωρούμενοι.
τοῦτο δ᾽ ἔστ᾽ ἄλγιστον ἡμῖν, ἤν τις ἀστράτευτος ὢν
ἐκφορῇ τὸν μισθὸν ἡμῶν, τῆσδε τῆς χώρας ὑπερ
μήτε κώπην, μήτε λόγχην, μήτε φλύκταιναν λαβών.
ἀλλ᾽ ἐμοὶ δοκεῖ τὸ λοιπὸν τῶν πολιτῶν ἔμβραχυ
ὅστις ἂν μὴ ᾽χῃ τὸ κέντρον, μὴ φέρειν τριώβολον.

C. Grammar and Philology.

5. Summarize what is known about the digamma.

6. Analyse the following words, with illustrations from cognate or parallel formations :—ἀμνός, ἁπλοῦς, ἐλαχύς, λεύσσω, Μουσῶν.

7. Translate and annotate :—

(a)   ἀλλὰ Θερσίτης τις ἦν
ὃς οὐκ ἂν εἵλετ᾽ εἰσάπαξ εἰπεῖν, ὅπου
μηδεὶς ἐῴη.—Sophocles.

(b)   οὐκ ἔσθ᾽ ὅπως λέξαιμι τὰ ψευδῆ καλά.—Aeschylus.

8. Emend or defend :—

(*a*) τοῖον γάρ οἱ πομπὸν ὀπάσσομεν Ἀργειφόντην
ὃς ἄξει εἶως κεν ἄγων Ἀχιλῆι πελάσσῃ.—HOMER.

(*b*) κἀμοὶ ἔδοξεν οὕτω θεῖα καὶ χρυσᾶ εἶναι, ὥστε
ποιητέον εἶναι ἐν βραχεῖ ὅ τι κελεύοι Σωκράτης.—PLATO.

LATIN.

Examiner—PROFESSOR SANDFORD.

1. Translate the following unprescribed passages :—

I.

Hui, ' Totiensne me litteras dedisse Romam, cum ad te nullas darem '? At vero posthac frustra potius dabo, quam si recte dari potuerint, committam ut non dem. Ne provincia nobis prorogetur, per fortunas ! dum ades, quicquid provideri potest, provide : non dici potest quam flagrem desiderio urbis, quam vix harum rerum insulsitatem feram.

Pompeius mihi quoque videbatur, quod scribis Varronem dicere, in Hispaniam certe iturus : id ego minime probabam, qui quidem Theophani facile persuasi nihil esse melius quam illum nusquam discedere. Ergo Graecus incumbet ; valet autem auctoritas eius apud illum plurimum. Ego has pr. Nonas Quinctiles proficiscens Athenis dedi, cum ibi decem ipsos fuissem dies.—CICERO, *Ad Att.* v. xi.

II.

Nunc quae mobilitas sit reddita materiai
Corporibus, paucis licet hinc cognoscere Memmi,
Primum aurora novo cum spargit lumine terras,
Et variae volucres nemora avia pervolitantes
Aera per tenerum liquidis loca vocibus opplent,
Quam subito soleat sol ortus tempore tali
Convestire sua perfundens omnia luce,
Omnibus in promptu manifestumque esse videmus.
At vapor is quem sol mittit lumenque serenum
Non per inane meat vacuum ; quo tardius ire
Cogitur, aerias quasi dum diverberet undas.

LUCRETIUS II.

III.

Lε. Edepol virtutes qui tuas nunc possit collaudare,
Sicut ego possum quae domi duellique male fecisti ?
Ne illa edepol pro merito tuo memorari multa possunt ;
Ubi fidentem fraudaveris, ubi ero infidelis fueris,
Ubi verbis conceptis sciens lubenter periuraris,
Ubi parietes perfoderis, in furto ubi sis prehensus.
Lɪ. Fateor profecto ut praedicas, Leonida, esse vera :
Verum edepol ne etiam tua quoque malefacta iterari multa
Et vera possunt : ubi sciens fideli infidus fueris,
Ubi periuraris, ubi sacro manus sis admolitus,
Ubi eris damno molestiae dedecori saepe fueris.

PLAUTUS, *Asin.*

2. Translate, with short notes where necessary :—

I.

Ille gener, ille in adoptando P. Clodio augur, ille resti-
tuendi mei quam retinendi studiosior, ille provinciae
prorogator, ille absentis in omnibus adiutor, idem etiam
tertio consulatu, postquam esse defensor reipublicae coepit,
contendit ut decem tribuni pl. ferrent, ut absentis ratio
haberetur, quod idem ipse sanxit lege quadam sua, Marcoque
Marcello consuli finienti provincias Gallias Kal. Mart. die
restitit.—CICERO, *Ad Att.* VIII.

II.

Dionysius quum ad me praeter opinionem meam venisset,
locutus sum cum eo liberalissime, tempora exposui, rogavi
ut diceret quid haberet in animo, me nihil ab ipso invito
contendere. Respondit se, quod in nummis haberet, nescire
quo loci esset, alios non solvere, aliorum diem nondum esse.
Dixit etiam alia quaedam de servulis suis quare nobiscum
esse non posset. Morem gessi, dimisi a me, ut magistrum
Ciceronum non lubenter, ut hominem ingratnm non invitus.
—CICERO, *Ad Att.* VIII.

III.

Nam quodcunque erit, esse aliquid debebit id ipsum ;
Cui si tactus erit quamvis levis exiguusque,
Augnime vel grandi vel parvo denique, dum sit,
Corporis augebit numerum summamque sequetur :
Sin intactile erit, nulla de parte quod ullam
Rem prohibere queat per se transire meantem,

Scilicet hoc id erit vacuum quod inane vocamus
Praeterea per se quodcunque erit, aut faciet quid
Aut aliis fungi debebit agentibus ipsum,
Aut erit ut possent in eo res esse gerique :
At facere et fungi sine corpore nulla potest res,
Nec praebere locum porro nisi inane vacansque.
Ergo, praeter inane et corpora, tertia per se
Nulla potest rerum in numero natura relinqui.

LUCRETIUS I.

(*a*) How does Lucretius prove that the universe is infinite?

(*b*) ' Religio peperit scelerosa atque impia facta.'
What example does he give?

(*c*) How does he illustrate the importance of the *positura*
of the *primordia* ?

(*d*) What does he say of Heraclitus ?

(*e*) What is *homœomeria* ?

IV.

Ev. Anus hercle huic indicium fecit de auro : perspicue
palamst :
Quoi ego iam linguam praecidam atque oculos ecfodiam domi.
MEG. Quid tu solus tecum loquere ? Ev. Meam pauperiem
conqueror.
Virginem habeo grandem, doti cassam atque illocabilem :
Neque eam queo locare quoiquam. MEG. Tace, bonum
habe animum, Eudio
Dabitur : adiuvabere a me : dic si quid opust : impera.
Ev. Nunc petit quom pollicetur : inhiat aurum ut devoret.
Altera manu fert lapidem, panem ostentat altera.
Nemini credo qui large blandust dives pauperi
Ubi manum inicit benigne, ibi onerat aliquam zamiam.
Ego istos novi polypos qui ubi quidquid tetigerunt tenent.

PLAUT. *Aul.*

Explain :—Ex me ut unam faciam litteram. Factiosus.
Trium litterarum homo. Pipulo deferre. Abstinebit cen-
sione bubula nec sua opera rediget unquam in splendorem
compedes. Aufer cavillam. Luci claro. Ne istuc dixis.

Scan :—
Confige sagitis fúres thensaurários.
Nímis male timuí: priusquam intro rédii exanimatús fui
In paúciore ávidos altercátiost.

s 2

(a) What is meant by 'hidden quantities' ? Illustrate your answer by reference to the words—illex, nundinae, infringo, consul, mollis, corolla.

(b) Comment on the spellings—contio, auctor, formossus, delero, sepulchrum, comminus.

(c) On what did Syncope depend ? Give examples.

(d) How is it that while the second conj. is generally intransitive, there is a small body of verbs of this conjugation with transitive meaning, e.g. *moneo* ?

(e) What old usages are found in Vergil of the following :—ni, atque, enim, quianam ?

(f) Translate and comment on the points of interest in— Neve aurum addito, at cui auro dentes iuncti escunt, ast im cum illo sepeliet uretve se fraude esto.

For Latin Composition.

I.

I am not at all troubled about what you tell me, that my letter has got abroad : indeed I have myself given it to several people to take a copy of; for, after all that has happened, and all that is hanging over us, I cannot but wish that it should be left on record what my views are about the terms of peace. Now in using arguments towards this end, above all when addressed to such a man as he is, I saw no more likely way of impressing him than by saying that my object in writing would commend itself to his 'wisdom.' If I have called that 'admirable,' inasmuch as my object was to urge him to do what is essential for the safety of our country, I had no dread of the appearance of flattering a man at whose feet in such a cause I would willingly have flung myself.—(*From Cicero.*)

II.

Dear Mr. Gray,

I write to make you write, for I have not much to tell you. I have recovered no spirits as yet; but as I am not displeased with my company, I sit purring by the fireside in my armchair with no small satisfaction. I read, too, sometimes : and have begun Tacitus, but have not yet read enough to judge of him; only his Pannonian mutiny in the first book of his Annals, which is just as far as I have got, seemed to me a little tedious. I have no more to say, but to desire you will write letters of a handsome length and always answer me within a reasonable space of time, which I leave to your discretion.

Yours very sincerely,

J. WEST.

POPE'S, *March* 28.

THE 'DR. AND MRS. W. A. BROWNE' SCHOLARSHIP.

GERMAN.

Examiner—PROFESSOR STEINBERGER.

1. Translate into German:—

It is somewhat curious that the admirers of Strafford should also be, without a single exception, the admirers of Charles; for, whatever we may think of the conduct of the Parliament towards the unhappy favourite, there can be no doubt that the treatment which he received from his master was disgraceful. Faithless alike to his people and to his tools, the King did not scruple to play the part of the cowardly approver, who hangs his accomplice. It is good that there should be such men as Charles in every league of villany. It is for such men that the offer of pardon and reward which appears after a murder is intended. They are indemnified, remunerated, and despised. The very magistrate who avails himself of their assistance looks on them as more contemptible than the criminal whom they betray. Was Strafford innocent? If so, what shall we think of the Prince, who having solemnly promised him that not a hair of his head should be hurt, and possessing an unquestioned constitutional right to save him, gave him

up to the vengeance of his enemies? There were some
points which we know that Charles would not concede, and
for which he was willing to risk the chances of civil war.
Ought not a King, who will make a stand for any thing,
to make a stand for the innocent blood? Was Strafford
guilty? Even on this supposition, it is difficult not to feel
disdain for the partner of his guilt, the tempter turned
punisher. If, indeed, from that time forth, the conduct of
Charles had been blameless, it might have been said that
his eyes were at last opened to the errors of his former
conduct, and that he gave a painful and deeply humiliating
proof of the sincerity of his repentance.

2. Translate into English:—

(*a*) Elisabeth gehörte zu den Fürsten, die sich im voraus über
die Pflichten der Regierung einen Begriff gebildet haben. Vier
Eigenschaften, sagte sie einmal, seien ihr dazu nothwendig erschie-
nen: Gerechtigkeit und Mäßigung, Großmuth und Urtheil. Der
beiden ersten dürfe sie sich rühmen: nie habe sie bei gleichem Recht
Einen vor dem Andern begünstigt, nie habe sie einem ersten Bericht
geglaubt, sondern bis zur vollen Kenntniß an sich behalten. Die
beiden andern wolle sie sich nicht anmaßen, denn es seien Tugenden
der Männer. Eben diese aber schrieb die Welt ihr in hohem Grade
zu. Ihr feines Urtheil erblickte man in der Wahl ihrer Diener
und der Verwendung derselben zu solchen Diensten, zu denen sie
eben geschickt seien. Ihre Großherzigkeit sah man in der Ver-
achtung kleiner Vortheile und ihrem unerschütterlichen Gleichmuth
in der Gefahr. Während des aus Spanien daherziehenden Unge-
witters habe man keine Wolke auf ihrer Stirn gesehen, durch ihre
Haltung habe sie Adel und Volk belebt, ihre Räthe beseelt. . . . .
Das Ideal einer Herrscherin darf man aber auch in Königin
Elisabeth nicht suchen. Niemand kann die Härten in Abrede
stellen, die unter ihrer Regierung, selbst mit ihrem Vorwissen,
begangen worden sind.

(*b*) Ich schreibe Ihnen, lieber Freund, mit wehmüthigem Herzen.
Ich kann sagen daß mich, seit ich lebe, jetzt das erste Unglück be-
troffen hat. Aber der erste Schlag ist auch fast der härteste, der
mich je hätte treffen können. Unser älteste Knabe, Wilhelm, dessen

Sie sich vielleicht dunkel erinnern, ist uns plötzlich an einem bös-artigen Fieber gestorben. Das arme Kind war kaum einige Tage krank. Auf einige leichte Fieberanfälle folgte plötzlich ein heftiges Nasenbluten. Wir waren auf dem Lande in Laricia, aber zufälli-gerweise hatten wir, und haben noch einen deutschen Arzt bei uns, einen trefflichen Menschen, von außerordentlicher Kenntniß und Erfahrung, dem theilnehmendsten Gemüth und doch der größesten Besonnenheit und Ruhe. Dieser — er heißt Kohlrausch und ist ein Hannoveraner — that was er konnte; aber die Gewalt des Uebels war zu heftig, und in kaum sechs und dreißig Stunden lebte er nicht mehr. Sein Tod war sanft, sehr sanft, er hatte fröhliche Phantasieen, litt nichts und ahnte nichts. Er liegt jetzt bei der Pyramide des Cajus Cestius, von der Ihnen Goethe erzählen kann. Ich habe mit diesem Kinde viel verloren.

———

GERMAN.

Examiner—Professor Steinberger.

Write, in German, an essay of about 100 lines on—

Kann man den Krieg in der modernen Civilisation rechtfertigen?

Or,

Morgenstund hat Gold im Mund.

———

FRENCH.

Examiner—Professor Steinberger.

Translate into French :—

History, at least in its state of ideal perfection, is a com-pound of poetry and philosophy. It impresses general truths on the mind by a vivid representation of particular characters and incidents. But, in fact, the two hostile elements of which it consists have never been known to form a perfect amalgamation; and at length, in our own time, they have been completely and professedly separated. Good histories, in the proper sense of the word, we have not. But we have good historical romances, and good historical essays.

To make the past present, to bring the distant near, to place us in the society of a great man or on the eminence which overlooks the field of a mighty battle, to invest with the reality of human flesh and blood beings whom we are too much inclined to consider as personified qualities in an allegory, to call up our ancestors before us with all their peculiarities of language, manners, and garb, to show us over their houses, to seat us at their tables, to rummage their old-fashioned wardrobes, to explain the uses of their ponderous furniture, these parts of the duty which properly belongs to the historian, have been appropriated by the historical novelist. On the other hand, to extract the philosophy of history, to direct our judgment of events and men, to trace the connexion of causes and effects, and to draw from the occurrences of former times general lessons of moral and political wisdom, has become the business of a distinct class of writers. Of the two kinds of composition into which history has been thus divided, the one may be compared to a map, the other to a painted landscape. The picture, though it places the country before us, does not enable us to ascertain with accuracy the dimensions, the distances, and the angles.

Translate into English :—

(*a*) M. Balthazar Cherbonneau avait l'air d'une figure échapée d'un conte fantastique d'Hoffmann et se promenant dans la réalité stupéfaite de voir cette création falote. Sa face extrémement basanée était comme dévorée par un crâne énorme que la chute des cheveux fasait paraître plus vaste encore. Ce crâne nu, poli comme de l'ivoire, avait gardé ses teintes blanches, tandis que le masque, exposé aux rayons du soleil, s'était revêtu, grâce aux superpositions des couches du hâle, d'un ton de vieux chêne ou de portrait enfumé. Les cavités et les saillies des os s'y accentuaient si vigoureusement, que le peu de chair qui les recouvrait ressemblait, avec ses mille rides fripées, à une peau mouillée appliquée sur une tête de mort. Les rares poils gris qui flânaient encore sur l'occiput, massés en trois maigres mèches dont deux se dressaient au-dessus des oreilles et dont la troisième partait de la nuque pour mourir à la naissance du front, faisaient regretter l'usage de l'antique perruque à marteux ou de la moderne tignasse de chiendent, et couronnaient d'une façon grotesque cette physionomie de casse-noisettes. Mais ce qui occupait invinciblement chez le docteur, c'étaient les yeux ; au milieu de ce visage tanné par l'âge, calciné à des cieux incandescents, usé dans l'étude, où les fatigues de la science et de la vie s'écrivaient en sillages profonds, en pattes d'oie rayonnantes, en plis plus pressés que les feuillets d'un livre, étincelaient deux prunelles d'un bleu de turquoise, d'une limpidité, d'une fraîcheur et d'une jeunesse inconcevables. Ces étoiles bleues brillaient au fond d'orbites brunes et de membranes concentriques dont les cercles fauves rappelaient vaguement les plumes disposées en auréole autour de la prunelle nyctalope des hiboux.

(*b*) Eh bien ! Malgré ces plates horreurs, si vous le compariez à la salle à manger, qui lui est contiguë, vous trouveriez ce salon élégant et parfumé comme doit l'être un boudoir. Cette salle, entièrement boisée, fut jadis peinte en une couleur indistincte aujourd'hui, qui forme un fond sur lequel la crasse a imprimé ses couches de manière à y dessiner des figures bizarres. Elle est plaquée de buffets gluants sur lesquels sont des carafes échancrées, ternies, des ronds de moiré métallique, des piles d'assiettes en porcelaine épaisse, à bords bleus, fabriquées à Tournai. Dans un angle est placée une boîte à cases numérotées qui sert à garder les serviettes, ou tachées ou vineuses, de chaque pensionnaire.

———

FRENCH.

Examiner—Professor Steinberger.

Write, in French, an essay of about 100 lines on—

Faut-il exciter l'émulation des élèves dans les écoles au moyen de prix annuels ou d'autres récompenses ?

Or,

A force de forger on devient forgeron.

LAW SCHOLARSHIP—FIRST YEAR.

REAL PROPERTY.

Examiner—PROFESSOR CAMPION.

1. A testator devises an estate to the person who is his heir-at-law. Does the latter take by 'descent' or by 'purchase' (so as to become the stock of descent)?

2. To what extent has statutory enactment preserved 'contingent remainders,' notwithstanding the original requirements essential to their validity?

3. Upon what legal principle did the ordinary 'Limitation to bar Dower' (before the Dower Act) operate to effect that result? State its terms.

4. Give examples of the following :—the doctrine of 'Cypres'; the operation of 'the rule in "Shelley's Case,"' and the legal grounds on which it is based.

5. A woman, married before the Married Woman's Property Statute, had, at the time of her marriage, the following properties :—An estate in fee-simple ; a leasehold for a term of years ; personal estate in possession, and in remainder, and debts due to her.

What right in these properties, respectively, did her husband acquire '*jure mariti*'?

6. In what particular case, and on what legal ground, does the 'remoteness' of the event on which an executory limitation is to take effect, not affect its validity?

7. Having regard to the pre-existing rule of law, in what manner did the Statute of Wills extend the operation of a residuary devise of real estate?

8. Compare the title of 'coparceners' with a tenancy in common as regards its derivative character and its subsequent devolution.

9. Upon what legal ground was it held that the following constituted an estate tail (originally):—a devise 'to A ; and, if he die without issue, to B'? and state the character of the tenure now resulting from the same terms.

10. Since the Married Woman's Property Statutes, what provision is thereby made as to the capacity of a married woman to contract, and the remedy to enforce such contract?

11. State the twofold classification of ' terms of years '; and, as regards long terms of years, the statutory enactment as to their termination when satisfied.

12. Define, and give an example of, ' Prescriptive right '; and state the material alterations introduced by statute.

JURISPRUDENCE.

Examiner—PROFESSOR BASTABLE.

1. Compare the conceptions of Jurisprudence presented by Austin, Maine, and Holland.

2. Draw up a table of the different classes of ' laws ' with which Jurisprudence deals in a form that will bring out their relation to each other.

3. Consider the advantages and disadvantages of the system of case law.

4. Summarise Holland's account of ' the object of law.'

5. Examine the distinction between *res corporales* and *res incorporales*, and estimate its importance.

6. Write short notes on the following terms :—(a) *Jus receptum*, (b) private international jurisprudence, (c) personal servitude, (d) *stipulatio*.

7. State carefully Maine's views on the origin of feudalism, adding any necessary criticisms.

8. Compare ' municipal ' with ' international ' law in respect to its (a) sources, (b) sanctions, (c) course of development.

9. Examine the views of Austin and Maine on the growth of the Roman system of equity.

10. What is meant by ' administrative law ' ? Enumerate the principal topics with which it deals, and consider its relation to ' constitutional law.'

LAW SCHOLARSHIP—SECOND YEAR.

PERSONAL PROPERTY AND LAW OF CONTRACTS.

Examiner—PROFESSOR CAMPION.

PERSONAL PROPERTY.

1. Define the distinctive classification of long terms of years, their limit and operation, and the amendment introduced by statute when satisfied.

2. A man having personal estate absolutely, settles it on himself for life or until his bankruptcy, and in the latter event, declares that it should pass to another. State the settled rule as to the legality of the latter, and any modification thereof.

3. Define a right of action, and distinguish the former and the present statutory right of a creditor to assign a debt (due to him) to a third party.

4. To what qualification is the legal right of 'stoppage *in transitu*' subject?

5. In an action of trover for goods illegally taken, state the extended statutory remedy (irrespective of the right to damages).

6. By what two modes may the absolute interest in *personal* property (as distinguished from *real* property) be transferred without a deed or any consideration?

LAW OF CONTRACTS.

7. In cases within the Statute of Frauds, upon what legal ground was it that the consideration should be in writing? State the present statutory exception.

8. On the point as to whether a contract is invalidated by illegality, state the difference between the following :—

    (*a*) Where part of the consideration is bad.

    b) Where one of the promises is bad.

9. Define the characteristic of a contract by 'specialty,' as distinguished from a simple contract; and define the doctrine of Estoppel by deed, and the qualification of the latter.

10. When an agent contracts with a third party without disclosing the name of his Principal, what are the respective rights and liabilities of the third party and the Principal when the name of the latter becomes known?

11. When a man undertakes to pay the debt of another, what is the true criterion by which to determine whether such constitutes 'a guarantee' within the Statute of Frauds?

12. State apparent exceptions to the ordinary rule, that mutuality of obligation is essential to the validity of a contract.

ROMAN LAW.

Examiner—PROFESSOR BASTABLE.

1. Give a clear account of Justinian's measures of codification.

2. Explain the method by which the prætors introduced changes into the law, giving illustrations.

3. What different views have been taken of 'the law of persons' as treated in the first book of the *Institutes*?

4. What duties did the freedman owe to his patron?

5. Describe the different modes of appointing a guardian.

6. Give an account of the rights and duties created under the contract of *mandatum*. Consider to what class of contracts *mandatum* belongs.

7. '*De obligationibus et Actionibus*' is the heading of a title in the Digest. What conclusion has been drawn from this? Define both terms; and consider how the objects that they denote are related.

8. Illustrate the influence of Roman Law on International Law.

9. Specify the conditions necessary for the validity of a will. What was the *clausula codicillaris*?

MEDICAL SCHOLARSHIPS—SECOND YEAR.

ANATOMY.

Examiner—PROFESSOR PYE.

1. Describe the sphenoid bone.

2. A vertical antero-posterior (sagittal) section is made through the middle of the knee-joint. Describe the appearance presented.

3. The triceps muscle of the arm: its anatomy (including nerve and blood-supply) and action.

4. Describe the astragalus.

(*Further Examination in Dissecting Room.*)

CHEMISTRY.

Examiner—PROFESSOR SENIER.

[*Formulæ, equations, and diagrams are to be used whenever possible.*]

1. Explain (*a*) the meaning of the terms 'molecule' and 'atom'; (*b*) the evidence leading to the molecular and atomic hypotheses; (*c*) the importance of these hypotheses in the development of chemistry.

2. It is required to prepare 100 grams of potassium chlorate. (*a*) What materials would you employ, and what quantities, supposing no loss to occur during the operation? (*b*) Explain the changes that would occur.

3. (*a*) How does phosphorus behave when heated in a current of chlorine? Explain (*b*) the changes which take place, and also (*c*) the reactions which occur when each of the products interact with water.

4. (*a*) Give the method by which 'tartar-emetic' is usually prepared. (*b*) Explain its probable constitution and the experimental evidence supporting it.

5. Describe and explain Maxwell Simpson's synthesis of succinic acid.

6. Well-known classes of compounds exist, which may be regarded as derivatives of ammonia, in which one of the hydrogen atoms is replaced by alkyl, aryl, or acyl radicles; for example, by ethyl, phenyl, or acetyl. Give (a) the name, (b) a method of preparation, (c) the chief distinguishing characters of one of each of these three classes of compounds.

————

ZOOLOGY AND BOTANY.

Examiner—Professor Richard J. Anderson.

1. Classify the Echinodermata. Refer to the chief distinctive marks in each order.

2. Write an account of the structure of a fresh-water Mussel.

3. Describe the respiratory apparatus in Fishes, and note the varieties.

4. What are the distinctive peculiarities of the Primate and Marsupial Orders?

5. Write an account of the anatomy and physiology of the Leaf. .

6. Define the Scrophulariaceæ, Geraniaceæ, and Caryophyllaceæ.

7. Give a list of orders in which the stamens are adherent to the Corolla.

8. How do light and heat influence or affect plants?

————

The following papers were also set for this examination :—

Natural Philosophy, see p. 326.
French or German, see pp. 318, 320.

MEDICAL SCHOLARSHIPS—THIRD YEAR.

PHYSIOLOGY.

Examiner—PROFESSOR PYE.

1. Show how the working of a muscle is influenced by temperature.

2. What effect has carbonic acid on the irritability or conductivity of a nerve?

8. Describe the histology of an air-vesicle of the lung.

4. How would you prove the presence of nitrogen as a constituent of a proteid?

5. Describe the left auricle of the heart.

(*Further Examination in Physiological Laboratory.*)

ANATOMY.

Examiner—PROFESSOR PYE.

1. Mention (without describing them) the parts of the body supplied with blood by the internal carotid artery.

2. Write a description (with diagrams if possible) of the forms assumed by the stomach in different conditions. What hardening methods of fixing are used?

8. Describe the septum lucidum.

4. The anatomy of the superior constrictor muscle of the pharynx.

(*Further Examination in Dissecting Room.*)

MATERIA MEDICA.

Examiner—PROFESSOR COLAHAN.

1. Compare the preparation of hydrargyri subchloridum and hydrargyri perchloridum. Explain the difference, and give the B.P. preparations and doses of each.

2. Contrast the action of belladonna and opium, and give the B.P. preparations of each drug, and their doses.

3. Enumerate the officinal compounds and preparations of arsenic ? What are the symptoms of (*a*) acute, and (*b*) chronic poisoning by arsenic. Mention an antidote.

4. What are the therapeutic values, and what are the ordinary doses of alum, tannic acid, and gallic acid ? Enumerate their B.P. preparations and doses.

5. How do you prepare hydrocyanic acid ? What are its uses ? How does it kill, and what are its antidotes ?

CHEMISTRY.

Examiner—PROFESSOR SENIER.

[*Give the results at which you arrive, together with full experimental proof.*]

1. A black powder. Identify it. (Cupric oxide or cobalt oxide.)

2. A metal. Identify it. (Magnesium, zinc, or cadmium.)

3. A colourless solution. Search for one basic and one acidic radicle. (Sodium pyroborate, ammonium oxalate, or disodiumhydrogenphosphate.)

MEDICAL SCHOLARSHIPS—FOURTH YEAR.

PHYSIOLOGY.

Examiner—PROFESSOR PYE.

1. Map out the motor areas of the cortex cerebri according to present evidence.

2. The functions of the spinal accessory nerve, and the evidence for them.

3. Give a short general account of the anatomy of the labyrinth of the ear (not microscopical).

4. Describe the epiglottis.

(*Further Examination in Physiological Laboratory.*)

MATERIA MEDICA.

Examiner—PROFESSOR COLAHAN.

1. Describe some of the most important symptoms produced by a fatal dose of strychnine, and contrast these symptoms with those present in a case of traumatic tetanus.

2. Enumerate the drugs you would use in the treatment of tape-worm, the ascarides, and the oxyurides, respectively; and write a prescription for the administration of the drug in each case to a child of ten.

3. Write a list of the official hypnotics or soporifics, and give the preparations and doses of each.

4. State shortly the reasons that would induce you to select the preparation of the iodides in preference to those of mercury in the treatment of syphilis.

MEDICINE.

Examiner—PROFESSOR LYNHAM.

1. Enumerate the conditions under which albumen is found in the urine.

2. Describe an attack of hepatic colic, and its treatment.

3. Give the causes and symptoms of secondary lateral sclerosis.

4. Write a short account of primary tuberculosis of the kidney.

5. Mention some varieties of dyspepsia, with an outline of their treatment.

SURGERY.

Examiner—PROFESSOR BRERETON.

1. Describe application of superficial, deep, and buried sutures.

2. Give the pathology of Colles' fracture, more particularly from knowledge obtained by Röntgen Rays.

8. In the anomalous dislocations of the femur, everted dorsal, supra spinous, and anterior oblique, what is the relation of Y ligament in each?

4. What are the symptoms of intersusception ?

5. In what portion of the intestine is obstruction most frequent ?

SENIOR SCHOLARSHIP IN ANATOMY AND PHYSIOLOGY.

Examiner—Professor Pye.

1. The position of the ovary. Write an account of the results of modern methods of fixing (freezing or hardening) in the study of this question.

2. Make diagrams to show the original position—fœtal, say, at 7th month—of liver, stomach, panereas, spleen. Your diagram is to show ligamentum suspensorium hepatis, lesser omentum, mesentery.

8. The regeneration of a cut nerve. Describe the process in a medullated nerve, and discuss the results obtained by joining afferent and efferent nerves after section—each to a different kind.

4. Describe the right pleural sac.

5. Describe the region exposed by detaching the complexus muscle from the occipital bone and seventh cervical vertebra, and throwing it outwards.

6. Discuss the following points relating to the physiology of the nerve cell—

(*a*) Is the possession of branches necessary to the functional activity of a cell ?

(*b*) The dendrites are always growing in number: does this imply new functions ?

(*c*) A stimulated cell shows shrinkage. Is this a fatigue phenomenon ?

7. How would you proceed to make dissections for demonstrating the anatomy of the inguinal canal ?

(Further examination in Laboratory.)

т

ENGINEERING SCHOLARSHIPS—SECOND YEAR.

MATHEMATICS.

FIRST PAPER.

Examiner.—PROFESSOR BROMWICH.

1. Solve the equations for x, y, z, t,

$$ax + by + cz = 0, \quad bz - cy = p - at, \quad cx - az = q - bt,$$
$$ay - bx = r - ct.$$

2. Given

$$\frac{1}{x} + \frac{1}{1-y} = \frac{1}{1-x} + \frac{1}{y} = 4,$$

find x, y. How many sets of values would you expect to find?

3. Verify, by continued division, that

$$(1 - x)^{-2} = 1/(1 - 2x + x^2)$$
$$= 1 + 2x + 3x^2 + \ldots + (n + 1) x^n$$
$$+ [(n + 2) x^{n+1} - (n + 1) x^{n+2}]/(1 - 2x + x^2).$$

4. Using question 3, prove that the value of $(\cdot975)^{-2}$ is given by

$$1 + \frac{2}{40} + \frac{3}{(40)^2}$$

correct to three decimal places; and calculate it.

5. In a plane triangle the sides are as $5 : 6 : 7$, find the angles, each to the nearest minute.

6. The internal bisector of the angle A of a triangle ABC meets BC in D; and the radius of the circumcircle drawn through C meets AD in E. Prove that the length of DE is

$$ab \cos A/(b + c) \cos (\tfrac{1}{2}A - B).$$

7. If $\theta = a$, $\theta = \beta$ are the two roots of the equation

$$\frac{\cos \theta}{\cos \gamma} + \frac{\sin \theta}{\sin \gamma} = 1,$$

prove that

$$\cos a \cos \beta = -\cos^4 \gamma, \quad \sin a \sin \beta = -\sin^4 \gamma.$$

8. Assuming that

$$\sin 18° = \tfrac{1}{4}(\sqrt{5} - 1), \quad \sin 15° = \tfrac{1}{4}(\sqrt{6} - \sqrt{2}),$$

find sin 3° in the form

$$\tfrac{1}{16}\left[(\sqrt{6} + \sqrt{2})(\sqrt{5} - 1) - 2(\sqrt{3} - 1)\sqrt{5 + \sqrt{5}}\right],$$

calculate this to four places of decimals, and compare it with the circular measure of 3°.

9. If p is the length of the perpendicular drawn from C on AB (in any spherical triangle), prove that

$$\sin c \cos p = (\cos^2 a + \cos^2 b - 2 \cos a \cos b \cos c)^{\frac{1}{2}}.$$

10. Solve the right-angled spherical triangle, given

$$A = 46°, \quad B = 54°, \quad C = 90°.$$

MATHEMATICS.

SECOND PAPER.

Examiner—PROFESSOR BROMWICH.

1. A, B, C, D are the angular points of a square whose side is a and whose centre is O : prove that

$$AP^2 + BP^2 + CP^2 + DP^2 = 4 . OP^2 + 2a^2$$

if P is any point in the plane of the square.

2. PL, PM, PN are perpendiculars drawn from P to the sides BC, CA, AB of a triangle ABC. Prove that, if the ratio $LM : LN$ is given, the locus of P is a circle with respect to which B and C are inverse points.

3. Divide a given straight line into two parts so that the difference of the squares on the two parts may be equal to the rectangle contained by them.

4. A, B, C, D are four points not in one plane: if the mid-points of AB, BC, CD, DA lie on a circle, then AC, BD are perpendicular.

5. Write down the expression for the area of a triangle in terms of the coordinates of its angular points. Prove that the area of the triangle formed by the lines

$$x = a, \quad y = b, \quad x/b + y/a = 1$$

is

$$\tfrac{1}{2}(a^2 - ab + b^2)^2/ab.$$

6. PQ, PR are chords of the circle $x^2 + y^2 = 1$, and pass through the points $(\frac{1}{2}, 0)$, $(-\frac{1}{2}, 0)$ respectively. Show that the equation to QR is

$$x \cos \theta + \tfrac{4}{3} \, y \sin \theta + 1 = 0,$$

if the coordinates of P are $(\cos \theta, \sin \theta)$.

7. Find where the parabolas

$$y^2 = ax, \quad x^2 = ay$$

intersect, and find the tangents at the points of intersection. Prove that the angle between the tangents (at the point of intersection other than the origin) is $\tan^{-1} \frac{3}{4}$.

8. Trace the graphs of

$$y = x^2 - 1, \quad y = x - 1/x, \quad y^2 = x^2 - 1.$$

9. Perpendicular lines on a plane slope make angles 30°, 20° with the horizon: find the angle of slope of the plane.

10. Find an expression for the area of a spherical triangle in terms of the spherical excess.

If θ is the side of an equilateral triangle, whose area is $\frac{1}{30}$th that of the sphere, prove that

$$\sec \theta = \sqrt{5};$$

and find θ from the tables.

CHEMISTRY.

Examiner—PROFESSOR SENIER.

[Formulæ, equations, and diagrams are to be used whenever possible.]

1. Explain (a) the meaning of the terms ' molecule ' and ' atom '; (b) the evidence leading to the molecular and atomic hypotheses ; (c) the importance of these hypotheses in the development of chemistry.

2. (a) What is meant by the ' nascent state ' ? (b) Give examples. (c) Suggest an explanation.

3. It is required to prepare hydrochloric, hydrobromic, hydiodic, and hydrofluoric acids. (a) What reactions would you employ ? (b) Give technical details of each operation. (c) Explain the changes that would occur.

4. Describe and explain the behaviour of the following substances when heated :—(*a*) lead nitrate, silver nitrate, potassium nitrate, ammonium nitrate ; (*b*) nitric acid and copper, silver, zinc, mercury, respectively ; (*c*) limestone and ammonium chloride.

5. Contrast and explain the behaviour of iron immersed in (*a*) pure water, (*b*) in water which has been exposed for some time to the air.

ENGINEERING.

Examiner—Professor Townsend.

1. Through a given point in the vertical plane of projection draw a plane making given angles with the horizontal and vertical planes, and state the relation that must exist between the given angles.

2. Through a given point draw a line perpendicular to a given plane, and find the length of the perpendicular.

8. In the accompanying diagram (P) of the projections of a sphere and of a line lying in the horizontal plane, you are required to construct the traces of a plane passing through the line and touching the sphere.

4. In the accompanying diagram (Q), the quadrilateral 1, 2, 8, 4, lying in the horizontal plane, is the directrix of an oblique prism, B, B' are the horizontal and vertical projections of the direction of its generatrices, and A, A' the projections of a line : find the projections of the points where the line meets the prism.

5. In the accompanying diagram (R), the figure 1, 2, 8, 4, 5, lying in the horizontal plane, is the base of a pyramid, V, V' the projections of its vertex, and A, A' the traces of a plane : construct the vertical and horizontal projections of their intersection, and develop the curve of intersection in the horizontal plane.

6. Construct the perspective of the object represented by the projections in the accompanying diagram (S).

7. Sketch an open timber-roof of the Perpendicular period

8. Sketch a doorway of the Early English style.

9. Sketch a plan of the Erectheium, and describe its general features.

10. On a French map 4 inches represent 10 kilometres: construct a scale of miles and furlongs sufficiently long to measure 10 miles.

———

The following papers were also set at this Examination:—

French or German, see pp. 818, 820.
Experimental Physics, see p. 826.

———

Drawings executed in the First Year.

———

ENGINEERING SCHOLARSHIPS—THIRD YEAR.

MATHEMATICS.

Examiner—PROFESSOR BROMWICH.

1. Solve the equations
$$x(1-y) = y(1-z) = z(1-x) = c$$
for the cases   (i) $c = \frac{1}{4}$,   (ii) $c = 1$.

2. A, B, C, D are the angular points of a square: find a point P on a given line (in the plane of $ABCD$) for which the sum
$$AP^2 + BP^2 + CP^2 + DP^2$$
is least.

3. A sphere passes through two fixed points and touches a fixed plane: prove that the point of contact lies on a fixed circle.

4. A, B, C, D are four points in order on a straight line, such that
$$AB = BC = CD,$$
and the angles subtended by AB, BC, CD at any point P are θ, ϕ, ψ, respectively; prove that
$$(\cot\theta + \cot\phi)(\cot\psi + \cot\phi) = 4(1 + \cot^2\phi).$$

5. The area of an equilateral spherical triangle is $\frac{1}{10}$th that of the sphere.   Prove that if θ is the side of the triangle

$$\sec \theta = \sqrt{5} \; ;$$

and find θ from the tables.

6. *PQ*, *QR* are chords of the circle $x^2 + y^2 = 1$, and pass through the points $(\frac{1}{4}, 0)$, $(-\frac{1}{4}, 0)$, respectively.
Show that the equation to *QR* is

$$x \cos \theta + \tfrac{4}{3}y \sin \theta + 1 = 0$$

if the coordinates of *P* are $(\cos \theta, \sin \theta)$.

7. Prove that the parabolas $y^2 = ax$, $x^2 = by$ intersect in the point

$$x = (ab^2)^{\frac{1}{3}}, \quad y = (a^2b)^{\frac{1}{3}} \; ;$$

find the tangents to the two curves at this point, and verify that the angle between them is θ where

$$\tan \theta = \tfrac{3}{2} a^{\frac{1}{3}} b^{\frac{1}{3}} / (a^{\frac{2}{3}} + b^{\frac{2}{3}}).$$

8. Differentiate with respect to x

$$\log (y \sqrt{a + ax + b})$$

and $\qquad \tan^{-1} \left[\{apx + b (x + p) + c\} / yq \right],$

where $\qquad y^2 = ax^2 + 2bx + c, \quad q^2 = - (ap^2 + 2bp + c).$

9. A circle of radius a rolls on the outside of a circle of radius $3a$: prove that the locus traced out by a marked point on the circumference of the rolling circle is given by

$$x = 4a \cos \theta - a \cos 4\theta, \quad y = 4a \sin \theta - a \sin 4\theta.$$

Find the equation to the tangent at the point $\theta = \tfrac{1}{4}\pi$.

10. Find the area cut off from the parabola $y^2 = 4ax$ by the line $x = b$.

11. Verify that

$$\int \frac{(Ax^2 + B)\, dx}{(x^4 + a^4)^2} = \frac{1}{4a^4} \left[\frac{Ax^3 + Bx}{x^4 + a^4} + \int \frac{(Ax^2 + 3B)\, dx}{x^4 + a^4} \right],$$

and complete the integration.

CHEMISTRY.

Examiner—PROFESSOR SENIER.

[*Give the results at which you arrive, together with full experimental proof.*]

1. A black powder. Identify it. (Ferrosoferric oxide.)

2. A metal. Identify it. (Cadmium.)

3. A colourless solution. Search for one basic and one acidic radicle. (Potassium sodium tartrate.)

ENGINEERING.

Examiner—PROFESSOR TOWNSEND.

1. In the accompanying map take out the acreage of each field in statute measure.

2. Describe the adjustments of the instrument set before you, and read the vernier.

3.

Depths in Feet.		Bidder's Tabular Numbers.		Distance in Chains.	Contents in Cubic Yards.	Square Yards in Slopes.
		Black.	Red.			
13	20	676	40·3	5		
20	25	1243	55·0	2¼		

From the above data of a cutting, calculate the contents in cubic yards, and the area of the slopes in square yards, of each section, the base being 30 feet, and the ratio of slopes 1½ horizontal to 1 perpendicular.

4.

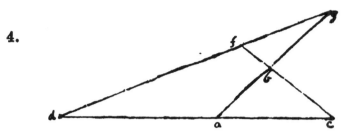

In the above figure given the triangles *abc*, *fbg*. Find the distance *ad*.

5. Calculate the discharge in cubic feet per minute from a V-notch, the angle which the sides make with the vertical being 60°, and the depth of the notch 15 inches.

6. Make a sketch of a double-acting switch-bolt at the points of a railway, and state the advantages which it possesses over the single bolt.

7. Make a large sketch of an ordinary cross-over road from down main line to up main line.

8. Make a *figured* cross-section of a double line of railway (English gauge), showing ballast, sleepers, and rails.

9. Make a sketch of a single hammer-beam roof, naming the different members, and state the structural advantage of this particular form.

10. Make a sketch showing the construction of a six-panelled square framed door, and write out the names of the different members.

———

The following paper was also set for this examination:—

Mathematical Physics, see p. 846.

———

Drawings executed in the Second Year.

SENIOR SCHOLARSHIP IN ENGINEERING.

ENGINEERING.

Examiner—PROFESSOR TOWNSEND.

1. In a masonry dam of triangular section the inner side being vertical, show how to calculate the limit of the depth to which the triangular section can be carried down when the reservoir is full, q being the density of the masonry, r the weight of a cubic foot of water, and s the limiting intensity of stress per square foot.

2. A cast-iron pillar 14 feet long supports a working load of 60 tons : calculate the thickness of the material, the external diameter being 8 inches, the factor of safety 6, and both ends firmly fixed.

3. A wrought-iron shaft 20 feet long and 6 inches in diameter is strained by an external moment of 6 foot-tons. Calculate the angle of torsion in degrees and minutes, the coefficient of torsional elasticity being 9,000,000 lbs.

4. In the accompanying diagram of a roof-truss, calculate, graphically, the reactions at the points of support, and the stresses in the several members, produced by the force P.

5. In the accompanying diagram of a girder, calculate the maximum stress in bay f, and the maximum compressive stress in diagonal d, resulting from an uniform load of $\frac{1}{4}$ a ton per foot, and a rolling load of 1 ton per foot.

6. A beam of memel 28 feet long and 12 inches wide supports an uniform load of 4·4 tons : calculate its depth, the coefficient of rupture being 1848 lbs., and the factor of safety 10.

7. Describe the manufacture of Portland cement, and write a specification for some of good quality.

8. Describe the manufacture of Bessemer steel.

9. Describe the recent method of forming a breakwater by means of concrete blocks on a foundation below low water.

10. Make a figured sketch of the mode of drawing off water from a reservoir under an earthen embankment 60 feet high.

———

Drawings executed in the Third Year.

STUDENTS' LITERARY AND DEBATING SOCIETY.

Patron,	President Anderson.
President,	Professor Richard J. Anderson.
Chairman,	James Flack.
Vice-Chairman,	Samuel Minnis.
Hon. Treasurer,	William J. M'Farland.
Hon. Secretaries,	Patrick J. Cusack. / John E. A. Lynham.
Committee,	Anthony Curran. / Thomas Walsh. / Patrick M. Walsh. / Thomas May. / Francis P. Byrne.

BIOLOGICAL SOCIETY.

(FOUNDED, 1889.)

This Society meets in the Physiological Laboratory on Friday evenings at 7.30 p.m.

President,	Professor Pye.
Secretary,	Samuel Porterfield.

CELTIC LITERARY SOCIETY.

atron,	Professor Pye.
resident,	Professor Trench.
Chairman,	Thomas Walsh.
Hon. Secretaries,	George A. Francis. / Stephen J. M'Donagh.
Hon. Treasurer,	John Holmes.
Committee,	Joseph J. O'Neill. / Gilmore Bell. / James Byrne. / Michael J. Glancy. / John O'Flaherty. / George M'Donnell.

ATHLETIC UNION.

President, ... Professor Trench.
Hon. Treasurer, ... Professor Senier.
Hon. Secretary, ... Robert M. Duncan.

General Committee, ... { The Professors.
Robert M. Duncan.
John A. Moore.
Joseph M'Causland. }

The Athletic Union embraces the following Clubs :—

FOOTBALL CLUB.

Patron, ... Professor Senier.
President, ... President Anderson.

RUGBY.

Captain, .. Robert M. Duncan.
Vice-Captain, John R. Burke.
Hon. Treasurer, John A. Moore.
Hon. Secretary, R. G. C. M. Kinkead.

Committee, { C. W. N. Anderson.
Isaac Flack.
J. J. A. Gannon. }

Delegates to Athletic Union. { Robert M. Duncan.
John A. Moore. }

Representative on Connaught Five. } Robert M. Duncan.

ASSOCIATION.

Captain, .. George Maxwell.
Vice-Captain, James J. Hannigan.
Hon. Treasurer, John A. Moore.
Hon. Secretary, John R. Burke.

Committee, { John C. Macaulay.
Samuel M'Causland. }

HOCKEY CLUB.

Patron, ... Professor Senier.
President, ... President Anderson.
Captain, ... John A. Moore.
Vice-Captain, ... George Maxwell.
Hon. Treasurer, ... William F. A. Carson.
Hon. Secretary, ... John S. M'Lachlan.

Committee, ... { Joseph M'Causland.
James J. Hannigan.
Richard G. C. M. Kinkead. }

Representative on Connaught Five, .. Joseph M'Causland.

U

TENNIS CLUB.

Patron,	.. ..	Professor Senier.
President,	.. ..	Professor R. J. Anderson.
Captain,	.. ..	John A. Moore.
Hon. Treasurer,	.. ..	Cuthbert F. Montagu.
Hon. Secretary,	.. ..	John S. M'Lachlan.
Committee,	.. ..	{ Robert M. Duncan. Robert B. M'Lachlan. Agnes M. Perry.
Delegate to Athletic Union,	.. ..	Joseph M'Causland.

CRICKET CLUB.

Patron,	.. ..	Professor Townsend.
President,	.. ..	Professor Senier.
Captain,	.. ..	Joseph M'Causland.
Vice-Captain,	.. ..	Samuel M'Causland.
Hon. Treasurer,	.. ..	James J. Hannigan.
Hon. Secretary,	.. ..	John R. Burke.
Committee,	.. ..	{ John A. Moore. John O'Flaherty.

CYCLING CLUB.

Patron,	.. ..	President Anderson.
President,	.. ..	Professor Steinberger.
Captain,	.. ..	Robert M. Duncan.
Hon. Treasurer and Hon. Secretary,	..	John L. Dunlop.

HANDBALL CLUB.

President,	.. ..	Professor Pye.
Captain,	.. ..	Patrick J. Cusack.
Secretary,	.. ..	James Flack.
Treasurer,	.. ..	Samuel Porterfield.
Committee,	.. ..	{ Francis P. Byrne. Michael J. Glancy. Charles W. Anderson.

Lightning Source UK Ltd.
Milton Keynes UK
UKHW021330250219
337978UK00013B/1517/P